Play for a Change

Play, Policy and Practice:
A review of contemporary perspectives

Stuart Lester and **Wendy Russell**
University of Gloucestershire

national children's bureau

Play England
Making space for play

Play England

Play England aims for all children and young people in England to have regular access and opportunity for free, inclusive, local play provision and play space.

Play England provides advice and support to promote good practice, and works to ensure that the importance of play is recognised by policy makers, planners and the public. For further information visit www.playengland.org.uk.

Play England is part of the National Children's Bureau, and is supported by the Big Lottery Fund.

National Children's Bureau

The National Children's Bureau (NCB) promotes the voices, interests and well-being of all children and young people across every aspect of their lives.

As an umbrella body for the children's sector in England and Northern Ireland, NCB provide essential information on policy, research and best practice for our members and other partners.

NCB has adopted and works within the UN Convention on the Rights of the Child.

National Children's Bureau, 8 Wakley Street, London EC1V 7QE
Website: www.ncb.org.uk
Registered charity number: 258825

Published for Play England by the National Children's Bureau

© Play England 2008
Published September 2008
ISBN: 978-1-905818-39-6

Front cover image: Natural England/Nick Turner Photography

Contents

Chapter 4: Children's play patterns

Chapter 5: From policy and theory into practice: provision for play

5

Acknowledgements

Our thanks go to Play England for initiating and funding the research and to Issy Cole-Hamilton for support and direction throughout and for close reading of draft versions; to Anna Kassman-McKerrell and Michael Welsh at the Children's Play Information Service for support in accessing the information both within the play library and the National Children's Bureau library; to Hilary Smith at the University of Gloucestershire for administrative and academic support and comments on early draft reports; to Louise Kennedy at the University of Gloucestershire for additional research; to members of the advisory group who read and commented on drafts: Jackie Boldon, Fraser Brown, Steve Chown, Phil Doyle, Tim Ferguson, Bob Hughes, Haki Kapasi, Julie Mattocks-Cawood, Frank O'Malley, Robin Sutcliffe, Wendy Usher, Adrian Voce, Ian Wellard.

Stuart Lester

Stuart Lester is Senior Lecturer in Playwork at the University of Gloucestershire and an independent playwork trainer and adviser. He has worked for over twenty years as a playwork practitioner, with a particular focus on adventure playgrounds and outdoor play. Recent publications include *Play, naturally* a review of children's playful relationship with natural spaces (with Martin Maudsley).

Wendy Russell

Wendy Russell started her first adventure playground job in 1975. She has worked in playwork ever since, in a number of roles, including playworker, play officer, play researcher and playwork trainer. Currently, she divides her time between being Senior Lecturer in Playwork at the University of Gloucestershire, working freelance, and her own research into play and playwork.

Foreword

Adrian Voce, Director of Play England

In a recent exchange, I was (gently) chastised for publicly making a connection (along with more than 270 children's professionals, writers and academics) between escalating mental health problems for children and their diminishing opportunities to play. I was told that 'a reading of the evidence base revealed nothing that could substantiate such a direct link'.

Strictly speaking, this criticism was perhaps justified. Robust empirical research on children's play provision that is of sufficient scope to be conclusive as to its impact, is thin on the ground. The University of Birmingham's national evaluation of the Children's Fund, for example, while suggesting there were indications that play provision may help to reduce young offending, also suggested that further, specific investment in long-term play provision and its evaluation was needed to provide more evidence.

This lack, as yet, of what is routinely referred to in policy circles as 'a robust evidence base' is presumably a main reason why, until very recently, the only significant national investment in play provision in England has been from the national lottery.

Yet, as this impressive literature review demonstrates, the evidence of the role that play has in children's lives and in human development is substantial and wide-ranging. It seems clear that the instinct to play is very deep, that it arises from very fundamental impulses. In playing, from the very earliest age, the human child engages with and learns about the world and about herself, builds crucial relationships with her carers, peers and siblings, and imagines the world she will partly inherit, partly create.

But the strongest message from this review is that all of these important functions of play are incidental in the child's own experience, which has little, if any, cognisance of 'outcomes'. Play is evidently simply how children enjoy being alive in the world now. After basic physical and emotional needs are met, children play. Even when they are not playing, the impulse to do so remains and can help to heal the effects of abuse and neglect.

There is an argument that this is all self-evident. Why do we need to research and validate such a primary form of activity, such an elemental aspect of children's behaviour? Is it not obvious, and have children not played happily without anyone researching it, for millennia?

The answer is both yes and no. Play does appear to be something that has been with us since our earliest evolutionary steps; indeed research of play in the animal kingdom shows that we share many play behaviours with fellow mammals. Some theorists suggest that our evolution itself is steered by the play of our young. And yet many human cultures, not least our own, have undervalued the significance of children's play, curtailing it for the more serious business of family or community survival which, in the modern world equates to academic attainment as a means to economic advancement.

If the research is not conclusive, perhaps this is because most of the studies have been attempts to broaden our understanding of children (and of ourselves) and their play, rather than to identify the role that it has in other outcomes for them. Policy-making must rely upon evidence, but, within an outcomes framework that largely identifies particular indicators of pathology, under-achievement or potential risk, the evidence that finds favour will tend to be that which can demonstrate an impact on these.

The case for children's play provision as an aspect of public policy is, first and foremost, that it is an established human right, recognised under the United Nations Convention on the Rights of the Child (UNCRC) of 1989. There is indeed an argument that the right to play is the one that is most distinctly children's; that it defines, almost, the right to be a child. The 1913 Declaration of Dependence by the Children of America in Mines and Factories and Workshops Assembled (McKelway AJ 1913), a forerunner to the Geneva Declaration of the Rights of the Child in 1924, that itself eventually led to the UNCRC, asserts as its first resolution 'that childhood is endowed with certain inherent and inalienable rights, among which are freedom from toil for daily bread; the right to play and to dream'.

Much of the current policy framework for children has been developed with a view to 'balancing rights and responsibilities' for children. Certainly before the departmental changes in government in June 2007, this had almost become a mantra to rival 'education, education, education'. But this very earliest declaration of children's rights in modern times implies that children have the right not to be responsible: for the adult world to be responsible for them. The world of the child, in which they form and rehearse their range of responses (which is another way of saying they become responsible), is the world of play. The richly imagined but ethereal landscapes – physical, social, cultural and emotional – of children at play are, to many of the researchers and theorists surveyed in this volume, both uniquely the real world of childhood and the training ground for the actual world that they will not simply inherit but create, as adults.

Some of the research reviewed within does suggest strong links between the enjoyment that children derive from play and its benefits for their all-round health and well-being now and in the future. But there are problems in producing longitudinal research that shows clear statistical cause and effect of an activity as elemental, innate and ubiquitous as children's play. How is the activity in question to be defined accurately when children have been shown to be able to play anywhere and with anything, given the space and permission? How is it to be measured? What price a study group?

Thankfully – for the time-being at least – the argument for investing in children's play provision and for seriously tackling the many barriers to their access to it, appears to have been won. The government, as of December 2007 (after this research review was complete) has adopted a substantive play policy as part of The Children's Plan (DCSF 2007), its ten-year strategy to make England the best place in the world to grow up. The government has now fully embraced the principle that there is a societal responsibility to enable 'children to enjoy their childhoods as well being prepared for adult life'.

The Children's Plan investment of £235m in play areas, adventure playgrounds and playworkers – within the context of a national play strategy that will attempt to coordinate planning, traffic, housing, health and children's services around the common aim of giving children more freedom to use these spaces – will not on its own transform the environments where children live and play. But because it is a strategic programme, designed to inform future policy, it should create the opportunity for that fuller evidence base.

Much of the research marshalled and elucidated so admirably in this volume has been instrumental, at least indirectly, in achieving this policy breakthrough. It should now provide future researchers, including the evaluators of the current and future government initiatives, with the map and the compass they will need to assess the real value of play provision. It is a value measurable, first and last, in the extent of children's enjoyment.

Chapter 1

Background, scope and key messages

Our aim in researching and writing this report is to produce an up-to-date review of research and literature on children's play, with a focus on evidence-based research that can inform policy. This document builds on the work carried out by Cathy Street (2001) of the New Policy Institute that was published as The Value of Children's Play and Play Provision, Section Two of *Making the Case for Play: Gathering the evidence* (Cole-Hamilton and others) published by the former Children's Play Council in 2002. The context of public provision for children's play has changed enormously over the last five years, and the time feels right for a fresh look at the literature underpinning our understanding of the importance of play in children's lives and how this might relate to social policy and public provision for play.

Scope

11

Our remit was to undertake a review of published research and other literature relating to children's play, focusing on works published since 2001, in order to update the information in *Making the Case for Play: Gathering the evidence* (Cole-Hamilton and others 2002). We have used this document as a starting point to identify three key strands of the literature review, namely:

- the policy context for supporting children's play, including an analysis of the literature on approaches to policy-making and the literature on children and childhood (Chapter 2)
- the literature on the benefits of children's play (Chapter 3) and on children's play patterns (Chapter 4)
- provision for play and working with children at play (Chapter 5).

The report draws on a diverse and at times disparate range of evidence sources. It has been difficult to set boundaries for this desk-based review, since play permeates every aspect of children's lives. We have drawn on a wide range of academic disciplines from the emerging studies of neuroscience, systems thinking and epigenetics to the more ethnographic studies of the geographies and sociology of childhood, stopping off briefly within philosophy.

Whilst not entirely forgetting the foundation that developmental psychology has given to theories about children and play, this review has largely focused on alternative approaches. We have reviewed the literature on the play of children and young people aged from birth to 18 years, although at times we have also used research on animals, because this provides data that would be impractical or unethical to gather on children and young people. We have drawn on international literature, most notably from 'western' countries such as the United Kingdom, Northern Europe, North America, Australia and New Zealand, as this provides a comparative perspective, particularly on play patterns and practice among similar countries, although demographic and policy data are for England or the UK only. The literature on play itself is growing, but the literature on children and childhood is much bigger, and we have tried to trawl a fair range of books and papers that may give some insights into children's play, even if that is not their main focus. Given the diverse and ambiguous nature of playing and the vast range of studies across these disciplines, we accept that what we offer here is partial and cannot be a wholly comprehensive review of the research. A detailed list of sources and approaches can be found in Appendix 1.

The authors would like to highlight three key limiting factors to the literature review. Firstly, whilst we both have extensive experience in playwork, neither of us is from a natural science background and we acknowledge our limitations in reading and interpreting complex scientific material, particularly that from neuroscience. Secondly, there were, of course, time constraints, which will inevitably lead to gaps in the evidence collected and reviewed. Finally, in terms of reviewing the literature on provision for play, we acknowledge that there is much taking place at local level that falls outside of this review: we have reviewed the nationally published literature rather than local practice.

Play, policy, practice and paradigms: a case for realignment

The three strands of the review identified above have formed a triangular framework for analysis as shown in the figure below. The model has been used for the purposes of analysis only, and is not intended to reduce the complexity of the range of influences on theory, policy or practice.

There is an assumption, or at least an aspiration, that all three points of the triangle align, that (recognising that the cycle can begin at any point) evidence informs policy, which then informs practice, this feeding into further evidence and research and so on. However, what the review unveiled is that this framework more accurately represents a 'tension field' in which the various points of the triangle may find themselves misaligned, or at times taking oppositional positions (Fig 1). This is due in no small part to particular understandings of children and play.

It is worth introducing here a few key concepts that underpin the literature review and are integral to understanding the key messages. One of the consequences of drawing on such a broad range of academic disciplines is an appreciation of diversity, not only in what is studied, but also in the methods of study, the conclusions drawn and, particularly, in the underpinning paradigms each discipline employs. Moss (2007: 243) defines a paradigm as 'an overarching system of ideas and beliefs by which people see and organise the world in a coherent way, a mindset for making sense of the world and our place in it'.

Recognition of the existence of different paradigms and discourses ('ways of naming things and talking about them', Moss 2007: 243) brings with it an appreciation of the implausibility of one single truth to explain a phenomenon as complex, multilayered and diverse as playing, or its relation to social policy. The exponential growth of policy initiatives relating to children

12

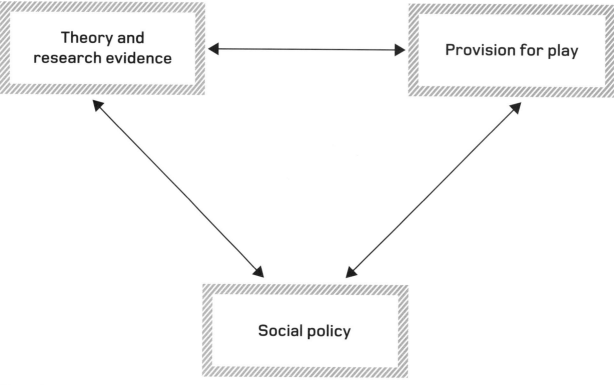

Figure 1

'Much of the evidence from neuroscience suggests that playing is a way of building and shaping the emotion, motivation and reward regions of the brain ...'

and young people over recent decades, and the last decade in particular (Roberts 2001; Mcneish and Gill 2006; J Brown 2007b) has been informed for the most part by one dominant paradigm and discourse that has marginalised other discourses and which assumes universal and rational truths about children. These truths include the belief that interventions have a direct and causal link to outcomes beneficial to society if only the right interventions can be identified, measured and embedded into increasingly technical, standardised and regulated practice at the right time in each individual child's life (Wyness 2006; Moss 2007). A key disciplinary perspective that informs this paradigm is child development, with its understanding of childhood as a period of preparation for adulthood (Mayall 2005; Meire 2007; Moss 2007). Key terms used in the discourse include 'development', 'children's needs', 'quality', 'best practice', 'benchmark' and 'outcomes' (Moss and Petrie 2002; Wyness 2006; Moss 2007).

This dominant paradigm embraces a particular view of play as a medium for learning and preparation for adulthood. This is what Smith (as long ago as 1988, and more recently in 2005) calls the 'play ethos', and Sutton-Smith (1997; 2003) the 'progress rhetoric'. The relationship between play, learning and development espoused by this paradigm is, according to Sutton-Smith (1997; 2003) based more on analogy, metaphor and self-referential presupposition than empirical evidence. Burghardt (2005: 381) asserts that 'common assumptions about play are often misleading and claims for the role of play are often suspect'. Smith (2005) suggests that children's play has been 'co-opted' in modern, industrialised societies as a way of improving cognitive and social skills.

These three references are from play scholars spanning academic disciplines from children's folklore, through developmental psychology to ethology. Such a widespread questioning of existing understandings of play demands more than a passing consideration. The uncritical assumption that playing is a mechanism for learning and development has come to be seen as a self-evident truth. It has also tended to lead to a rather romanticised view of playing that glosses over (or attempts to control) some of the nastier or more disturbing ways of playing (Sutton-Smith 2003; Holland 2003; Kalliala 2006). Meire (2007: 3) summarises this paradigmatic understanding:

> Understood as rational, orderly, and rule-governed, play is a civilizing activity and its value lies in its socializing force. This implies, however, that play must be guided in the right, future-oriented directions – into those that are productive and socializing.

In this rational, measurable and technical paradigm, play has a purpose: it is seen as being 'instrumental' in the overall child development project. For this reason, play advocates have tended to focus on this understanding of the purpose of play (Meire 2007). It is particularly evident in social policies which encourage active playing as a way of tackling obesity, or which use playing as a vehicle for academic learning, social development, crime reduction or

13

'Play can help build resilience – the capacity for children to thrive despite adversity and stress in their lives.'

community cohesion. Powell and Wellard (2008) refer to this as a 'utilitarian' view of playing; throughout this report we refer to it either as 'utilitarian' or 'instrumental'.

The sources drawn on in this literature review offer additional perspectives on the key concepts of play and development that are more complex, differentiated and relational. In some ways this is unsettling because it becomes difficult to make (with any certainty) specific claims for the importance of playing in the lives of children. For example, to recognise the interconnectedness of genes, brains and bodies, and physical, social and cultural environments, opens up infinite and reciprocal possibilities for influence rather than singular cause and effect, as does recognition of children themselves as active agents in their own lives. This makes it almost impossible to make generalisations or universal claims regarding interventions.

Within these alternative paradigms, an 'instrumental' or 'utilitarian' understanding of play becomes questionable, and we can begin to look at a more intrinsic (sometimes referred to as 'autotelic') value drawn from the process of playing for its own sake rather than from its content (Hakarrainen 1999) or from its purported role in specific learning or developmental progress. As Burghardt (2005: xiii) says, 'much of what play entails may not be as it seems'.

Recent studies of the place of children's play within public policy (Santer 2007; Powell and Wellard 2008) find play to be poorly defined with no coherent understanding across or among policies. This is not surprising, since play scholars themselves are unable to agree a definition (Sutton-Smith 1999; Burghardt 2005). However, as Burghardt (2005: xii) says, this does not diminish its importance:

> The problem of defining play and its role is one of the greatest challenges facing neuroscience, behavioral biology, psychology, education and the social sciences generally. Alas, it is rarely recognized as such… In a very real sense, only when we understand the nature of play will we be able to understand how to better shape the destinies of human societies in a mutually dependent world, the future of our species, and perhaps even the fate of the biosphere itself.

In his overview of attempts to define play both in animals and children, Burghardt highlights the difficulties of identifying characteristics that apply always and only to playing. Harker (2005, cited in Meire 2007: 10) advocates modesty in theorising about play. Many of the key characteristics often cited, such as freedom of choice, may not always apply absolutely (in group play, there has to be some compromise in order for the play to continue; not every player can do exactly as she or he chooses if they want to remain with the play group) and may also apply to behaviour that might not be play (such as exploration, curiosity or excitement-seeking). That said, the idea of personal choice and control can be found consistently within lists of defining characteristics. Lindquist (2001, cited in Meire 2007: 11) highlights the importance of feelings of power and control within playing, either for the individual or for the group as a whole. Other

14

characteristics of children's play from the literature are that it is 'non-literal' ('as-if' behaviour, the opportunity to turn the world upside down or rearrange it or behave in ways that would not normally be acceptable) whilst having some relationship with non-play behaviours; it is intrinsically motivated (undertaken for its own sake rather than for any external goal or reward); it is accompanied by positive affect (that is, it is pleasurable and enjoyable, positively valued); it is flexible and adaptive (using objects and rules in a variety of ways). Play can also often be repetitive, unpredictable, spontaneous, innovative and creative (Burghardt 2005).

Chapter 3 considers the nature of playing in detail and highlights its diversity. At this stage, given the lack of agreed definition, this report draws on the understanding of play from *Getting Serious About Play* (DCMS 2004: 9), which is also the definition used by the Big Lottery Fund for their Children's Play programme, namely:

> **what children and young people do when they follow their own ideas, in their own way and for their own reasons.**

Such a definition represents a significant field of tension and misalignment in the triangle of evidence, policy and practice. Whilst the idea of self direction might be espoused in policy terms as empowering, or as encouraging autonomy as a developmental milestone, it is likely to be supported only insofar as the play behaviour mirrors or simulates socially acceptable behaviour, or is understood (by its content) to show a direct relationship with instrumental policy objectives. Yet, what the evidence seems to point to, across both natural (neuroscience) and social (ethnography) science perspectives, is that children deliberately seek out uncertainty (both physical and emotional) in their play (for example, Spinka and others 2001; Sutton-Smith 2003; Kalliala 2006). Such playing with uncertainty is likely to be manifested in play behaviours that may not appear to be 'positive' in any linear or causal way. Examples might include war and superhero play, rough and tumble play and play fighting, teasing and bullying, jokes and obscenities, thrill seeking play such as parkour or skateboarding, adolescent experiments with drugs and sex, as well as behaviour in the public realm that is increasingly understood as dangerous or antisocial.

15

Much of the evidence from neuroscience suggests that playing is a way of building and shaping the emotion, motivation and reward regions of the brain rather than rehearsing specific skills that may be needed later in adult life (Burghardt 2005), and also that playing is a way of building a range of flexible responses across a number of adaptive systems that link the brain, the body and the social and physical environment. First-hand experiences of the raw, primary emotions of fear, anger, sadness, happiness, surprise and disgust (Damasio 2003) are essential for these processes to take place, and are evident in these kinds of playing.

Sutton-Smith (2003) suggests that play provides an excellent safe frame for the expressions of these primary emotions that can be held in check by the rules, rituals and play signals that define the game being played. These rules, rituals and play signals are driven by the more social, secondary emotions (for example, pride, shame, sympathy). This theorising is supported by studies which show that engagement in play helps to develop emotion regulation (for example, Panksepp 2007; Sutton-Smith 2003), peer and place attachment (for example, Gayler and Evans 2001; Mathur and Berndt 2006; Goodwin 2006; Korpela 2002; Corsaro 2003), emotional health through pleasure and enjoyment (for example, Tugade and others 2005; Gervaise and Wilson 2005: Martin 2007) and physical health (for example, Mackett and Paskins 2004).

A key point highlighted by much of the research is the importance of understanding these aspects as being interconnected and mutually dependent (Diamond 2007). Human development is a lifelong process of experiences that connect the brain, the body and the environment in a constant, mutually influencing shaping process (Thompson and Varela 2001; Edelman 2006). Through their play, individual children both adapt to and shape their environments. Such an understanding allows a breaking down both of the concept of the universal child developing through fixed stages towards the goal of adulthood (Wyness 2006) and also of the fixed and opposite understandings of difference as understood through adult/child, girl/boy, black/white, rich/poor and other binaries (Prout 2005). The dominant paradigm of preventative policies aimed at children 'at risk' of social exclusion has been criticised for focusing too much on the individual child and family. Evans and

Pinnock (2007) note that this deficit model overlooks the importance of children's relationship within their social and cultural networks and with their physical environments.

The sense of pleasure and reward derived from play generates an appetite or urge to seek out further stimuli that afford opportunities to play. The expression of this urge is not confined to the times and places that adults set apart for playing. Ethnographic studies of children's own experiences of playing in their local environments and in the school playground show that children continue to use space and time to play in ways that evoke adult nostalgia (challenging the perception that children no longer know how to play), anxiety and recrimination (for example, Percy-Smith 2002; Cloke and Jones 2005; Armitage 2004). Children's ability to engage playfully with their local environments and to actualise what these spaces afford for play depends on their ability to move independently within and across spaces. Restrictions to mobility, a heavy promotion of adult agendas and the determination of outcomes from play, prohibitions and constraints about the use of space and/or dull and featureless environments will narrow the potential of local environments to support children's play (Kytta 2004). Gill (2007) suggests that there is a need to move from a philosophy of protection towards a philosophy of resilience. Understanding children's play patterns can help adults to appreciate how to design spaces that support children's play, or indeed to acknowledge the existence of such patterns and do little other than protect children's right to participate within their local environments (Blinkert 2004).

Key messages

Play for a change has revealed a resonance between the academic research on the benefits of play for children's health and well-being and the broad aims stated in current policies for children and young people. However, policies and practice do not reflect this resonance because of their instrumental understanding of play and the nature of childhood. These key messages distil the findings of the review.

1. The well-being of children in England
A 2007 Unicef report on the well-being of children in 21 of the world's richest countries ranked the UK bottom. This sends a strong message that we need to think again about children's experiences of childhood. There are many statistics and many moral panics about the lives of children in England. Policy-makers need to heed the fact that, when children and young people themselves are asked about what is important in their own lives, playing and friends are consistently at the top of the list.

2. Play, development and well-being
We are now beginning to understand the interrelationship between genes, the brain, the body, behaviour and the physical and social environment. This has enabled a deeper understanding of how play contributes to children's physical and emotional well-being and to their development. Contrary to the dominant belief that it is a way of learning specific motor, cognitive or social skills, play has an impact on the architectural foundations of development such as gene expression and physical and chemical development of the brain. In turn, these foundations influence the child's ability to adapt to, survive, thrive in and shape their social and physical environments. Children's development and well-being cannot be understood as separate from their environment.

3. Play and resilience
Play can help build resilience – the capacity for children to thrive despite adversity and stress in their lives. Emotions have a key role in playing and play makes a major contribution to developing emotion regulation, building strong attachments and peer friendships, engendering positive feelings, and enabling children to cope with stressful situations through developing creative approaches and problem solving skills.

4. Play and social policy
The role of play in building children's resilience and in their health and well-being chimes with the emphasis on building resilience in social policy. The evidence is compelling. However, there is a need

to move away from an instrumental view of play that *Play for a Change* has found in much policy and practice, and towards a recognition that the benefits of play accrue from its characteristics of unpredictability, spontaneity, goallessness and personal control, rather than directly from its content. If policy-makers accept the evidence for the significance of play for children's well-being and development, then play provision should be judged on whether it enables children to play rather than on more instrumental outcomes. Because of the interrelationship with the environment there is no guarantee that playing will deliver on the five Every Child Matters outcomes; we can, however, be confident that these outcomes are more likely to be realised if children can play.

5. Time and space for play

The pleasure and enjoyment that children gain from playing leads them to seek out time and space to play. The prevailing understanding of childhood and play has led to an increase in adult control of children's use of time and space which in turn constrains the ways in which children can exploit the opportunities that local environments offer for playing. Where children can range independently, their environment becomes a field of 'free action' in which they can follow their own desires and create situations of wonder and uncertainty (Kytta 2004). An appreciation of the relationship between the nature of play and an environmental field of free action is crucial in designing play friendly neighbourhoods. This calls for partnership and cross-departmental working at local and national level.

6. The children's workforce

Evidence from the brain sciences shows that benefits accrue in part from the very characteristics of playing that adults often find uncomfortable and so seek to suppress. This raises questions, for example, about the effectiveness of anti-discriminatory practices, approaches to challenging behaviour, and if, when and how to direct or intervene in play. The evidence from ethnographic studies of children's play provides an excellent foundation for building an understanding of play through the eyes of children themselves. Given the significance of play in the lives of children, both from their own accounts and from the brain sciences, it would seem that it should, as a minimum, be part of the common core of knowledge that every adult needs when working with children.

7. Gathering the evidence from practice

The rich source of research about play, drawn from a range of academic disciplines, provides evidence of the need to ensure that children can play. However, this review has shown that there is a dearth of academically rigorous research into how best to make sure that children are able to play, either in the general environment or in children's spaces. Much of the literature on practice aims to show instrumental outcomes for play provision, whether that be motor, cognitive, social or emotional skills, physical activity or crime reduction. There is a need to gather the evidence on what works best in providing for play for its own sake.

Chapter 2

National and local socio-political context

This section provides the broad social and policy context for
a consideration of children's play as a matter for public policy.
It summarises the literature on the numerous measurements
of the lives of children and young people in England and the
areas of concern voiced about children and young people today.
It then draws briefly from the growing field of social studies
of childhood to consider how childhood is conceptualised or
constructed before moving on to review the literature on
children and social policy. Having laid this foundation of how
childhood is experienced and conceptualised, the place of
children's play in social policy is reviewed. The section finishes
with a review of the literature on policy making and particularly
on the concepts of risk, prevention and resilience within
approaches to policy-making.

Contemporary childhood in England: children's well–being

Children's well-being is the focus of much research; however, despite play being a defining
characteristic of childhood (Mayall 2002), it does not feature in any specific measurement of
well-being other than in children and young people's own accounts of their lives.

When Unicef released its report on the well-being of children in 21 of the richest countries in
February 2007, the British were horrified to discover that the UK ranked bottom of the list. *The
Sun* newspaper's political editor said that the 'bombshell report' identified Britain as 'the worst
country in the developed world for kids to grow up in' (Pascoe-Watson 2007). *The Independent*
ran with 'Britain's children: unhappy, neglected and poorly educated: damning verdict on the
ordeal of growing up in Britain today' (J Brown 2007a).

The Unicef report uses available data from 40 separate indicators across six dimensions:
material well-being, health and safety, education, peer and family relationships, behaviours
and risks, and young people's own subjective sense of well-being. There is recognition that
the best available data have their limitations and that there are several omissions, however,
a comparison of the data shows what is possible and 'demonstrates that given levels of child
well-being are not inevitable but policy-susceptible' (Unicef 2007: 3). For example, under the
heading of 'material well-being', the following observation is made:

> Higher government spending on family and social benefits is associated with lower
> child poverty rates. No OECD country devoting 10% or more of GDP to social
> transfers has a child poverty rate higher than 10%. No country devoting less than 5%
> of GDP to social transfers has a child poverty rate of less than 15% (Unicef 2007: 7).

Bradshaw and others (2007) report in more detail on the indicators and data used in the Unicef
report, comparing national indicators and discussing a framework for the analysis of children's
well-being. They note that many surveys exclude those who are structurally disadvantaged
(for example disabled children, children living in institutions and refugee children), since they
tend to target those living in family households and in mainstream education. Of particular

interest to this review, however, is the lack of any explicit reference to children's play within the Unicef indicators. Bradshaw and others acknowledge the importance of play and recreation to children's well-being as recognised in the United Nations Convention on the Rights of the Child (UNCRC), yet its inclusion in the indicators used is implicit within measures of leisure and friendship, and there is no recommendation in Bradshaw's analysis of data collection methods to develop explicit indicators on this defining feature of children's lives. As Mayall (2002: 132) notes, 'play features … prominently in young people's accounts of childhood', and this has been shown time and again when they are asked about their lives (for example CYPU 2002; Camina 2004; The Children's Society 2006). This appears to be a significant discrepancy between the ways in which children and young people and adults understand childhood. Given the relationship between play and well-being outlined in Chapter 3 of this review, there is a strong argument for paying it more attention.

The UK Government submitted its third report on its implementation of the UNCRC to the United Nations Committee on the Rights of the Child in July 2007. In preparing for this report, the government commissioned a review of the views of children, and reports (UK Government 2007: 27):

> While nearly 80% of children said they had opportunities to relax, play and have fun most days or every day, more opportunities for leisure and socialising was the most common response when children were asked what would make life better for them and their friends.

The report has a chapter on education, leisure and cultural activities, which covers Article 31 of the UNCRC. There are 104 paragraphs reporting on education across the four nations of the UK, one on play generally and one on play in each of the four nations (totalling five), a further 17 on sport and the arts and eight on youth policy. Whilst this is a very crude method of analysis, it is notable that the government put very little emphasis on an issue that children and young people themselves consider so important.

Statistical and qualitative information on children's lives today is abundant, as Thomas and Hocking (2003: 9) show:

> British children are among the most measured in the world, and there are innumerable sources of evidence regarding their well-being — from hard facts depicting their health, wealth, academic achievement, criminal behaviour and family circumstances, to softer impressions of how they are portrayed in the media, and the anecdotal evidence we all carry with us about how we respond to, interact with and observe our own and other people's children.

One such assessment of children's well-being in the UK was carried out by Save the Children (Bradshaw and Mayhew 2005), and some of the findings are given here as overall contextual information. The report found that well-being was steadily improving for most children in the UK, with falling levels of child poverty, improved educational attainment, lower infant death rates and child pedestrian death rates and a levelling of youth crime rates. However, the report also notes a rise in the number of children living in workless households, a continuing decline in children's use of public spaces, a rise in school exclusions, little improvement in literacy and numeracy, a downward trend in many health indicators and a rise in homelessness.

Despite overall falling levels of child poverty and rising attainment, this is not evenly spread across all children: 'although children in ethnic minority families make up 14 per cent of the total child population, they make up 25 per cent of all poor children' (Department for Work and Pensions 2007: 12). Similarly, Preston and Robertson (2006) report that over half of disabled children live on or near the margins of poverty.

The Good Childhood Inquiry describes itself as 'the UK's first independent national inquiry into childhood' (The Children's Society 2006: 7) and is asking three key questions:

• What are the conditions for a good childhood?

• What obstacles exist to those conditions?

• What changes could be made that would be likely to improve childhood?

The launch report includes findings from a preliminary survey of over 8000 young people aged between 14 and 16 years, which asked the first two of these questions. Leisure was the third most important aspect of the respondents' lives, with requests for accessible places to go and things to do. The case for the importance of play in children's lives across these headings has been put by Play England (2006: 2):

> [A] good childhood involves all children and young people being able to find places, near their homes, where they can play and meet their friends free of charge.

Yet explicit mention of the importance of play in children's lives and the contribution it can make to well-being (see Chapter 3), other than its broader cousins such as 'leisure' or 'friendships', remains notable by its absence in the official documentation both in measurement of children's well-being and in policy aimed at improving it.

The New Economics Foundation (2004) focused on subjective perceptions of well-being in their survey of Nottingham children and young people. They identified two aspects of well-being: life satisfaction and personal development. Personal development is defined as 'being curious and engaging in challenging and absorbing activities' (NEF 2004: 2). Whilst play is not a focus of this report, it could be argued that it is an excellent expression of and mechanism for this aspect of well-being. Using these indicators, the study found that well-being fell substantially as children grew older; children at the top academically performing primary school showed lower well-being than other primary schools; children who were unhappy at home were three times more likely to have lower well-being than the average; and those who engaged in sport had substantially higher well-being.

Madge (2006) provides a snapshot of children's, young people's and adults' views on childhood and youth today from 2000 young people aged 7-15 years and 500 adults, both parents and non-parents. The key messages from this survey were that most children described their childhoods as happy, that they valued what they saw as a freedom from responsibility although, as they became older, they wanted to be given more independence. Children also wanted to feel safe, yet at the same time wanted freedom to make their own choices. With reference to antisocial behaviour and criminality, Madge (2006: 142) suggests a need to put the issue into perspective and to 'convey the message that most kids are okay'.

'The way in which childhood is conceptualised and understood has a significant impact on how play is understood and particularly on the way in which it is addressed in social policy.'

Adult concerns about children

It would seem, however, that adult perceptions of children in England today do not necessarily reflect Madge's conclusion. Adult concerns about children generally affect the way that children's play is understood, so these concerns are reviewed here to provide a general backdrop to the specific review of the literature on children's play in Chapters 3 and 4.

A MORI survey (2004, cited in Madge 2006) highlighted the predominance of negative images of young people in the media (71 per cent), with only 14 per cent positive and 15 per cent neutral, despite International Federation of Journalism guidelines agreed in 1998 to 'avoid the use of stereotypes and sensational presentation ... involving children' (Madge 2006: 144-145). The Children's Society (2006: 6) highlights the contradictory nature of reporting on children and young people:

> A brief scan of recent headlines in the UK press quickly illustrates our contradictory and dichotomous attitudes towards children and young people: our angels or demons, innocents or deviants. Our fear for children 'Get these perverts off the street… or parents will' (*The Sun*, 14 June 2006), 'Betrayal of innocence' (*The Mirror*, 27 July 2006) contrasts sharply with our fear of children, 'Let's tame these feral children now' (*The Independent*, 29 April 2002), 'A generation of young savages' (*The Mail* on Sunday, 17 April 2005), 'Yobs are laughing off their Asbos' (*The Daily Mail*, 14 January 2006).

It is not only the media and well-being surveys that express concerns about today's children and young people. Parents, practitioners and academics have all added their anecdotes, observations and research to create a general zeitgeist that says all is not well with our young. Mayall (2005) cites Simon Hoggart (2005: 14) writing in *The Guardian*:

> [O]f the top 10 hardback and 10 paperback bestsellers in March 2005, nine are about child abuse, bullying, anorexia, childhood 'in care'. This amounts to 'thousands of volumes packed with childhood misery and youthful torment sold every week'. Why do people want to read about such matters? he asks.

The debate centres around whether changes are in children themselves or in adult perceptions, or a mixture of both. Gill (2007b: 78) suggests that 'what were once deemed "normal" behaviours in growing children – unruliness, tantrums, quarrels, play-fighting, shyness, introspection – seem to have become pathologised as psychological problems'. From assertions of the disappearance of childhood due to children's exposure to adult images via technology (Postman 1983), through teachers reporting an increase in verbal abuse against and physical attacks on staff (Smith 2007) and an increase in cyberbullying of peers and of teachers (ATL 2007), to Palmer's (2006) thesis of 'toxic childhood syndrome', a number of contested areas for adult concerns about childhood and youth emerge. Some of these are reviewed very briefly here, more to illustrate how adult understandings of childhood and youth are contested than to give any hard statistics.

• **The rise in mental health problems, particularly conduct and hyperkinetic disorders such as Attention Deficit (Hyperactivity) Disorder (ADHD),** although the evidence is inconsistent: Green and others (2005) report that there is no change in the prevalence between 1999 and 2004; NICE (2005) report that prescriptions rates in England for stimulant drugs (methylphenidate and dexamfetamine) in the same period have almost doubled; Palmer (2006) talks of the special needs explosion; Rose (2005: 256) suggests 'there are no manifest structural or biochemical abnormalities in those diagnosed with ADHD' and Timimi (2005: 35) queries the validity of diagnoses and proposes that the current trend towards the medicalisation of childhood is 'an (inadequate) response to the social and economic conditions of the time'.

• **The rise in anti-social behaviour and youth crime:** Hough and Roberts (2004) found that 75 per cent of people polled in their survey thought that the number of young offenders had increased, whereas numbers coming to the attention of the police had fallen by 9 per cent.

- **The effects of technology on children:** Palmer (2006), whilst acknowledging the benefits of technology, lists research on the dangers of TV, mobile phones and the internet; Cunningham (2006), whilst recognising the potential pitfalls, draws parallels with adult concerns at each new technological innovation from books to the cinema to rock and roll music, and suggests that children are more sophisticated and discerning than some adults assume; Livingstone (2003) notes the growing research in children's and young people's use of the internet for building existing real social networks.

- **The rise in obesity:** statistics for childhood obesity clearly show a rise, with 27.7 per cent of 2- to 10-year-olds being either overweight or obese in 2003, a rise from 22.7 per cent in 1995 (Jotangia and others 2006); the disagreements arise over how best to tackle the issue through changing eating and exercise habits, with the BMA (2005) recognising the range of individual, interpersonal, organisational and policy level factors as well as psychosocial influences.

- **The commercialisation of childhood:** Williams (2006) highlights how marketing aimed at children, in a child-oriented market worth £30 billion, is affecting the way they eat, learn and play. The 'cool factor' requires certain clothes to be worn and fear of teasing or bullying in the school playground gives weight to 'pester power'. Commercially produced toys are perceived as restricting imaginative and active play. Hill (2003) debates whether the all-pervasiveness of marketing to children is encouraging consumerism, bad eating habits and sexualised behaviour or whether adults' concerns are based more in a fear of children embracing modern life and other misplaced anxieties; running alongside these concerns is also the concern about the commodification of childhood (McKendrick and others 2000) through conceptualising children (or their parents) as consumers or customers of services such as education, and through the growth in areas such as the children's fashion industry or commercial play sector.

Many of these issues are explored further in Chapters 3 and 4. In addition, fears for children's safety have an impact on their independent mobility and their play and friendship patterns, as is outlined in Chapter 4.

The Rt Hon David Lammy MP recognises that these concerns about children 'lack a coherent political narrative'. He goes on to say that debates about childhood 'tend to be framed either by anxious reactions to specific trends which tend to condemn the modern world as the enemy of real childhood or in notions of youth and childhood themselves being out-of-control, the enemy of civic and cultural life' (Lammy 2007: 1).

The concept of childhood

The way in which childhood is conceptualised and understood has a significant impact on how play is understood and particularly on the way in which it is addressed in social policy. The late twentieth century saw a growth in the development of social studies of childhood (for example, Hendrick 1997; James and Prout 1997; James and others 1998), which challenged the thinking from psychology that had dominated childhood studies for the previous half-century. The notion of a universal or 'natural' childhood consisting of ordered stages of development was countered with the concept of childhood as a social construction. As Madge (2006: 2) says:

> Although the biological immaturity of children is a fact of life, the ways in which this is understood and made meaningful is dependent on culture.

A number of varying ways of conceptualising childhood have been developed, including the innocent child in need of protection, the evil child in need of correction, the child as adult-in-waiting in need of education and socialisation, the child as investment in the future and children as a minority group (Hendrick 1997; James and others 1998). The key aspects of childhood that these theorists highlight is the diversity of children's lives and experiences across class, ethnicity, gender, disability and other social divisions: 'there is not one childhood but many' (Fawcett and others 2005: 19), together with the concept of children's own agency and their social competence in being children

(Mayall 2002; Hutchby 2005). Much current social policy focuses on the future of children's lives – the adult citizens they will and should become – rather than their lives as experienced in the here and now (Mayall 2005).

After 20 years or so of studies into the socially constructed nature of childhood, Prout (2005) questions whether the focus has shifted too far, and suggests that a simplistic binary opposition of biology and culture is counterproductive in our understanding of childhood. Fawcett and others (2004) criticise the tendency of constructionist theorising to dismiss developmental psychology outright, claiming there is much of value to be found in the detail and complexities of this discipline.

Two particularly interesting arenas for debate have emerged from these studies, and particularly from the ESRC Children 5-16 Research Programme (Prout 2002). The first of these is the idea of children as social actors: children are not merely passive recipients of education, socialisation and other environmental stimuli, but they act upon and influence events and contribute to social and cultural change. This became particularly apparent through the involvement of children and young people themselves throughout the ESRC Children 5-16 Research Programme. As Prout (2002: 68) concludes:

> By engaging children in research they have been shown to have a 'standpoint', from which social life often appears differently from how it looks from an adult perspective.

The second aspect develops from the understanding of children as social actors and is the exploration of adult-child relations. From a philosophical perspective, Archard (2004) draws distinctions between adults' liberationist and paternalistic (caretaker) approaches to their relationships with children. Alanen (2001b) suggests that considering adult-child relations through the theoretical lens of generational relationships allows a useful examination of agency, power and influence (or lack of it) in children's everyday lives. This area is explored further in Chapter 5 in relation to adult involvement in children's play.

Moss and Petrie (2002) suggest that the current focus on evidence-based policy masks an underpinning construct of the child as weak and needy, as innocent or threat, leading to an ever-increasing surveillance and control of children and young people. Moss and Petrie (2002) advocate moving away from a top-down, linear, instrumental approach to children's services towards a concept of children's spaces where children are recognised as competent and active agents in their own lives. Their book opens with a description of The Venture, an adventure playground in North Wales, as an example of a children's space.

'Much current social policy focuses on the future of children's lives – the adult citizens they will become – rather than their lives as experienced in the here and now.'

Children and social policy

More recently, Moss (2007) continues to expose a deep 'paradigmatic divide' between the dominant and alternative discourses on childhood within the early childhood education and care sector. The dominant paradigm sees children as the future of the nation, and professional, technical interventions as the means to ensure an economically and socially effective future society. The values and assumptions of the dominant paradigm lie in a

> particular form of modernity … [that is] highly regulatory, foregrounding order, control and certitude and privileging a particular concept of reason and knowledge: an instrumental, calculating and totalising reason and a scientific knowledge that is unified and claims to reveal an objective and universal truth about humanity, history and nature. (Moss 2007: 230)

Within this paradigm, professional and technical inputs lead to measurable outcomes in the lives of children. Much of the literature on playing, development and well-being within this review bring into question the possibility of any certitude of cause and effect in such a singular, universal and linear manner.

Children and young people have been the focus of a plethora of social policy initiatives and strategies since the Labour Party came to power in 1997. The Social Exclusion Unit, Sure Start, Health Action Zones, Education Action Zones, the National Childcare Strategy, Working Families Tax Credit, are but a few of the projects established in the first term (Roberts 2001). Since then, the work has continued to grow, with the appointment of a Children's Commissioner, the Children Act 2004, the Childcare Act 2006, Every Child Matters and more (Mcneish and Gill 2006). Running alongside this has also been a range of measures to tackle youth crime, including Antisocial Behaviour Orders (ASBOs), Youth Offending Teams, Preventative Strategies, Parenting Orders and the Respect Agenda (Goldson 2002; J Brown 2007b).

As Reeves (2003, cited in Madge 2006: 5) shows, there is a conflation of several constructs of the child within this 'growing child-centred political consensus':

> … treacly words mask a deep-seated uncertainty about the nature of children and childhood. Are children mini-adults, able to manage a sophisticated consumer environment and influence events? Or are they large toddlers requiring constant protection, not least from the state, against a predatory society? Does their youthful vigour represent the long-term solution to our problems, or are their delinquency and disenchantment the cause? Perhaps most important – with whom does responsibility for their welfare rest?
>
> Listen to Gordon Brown [then Chancellor of the Exchequer], and children are the little angels who will bear us to a fairer world. Listen to Charles Clarke [then Education Secretary] and they are the army of the new economy. Listen to David Blunkett [then Home Secretary] and they are the thugs blighting our cities. Listen to Tony Blair [then Prime Minister] and, depending on the day, they are all of the above.

Hood (2007) suggests that the way data about children are gathered and categorised reflects how children are understood, and the goals and priorities that adults set for them through social policy. Traditionally, the focus has been on service delivery, largely around health, welfare and education. Recently this has shifted to a more holistic approach to planning and a greater commitment to seeking the views of children and young people themselves.

In 2001 a Children and Young People's Unit (CYPU) was established within the Department for Education and Skills (DfES) although this has now disappeared as a discrete unit. During 2001-2002 the CYPU carried out a major consultation on a proposed Strategy for Children and Young People (CYPU 2001a), consulting separately with children, young people and adults. This consultation document formed the beginnings of the current Every Child Matters (DfES 2004) outcomes framework for every child to be healthy, stay safe, achieve and enjoy, make a positive contribution and achieve economic well-being. The original consultation document included the outcome of 'achievement and enjoyment' where the 'aspiration' was defined as:

> Children and young people should have the opportunity to fulfil their personal goals and ambitions, to make mature choices about their future lives, to achieve success in their academic, social and cultural development; to be recognised, to enjoy the fruits of their achievements when they begin work, and have the means to engage in constructive play and leisure pursuits for their own sake.

and the measurement of success being through outcomes, including:

> educational attainment; first employment and employability; engagement in the arts, music, sport and wider leisure activities; access to popular play and leisure facilities; engagement in community and voluntary activities; a sense of achievement and self-esteem. (CYPU 2001: 22)

The responses to the consultations with children and young people, across all ages and consultation methods (events, questionnaires, booklets, postcards), consistently prioritised more places and opportunities for play and leisure. These responses were taken forward within the government's Every Child Matters and Youth Matters agendas. However, the combining of 'enjoyment' with 'achievement', together with the filtering of children's and young people's responses through the lens of adult understandings of childhood, has meant that children's and young people's play and informal recreation has taken a lower priority in the focus on academic achievement. Hood (2007), in discussing the framework for the second State of London's Children Report (Hood, 2004), felt the need to reflect children's and young people's views of what was important in their lives through separating out enjoyment and achievement.

> This aims to do justice to the concept of enjoyment as an important outcome in its own right and to reflect young people's own expressed concerns about the opportunities that are available to them in their non-school and leisure time. (Hood 2007: 255)

A similar move was made by Hull City Council in their Children and Young People's Plan, which is organised around six rather than five outcomes:

> The Every Child Matters framework sets out 25 aims under five outcomes. We will work towards achieving the 25 aims under six, rather than five, outcomes, separating Enjoy and Achieve. This will ensure the Enjoy Life outcome receives as much focused attention and activity as the other outcomes. (Hull City Council 2005: 11)

Children's play and social policy

Alongside the Every Child Matters programme, the social policy context for children's play has also changed enormously in the last five years. *Best Play: What Play Provision Should do for Children* was published in 2000 by the National Playing Fields Association, the Children's Play Council and PLAYLINK in response to a challenge from the then Culture Secretary, the Rt Hon. Chris Smith MP. This kick-started a process within government that eventually led to the Play Review, a consultative process led by the Department for Culture, Media and Sport, which made recommendations on the use of lottery funding for children's play (DCMS 2004). *Making the Case for Play* was published by the Children's Play Council in 2002 (Cole-Hamilton and Gill 2002) and drew on an 18-month research project to show how, despite a growing interest in play, children's opportunities to play varied according to where they lived and their particular needs, and was restricted by fear, lack of adequate play spaces, a replacement of open access play provision with childcare, varied levels of strategic planning and wide variations in support for staff. The report made a number of recommendations, including calling for a national strategic approach to address these variations.

This publication fed into the DCMS Play Review and eventually the framework for the Big Lottery Fund's £155 million Children's Play initiative. Play England, a five-year national programme to 'promote strategies for free play and aims to create a lasting support structure for play providers in England' (www.playengland.org.uk), was launched in 2006 as one element of this initiative. The main element, the Children's Play programme, allocated a total of £124 million to English local authority area play partnerships which were invited to make applications for a portfolio of projects as a part of their overall play strategy. The third element of the initiative was Playful Ideas, making £16 million available to support innovation and new ways of providing for children's play.

> There has been real progress for the play sector since the publication of *Best Play* in 2000, *Making the Case for Play* in 2002 and *Getting Serious About Play* in 2004 … There have been huge changes for the play sector through the Big Lottery Fund's play initiative and the establishment of Play England. These have been taking place at the same time as the increased recognition of the importance of play at a national level … The concept of play is now embedded in a way that it never was before, thanks in no small measure to the work of CPC [the Children's Play Council]. (DCMS 2006a: 43)

The DCMS (2006a) publication *Time for Play*, cited above, came out of the DCMS-led cross-departmental group on play that was established following the publication of *Getting Serious About Play* (DCMS 2004) and a recognition of the need for a 'more strategic approach to play policy', highlighted by the then Culture Secretary, the Rt Hon Tessa Jowell MP (Davis 2006b). The document shows how play contributes to many government priorities and outlines national government support for play, including:

• the Department for Culture, Media and Sport's funding of national organisations and support for play through cultural programmes;

• the Department for Education and Skills' Every Child Matters programme, Sure Start and Youth Matters;

• the Department for Communities and Local Government's Cleaner, Safer, Greener programme to improve public spaces in neighbourhoods;

• the Department of Health's Healthy Schools programme which recognises the importance of play in tackling obesity;

• Home Office support for work with the families of those in prison, including play facilities for children visiting prison;

• the Department for the Environment, Food and Rural Affairs support for play provision in rural areas through parish councils, and support for the work of organisations such as the Forestry Commission, the Countryside Agency, English Nature and Natural England in encouraging children to play in the natural environment;

• the Department for Transport's support for Home Zones through publishing guidelines as well as encouraging local authorities to consider how children and young people can access spaces to play.

Time for Play was broadly welcomed by the play sector, with some reservations, including a comment from Shola Shobowale of Lambeth Youth Council, who pointed out that 'the document seemed to describe progress to date from government rather than what is going to be done' (Shobowale 2006).

The initiatives listed above show that, despite a stated commitment to children's play, its place in national policy is subsumed within broader policies with no statutory duty attached, and is therefore simultaneously a mechanism for government targets and without weight. Powell and Wellard (2008), in their analysis of 43 government policy and legislative documents that have an impact on children's play, found that there was no single coherent understanding in government policy of what is meant by play and often, whilst play is recognised as important in the policies, this is not followed through into performance measurement. Generally speaking, they found that adult-led, structured activities were more commonly endorsed by government than play and informal recreation, particularly in legislation and statutory guidance.

> While the importance of play appears to be recognised by Government departments, in some cases its value seems predominantly to be utilitarian, the text demonstrating how its known benefits effectively can contribute to departmental priorities and targets. An alternative view recognises play's intrinsic value to children; this is less commonly supported by policy documentation.
> (Powell and Wellard 2008: 10)

Such utilitarianism tends to focus on two main adult-perceived benefits of play and play provision. The first of these is its role in learning and development, particularly in the early years, for example the Curriculum Guidance for the Foundation Stage (QCA 2000: 25) states that 'well planned play is a key way in which children learn with enjoyment and challenge'. The National Standards for Daycare and Childminding (DfES 2003: 12), applicable for settings which provide for children under eight-years-old, but which also have a knock-on effect on supervised play and out of school settings that cater for both under and over eight-year-olds, require the registered person to 'plan and provide activities and play opportunities to develop children's emotional, physical, social and intellectual capabilities'. Santer and others (2007: 18) highlight the lack of an agreed understanding of what is meant by play, saying, with reference to the Early Years Foundation Stage:

28

> The lengthy consultation document made explicit that play is to be fostered in young children. However, a close reading of the document reveals that more emphasis is placed on 'purposeful' and 'planned' play than on children's free play. Whilst many early childhood practitioners understand this to mean that adults structure and plan the environments for play, rather than the play itself, this is not made explicit and may not be understood in this way by all practitioners.

This leads Santer and others (2007: 20) to draw the following conclusion regarding the place of play in early childhood policy:

> Play is enjoying a renaissance at present. The programmes mentioned ... suggest that play is positively regarded in the lives of young children and an integral element of high quality provision. Large-scale projects such as the Effective Provision of Preschool Education (Sylva and others 2004) funded by the government, and the Study of Pedagogical Effectiveness in Early Learning (Moyles and others 2002) both talk of the importance of play in high quality provision. Generally, however, 'play' is an ill-defined and all-encompassing term that requires further examination.

Space for play and informal learning in primary and secondary schools, through the Building Schools for the Future agenda, as well as the focus on the play-based curriculum in the early years, is seen as essential for nurturing creativity in young people (DCMS 2006b).

The second utilitarian focus for play in social policy is its role in crime reduction. An example of this is the multi-departmental Positive Activities for Young People programme that ran from April 2003 to March 2006 with a budget of £124.5 million. The programme brought together several pre-existing initiatives and projects into one and was 'aimed at those young people aged 8-19 years most at risk of social exclusion, committing crime or being a victim of crime' (DfES 2006a).

A similar focus on 'positive activities' can be found in the Youth Matters programme (DfES 2006b), the development of which was influenced by research from Feinstein and others (2005). Drawing on the 1970 Cohort Study to consider relationships between choice of leisure activity in mid-teens and social exclusion later in life, the research found that those who attended the less structured youth clubs tended to come from socially excluded backgrounds, whereas the opposite was true for those who attended uniformed groups or church-based activities.

Attendance at sports centres and clubs showed no such differentiation. Allowing for a number of variables, the research concludes, 'participation in youth clubs was associated with adult social exclusion, particularly in terms of criminal offending or poor educational attainment' (Feinstein and others 2005: 19). Whilst the authors urge caution in attributing straight causality between youth club attendance and later social exclusion, they do suggest that a lack of structure and therefore stronger peer group influences were linked to negative outcomes in this way. The authors also recognised the challenge of developing services that would attract such young people whilst still providing a level of structure that would counteract negative peer group influences.

McArdle (2001) draws on research to show how play is important both in terms of emotion regulation and in terms of developing social networks and social skills. Play in middle childhood is dependent on the availability of safe spaces, and McArdle notes that the reduction in adult social networks, together with the rise in traffic and loss of play space, has a bigger impact on children from poorer housing areas than for their better off counterparts. These children, particularly boys, are

> deprived of a safe and regulated outlet for negotiating dominance, saving face and teamwork and of opportunities for exploratory play. As a consequence … it may be that human adolescent males from such a background may tend to engage more often in dysfunctional competition, perhaps contributing to the rise in violent behaviour among urban youths. (McArdle 2001: 512)

He suggests that national and local government should consider opportunities for play as 'a serious candidate for the prevention of adolescent problems' (McArdle (2001: 512).

Young people themselves cite boredom as a key factor in involvement in crime (Adamson 2003). The New Deal for Communities (NDC) programme included what was termed 'diversionary' activities as part of the strategy for crime reduction, and these activities varied in the level of direction and supervision by adults.

29

'… play is important both in terms of emotion regulation and in terms of developing social networks and social skills.'

In discussing the Youth Matters agenda, Smith (2005) highlights the tension within the youthwork sector between youthwork as social education and youthwork as recreation, parallel debates to those in the playwork sector on the tensions between the instrumental and the intrinsic value of play and consequent debates on levels of adult direction and ways of measuring the effectiveness of provision.

In addition to the policy focus on play's role in learning and crime prevention, there is also a growing awareness of the role of play in combating childhood obesity. The target to halt the increase in child obesity by 2010 became a Public Service Agreement (PSA) in 2004. Whilst recognising that obesity is a complex issue, and that 'the degree to which inactivity is responsible for the rising levels of obesity in children has not been established' (DH 2004a: 32), it is accepted that children need to be encouraged to take part in physical activity in order to prevent and treat obesity, and in 2004 the Chief Medical Officer recommended that children should take at least an hour of at least moderate physical activity each day (DH 2004a), and that there should be a good variety of physical activity including spontaneous play, climbing and rough and tumble. The report also recommends that local authorities should take steps to make neighbourhoods more conducive to activities such as walking and playing. In follow-up guidance play features as a key contributor to physical activity and to laying the foundations for an active adult life (DH 2004b) and play is included in measures for schools, extended schools, children's centres and local authorities to take in order to encourage an increase in children's and young people's physical activity (DH 2005). The Big Lottery Fund's Children's Play programme is listed as a key programme contributing to the delivery of the government's child obesity PSA target (Comptroller and Auditor General 2006).

The relationship between playing and both physical and mental health is explored in more detail in Chapter 3 where the evidence suggests that, for the optimum health benefits from physical activity, it needs to contain elements of non-routine movements, uncertainty, and a sense of enjoyment, control and efficacy (Poulsen and Ziviani 2004; Burdette and Whittaker 2005). Whilst social policy measures can help to create the opportunity for such playful physical activity experiences, it would be difficult to prescribe them.

Finally, in terms of the discussion on utilitarian underpinnings for children's play in social policy, attention must be drawn to the place of childcare provision. The government's 10-year childcare strategy (HM Treasury and others 2004) is a major element of the drive to eradicate child poverty through enabling parents and carers to take up paid employment, mainly through the introduction of tax credits. The utility here is economic, but there is evidence to show that the rise in out-of-school childcare provision has also led to a reduction in open access play provision (Head and Melville 2001; Hallsworth and Sutton 2004; Play England 2006). The extent to which out-of-school childcare can provide for children's play is a contested area, particularly where provision is run on school premises with the restrictions that brings (for example, Smith and Barker 2000). However, there is also evidence (Hallsworth and Sutton 2004; Smith and Barker 2004) that particular groups of children (for example, children from Black and minority ethnic groups, refugees and asylum seeking children, looked-after children and those from low income families) who would be able to access open access play provision are more likely to be excluded from childcare provision.

Whilst policies aimed specifically at children and young people tend to promote a utilitarian or instrumental view of play, those that relate to the population as a whole, and particularly to communities, neighbourhoods and the environment, are more likely to acknowledge play's intrinsic value (Powell and Wellard 2008).

The government's Cleaner, Safer, Greener agenda (ODPM 2002a), aimed at improving the quality of public space, recognises the importance of ensuring that children can play, citing evidence that good quality public space and children's play areas are important to people and have an impact on community well-being. The programme specifically lists creating attractive and welcoming parks, play areas and public spaces, and ensuring appropriate provision for children and young people in its key targets, and is supported by the Public Service Agreement (PSA) Target 8 (Liveability). CABE Space was created as a part of this agenda, coming out of the Urban Green Spaces Task Force in 2002, and they have played a major role in consulting with children and young people over the design and maintenance of public spaces where they can meet and play (CABE Space 2004). These developments also tie in with the neighbourhood renewal agenda and programmes such as New Deal for Communities, which have also recognised the need for quality play space for children in their own neighbourhoods (for example, Barraclough and others 2004).

Planning Policy Guidance 17: Planning for open space, sport and recreation (ODPM 2002b), requires local authorities to carry out a quantitative and qualitative assessment of need for and audit of existing open spaces and sport and recreation facilities. This includes children's opportunities for play. The Children's Play Council (2006a) recommends that the development of play strategies can complement or support this work.

The Rt Hon. David Lammy MP suggests that these two currently separate spheres of policy (children's services and local regeneration) need to be brought together:

> After a decade of investment in children's services and in the wider public sphere, I believe the challenge is to connect two of this Government's most successful policy agendas: children's services and local regeneration. We need to put children at the forefront of our efforts at urban renewal. (Lammy 2007: 1)

Risk, prevention and resilience as themes in social policy

Having considered the social policy context for children's play through reviewing the literature on adult understandings of children and young people and the dominant paradigm highlighted by Moss (2007) of an instrumental and technical approach to services for children and young people, this section returns to the literature on policy-making to examine a particular paradigm (or theoretical framework) that offers the potential for recognising the intrinsic value of children's play within social policy.

France and Utting (2005) note a shift away from a focus on children in need, which formed the basis of the Children Act 1989, towards a focus on prevention: rather than focusing scant resources on services for children and young people in need, the prevention discourse suggests that there are moral and economic gains to be had from investing resources in prevention. Policies introduced by the Labour Government since 1997, such as On Track, Sure Start and the Children's Fund, were all within this prevention paradigm, as was the requirement on local authorities in 2002 to develop preventative strategies. Two aspects of the prevention approach are the identification of risk and protective factors.

The 'risk-focused prevention paradigm' seeks to find ways of addressing a number of social problems (such as educational underachievement, crime, substance misuse and mental health problems) through early intervention with children and young people identified as being 'at risk' of problems later in life. The interventions are based on seeking to reduce known risk factors – not causes or predictors of later problems, but factors that have been seen to be present in the lives of those who manifest problems in later life. Drawing on Farrington (2000), France and Utting (2005: 79) explain that:

> knowledge of risk factors for problem behaviour, derived from prospective longitudinal research, can be used to design prevention programmes. No single factor among the risk factors consistently identified in children and young people's lives, can be said to cause later problem behaviour, but by reducing them, their incidence can be reduced.

Hansen and Plewis (2004: 6) also highlight the difficulty of attributing risk factors to eventual adverse outcomes. Although children born and raised in particular circumstances (for example, poverty, family breakdown or low academic achievement of parents) tend to show poorer outcomes, it should not be assumed that this is always the case or that risk factors are the same thing as predictors of later problems. Feinstein and Sabates (2006: iii) show in their analysis involving data from 1958 and 1970 British Cohort Studies that there is a 'high level of

31

capacity to identify early on those at risk of high cost, high harm outcomes'; yet they caution that identification is not the same as causation: the measures used to identify those most at risk are not the same thing as the causes of poor outcomes, and the holistic local picture needs to be studied rather than developing universal and technical policy or practice solutions.

In addition to identifying risk factors, the prevention approach also uses knowledge of 'protective factors' that have a parallel relationship to good outcomes for children and young people who grow up in situations where they are likely to be exposed to many of the risk factors. Protective factors include strong social bonds with friends, family and other adults.

Detractors of the paradigm argue that early assessment can stigmatise children and is fraught with ethical problems, including increased surveillance and monitoring. The generalisations of both risk and protective factors may not apply to each individual case. Nevertheless, France and Utting suggest that, notwithstanding some of the weaknesses, this is a model that is worth pursuing. It can be seen in several recent and current government initiatives including Sure Start, On Track, the Children's Fund and Connexions (Evans and Pinnock 2007). It can also be seen in many of the aims, targets and indicators of the Every Child Matters framework, for example promotion of breast-feeding, reduction in teenage conceptions, alcohol and drug consumption, crime and antisocial behaviour, and educational achievement. What is worth consideration here is research data that shows how playing in childhood can be seen as a protective factor, particularly through its relationship to resilience and coping strategies (see Chapter 3).

The Children's Fund, a preventative programme with an overall budget of £960 million over the first eight years (Edwards and others 2006) targeted its work at children and young people aged five to 13 years considered to be 'at risk of social exclusion'. One of the findings of the National Evaluation of the Children's Fund was that, despite the innovative emphasis within the Children's Fund on partnership working and the importance of professional networking, the model of prevention used across the Children's Fund focused on the individual and family levels of prevention and building resilience, rather than the community level. As a result, the design and implementation of services focused attention 'on individual children rather than on the processes by which they came to be excluded' (Barnes and Morris 2007: 194). This raises some concern about the sustainability of the effects of any preventative intervention within communities in the long term, as well as a tendency to see services as a one-way process of professional experts acting upon needy and incompetent children, rather than recognising children's own agency and strength to develop coping strategies through their relationships (Edwards 2007). The recognition of the role of children's social networks in their well-being and their sense of connectedness or disconnectedness is highlighted by Barnes and Morris (2007). Although they do not mention play specifically, this raises interesting questions for social policy approaches to helping to build strong social networks, given that playing is a key process for building and maintaining social relationships, and particularly one that affords children agency. As Hine (2005: 129) says:

> Qualitative work with children and families … increasingly highlights the resilience of children and young people living in what many of us would consider to be extraordinary and difficult environments. The challenge for interventions is to provide services that acknowledge their realities and support children and young people's own efforts to lead pro-social lives.

Evans and Pinnock (2007) argue that whilst many services target support at individual children, more could be done in building services that take children's wider domains into account (family, school, community) and so tackle the wider, more ecological and structural aspects of social exclusion. Their research draws on qualitative data gathered from children and young people and their families, echoing Mayall's (2001, 2005) emphasis on the importance of taking children and young people's perspectives into account in policy development, implementation and evaluation. The focus on the individual child privileges biological and psychosocial aspects over environmental and structural ones (the way that society is structured); such an approach can stigmatise individuals who are often labelled as vulnerable or at risk because 'their appearance, language, culture, values, home communities, and family structures do not match those of the dominant culture' (Evans and Pinnock 2007: 23). Such an argument would support the idea that children's social networks can play a large part in helping to develop resilience (as advocated in Gilligan 2000 and Little and others 2004), and an extension of the argument would be to suggest that such networks are often developed through play (Weller 2007a).

The need to take community and neighbourhood factors into account is also highlighted by Jack (2006), who cites evidence to show that families living in disadvantaged areas are less able to develop social networks and are subject to more stress as a direct result of the areas in which they live, irrespective of the individual characteristics of the families themselves. He notes that the most significant 'neighbourhood characteristic correlated with different levels of health and well-being for parents and children, noted in study after study, is the nature of the social environment in which they live' (Jack 2006: 339).

In his discussion on resilience, Gilligan (2000) reports that multiple adverse factors in children's lives increase the likelihood of negative outcomes. The effect is cumulative, and reducing or mitigating one factor can have a significant impact. Favourable experiences, even minor ones, can be 'turning points' in a child's developmental trajectory: 'relatively little things can make a big difference' (Gilligan 2000: 39). However, there is no clear relationship or universal guarantee that one specific input will lead to one specific change. Drawing on the research into attachment, Gilligan suggests that although effective attachment to primary carers provides a secure base, other attachments with less significant people can also have a positive impact. In addition to this secure base, Gilligan adds two further sources of resilience: self-esteem and self-efficacy. He suggests that policy-makers should acknowledge the small ways in which professionals and others can contribute to developing these sources of resilience through showing a genuine interest and care for children and through the daily routines and rituals of settings.

33

> Research evidence seems to underline the importance for those children who experience adversity at home to have havens of respite or asylum in other spheres of their lives. (Gilligan 2000: 38)

The final report on the policy review on children and young people (HM Treasury and DfES 2007a), a part of the Comprehensive Spending Review, announces a new emphasis on building resilience, with a focus on three protective factors: high educational attainment, good social and emotional skills and positive parenting. The section on social and emotional skills highlights self-awareness, the ability to manage feelings (emotion regulation), motivation and empathy. The role that play has in building these abilities is discussed in Chapter 3.

'Favourable experiences, even minor ones, can be "turning points" in a child's development trajectory ...'

The importance of play in children's lives

Photograph: Play England/Philip Wolmuth

This chapter reviews the current research on play, drawing on studies on both animals and children across a number of academic disciplines. It presents an alternative understanding of play to that of the dominant framework described in Chapter 1, which sees play as having direct instrumental value in terms of specific skills acquisition across a number of domains such as cognitive, social, emotional and physical. An attempt to summarise the benefits of play from this alternative perspective is offered here, but what the research shows is that playing is a highly complex process which operates at multiple and interconnected levels of organisation, so any attempt at summarising is vulnerable to both oversimplification and incomprehensibility. That said, the summary statement here attempts to draw together the social and emotional motivations for engaging in play, its 'as-if' and non-literal nature, and its role in children's health, well-being and development.

Playing is a way of experiencing bodily and emotional sensations through engaging with the immediate real and imagined social and physical environment in any number of ways, and where the player has a sense of control. This engagement with the environment has an impact on the way in which genes are expressed (activated) and on the structural development of the brain. This change leads to further motivation for playful engagement with the environment, seeking out the bodily and emotional pleasure that playing with uncertainty in novel and flexible ways brings. This cyclical process, what Thompson and Varela (2001) refer to as dynamic coupling, enables children both to adapt to the physical and social environment and to construct their own niche within it (Pellegrini and others 2007).

From this perspective, playing is understood as a way of building and shaping the architecture of the brain in a unique manner, through its relationship to the body and to the environment rather than as a way of learning specific skills. Such a view of playing highlights the motivation (arousal and seeking out of stimuli, bodily and emotional pleasure often referred to as positive affect) and the process (engagement with both real and imagined physical and social environments), and suggests that the content of playing has little to do with the learning of any specific skills the playing may appear to represent. This has implications for the way in which adults understand the kinds of playing that have been deemed dangerous and harmful or merely frivolous and non-productive.

The structure of this chapter

As a way of setting the context for presenting recent research, the chapter opens with a brief discussion on how play has historically been understood and some contemporary challenges to that understanding. Given the challenge to our understanding of play, the core concept of development is then reframed to highlight the interconnectedness and mutual influences of genes, the brain, the body and the physical and social environment and also the lifelong nature of development.

This foundation then allows us to explore a reframing of our understanding of play, particularly through a review of the literature on play and brain development, including some contextual information on the brain. A key finding to emerge from this review is play's role in the development of systems within the brain of reward, motivation and emotion, rather than specific cognitive skills. Following on from this is play's role in developing resilience, a finding that has implications for policy-makers, since resilience has been identified as a key protective factor within preventative social policies for children and young people.

The research on resilience forms the central part of this chapter, and seven aspects are explored, which allow for an understanding of play to be framed within this central concept of resilience:

- emotion regulation
- pleasure and enjoyment
- stress response systems, uncertainty and risk
- playing and creativity
- playing and learning
- attachment and the development of peer play culture
- children's play and environmental interaction.

The section on play and resilience highlights play's role in developing adaptiveness; however, there are factors that impinge on the ability of children to play in ways that enable this development. These factors can be endogenous (from within the child) and/or exogenous (external to the child), although there will always be a relation between the two. This section explores Attention Deficit Hyperactivity Disorder (ADHD), autism and play deprivation as illustrations of factors that can impinge on playing.

Finally, the chapter considers the nature of well-being and how a reframed understanding of play might be understood to contribute to this and to particular outcomes such as health, social capital and learning.

Perspectives on play

Lytle (2005: 149) notes that 'play is complex for it is biologically and socially given, involving order and disorder, display, entertainment, imitation, inversion and marginality'. The review of research presented here suggests that play operates at multiple levels of analysis. A full appreciation of the nature of play requires the concurrent examination of biological, psychological, and environmental/social processes and their interplay at varying developmental periods. Such an analysis is more likely to provide an integrated conceptualisation of the nature of this behaviour

In his preface to *The Ambiguity of Play*, Sutton-Smith (1997) comments that following his 40 years of studying play, an appreciation of the essential ambiguity of this behaviour requires multiple perspectives. Sutton-Smith (1997: 1) commences his analysis with this statement:

> We all play occasionally, and we all know what playing feels like. But when it comes to making theoretical statements about what play is, we fall into silliness. There is little agreement among us and much ambiguity.

This ambiguity may arise from the considerable diversity of play forms and behaviours, the diversity of players and the diversity of play scholarship and academic perspectives that seek to explain this ludic (playful) form.

Burghardt (2005) provides a detailed review of the modern history of studying play and notes that the 'footprints' established by early scholars have established the foundations for almost the entire body of modern play research. Drawing on a wide range of studies into animal and human play, Burghardt notes that for over a century many claims have been made about the role of play for the mental life and behaviour of animals (for other reviews of the study of play see Sutton-Smith 1997; Power 2000; Pellegrini and Smith 2005). Generally accepted claims of the benefits would acknowledge that 'play allows children to use their creativity while developing their imagination, dexterity, and physical, cognitive and emotional strength' (Ginsberg 2007: 183).

Brown (2006a) provides a useful summary of traditional approaches to describing the benefits of play:

Generally accepted claims	
Arousal seeking, fun and enjoyment	Children seek novelty and stimulation; play maintains arousal at optimum level.
Freedom to act independently	Play allows children to explore and experiment within a safe play frame.
Flexibility	Play supports the opportunity to try out novel combinations of behaviour; through playing children acquire a flexible approach to the world.
Social interaction and socialisation	Play enables children to develop social skills; through play children acquire an understanding of customs, rules and relationships.
Cognitive development	Play has traditionally been associated with supporting the learning process; in play children come to recognise the properties of objects and relationships between them; play is associated with higher order thinking skills.
Physical activity	Play contributes to the development of motor skills and co-ordination of their bodies in relation to the physical environment.
Creativity and problem solving	Children play with meanings, create new possibilities and combinations of behaviours and resolve tensions that may exist in play frames.
Emotional equilibrium	Play supports emotional growth; children 'play out' painful emotional experiences.
Self discovery	Play supports the development of self-identity.

The precise nature of the benefits of play remains a matter of conjecture, and there may be little concrete evidence to support the many claims made on its behalf. Many studies of play remain controversial, contradictory and often lack empirical support (Bateson 2005; Burghardt 2005).

However, in spite of the lack of research evidence, claims to the central importance of play have been widely discussed and debated:

> Play may actually have an important role in the behavioral, social, emotional, cognitive, physiological, and developmental realms in the lives of many animals, including people. However, this role is likely to be multifaceted, variable, and often involve complex, indirect and subtle processes ... It is this protean complexity that makes play an often paradoxical and socially controversial topic. (Burghardt 2005: 114)

Burghardt suggests that the historical claims for play as providing deferred benefits for the young of the species (that is, the benefits of play are not for the present but help prepare children for becoming an adult) are not matched by research evidence and indicates that perhaps the focus on studying play should centre on the immediate benefits for children. Pellegrini and others (2007) comment that play in juvenile forms is qualitatively different from adult forms of this behaviour. As such, play is more likely to have an immediate effect and the benefits are not necessarily deferred until adulthood, requiring the evaluation of this form of behaviour to be in terms of the specific age period in which they occur, and not necessarily of future benefits.

Pellegrini and Smith (2001) also suggest that the role of play in development remains controversial. Using a cost-benefit approach, they suggest that there should be benefits associated with play but they may be limited to the period of childhood rather than deferred until after this period. Suggested benefits may be physical fitness (for physical play), fighting and dominance skills (for rough and tumble play), and affiliative and theory of mind skills (social and pretend play).

Prout (2005), citing the work of Rubenstein (2002), comments that play may be connected to the enhancement of social, physical and cognitive skills. This is not necessarily to prepare a child to become a better adult; rather the benefits of playing in the present moment help to make a better child. Of course, such claims immediately raise questions about descriptions of play as purposeless and non-functional (Burghardt 2005). However, these behaviours may have benefits that extend through development and subsequent environments encountered (Pellegrini and others 2007).

Herein lies a fundamental dilemma: for the past 30 years or so, attempts at interpreting the benefits of play for children, particularly from an early childhood perspective, have been largely instrumental – explanations that see play as serving a specific purpose and outcome. Children's play activities have been given value only to the extent that they contribute to socially valued aspects of later life or to higher level cognitive functions, what Sutton-Smith (1997) refers to as the progress rhetoric. From this perspective, play becomes a tool for guiding the development of children, giving licence for adults to determine desirable goals and censure other forms of play that appear not to contribute to this (Brown and Cheeseman 2003). The prevalence of this perspective on play has been evident throughout this literature search from the considerable volume of research studies that focus on children's cognitive development, particularly in pretend play, and the paucity of materials that explore other forms of children's play, notably those that adults find distasteful or worrying.

Before proceeding to consider how recent research may extend our understanding of the nature and benefits of play, it is important to explore and establish the concept of 'development'. This following section thus briefly introduces some essential background that will help frame and situate the diverse range of recent research into children's play.

Reframing 'development'

Child development is mostly understood from the perspective of the dominant framework described in Chapter 1, a framework that is based on 'certain principles that have for most of the last century governed research, social policy, professional practice and in many ways commonsense thinking about the nature of adult/child relations' (Wyness 2006: 117).

Often termed 'developmentalism', this view is based on the idea that childhood is a universal experience during which all children progress through uniform, linear and progressive stages towards a state of completion called adulthood. Developmental psychology focuses on the individual child's progress in adapting to a fixed environment, and socialisation theory sees the environment acting upon children as passive recipients of its influences (Wyness 2006).

For the purposes of this review, development is seen as a 'heterogenous and complex mix of interacting entities and influences that produces the life cycle of an organism' (Oyama 2000: 1). Rose (2006) suggests that organisms construct themselves, their brains and their behaviour out of the raw material provided by their genes and the environmental context with which they interact. Thus, development entails profound and multilayered interrelations between genes and the social, physical and cultural environment; human beings are each the product of a unique genome and a unique set of experiences. The environment in which an individual develops influences the ways in which an individual's evolutionary acquired history is expressed (Rutter 2007; Chakravarti and Little 2006; Diamond 2007; Pellegrini and Smith 2005). On the one hand, our genetic make-up frames our mind/body responses to environmental factors, while on the other genetic expression is shaped by experience. As we grow, our brains and bodies continually change in response to this highly complex interrelationship; development is a lifelong process, not only limited to childhood.

This perspective allows for a replacement of the nature/nurture and biology/culture debates by a perspective which sees an intimate and dynamic interconnection between 'an embodied mind, embedded in the world' (Thompson and Varela 2001; Edelman 2006). As Prout (2005) observes, the old polarities of nature/nurture, mind/body, adult/child and so on are starting to fall away to be replaced by more holistic and inclusive approaches. Such integrated approaches attempt to explain the way that brain, body and environment exhibit self-organising and emergent processes at multiple levels. This perspective frames the exploration offered here of the relationship between play, well-being and development, based on an understanding of the playing child that:

> contains ideas of evolution and adaptation, of environment and ecology, of deep laws, of nature and nurture, of genes and inheritance, of emotional repertoires, of identity and self. (Conway and others 2004: 2)

This is echoed by Bjorklund (2006) who, in his review of the emerging science of epigenetics (the biological study of the causal interactions between genes and their products), notes that development occurs as a result of continuous and bi-directional interaction between various components of developmental systems (gene-environment expression, sometimes referred to as GxE[2]). Environmental experiences, and the behaviours adopted to respond to these, can trigger or deactivate the expression of genetic material. This review considers that this emerging discipline holds great promise for appreciating the importance of the relationship between play and development. Bjorklund (2006: 215) summarises the central foundation for this field: 'individuals that display a high degree of behavioral plasticity, defined as the ability to modify behaviour as a result of environmental input, are better able to adapt to novel environments than less plastic individuals'. This behavioural plasticity is especially apparent during the stage of childhood. The increased ability of 'adaptedness' allows individuals to enter new environments where, in response to the pressures they encounter, they can change their behaviours in more adaptive ways than their less flexible peers. As well as responding to the pressures presented by their environments, over time individuals can also change and adapt the environments in which they live (a process of niche construction). This in turn may have major evolutionary and ecological consequences for future generations as well as changing the conditions for themselves (Odling-Smee and others 2003).

As discussed later in this review, research suggests that play performs a pivotal role in developing this behavioural flexibility and niche construction.

---

[2] It should be highlighted that genes do not directly link to behaviour. As Pellegrini and others (2007: 271) suggest, there are many steps between genetic activity and production of proteins and behaviour in a 'complex system with possibilities of short-term and long-term feedback loops'.

39

A significant feature of child development research has been its emphasis on early childhood, identified as a critical period of accelerated growth and change and as central to successful adaptation in later life. It is a time when children are perceived as vulnerable, immature and in need of constant care and protection in order to flourish (Boyden 2003). This focus on the early years has not been matched by the degree of attention given to the nature of children's experiences and development during the middle and late periods of childhood. As such, the nature of child development after early childhood is less well researched and understood.

Thompson and Nelson (2001), in their review of the dominant developmental status of the 'first three years' and the application of research from neuroscience to support the primacy of this period to successful development, suggest that this focus ignores the fundamental plasticity of the developing brain, certainly through the childhood and adolescent period. Also, as emerging research identifies, the brain retains an element of plasticity throughout its lifetime. Thompson and Nelson (2001) indicate that the brain regions involved in higher cognition, reasoning, planning and problem solving, have a maturational course that extends well into adolescence. Research suggests that neurogenesis (the production of new neurons) and the formation of new synaptic connections is evident in adult brain regions (Gritti and others 2002; Harms and Dunaevsky 2007).

Whilst it is recognised that childhood is a period of immaturity during which children grow and develop, the social studies of childhood introduced in Chapter 2 allow for a recognition of differences between children and their environments and also introduce the concept of children as active agents in their own lives and the importance of seeing children as human beings and not only human becomings (for example, Prout 2005). This perspective sits well with the principles of interconnectedness between brain, body and environment, and also with the suggestion, explored in this chapter, that the benefits from playing are immediate rather than deferred (Burghardt 2005; Pellegrini and others 2007). In other words, playing helps children adapt to and co-construct their immediate environments as children, rather than practising skills needed in adult life.

This review of research considers the relationship between play and development across the extended period of childhood and adolescence. While not explicitly exploring beyond the period of childhood, we may also suggest that the benefits of play are not simply restricted to this period.

Reframing play

The concept of development as a continuous process, which involves a dynamic relationship between mind, emotions, body and environment, offers a broader perspective for considering the benefits of play in the context of development than one that focuses on specific skills acquisition. Childhood marks an extended period of immaturity. It is suggested that this is to enable children to best 'fit' the complex environments in which they find themselves. Given that children are active agents in their own development, seeking out and acquiring experiences that will shape their future behaviour (Bateson and Martin 1999), it is also suggested that play during this extended period of childhood is an 'important strategy used to develop behaviours that are adaptive to the niches that young children and adults inhabit' (Pellegrini and others 2007: 263).

The extended juvenile period of humans is crucial in developing plasticity and the complex set of skills necessary for survival, given that they live in highly complex and unstable environments (Burghardt 2005; Pellegrini and others 2007). The key purpose of this lengthy period is to acquire the knowledge and practice to develop and refine social skills and to establish coalitional relationships necessary for adapting to the increasingly intense and complex social landscape (Flinn 2006). This perspective is reinforced by Panksepp (2007: 7) who, in his review of research into animal laughter and play behaviour, notes 'the play urge may be one of the few innate tools of nature that evolution provided for the epigenetic construction of fully social brains in mammalian species'.

Given the complexity of contemporary social and physical environments, it is suggested that the necessary skills required for survival in these diverse environments cannot be genetically pre-ordained but instead young animals use the resources afforded them (the safety and provisioning given by parents that help to create an environment conducive to play – a 'relaxed field') to explore their environments and try out a wide range of strategies that may be effective within the specific environment (Burghardt 2005; Bateson 2005; Edelman 2006). Play enables children to 'sample their environments and develop behavioural responses in a relatively low-risk fashion' (Pellegrini and others 2007: 268). While other forms of behaviour may contribute to this, play has design features that make it especially suitable for finding the 'best way forward' (Bateson 2005). The key element within this is the flexibility of responses generated through the play process. Pellegrini and others (2007) note that more formal learning methods and adult tuition replicate existing practices rather than facilitate innovative approaches. As discussed later in this chapter, peer play demonstrates more flexible and complex patterns of behaviour than does adult-child interaction.

Bailey (2002: 171) notes that play provides children with a dimension that is unique and not replicable in other aspects of their lives, citing the work of Humphrey (1986: 63):

> If there is one element common to all kinds of play – from rough-and-tumble in the playground, to the most intense and secret fantasy-games behind the henhouse – it is surely this: play is a way of experimenting with possible feelings and possible identities without risking the real biological or social consequences. Cut! Time for tea, time to go home – and nothing in the real world has changed, except perhaps that the child is not quite the person that he was before, he has extended just a little further his inner knowledge of what it can feel like to be human.

Bateson (2005: 23) observes, 'aspects of play can indeed increase the total sum of spontaneously developing behavioural structure that serves to solve complex problems'. When faced with a novel or uncertain situation, play affords the opportunity for innovation and subsequent practice of newly developed behaviours and strategies.

From this perspective Burghardt (2005) indicates that some of the immediate benefits of play would include:

- providing important physical exercise that develops endurance, control of body movements and perceptual-motor integration (the ability to coordinate ones body in relation to the information received about the environment through our senses)

- testing objects that may represent food or danger;

- establishing roles and developing communication skills that may contribute to current survival;

- enhancing psychological and physiological well-being and resilience.

Palagi and others (2004) evidence this process through their study of the frequency and nature of play in a group of chimpanzees at feeding time. Research into the feeding habits of chimpanzee groups would indicate that the period before feeding is highly competitive. Palagi and others' observations of this period note that play is used in anticipation of the stress associated with feeding. Chimpanzee play reduces the risk of aggression, increases social grouping and acceptance, provides a safe frame for testing personal abilities and the strengths and weaknesses of playmates and enables the animal to assess the degree of cooperation present within the relationships. Certainly, from this perspective, the benefits of playing are immediate and far from being a purposeless activity.

The key themes identified by Burghardt's analysis of the immediate benefits of play, in relation to humans, are explored in more detail in the following section.

Play and brain development

> The very fact that play contains so much nonsense, so much replication, and is so flexible certainly suggests that it is the prime domain for the actualisation of whatever the brain contains. (Sutton-Smith 1997: 226)

Making the Case for Play: Gathering the Evidence (Cole-Hamilton and others 2002: 59) briefly highlighted emerging research into the connection between play and brain development suggesting that: 'play creates a brain that has greater behavioural flexibility and improved potential for learning later in life'. The report notes that this area is attracting more interest and may in time produce more robust data concerning the effects of human play activity. This next stage of the review explores some of this research.

Attempts at understanding play and its relationship to development and well-being highlight the complexity and heterogeneity of this form of behaviour. This becomes even more problematic when we start to explore the possible relationship between play, brain and development. As Edelman (2006) acknowledges, the human brain is one of the most complicated material objects in the known universe. To give a measure of this complexity, Edelman notes that the cortical region alone contains about 30 billion nerve cells (neurons) and about one million billion connections.

Smith (2002) highlights some of the dilemmas facing attempts to relate research from the neurosciences to other disciplines, and in the context of studying children's play we should acknowledge that neuroscience is not a unified field and that there are diverse theoretical approaches that inform research. The conditions under which laboratory testing of specific aspects of brain structure and development in animals takes place do not correspond to the complex environments inhabited by humans, and each individual brain is a unique representation of gene-environment expression (environmental experiences, and the behaviours adopted to respond to these, can trigger or deactivate the expression of genetic material). In this context, it is essential to balance findings from animal research with caution about the limits of what is understood today (Shonkof and Philips 2000). Burghardt (2005) acknowledges that there are great logistical problems in carrying out experimental research into animal play behaviours, and it is very difficult to isolate one single variable from overall behaviour patterns.

However, the emerging findings may have implications for the study of human play. Panksepp (2002: 227) notes:

> If modern molecular biology has taught us anything of profound general significance, it is that we are really not that different from other animals in the biological realm, even in most brain matters.

In addition, caution is needed in terms of interpreting information from the brain sciences. Whilst experimental research can discover, through the use of brain imaging technology, which sections of the brain become active under which conditions, quite what this may mean for humans is a matter of interpretation. For example, emotions can be seen as chemical or electrical activity in the brain, yet what these emotions actually mean, and their expression

'Play opens up possibilities in the brain that may be picked up later or discarded ...'

through bodily changes or behaviour, depends very much on the cultural environment in which people live. Emotions may be a matter of natural science; their meaning is also culturally constructed (Turner and Stets 2005).

With this in mind, some of the key features from brain science research are developed here; however, the intention is not to produce a definitive account of such a complex field of study, but to establish a basic framework for situating some of the ideas that have emerged and highlight areas that might warrant further exploration.

Before looking at recent research into the relationship between play and brain development, it is necessary to briefly introduce some of the key processes and structures associated with the ways in which the brain develops (again bearing in mind that this is still a highly contentious area and that attempting to provide a basic overview runs the risk of reducing high complexity to a simplistic and unrepresentative analysis). The intention of this introduction is to establish some context and background to the evidence that is presented later in this section.

The connectivity of the brain

The brain is remarkably flexible and malleable. Plasticity in brain function is evident not only during the period of childhood but also in adults (Harms and Dunaevsky 2007). This plasticity is evident through the ways in which brain cells (neurons) establish connections with each other via synapses. This connection is critical to ensuring the functioning of brain circuits (Edelman 2006). Synapses operate through electrical and chemical signals (neurotransmitters) which enable neurons to connect and send messages to each other. Synaptic communication takes place between neurons at all levels: locally between neighbouring neurons and globally through the production of neurochemicals that reach all regions of the brain (Lewis 2005).

Various activities and biochemical events can change the strength and connectivity between neurons. Connections that respond most adequately to a stimulus will survive, those that do not will disappear (Edelman 1992; Schore 2001). Adaptation depends on the speedy reaction and consolidation of behaviours essential to survival and the ongoing flexibility to adjust to changing events and environments (Balbernie 2001). The developing brain is 'under construction' well past the first decade, and this is responsible in part for its plasticity or capacity to be shaped or moulded by experience.

While guided and framed by genetic information, a great deal of neural patterning occurs through the child's interaction with her or his environment (often referred to as experience-dependent plasticity). Experience-dependent plasticity is idiosyncratic, designed for the survival of an individual, and optimises the individual's adaptation to specific and possibly unique features of the environment. These processes need to be flexible, 'such that at any time neural connections may need to be altered to reflect the unique experiences of the animal' (Black 1998: 169). Thus, the brain is continually reorganising itself through the activities of everyday living, and the laying down of neural structure is highly individual rather than pre-established.

The structure of the brain

Lewis (2005: 257) suggests that the brain may be roughly divided into four systems, each more advanced and appearing later in evolution than the previous one:

- The brain stem forms the core of the brain and processes relatively basic response patterns. It is the seat of primary or basic emotions (including fear, anger, sadness, joy, excitement, attachment and sexual desire). This region displays little evidence of plasticity, but has wide reaching connections to other brain regions and influences these through the global transmission of neurochemicals, in particular dopamine.

- The hypothalamus acts as a central regulator of body responses to external events and again transmits neurochemicals that influence goal-directed states and helps to maintain lasting emotions or moods.

- The limbic region mediates emotional states and orientates action and attention to whatever is of current interest to the system and thus has connections 'up' (to the cortex) and 'down' (to the hypothalamus and brain stem) the brain. This area retains plasticity and is open to change on the basis of experience.

- The cerebral cortex is the key system for cognition, perception and attention and the cognitive control of emotional responses, often referred to as emotion regulation (Damasio 2003). Again, there are intimate connections between the cortex system and the limbic area.

While the brain has distinctive regions and structures, the connectivity and chemical signalling enables these regions to work together in highly co-ordinated and synchronsied ways (Lewis 2005; Edelman 2006).

Lewis (2005) explains that the traditional view of top-down control and domination of emotions by the 'rational' cortex is not an accurate picture of the coordination of brain activity. Rather, we depend equally on our autonomic system (the parts of the nervous system that operate unconsciously), our ability to move, our memory and emotions, and thinking and communicating. Our brain needs all its parts to enable us to survive in our surroundings. Each animal's brain enables it to live in its own world. As Lewis (2005: 260) notes, the evolved areas of the brain work in concert or 'vertical integration':

> Primitive agendas and requirements ... flow up the neuroaxis from its most primitive roots at the same time as executive attention, planning and knowledge subordinate each lower level by the activities of the cortex. If not for the bottom–up flow, the brain would have no energy and no direction for its activities. If not for the top down flow, recently evolved mechanisms for perception, action and thought would have no control over bodily states or behaviour.

Relationship to play

This brief overview of the significant processes that inform brain function and development establishes a background for a review of the work that has taken place since the publication of *Making the Case for Play* (Cole-Hamilton and others 2002).

The increasing interest in the relationship between the brain and play has some significant foundations. Sutton-Smith (1997) notes the enormous variability of play and suggests that this heterogeneity may indeed be the central feature of the function of play. Drawing on the work of Gould (1996), Sutton-Smith notes that successful biological evolution, rather than being dependent on precise adaptations, requires opposite characteristics:

> In our world of radically and unpredictably changing environments, an evolutionary potential for creative responses requires that organisms possess ... [a] set of characteristics usually devalued in our culture: sloppiness, broad potential, quirkiness, unpredictability, and above all, massive redundancy. The key is flexibility, not admirable precision. (Gould 1996: 44; cited in Sutton-Smith 1997: 221)

Given the over-production of neurons during early childhood, Sutton-Smith (1997: 225) proposes that play's function may be 'to assist the actualization of brain potential without as yet any larger commitment to reality'. Play opens up possibilities in the brain that may be picked up later or discarded; the important feature is that the potential is kept alive, more so than if play never occurred in the first place. Evidence to support this claim is emerging in animal-based research, for example, Gordon and others (2003) note that rats who play in play arenas, and engage in rough and tumble and chase play have significantly elevated levels of brain-derived neurotrophic factor (BDNF), recognised to be a 'key modulator of neuronal development, plasticity and survival' (Gordon and others 2003: 17). Research by Van Praag and others (2005) highlights how locomotor activity in rats contributes to maintaining neural plasticity.

Spinka and others (2001: 143), in an attempt to explain how and why play behaviour evolved, suggest that a 'major ancestral function of play is to rehearse behavioural sequences in which animals lose full control over their locomotion, position, or sensory/spatial input and need to regain these facilities quickly'. By deliberately seeking out and placing themselves in these uncertain situations, animals can begin to improvise their responses to the unexpected, drawing on conventional movements alongside atypical movements and actions to regain control and re-establish a sense of balance.

Spinka and others (2001) claim that this process does not simply relate to locomotor versatility but also extends to dealing with the emotional aspect of being surprised or disorientated. In their hypothesis of play as 'training for the unexpected' the importance of play lies with developing emotional flexibility by rehearsing the emotional aspect of being surprised or temporarily disorientated or unbalanced – that is by playing in a relatively safe context, emotions are modulated in play by the frame in which play occurs and the lack of serious consequences from losing control. Such uncertain experiences develop repertoires for avoiding emotional over-reaction, the ability to mediate responses and avoid harmful stress. Pellegrini and others (2007) note that the possible benefit of play, relative to other strategies, is that the behaviours generated through play can be more innovative and allow for further practice of newly developed behaviours. Play appropriates stimuli, experiences, or objects from their original meanings, creating a new frame that allows for greater freedom, interactivity and creative possibilities (Gordon and Esbjörn-Hargens 2007).

A central feature of playing is the ability to hold a paradox that something is simultaneously what it represents and not what it represents, and this enables the players to engage with 'real' concerns without losing full control. As Gordon and Esbjörn-Hargens (2007: 216) comment:

> The implicit or explicit limits that bind play in space and time make it safe for the player to surrender to the playful urge, take chances, try on new roles, and attempt tasks that, under normal circumstances, might be avoided as too difficult or unpleasant. It is a place where the novelty and risk of a new situation or experience only add to the intensity and pleasure of play. The player is able to be in control of being out of control and so enjoy a sense both of risk and of mastery simultaneously.

Because play provides the opportunity for new, and possibly adaptive, responses to novel environments, it may become 'an exemplar of behaviour affecting evolutionary processes' (Pellegrini and others 2007: 270). This idea suggests that changes made during the period of childhood may 'launch' the child into new developmental trajectories for the rest of their life span.

This parallels ideas from the study of gene-environment expression (GxE) on the interconnectedness of environmental experiences, behaviour and the activation or deactivation of genes. Hughes (2006: 109) also suggests that 'play can operate both inside and outside the body': the process of playing impacts on the organisation and structure of the brain while at the same time, the reorganisation of structure allows for further and more complex and variable play behaviours. Burghardt (2005: 177) makes a similar point by remarking that play may involve some role in refining behaviour, performance and capability and thus:

> … play gets animals doing things, and doing things may cause rapid changes in dendritic spines as well as activating chemical changes and brain areas. Animals capable of being more active and active in diverse ways are going to have more opportunities for these brain changes to take place and lead to even more behavioral change in a positive feedback manner.

Thus, play can increase the total sum of spontaneously developing behavioural structures that serve to support adaptation and survival in complex environments (Bateson 2005).

In summary at this stage, research from the (limited) evidence suggests that somatosensory (the area that responds to bodily sensations and touch), emotional and motor centres of the brain are affected by play experiences (Spinka and others 2001). Burghardt (2005) proposes that play may serve as an enhancement of brain development, not specifically to cognitive areas as much of the research into play indicates, but more accurately to the areas that link emotion, motivation and reward. It may be that play supports integration of the brain systems involved in the play process, from the brain stem and instinctive behaviours, through the limbic (emotion) regions and the paralimbic (the areas that connect the limbic and cortex systems) areas.

45

Making connections

Support to the above may be found in perhaps one of the most significant discoveries in terms of understanding the relationship between the brain and play – the mirror neuron system. Again, it should be acknowledged that the emerging research from the study of this neural mechanism is in its infancy and the implications for understanding play have not been fully explored.

Rizzolatti and others (2001) suggest that we understand the action of others through matching their actions through our own neuronal pathways. Following research with monkeys, Rizzolatti and others propose that there are specific neurons within key brain regions – mirror neurons – that perform this matching function. Research (Gallese and Lakoff 2004) shows that when monkeys watch others, the same neurons fire in their brains as those that fire when they actually perform the actions observed.

From this basic principle Gallese and others (2004) suggest that this mirroring mechanism may make a significant contribution to the ways in which we come to understand the actions and emotions of others. This is a complex area, but Gallese (2003: 524) summarises the key features that have emerged from research:

> … motor imagery, action observation, imitation and empathy all share the same basic neural mechanisms, the mechanism of embodied simulation … Embodied simulation enables models of real or imaginary worlds to be created. These models are the only way we have to establish a meaningful relationship with these worlds, because these worlds are never objectively given, but always recreated by means of simulated models.

Burghardt (2005) extends this into recognising that the act of imagination provides a bridge between perception and motor control. The inference is that the practice and repetition of similar (but not identical) patterns in play may establish a close integration of the physical motor areas of the brain and higher cognitive function. From this integration, individuals may then begin to develop behaviours that become separated from the actual physical actions, giving rise to pretence, fantasy and novelty of ideas. In other words, playing with others, and matching their movements and emotions also leads to developing the capacity for imagining these situations. The very act of imagining movement and action promotes activity in the brain systems associated with that motor activity. Burghardt (2005:395) continues with the recognition that this ability to imagine activity then offers the opportunity to 'mentally rehearse different actions', which in itself offers a valuable adaptive strategy.

Again, this connects with Spinka and others' (2001) observations that play is essentially about learning how to respond to uncertain situations. Mental rehearsal and simulation support creativity, planning, and imagination. They suggest that play results in 'measurable changes and enhancements in the brain systems that receive and integrate novel and complex sensory messages from the environment, control motor patterns and mediate emotional reactions to these situations' (Spinka and others 2001: 147). The novelty and unpredictable situations generated in play cannot be resolved by existing rules and patterns but must be resolved by improvisation that draws upon existing patterns and adds new dimensions to thinking, moving and emotional flexibility.

Lytle (2005: 144) asserts that the discovery of this system may be very significant for psychology; from the studies it has been confirmed that 'humans are special empathetic, playful creatures, neurocortically driven'. Riihela (2004) comments on the ways in which young children demonstrate an innate ability to imitate and share experiences with each other. But this is not simply a straightforward copying of actions. Mirroring or imitation requires a decision about what to imitate, a selection from a diverse range of stimuli that is likely to create a desirable response from the environment. This amazing ability to imitate is one way of opening and maintaining interaction, leading to shared activity, dialogue or play.

Further understanding of this mirror neuron system and the ways in which physical, affective and imaginative behaviours are integrated may prove to be significant to the future study of play.

Play types

Burghardt (2005) highlights the importance of attempting to classify the diversity of play in order to appreciate its role. Attempts at classification provide accounts of the qualitative distinctions among play forms. Traditional taxonomies of play have drawn distinctions between three basic categories of locomotor, object and social play.

Hughes (1996a, 2002, 2006) provides a taxonomy that is now generally accepted in the playwork field in the UK. He identifies 16 different forms that 'range from three-dimensional movement to rough and tumble, and from exploration of, and experimentation with, objects and spaces, to dialogue and symbolism' (Hughes 2006: 35). Taking the original ideas forward, Hughes (2006) develops a deeper exploration of the concept of play types to suggest that perhaps each play type may contribute to enhancing development in different brain regions. This idea would find support from Burghardt (2005), who acknowledges the diverse nature of play and suggests that different types of play may have their own phylogenetic (evolutionary) and ontogenetic (developmental) trajectories. Equally, Bateson (2005) suggests that play has more than one biological function: some aspects of play may support the development of the nervous system and musculature while others may primarily be concerned with survival skills both in the present and the future.

However, whilst these discrete functions may be identifiable, they exist within the overall interconnectedness of brain, body and environment. Recognising the relationship between play types and brain development leads Hughes (2006) to suggest that each play type must inevitably make its own unique contribution to supporting brain growth. Studies into the developmental timings and sequences of play would suggest that physical forms of play might be an important precursor to mental play behaviours (Burghardt 2005). As previously identified, the brain works in a highly integrated manner (Lewis 2005; Edelman 2006) and, as synaptic connections are formed and strengthened through play, it is likely that play operates across brain regions. Bateson (2005: 18) notes that human play has acquired more complex cognitive forms and functions during the process of evolution, enabling children to 'rearrange the world in ways that ultimately enhance understanding'. Again this would find support from Spinka and others' (2001) proposition that physical play with self, others and objects leads to developing strategies for responding to uncertain and unpredictable situations involving mental rehearsal, the use of imagination, ability to predict and solve problems, and developing creative responses. Thus, as play occurs, the results of the experiences will lead to more complex and amalgamated play forms that show greater integration of both play types and brain connectivity, a point developed by Hughes (2006) in his proposal that increasing sophistication in brain connectivity patterns would be reflected in further sophistication in the types of play displayed.

The opening stages of this review suggest that play is a unique form of adaptive behaviour. Taking Thompson and Varela's (2001) study of the relationship of mind, body and environment as a dynamic and emergent coupling process, the evidence suggests that play operates across levels of:

- basic life regulation (homeostasis/homeodynamics and the sense of being alive)

- sensorimotor coupling with the environment (situated activity based on what the organism senses and how it moves and behaves in response to this, which in turn will impact on the neural systems that modulate and coordinate senses and movement)

- intersubjective interaction (the ability to interpret the actions of others and respond accordingly). The next stage of this review will begin to look in more detail at the nature of play and its relationship to these dynamic coupling processes.

Play and resilience

A key and fundamental finding from the evidence presented in this section is that children's play provides a primary behaviour for developing resilience, thereby making a significant contribution to children's well-being. There is a wide range of research from a variety of disciplines including biology, neuroscience, psychology, sociology (in particular the growing field of the sociology of childhood), education, health, cultural studies and children's geographies. While much of the research from these disciplines is specific to its disciplinary base, collectively they provide a rich mosaic of the relationship between play and resilience.

As an introduction we consider in more depth the possible connection between play and resilience, particularly in relation to Sutton-Smith's (2003) assertion that, where children cannot wilfully act out beliefs in their own agency and their future through play, then depression will be the outcome.

The nature of resilience

Rutter (2006) identifies resilience as an ability that allows individuals to overcome or resist severe risks or chronic stress factors in the environment. As a concept, resilience is a very broad idea which refers to the capacity of dynamic systems to withstand or recover from significant challenges and, as such, can be studied at many levels of analysis that range from 'the molecular to the global' (Masten 2007: 923). Threats to the well-being of young children are commonplace. Resilience marks the ability to spring back from and successfully adapt to adversity. Masten (2001) makes the point that the most surprising result from a range of studies with children is the 'ordinariness' of resilience:

> Resilience appears to be a common phenomenon that results in most cases from the operation of basic, human adaptational systems. If these systems are protected and in good working order, development is robust even in the face of severe adversity; if these major systems are impaired, antecedent of or consequent to adversity, then the risk of developmental problems is much greater, particularly if the environmental hazards are prolonged. (Masten 2001: 227)

The evidence presented in this literature review suggests that play operates across adaptive systems and supports the development of this 'ordinary magic' (Masten 2001). Research indicates that the basic foundation for resilience is a sufficient stock of 'good things' laid down through childhood, however partial these may be, since there is no 'happy childhood' that will guarantee a life free from conflict (Vellacott 2007).

Van der Hoek's (2005) study of children growing up in poverty in an area in the Netherlands notes that not all children show problematic outcomes in the presence of stressful situations. Understanding what enables some children to do well in the face of stressful situations, while others show social-emotional or behavioural problems, may provide essential information on the mechanisms by which stressful situations, such as growing up in poverty, affect children's lives. Finding ways to enhance resilience is a major task for child mental health professionals (Leckman and Mayes 2007).

While we do not know the degree to which negative experiences in childhood influence development, research indicates that early emotional challenges may have a significant impact; while children may be resilient in recovering from severe adversity it is not fully understood how these experiences may alter the 'quality of their inner lives' (Panksepp, 2001: 135). It is generally recognised that certain positive emotional experiences promote optimism, resilience and well-being, while negative emotional experiences have the opposite effect. In exploring this, Panksepp notes that more is known about the effects of negative experience than the long term 'fertilising' influences within the socio-emotional environment that support positive affect. While genetically encoded emotional systems provide developmental springboards, they emerge in many different ways according to the environments in which children grow. As discussed previously, the brain exhibits enormous plasticity in childhood, and early positive emotional experiences, and even mildly negative ones help to shape the brain in highly adaptive ways.

The early approaches to the study of resilience received critical attention for adopting the idea of childhood as a universal life phase that is marked by dependence and vulnerability. Using a developmental psychology approach based on the ages and stages of childhood, any response to adversity could be measured against standard norms. Those that fall outside of this are seen as children (or 'victims') in need of remedial care (Boyden 2003). A biomedical approach to adversity tends to provide uniform and decontextualised measures and models used to assess all children, and fails to take into account children's agency and the multiple ways of responding to these situations (Boyden 2003).

Rutter (2006) explains that resilience is a highly complex concept that cannot be reduced to standard research techniques; it is not possible to apply questionnaire or interview methods to identify the presence or absence of specific traits:

> … resilience is not a single quality. People may be resilient in relation to some sort of environmental hazard but not to others. Equally they may be resilient in relation to some kinds of outcomes but not others. In addition, because context may be crucial, people may be resilient at one time period in their life but not at others. (Rutter 2006: 4)

Consistent with the themes developed in this review to date, Cicchetti and Blender (2006) highlight the importance of adopting an interdisciplinary approach to the study of resilience which draws on interrelated perspectives that range from the cellular to the cultural. Cicchetti and Blender recognise that mechanisms of neural plasticity are integral to an appreciation of the biological aspect of resilience.

Resilience has a relationship to well-being. Contemporary approaches to well-being (considered at the end of this chapter) accept a dynamic view of resilience that acknowledges children as active beings who can interpret the world around them, make choices, define their role and identities, solve problems, reach decisions and work collaboratively with others (Masten 2006). These choices can play a substantial role in the course of development, including the course of physical and mental health or illness. Increasingly, it is recognised that any appreciation of the ways in which children develop coping strategies arises not only from psychological qualities of the child but also from factors in the child's social context such as the family, wider social networks and the quality of the local neighbourhood (Masten and Obradovic 2006). A systems perspective on resilience allows for a growing appreciation of the multilevel dynamics involved in this concept and the ways in which resilience is shaped by interactions across levels of analysis.

Van der Hoek (2005) highlights the importance of exploring resilience from a child's perspective. She notes two key considerations for adopting this approach:

• What are children's own perceptions of the stressful situation? Do they actually appraise the situation as stressful? What may appear challenging to an adult may not be as challenging to the children who are confronted by it. For example, the study highlights that for some children, the relationship with their peers was not affected by poverty, while for others this was a more serious issue leading to rejection and ridicule.

• What coping strategies do children use when confronted by a stressful situation? Van der Hoek suggests that coping may operate in a positive or negative manner, citing research which indicates that active coping, problem solving and cognitive appraisal of stressful situations are related to lower mental health problems, while avoidance and withdrawal from the situation is generally related to higher stress and mental health problems.

Through her research, van der Hoek identifies a range of coping strategies used by children to overcome the challenges associated with poverty. The results of the study indicate that children have to deal with this at every level of their daily routines and activities – home, school, peers and neighbourhood – and children vary their strategies according to where they are. The coping strategies that rely on withdrawal methods are less likely to be effective in supporting children's sense of well-being. In summary, van der Hoek notes that the act of listening to children as they relate their lived experiences provides an insight that should help to form policy interventions that take into account children's expressed needs, for example for free places to use in their social time.

Suomi's (2006) research with primates suggests that the development of resilience is a highly complex process of gene-environment interaction. Suomi comments that in their 'normal' development pattern, rhesus monkeys move from the intimate comfort of and attachment to their mother to exploring their physical and social environment. Following this initial separation, increasing time is spent in developing social relationships, especially with same-aged peers in social play. Yet a number of monkeys show significant deviation from this 'normal' pattern through either excessively fearful or overly aggressive behaviour, with significant consequences for their developmental trajectory. Fearful monkeys spend less time playing with peers, and overly aggressive monkeys, who may be dominant in initiating play bouts, are avoided by potential playmates. Exploring this, Suomi highlights the significance of the expression a specific gene (5-HTT) in development. Variations in gene expression may 'protect' monkeys from the impact of a harmful environment, or a good environment can protect or buffer the individual from the expression of a 'bad' gene. Luthar and Brown (2007: 934), drawing on research from animal studies, suggest that different social experiences can lead to 'substantial and enduring changes in the expression of genes'. Suomi also suggests that individual differences in resilience to environmental adversity represent the product of complex interactions between genes and characteristics of the physical and social environment in which development takes place. Citing similar research into gene expression in dogs, Suomi highlights that it is highly possible that early social experiences can alter gene expression in primates which, in turn, will influence future behaviour patterns, a point made in relation to play by Bateson (2005) and Pellegrini and others (2007).

Masten and Obradovic (2006) recognise that the new wave of research into resilience has overcome many of the criticisms targeted at the earlier research efforts. Their review of the current research perspectives in studying resilience leads to a suggestion that there are recurring attributes of person, relationships and context, which serve as general predictors of resilience across diverse situations. It is evident that resilience is a multifaceted concept that draws on a wide range of internal and external factors. Increasingly, research is focused on the interrelationship between these factors and the possible ways in which they combine to produce protective effects (Atwool 2006). Given the nature of play in supporting adaptation to the unique environments that children inhabit, we would anticipate a relationship between play and resilience. The next stage of the review examines in more detail how play has a great deal to contribute to an understanding of the processes underpinning resilience.

Masten and Obradovic (2006) identify a range of common adaptive systems, including learning systems and the ability to process information and solve problems; attachment system; mastery-motivation system and self efficacy; stress response systems; self-regulation systems; family system; peer system and cultural and societal systems. This summary of adaptive systems of agreed resilience factors has been adapted to provide a framework for presenting research which indicates that play makes a significant contribution to developing resilience across a number of interrelated adaptive systems:

• emotion regulation
• pleasure and enjoyment and the promotion of positive feelings
• stress response systems and the ability to create and respond to uncertainty
• creativity and the ability to make novel connections
• learning
• attachment to people and place.

It should be stressed that the separation of research findings across these systems is largely one of convenience and ease of presenting the diverse materials. There are reciprocal relationships that run across all of these areas; it is hoped that the connections and overlap will become fully apparent.

Emotion regulation

Perhaps one of the most interesting themes to emerge in the study of the relationship between play and development has been the exploration of play and emotions, largely driven by the work of Sutton-Smith (2002; 2003). The key theme proposed in this section is that play is central to emotion regulation and children's ability to manage their own behaviour and emotions (Singer and others 2006).

The nature of emotions

Emotions may be viewed as part of the basic mechanism of life regulation (Damasio 2003). Because of their remarkably ancient lineage in the evolution of the brain, it is recognised that these underlying brain systems serve as a foundation for the emergence of basic social and cognitive abilities (Panksepp 2001).

Sutton-Smith (2003) acknowledges the work of Damasio (1994; 2003) in framing his hypothesis about the relationship between emotional systems and play. As an introduction to these ideas, Damasio (2003) explains that primary emotions (listed as fear, anger, shock, disgust, happiness and sadness), largely arising in the more 'primitive' brain regions of the hypothalamus and brain stem, are involved in the immediate tasks of survival, and provide an 'anchor' (Lewis 2005) to the self-organisation of the brain. They show little evidence of plasticity and change little with experience. These systems have a key role in the vertical integration of neural activity through the transmission of neurochemicals (such as dopamine) across all brain regions.

The secondary, more social emotions (such as pride, guilt, embarrassment or sympathy) emerged with the evolution of the 'higher' brain regions and facilitate a more delayed and considered response to external stimuli. These brain regions retain plasticity through childhood and are constantly shaped by experiences. Effective responses to external stimuli require an integration between these two systems – primary emotions can modulate and focus cognition, while at the same time cognition can moderate emotions (Gray 2004).

Lewis (2005) attributes emotions and motivations as prime processes in developing synaptic connections. Emotional activity in the limbic and paralimbic regions (generally recognised as the emotional centres of the brain), and the associated release of neurochemicals, promotes synaptic change and yields 'novel synaptic configurations' (Lewis 2005: 262). At the same time, emotional responses may operate to reinforce existing patterns of synaptic activity and thus minimise synaptic change.

Emotion regulation

The concept of emotion regulation has been used in such a diversity of ways within child development research as to lead some to question its validity as a scientific concept. Cole and others (2004: 318) note that emotion regulation is not a matter of expressing only positive emotions and not negative ones that are often understood as 'culprits that disorganize functioning'. They argue that it is not the emotions themselves, or their expression, that is at issue; rather it is their effect on cognition and behaviour. The concept of emotion regulation is useful 'as a tool to understand how emotions organize attention and activity and facilitate strategic, persistent or powerful actions to overcome obstacles, solve problems, and maintain well-being at the same time as they may impair reasoning and planning, complicate and compromise interpersonal interactions and relationships and endanger health' (Cole and others 2004: 318).

A 'resilience' perspective on emotion regulation applies the concept as the role of maintaining a level of arousal that is both tolerable and flexible enough to support adaptive behaviour (Gayler and Evans 2001). It is an 'enduring capacity for flexibility and change, in one's goals, one's affective states, one's use of different cognitive, behavioural and social strategies and one's reliance on intrapsychic versus interpersonal processes' (Diamond and Aspinwall 2003: 150).

From a neuroscience perspective, emotion regulation, whilst difficult to separate from emotion activation, can be seen as the reciprocal and simultaneous interplay among regions of the brain leading to a vertical integration and co-ordination. The different regions combine to regulate each other to produce specific plans of action, a coherent cognitive appraisal, focused attention and a distinct feeling (Lewis and Stieben 2004). Where this regulation process is not effectively integrated it is likely to result in a range of psychopathological states that may be evidenced through poor habituation to novel stimuli, a hyperattentive bias to threat information, deficits in working memory and executive function (Thayer and Broschott 2005). Deficits in emotion regulation have been associated with common emotional and behavioural difficulties. These include poor adjustment to school, poor peer relations and social competence, and depression (Gayler and Evans 2001).

The human need for complex, flexible regulatory systems that can cope with a wide array of environmental conditions means that the development of emotion regulation begins early, takes place over an extended time period, and requires substantial external support (Berk and others 2006). Emotion regulation and modulation is about variability and flexibility, and corresponds with mental and physical health. Spinka and others (2001) acknowledge that play enables animals to develop emotional flexibility by rehearsing wide ranging emotions, but modulating these within the relatively safe context in which play occurs. This will be explored in more detail in the next section.

Emotions and play

The opening analysis to this section provides the background for Sutton-Smith's (2003) proposition that play is a parody of emotional vulnerability. Lester and Maudsley (2006: 15) summarise Sutton-Smith's basic proposal:

- primary emotions are still needed in survival emergencies
- because of this, primary emotions need to be exercised (which is what happens through play)
- at the same time, primary emotions need to be kept in check within the newer social emotions.

Sutton-Smith (2002; 2003) suggests that primary emotions can be both experienced and kept in check through children's play. Children can experience the primary emotions within the play frame; the framing is held in place by rules, rituals and metacommunications (play faces and other signals that send the message 'this is play'). So, although anger may be experienced in play fighting or games of contest, the players do not give way to outright aggression and violence but instead display strategy and control. Displays of courage and bravado can help to mediate the feelings of fear in deep play. Games that develop ways of bonding and developing a group identity mediate feelings of sadness and loneliness. Sutton-Smith's analysis, according to Lester and Maudsley (2006: 15) suggests:

> ... it may be possible to connect certain types of children's play with this mediating process, for example play fighting and the balance between anger and contest; den making as a mediation of sadness and loneliness through developing shared spaces; fear mediated through deep play; disgust mediated through playful obscenities and so on.

The process of exploring this interplay of primary and secondary emotions leads Sutton-Smith to suggest that play may have adaptive value as children regulate their emotions in terms of 'performance strategy, courage, resilience, imagination, sociability or charisma' (Sutton-Smith 2003: 15). Through playing, individuals may find and develop their own highly personal methods for dealing with different kinds of misfortunes. The emotional nature of playing may enhance the development of connections between cortical and limbic regions, developing neural mechanisms of affect synchrony (tuning into the emotional states of others), self-other awareness and the ability to take another's perspective. As Sturrock (2003: 4) comments, 'the negotiation of the stairs leading between upstairs (the neocortical region) and the downstairs of the brain (subcortical) is the province of the ludic'.

Tellingly, Sutton-Smith (2003) sees play as the capacity for creating an alternative or virtual reality that offers amusement as well as excitement. The establishment of this play frame temporarily removes the limits of the everyday world and allows positive affective substitutes to emerge. In other words, children can make their worlds more exciting through play. Basically, what play prepares you for is more play, and what that gives you is more satisfaction in being alive.

Evidence from research

This section briefly considers some of the evidence to support Sutton-Smith's exploration of the relationship between play and emotion regulation.

Rough and tumble play: Studies of rough-and-tumble play provide good examples of the nature of emotion regulation. Panksepp (2007) explores the correlation between animal and human brains with particular reference to neural emotional systems. Two powerful emotional circuits can be found in children: separation-distress states and rough and tumble play. The separation-distress state leads to a valuing of the company of others, particularly those who will support their welfare. Panksepp proposes that an even more 'wonderful tool' for supporting the fuller socialisation of the brain is rough and tumble play (in a wide ranging definition of this ludic behaviour). His review notes that feelings of mirth and fun are initiated by positively valued emotion systems of the brain and suggests that the play urge 'is one of the more genetically provided tools for facilitating the epigenetic construction of social brain':

> Although all emotional systems surely help contribute [to social brain development] a case can be made that strong and flexible prosocial strategies are critically molded through the living dynamics of play and separation distress circuits. It is through these systems in social contexts that animals come to understand what they can do to others and what they want others to do to them – it is through these comparatively 'simple' genetically provided emotional urges that animals may get woven naturally into their social structures. Such epigenetic effects that help refine neural circuits for social conduct might be achieved through arrays of brain-gene activational effects instigated by playful activities. (Panksepp 2007: 7)

Smith and others (2004) note that play fighting is a form of social play that may appear to be an act of aggression. Closer observation of these forms of behaviour highlight the ways in which vigorous physical behaviours (such as grappling, swinging or jumping) are mediated by the 'play tenor' of positive affect (laughter and the play face) and very controlled physical moves and contact. This form of play is a prime example of Sutton-Smith's (2003) emotion-based analysis. The play frame allows for displaying a parody of the primary emotion of aggression, mediated by the secondary emotional controls that players bring to this play behaviour. Alongside this, studies of the nature of rough and tumble play indicate that there is a great deal of reciprocity in taking superior and inferior roles within the play, and that such playing is common among close friends (Smith and others 2002; Smith and others 2004).

'... play [is a] capacity for creating an alternative or virtual reality that offers amusement as well as excitement.'

Given the importance of this play type for the development of the social brain, the evidence presented in Chapter 5, which shows that it is a form of playing that adults suppress is a cause for concern.

Pretend play: Russ (2004), approaching play from a psychoanalytical perspective, explores the nature of pretend play and affective/cognitive interactions. Russ's review of research on the importance of this form of play acknowledges that play 'is a major arena in which children learn to express emotion, process emotion, modulate and regulate emotion, and use emotion in adaptive ways' (Russ 2004: 5). Russ also comments that this perspective is consistent with research into the relationship between emotions and mental health.

Mohaupt and others (2006) note that pretend play is important to the process of mentalisation. Through these play forms, children use the 'as if' nature of pretence, fantasy, imagination and daydreaming to externalise feelings positively and naturally. By doing so, the child can explore their own emotions and form mental representations of them. Similarly, Russ (2004) comments that children can express a range of emotions in a pretend play situation, express affective themes within the play frame, gain comfort and enjoyment in their play and experience pleasure and immersion. The expression of material within the safe frame of pretend play may include both positive and negative emotions. Negative affect 'can be expressed, worked through and mastered' (Russ 2004: 25).

In his study of children's pretend play, Ariel (2003) observes that children draw on their emotions in the selection of play themes, and by exposing these in the play frame may modulate them or change the theme if the emotions become too unpleasant. Thus play may act as a homeostatic mechanism that regulates the level of emotional arousal within the play frame. High levels of sociodramatic play and conflict-resolution themes in play narratives are linked to good emotional self-regulation in preschoolers (Fantuzzo and others 2004). Sutton–Smith (2004) notes that the themes demonstrated through children's stories and play scenarios contain strong elements of attack, escape, accident, uncleanness and alienation. As previously discussed, these 'perils' can be connected to the primary emotions of anger, fear, shock, disgust and sadness. Following a study of children's stories, Sutton-Smith suggests that children construct and enjoy these stories because of the pervasiveness of these themes within their culture. By doing this, children create situations of pleasurable mild stress which they can overcome through their play. As such, the stories represent an early effort to achieve mental health.

Smith and Pellegrini (2005) note that pretend play is more prevalent and more encouraged by adults in modern urban societies than in foraging societies and suggest that this is an adaptation to the complexity of the society rather than a deficit in simpler societies. This cultural difference is explored in more detail in the section on children's play cultures.

Emotion regulation and environmental interaction: Studies in the field of environmental psychology highlight the significance of children's environmental transactions in supporting emotion regulation. Korpela and others (2002) review the significant findings from research into children's use of special places. They note that studies of adult memories of their favourite places indicated that they provided 'security, privacy and control'. The authors note common themes of expressed needs to be alone, the importance of hiding places and the need to escape from social demands. Their research highlights that all children from their sample could readily identify a favourite place. The majority of children and young people did consistently respond that they saw their favourite places as places to 'pour out troubles, reflect on personal matters, to clear one's mind and feel free and relaxed' (Korpela and others 2002:388). In the conclusion to their research Korpela and others (2002: 396) speculate that:

> This suggests that pouring out troubles and clearing one's mind can take place in conversation with friends in a place where children can feel free away from parents' supervision.

Pyle (2002: 319) notes the increasing lack of opportunity for children to encounter natural habitats and calls for protection of the 'unofficial countryside', the places that are the domain of unsupervised outdoor play. This aspect is further explored in Chapter 4.

Emotion regulation and social interaction: Research also indicates that emotion regulation and emotion understanding play a pivotal role in developing competence with peers (Lindsey and Colwell 2003; Gayler and Evans 2001). Gayler and Evans (2001) note that children's pretend play is a mode of social interaction which enhances the development of emotion regulation ability. Their study of pretend play with children aged 4 –5 years concludes:

> Children who demonstrated emotion regulation skills in a pretend play situation were rated as having better emotion regulation in every day life. Regular pretend play with a more experienced play partner was related to higher frequency of adaptive affect displays, empathy and emotional self-awareness in everyday interactions. Continuing a pretend play game when faced with a negatively valenced event was related to emotion regulation in the wider context, whereas effective solutions for this event were not. (Gayler and Evans 2001: 1903)

Therapeutic value: Russ (2004) considers the emotional coping strategies developed in the play frame and the possible transfer to non-play contexts. Reviewing the research evidence, Russ indicates that a limited number of empirical studies suggest that children are able to draw on the 'skills' developed through play into other situations; for example, Goldstein and Russ (2001) found that the level of fantasy and imagination in children's play correlated with the number and variety of coping strategies employed in a scenario requiring impulse control over aggression.

The concepts associated with 'psycholudics' (the study of the mind at play) developed in the UK by Sturrock and Else (1998) recognise the significant emotional content that children bring into the play frame. The establishing of play frames is a metacommunication process in which children use emotional communication through cues, non-verbal signs, prosody (the patterns and rhythms of verbal communication), laughter and directly issued verbal cues. The frame is maintained through a shared simulation and reading of the cues and returns from others in the play frame. Sturrock (2003: 4) explains that a significant purpose of play is the creation of 'lexicons' of emotion that play through the body in response to the external circumstances. Again, this would suggest that play establishes a repertoire of flexible emotional responses that have adaptive value.

Russ (2004) examines evidence from child psychotherapy and other play intervention studies and indicates that play interventions, if they are focused and controlled, do reduce fears and anxieties in various areas, including children about to undergo medical procedures or problems of separation or loss. Moore and Russ (2006) note that pretend play interventions with children are effective in both inpatient and outpatient settings for preventing and reducing anxiety and distress. Pretend play also has effects on reducing pain and adaptation to chronic illness.

Russ' analysis of research into the value of play also points to the general value of imaginative play in anxiety reduction. By creating manageable situations in a pretend frame, negative emotions can be expressed and, through playing, children can increase positive affect and reduce negative affect. Russ (2004) cites the work of Strayhorn (2002) who suggests that pretend play can be used for fantasy rehearsal: the child can try out the adaptive pattern of thoughts, plans, behaviours and emotions in their imaginative play frames. This fantasy rehearsal can help a child build up habits to cope with conflict situations in 'real life':

> Using this framework, a child could reduce fears and anxiety around separation or other issues, by acting out the adaptive ways of handling the separation and feelings around it in a pretend play situation. (Russ 2004: 73)

Thus play may provide a positive way of coping with anxiety rather than adopting avoidance strategies which give little opportunity to process difficult thoughts, emotions and experiences. Again, this perspective raises questions about an adult focus on the content of playing rather than on any benefits in terms of safe expression of emotion within the play frame as a contributor to emotion regulation.

The importance of empathy

Empathy is of considerable importance in developing and maintaining friendships, and in turn supporting children's well-being. As in other areas discussed in this review, the research into this specific and vital human characteristic is wide ranging and offers diverse approaches. There appears to be general agreement that the key components of empathy involve shared neural representations, self-awareness, mental flexibility, and emotion regulation, all underpinned by specific neural systems.

Gallese and others' (2004) research indicates that the mirror neuron mechanism (discussed in the 'Play and brain development' section) is involved in an ability to understand and experience the emotional states of others. This system enables an observer to resonate with the state of another individual through an internal representation of the movements and emotional expressions displayed. Preston and De Waal (2002) explain that the complex social world of humans requires that we can perceive the facial expressions, body postures, gestures and vocal intonations of others quickly and accurately to generate an appropriate response. The same nervous system link between perception and motor action that helps us to navigate the physical environment, also helps us to negotiate the social environment. The perception-action system allows for the perception of external conditions and the adjustment of our actions in response to these. Empathy also requires self–other awareness (the ability to distinguish oneself as separate from others) and mental flexibility (the ability to mediate one's own responses triggered by the interaction).

Preston and De Waal's (2002) review of the research evidence indicates that from very early on in development infants are capable of emotional resonance. With increasing age, knowledge and experience, individuals become better able to interpret and predict the emotional states of others and to separate them from their own internal states. The extended period of childhood and associated plasticity in brain connections gives individuals more time to intergrate these systems.

Decety and Grezes (2006) suggest that this could be important because, by becoming aware of the actions, emotions, motivations and desires of others, individuals can monitor and self-regulate their own actions. Their research notes that a fascinating characteristic of human nature is the ability to use imagination consciously to simulate reality as well as fictional worlds, and explains that the deliberate use of imagination fosters creativity. Using imagination enables children to plan actions, anticipate their own and other people's behaviour and to empathise with others. Through the use of imagination in play, real emotions can be expressed even though the characters and scenes are not 'real'. Yet at the same time, there is generally no confusion between reality and imagination (Decety and Grezes 2006).

Brownell and others (2002: 28) note that in peer play, children not only accommodate their behaviour to one another and share emotional expression and behaviour during play, they 'also share one another's goals, desires and beliefs'. Children's ability to cooperate in their play is enhanced by their emerging ability to infer the intentions of others, to recognise their feelings and thoughts and to attune their own play behaviours in response to a peer's assumed mental state and overt behaviour. As such, the development of empathy in peer play is not simply an unconscious mirroring of the actions and emotions of others but requires higher-level

'... fun [is] a central defining quality of children's play.'

representations and interpretations of the actions and emotions. Children must 'read well beyond other children's emotion behaviour to understand and respond appropriately both to their intentions or desires and to the emotions that follow from the other's success or failure in fulfilling those desires' (Brownell and others 2002: 28). With increasing complexity in play forms, children develop a whole series of masking and exaggeration techniques to transform emotional responses, and this in turn requires ever more sophisticated cognitive and emotional inferential abilities. Here again we may find a connection with Sutton-Smith's (2003) concept of play as mediation of primary emotions by secondary emotional systems.

Russ (2004) highlights the significance of pretend play in supporting interpersonal processes, specifically the development of empathy and ability to show concern for others, developing self–other differentiation and trust in the play relationship, and the ability to express and share ideas with others. Bailey (2002) notes that play is a precondition for the acquisition of these skills. In other words, it is through play that children first come to understand self-awareness, the distinction between appearance and reality, and possibly even the intentions of others, which seem to underpin the development of mindreading skills.

Pleasure and enjoyment

Recent research has reflected increasing interest in the influence of positive emotions (or affect) on cognitive processes and behaviour, although interest in this field is relatively new. As Pressman and Cohen (2005) note from their review of research there are over 20 times more studies on depression and disease than there are on happiness and health.

Research into positive affect investigates the impact that affect has on a wide variety of behaviour and thought processes, including memory, decision-making, risk preference, problem solving and creativity, to name just a few. Much of this work indicates that positive affect facilitates flexible thinking and problem solving, mastery and optimism and enhances performance (Isen and Reeve 2005; Pressman and Cohen 2005; Haglund and others 2007). Tugade and others (2005: 6) review a range of studies that demonstrate a high correlation between resilience and positive emotions, noting that resilient individuals have 'zestful and energetic approaches to life, and they are curious and open to new experiences … they also use positive emotions to achieve effective coping outcomes by using humour, creative exploration, relaxation, and optimistic thinking as ways of coping'. Haglund and others (2007) suggest that positive emotions play an important role in the capacity to tolerate stress, and research indicates that they are associated with a decreased incidence of stress-related illness.

Equally, children who report reduced subjective experiences of positive affect are more likely to display affective disorders including depression and aggressive behaviour which, in turn, may lead to negative social interactions and peer rejection (Forbes and Dahl 2005; Dougherty 2006).

Play and enjoyment

While children experience a range of emotions and experiences in play, it is generally acknowledged there is a prevailing mood of pleasure and enjoyment. Burghardt (2005: 138) comments that the joy, fun, thrill or pleasure associated with play behaviour is 'surely real in many cases and is an important perhaps critical issue in the analysis of play'. It is perhaps a taken for granted that play is generally pleasurable, although there will not always be visible signs of this. Turnbull and Jenvey (2004) acknowledge that there is now a consistent pattern of evidence indicating that play encompasses the behavioural element of positive affect and suggesting that this criterion should be seen as a key critical marker in definitions of play. Meire's (2007) review of research into children's play considers the element of 'fun' to be a central defining quality of children's play. In expanding on this, Meire distinguishes three main and interconnected sources:

- The feeling of agency and control that play offers for children represents an expression of personal power, which operates both individually and collectively. This enjoyment of agency has diverse expressions. For example, it may be through physical movement and achievement, what Spinka and others (2001) refer to as creating disequilibrium and uncertainty and restoring balance, or through the creation of imaginary and material worlds.

- The sharing of play represents a significant element in the enjoyment of play; the co-construction of the play frame enables children to do things together. The 'as if' nature of play provides improvised and stylised narratives that establish shared excitement and emotional security.

- The enjoyment in the bodily experiences of playing: play generally has an embodied element which finds expression in the somatosensory systems (perception and emotion).

Laughter appears to have originated in social play behaviours and may have evolved from primate play signals. It is part of a nonverbal 'gesture-call' system and considerably predates the evolution of formal language. Laughter in children occurs most frequently in the context of play (Martin 2007). Martin's (2007: 6) review of the nature of laughter and play notes that:

> … our ability to create humor to amuse one another and evoke laughter appears to have evolved as a means of providing us with extended opportunities for play. Play seems to serve important social, emotional, and cognitive functions (Bateson 2005). Indeed, all mammals engage in play as juveniles, but, unlike most other animals, humans continue to play throughout their lives, most notably through humor. When they engage in play, people take a nonserious attitude toward the things they are saying or doing, and they carry out these activities for their own sake – for the fun of it – rather than having a more important goal in mind.

Sutton-Smith (2002: 19) largely concurs with the above analysis:

> Play's function is most centrally that of emotional joy and emotional peace, but its variant actions must inevitably provide some trickle down of functional transfers – a kind of functioning … as an adaptive potentiation.

Positive emotions can undo the impact of negative emotions, which reduce tendencies to play and can have harmful effects on individuals over the long term (Gervais and Wilson 2005). Positive affect fosters 'intrinsic motivation': enjoyment and performance of enjoyable tasks lead to the desire for more of these experiences (Isen and Reeve 2006); what play essentially prepares for is more play (Sutton-Smith 2003). In the long term, the cognitive-emotional states we inhabit most in childhood sculpt the 'neural parameters that determine who we are as persons for the rest of our lives' (Lewis 2005: 268).

Burghardt (2005) recognises that these qualities of play are not easily measurable. However, the recent increasing interest in the significance of positive emotion and pleasure may help us to appreciate the importance of children's play. Loizou's (2005) study with 1-2 year-olds in a childcare setting gives a vivid example of how children, even at this young age, can carry out sophisticated and intentional acts of absurd and humorous play. As they play and explore, children watch the consequences of their actions, including the responses of the adults and their peers. Two central themes were observed in children's humorous play: incongruity and empowerment. The notion of incongruity is a sophisticated kind of novelty. More specifically an incongruous event differs from what we are used to and contravenes existing conceptual frames. Loizou (2005: 44) sees this as a 'higher cognitive function operating in a playful mode'.

This notion of incongruity also connects with Spinka and others' (2001) analysis of play as training for the unexpected. As Boyd (2004) observes, much of what children do when they play represents highly exaggerated and exuberant movements, testing the limits of balance and actively putting themselves in situations that may lead to loss of control, what Kalliala (2006) refers to as 'dizzy play'. While this may be done as a solitary form of play, a high percentage of these forms take place in a social context, and the use of laughter may be an important social control, as suggested in the section that considers the contribution of play to developing empathic responses. Boyd (2004: 10) comments:

> Shared expectations that allow for surprises that catch us off guard, that simulate risk and stimulate recovery, are the key not only to play of all kinds but also to

humour. In jokes we are often primed for surprise, but despite our actively seeking
to anticipate an unexpected resolution, the punch line still takes us unawares, but
in a way that allows the tripping up of our expectations to be followed by a swift
regaining of balance.

Drawing on the work of McGhee (1989), Loizou suggests that the use of playful humour develops
social competence in children through enabling the achievement of social goals, controlling their
aggressiveness and redirecting their hostile feelings. Examples observed in the research include
events that children produced or appreciated which were related to the alteration of different
positions, sounds, gestures or words. Loizou (2005: 48) gives an example of this play:

> ... children enjoyed bending their knees, lifting their bottom up and looking through
> their legs. This was one of the favorite activities that brought smiles or laughter to
> the producer of the activity as well as to the partner of the activity.

Similarly children were observed using the range of play materials in incongruous ways that
provoked humorous responses. The second theme, empowerment, was represented by the ways
in which children used intentional playful humour to subvert adult expectations. An important
aspect of this form of play is the expectation of a reaction from their caregiver, and that
makes it even funnier for them. Loizou concludes that this form of behaviour helps them to
learn about the appropriateness of using different materials, the accepted behaviour within
the care setting and the limits within which they can act.

Tickling play

Provine's (2004) study of the evolutionary nature of laughter refers to the game of 'tickling
battles' as the most benign form of human conflict. This game may 'bind us together in a laugh-
filled give and take that may be the basis of all social play' (Provine 2004: 217). The key feature
of this primitive form is reciprocity of action: the child being tickled may seek to escape from
being tickled, only to return and renew the interaction or begin a counter-tickling offensive.
Selden (2004) highlights the apparent paradoxical nature of this game and suggests that the
simultaneous expression of discomfort and laughter might be adaptive; discomfort motivates
the child to escape while the presence of laughter encourages the 'tickler' to continue and
thus helps the child being tickled to further develop skills useful in defence and combat.

For young children who cannot talk, this may be an important aspect of affect synchrony
(Schore 2001; discussed in the 'Attachment' section in this chapter) and entry into a mutual
social relationship in which the infant has a degree of control by, at times, expressing their
discomfort with the situation. If the situation is not perceived as safe, or if the incongruity is
too intense, the playful stimulus can evoke a distress or crying response (Gervais and Wilson
2005). Provine (2004) also suggests that tickling may be a novel approach to developing a sense
of self, based on a realisation that you cannot tickle yourself.

Laughter

An obvious expression of pleasure may be through the amount of laughter displayed by children
when they play. Thus, in the tickle-battle, laughter may be a signal that the play is pleasurable,
desired and non-aggressive (Selden 2004).

Laughter is marked by its inherent link with emotional experience generally referred to as
mirth, amusement, joy, exhilaration or positive affect (Martin 2007) and it appears to be linked
to the brain structures that underlie rough and tumble play (Panskepp 2001, 2007; Gervais and
Wilson 2005).

Rizzolatti and others (2001) comment that laughter is prone to be immediately reproduced
by others because its perception directly activates neurons that simulate the same motor
movements. A laughter message is likely to elicit positive affect, a generation of positive
feelings through a simulation of the emotional cause of the laughter. Thus, laughter is
contagious; heard laughter is a sufficient stimulus to create laughter. Martin (2007: 10)
also suggests that laughter may motivate others to behave in particular ways. For example,

laughter can be a method of positively reinforcing others for desirable behaviour ('laughing with'), as well as a potent form of punishment directed at undesirable behaviours ('laughing at').

Laughter, positive emotions and peer relationships

Dougherty (2006), in her review of research evidence into the relationship between emotions and peer friendships notes that positive emotion facilitates the initiation and regulation of social interactions, which may promote greater peer acceptance.

Panksepp (2007), in his review of research evidence on the nature of laughter and joy, concludes that social play and humour appear to share common neural substrates. Not only does their emotional impact use the same neural mechanisms of the subcortical brain region, but also functionally they may both serve to enable animals to navigate their way through a complex and ever changing social space.

Martin (2007) cites research (Shiota and others 2004) which also proposes that positive emotions may play an important role in the regulation of interpersonal relationships. The research suggests that positive emotions play a role in accomplishing a number of interrelated tasks in building relationships: identifying potential relationship partners; developing, negotiating, and maintaining key relationships; and collective agency (working together with others to achieve goals that could not be accomplished alone). Shiota and others suggest that the humour-related positive emotion of mirth is effective for accomplishing all three of these tasks and we may infer that they form a significant role in the ways in which children initiate and maintain their play activities.

Humour and communication

Within play, laughter becomes an expression that has an important communication role. More recently it has been suggested that laughter is not simply about communicating that an individual is in a playful state but may also induce the positive affective state in others. Laughter serves to smooth interactions and lessen tensions within play frames.

Coates (2007) analyses the nature of humour in informal conversations and notes the way that these conversations are supported with humorous stories, banter, teasing or spontaneous creative play with words. These conversational forms are used to establish a play frame; communication and non-verbal gestures indicate that the conversation is play. Where children collaborate to develop this, we see a highly sophisticated form of play emerge. As Coates (2007: 31) suggests from her observations, shared laughter arises from this play and is a 'manifestation of intimacy, with the voice of the group taking precedence over the voice of the individual speaker'. It may be that this co-construction of the frame demonstrates the fine attunement present among the players. This form of communication is qualitatively different from 'serious' talk, and Coates refers to the development of this form of play as closely resembling a jazz performance; improvising while co-constructing the themes.

Cekaite and Aronsson's (2005) study of child initiated and collaborative humorous language play in a classroom demonstrates how playful mislabeling and speech errors, for example, leads to joking repetitions and further expressions of mispronunciations, repairs and laughter, that is, more language play. They note that although the joking was quite rudimentary it included 'artful performance and collaborative aestheticism, involving alliteration and other forms of parallelisms, as well as code switching, laughing, and artful variations in pitch, volume and voice quality' (Cekaite and Aronsson 2005: 169).

Positive affect and further benefits

Research into the nature of human laughter, while still in its infancy, offers the promise of establishing a relationship between the tendency to laugh and play and mental health (Panksepp 2001; Gervais and Wilson 2005). Pressman and Cohen (2005) report that laughter and a state of positive affect and arousal may have an impact on neurochemical activity which assists resistance to health risks.

Forbes and Dahl (2005) comment that emotions represent an inherent tendency to act, and where the prevailing theme is one of positive affect, there are likely to be associated behaviours such as social engagement, initiating and maintaining relationships, reward seeking and motor activity.

Returning to Spinka and others (2001) and their analysis of play as uncertainty, it is suggested that the essence of humour seems to be incongruity, unexpectedness, and playfulness (Martin 2007), referred to by Gervais and Wilson (2005) as 'nonserious social incongruity'.

Play, as an enjoyable experience, promotes positive affect, which in turn encourages further exploration, novelty and creativity. Increasingly, research highlights that the experience of positive emotion is thought to be adaptive because it allows individuals to think in a broad and flexible manner which facilitates the acquisition of long lasting personal resources that can be drawn on in times of need, a 'broaden and build' theory by which positive affect broadens cognitive processes (Frederickson 2006). Through play children build social, cognitive and physical resources by broadening their repertoires of actions and behaviours.

Similarly, Salovey and others (2000) suggest that positive emotions generate psychological resources by promoting resilience, endurance, and optimism. Although the positive emotions themselves may be short-lived, these resources are long lasting and may be drawn upon in moments of need, for example, when challenged by stressful events. As Siviy's (1998) synthesis of animal research suggests, these resources may enable individuals to 'roll with the punches' and reduce the potential for harm when faced with stress. Another feature of positive affect may be related to the facilitation of recovery from stressful experiences, as suggested by research into the restorative effects of children's place making and play in natural spaces (Korpela and others 2002; Kaplan and Kaplan 2005).

Being in a positive emotional state increases the ability to maintain attention, allowing individuals to focus on a wide array of information and facilitating a global visual processing bias (Strauss and Allen 2006). Strauss and Allen also highlight a range of research studies which indicate that positive affect can increase verbal fluency, problem solving and creativity, verbal recall memory, attentional scope and abstraction-flexibility.

Summary
Gervais and Wilson (2005) identify the following key features associated with the nature of spontaneous laughter as an indicator of positive affect. It:

- increases positive affect and improves mood

- mitigates negative affective responses to stressful events and acts as a defence mechanism by trivialising stressful circumstances (nervous laughter)

- enables children to maintain interactions in novel, mildly stressful situations

- acts as a 'social lubricant' in conversations, working to lighten mood and increase a sense of belonging within a group

- can equally 'manipulate' the emotions of others by reducing friction and lessening competition

- may enable new members to integrate into the group (but may also act to establish boundaries and exclude others from participation: Panksepp (2001) refers to the 'dark side' of laughter, the derisive laughter that arises from feelings of social scorn, where laughter becomes a tool for teasing and taunting, where group members find enjoyment in the misfortune of others)

- with its associated feelings enables young children to maintain interactions with mildly stressful stimulation so they can increase their knowldge of the world and develop social competency

- can support playful interaction.

It should be recognised that the human condition is not simply about correcting weaknesses and deficiencies, but is about strengths and resilience. Humans desire lives that are imbued with meaning and purpose, a preference for being at ease and feelings of joy (Damasio 2003) and these states do not arise automatically by removing suffering (Duckworth and others 2005). Play is, in essence, a statement made by children that their lives are pleasurable and meaningful during the time of playing (Sutton-Smith 2002). In exploring the nature of being 'happy', Duckworth and others (2005) propose three interconnected domains of 'well-being', the first of which – the pleasant life – may exemplify Sutton-Smith's (1997) analysis of play as ludic virtual reality. The 'pleasant life' (or play) involves positive emotion about the past, present, and future:

> Positive emotion about the past includes contentment, satisfaction, and serenity. Positive emotion about the present includes the somatic pleasures (i.e., immediate but momentary sensory delights) and the complex pleasures (i.e., pleasures that require learning and education). Positive emotion about the future includes optimism, hope, and faith. The pleasant life is a life that maximizes positive emotions and minimizes pain and negative emotion. (Duckworth and others 2005: 635)

As Tugade and others (2004) comment, positive emotions can be an important factor that buffers individuals from maladaptive health outcomes. It may well be that play represents a vital evolved behaviour that is a critical necessity for optimal physical and emotional functioning.

Stress response systems, uncertainty and risk

There is an intuitively held notion that challenge and risk are important developmental processes in play (Burghardt 2005). 'Risk' is a daring venture, a balancing act with future possibilities as its ultimate goal. To place oneself at risk does not only mean that one places oneself in jeopardy, but also that one is situated in a zone of potential and development (Lindqvist and Nordanger 2007). Little (2006) notes that a considerable amount of children's daily activity involves an element of risk, particularly as they play with uncertainty and extend beyond their current experiences. Yet this positive aspect of risk-taking and its benefits has very little prominence in the 'risk' literature. An emphasis on the positive aspects of risk-taking is perhaps particularly timely given the increasing over protection and aversion to risk that permeates many of the approaches to working with children (Little 2006).

Spinka and others' (2001) exploration of playing with uncertainty suggests that play will inevitably contain an element of stress and risk. An example of this can be seen in Kalliala's (2006) observations of 23 six-year-old children in Helsinki. During the period of the study Kalliala (2006: 94) observed occasions when children engaged in 'swivelling' and the feeling of dizziness that accompanies this action, referred to by Kalliala as 'dizzy' play (drawn from Caillois 1961), and notes that a 'momentary need to turn the world upside down and fool about together seems to be a universal phenomenon'. Kallialla (2006) refers to the characteristics of dizzy play as fighting, playing noisily and chaos. The play, especially for young children, may be framed within a pretend or fantasy context. Also, it may contain 'forbidden' elements, both in terms of language and behaviour. Children create situations of unbalance in an attempt to regain equilibrium (Spinka et al 2001), what Sutton-Smith (1999) refers to as a ludic dialectic in which the need for excitement and novelty is balanced with safety controls within the play frame.

Playing allows for the arousal and expression of a range of emotions such as anger, fear or disgust, which may have undesirable consequences in the 'real' world but do not carry such consequences within the 'as-if' play frame (Sutton-Smith 2003). For example, research into rough and tumble play suggests that this broad range of play behaviours seems to be agonistic but in a non-serious, playful context (Fry 2005; Sheets-Johnstone 2003). Within the play frame of rough and tumble play, children describe the experience as 'being fun' and this is evidenced by the laughter and humour that accompanies these playful behaviours (Smith and others 2004). It appears that children's reflective accounts of their rough and tumble play experiences clearly demonstrate an underlying friendship within the play encounters. The locomotor element of rough and tumble play provides a way of coming to grips with our vulnerabilities (Sheets-Johnstone 2003). Through physical contact, children learn about their bodies and learn to move themselves, recognising that bodies can be hurt, others can shove or hit too hard, or inadvertently cause pain and so on. But rough and tumble play 'is all the same a sane and safe way of putting our vulnerabilities on the line' (Sheets-Johnstone 2003: 412).

At a more serious level, Hughes (2006: 41) discusses the nature of 'deep play' as children's confrontation with their significant fears, namely the human condition of mortality and death. In approaching these play situations, children believe in their ability to successfully overcome the challenges they face and display a sense of optimism.

Risk and beneficial stress

Despite an everyday understanding of stress as a negative or harmful experience, not all stress is necessarily damaging. The US National Scientific Council on the Developing Child (2005) identifies three kinds of stress in children's lives:

- **Positive stress:** moderate and short-lived bursts of increase in heart-rate or stress hormone levels are a normal part of life and, when experienced within an overall secure context, help to develop appropriate responses to new or unusual situations.

- **Tolerable stress:** refers to traumatic events (such as an accident, or parental divorce) from which children can recover and not suffer long-term harmful effects, particularly if they are in supportive relationships.

- **Toxic stress:** this is strong, frequent and persistent events that the child cannot control and which can have harmful effects on the development brain architecture and on the ability to cope with other stressors.

This section examines the literature on positive stress and its relationship with playing.

Rutter (2006) suggests that there is evidence that in some circumstances the experience of stress or adversity can strengthen resistance to later stress. Under normal conditions of temporary stress there may be a brief enhancement of immune and cognitive function (Flinn

'Through physical contact, children learn about their bodies and learn to move themselves, recognising that bodies can be hurt, others can shove or hit too hard, or inadvertently cause pain and so on.'

2006). Temporary elevations of cortisol could have beneficial developmental effects involving synaptogenesis (the creation of new synapses) and neural reorganisation:

> … if such changes are useful and necessary for coping with the demands of an unpredictable and dynamic social environment, elevating stress hormones in response to social challenges makes evolutionary sense if it enhances specific acute mental functions and helps guide cortical remodeling of 'developmental exuberance'. (Flinn 2006: 151)

Burghardt (2005) also notes that for many tasks, a moderate level of arousal or anxiety may be beneficial, with increased corticosterone levels enabling enhancement of synaptic reorganisation to respond in appropriate ways to the stimulus. Haglund and others (2007: 890) comment that exposure to mild and manageable forms of stress appears to contribute to building a 'resilient neurobiological profile', and they term this 'stress inoculation':

> Children who are faced with and overcome moderately stressful events seem better equipped to deal with significant stressors later in life … Children who learn to cope with stress also seem to gain the ability to effectively regulate their stress response systems over the long term.

However, if the stress is prolonged and severe, there are likely to be harmful outcomes.

Studies with rats (Arco and others 2007) indicate that different mild stressors increase the production of dopamine in the prefrontal cortex, and this is related to the activation of behavioural processes to cope with the stressor and the optimisation of cortical networks necessary for adaptive behaviour; the brain has design features that can readily adapt and cope with moderately stressful situations. Their research indicates that animals reared in enriched environments (with the presence of novelty and stimulation) that are used to coping with mild stressful stimuli have a reduced reaction to acute stress. In other words, they are better able to organise responses and deal effectively with these situations.

Greenberg (2004) comments that the modern medical concerns about stress focus on its potential for harm. Yet the neural coping systems that humans possess are very efficient in dealing with a moderate and short-lived amount of stress. Developing this, Greenberg highlights two significant features associated with stress response: the positive or negative affect associated with the stressor and the sense of control over the source of stress. Where there is a sense of helplessness and associated negative affect, there is likely to be a harmful impact. Haglund and others (2007) also highlight research with animals which suggests that the degree of control an organism has over the stressor will play a central role in determining whether the stressful event will lead to subsequent vulnerability or resilience. Again, returning to the outline of the nature of play in the earlier section, and drawing on Spinka and others' (2001) analysis, we may see that the playful disequilibrium generated in play may promote stress, but this stress is deliberately and positively initiated, valued and manageable within the play frame. Greenberg comments that the tendency associated with mild stress is to energise activity, while intense stress may have the opposite effect.

Yun and others (2005) question some therapeutic treatments that are designed to reduce stress symptoms as actually contributing to the buffering of natural variation patterns and perhaps have little impact on long-term health benefits. They conclude that potential benefits to health and well-being may arise from adopting approaches that expand, rather than reduce, the dynamic range of biological experiences and environmental cues.

Panksepp (2001) also notes that modest stressors strengthen emotional and brain executive systems and may have substantial positive effects in tuning neurochemical systems. We may find that this connects with Siviy's (1998) explanation that dopamine, norepinephrine and serotonin (key neurochemicals) have a role in orchestrating play behaviours. These are also important in co-ordinating responses to stress, and any behaviour that activates these systems in such a global manner as play must inevitably influence the future sensitivity of these systems. Siviy (1998) cites evidence that early social experiences can alter the function of these systems, largely based on research in isolating rats in captivity. Isolated rats tend to display reduced ability to deal with social stressors. Although the evidence is far from conclusive, Siviy's research with animals suggests that play experiences may result in a brain that is better able to deal effectively with different types of social stressors:

> In other words, those of us who have had an ample opportunity to engage in play as juveniles may be better equipped at a neural level to 'roll with the punches' associated with daily social interactions than those who haven't had this opportunity. (Siviy 1998: 236)

Yun and others' (2005) research suggests that the dynamic range of environmental cues that humans have experienced may have significantly diminished over time due to increasing human interventions. Modern lifestyle changes mean that we have reduced our contact with environmental variability and stress, citing examples of extremes of temperature, hunger/satiety, experience of pain and variations in natural light.

Given that our biological system is designed to operate in complex environments, this reduction may have harmful consequences arising from the under-utilisation of compensatory biological mechanisms. Drawing on a range of research studies, Yun and others (2005) explain that the body requires a variation of input stressors for maintaining the dynamic range of the autonomic system. Heart rate variability, a measure of the dynamic range, can decline under various circumstances and lead to increased risk of heart disease. High heart rate variability is consistent with a healthy body response system. Thayer and Broschott (2005) note that low heart rate variability is a marker for a reduced ability for restoration, under-activation in the prefrontal cortex, and may be consistent with a range of conditions, including immune system dysfunction.

Yun and others (2005) also suggest that a consequence of an increasingly sedentary lifestyle may be a reduction in the dynamic range of movement. Body muscle groups exhibit great plasticity, yet this can be significantly reduced through immobilisation, even for short periods of time. Research indicates that reduction in the range of movement leads to 'muscle atrophy, fatty deposition and inhibition of protein synthesis which may promote systemic disturbances' (Yun and others 2005: 176).

To counteract this, Yun and others suggest that exercise-associated intermittent challenge, with irregular and unpredictable input patterns that induce wide ranging emotions along with short term and manageable stress, can increase heart rate variability, maintain fluid range of movement and increase variation of dynamic blood flow. This is also consistent with Burdette and Whitaker's (2005) analysis of the health benefits of play. Rather than simply encouraging more physical exercise, health promotion should be seeking to enhance the resilience factor of increasing the dynamic range of physiological, psychological and social experiences.

Children as risk-takers

Morrongiello and Matheis (2004) examine the role of emotions in children's approach to risk-taking through a study of children's decision-making when presented with a variety of potentially risky situations. As a starting point they acknowledge the motivation for feelings of excitement, and fun is a key predictor of risk-taking behaviour among those high in sensation seeking. Their research concludes with an acknowledgement of the complexity of the interplay between emotions, cognition and the social-situational context of the risk, giving a unique and dynamic personal quality and perspective to risk-taking that will be situationally specific. The significance of these studies may also lie with the recognition that the widely researched approaches that adults have to assessing risk are also fully operational in children. Similarly, research by Levin and Hart (2003) notes that children as young as four years old can understand and follow procedures for risky decision-making tasks and are able to distinguish clearly between choices that will achieve gains and avoid losses. The research highlights comparative results for children and adults in their responses to test situations, and their results question traditional perspectives which generally hold that children are incompetent in their ability to perceive and manage risk.

Risk aversion

The current societal response to many forms of children's play behaviours, and children's relationship with their immediate environments may suggest that there is a prevailing over-controlling and fearful attitude to forms of play that contain seemingly risky elements. The emerging research suggests that this is likely to reinforce fearful behaviours in some children, increasing their anxiety and lessening their ability to cope with novelty and threat. Tonucci (2005) suggests that the current focus on continuous adult supervision of children restricts children's opportunity to explore, discover or be surprised, since adults tend to explain, anticipate and prevent any exposure to risk. To Tonucci, this presents an even more serious risk of 'never risking anything'. A comparative study with children from a working class estate and a middle class area in the UK indicates that the estate children, through a range of parenting strategies and their own agency, were able to look after themselves, and 'being streetwise meant being able to make informed decisions and take appropriate actions' (Sutton and others 2007: 32). By contrast the children from the middle class area faced more 'latent' risks, which were largely induced by parental anxiety and media reports. The chaperoning of children by parents to structured activities restricts the acquisition of competent risk assessment strategies and inculcates fears of other children in public space.

Emerging research suggests that children who develop attention bias to threat, and whose environment supports this temperament, are likely to have these behaviours significantly reinforced (Fox and others 2007). Attention bias is an over-vigilance towards stimuli that present a threat. While obviously vigilance to threat is beneficial to survival, a child with attention bias will take longer to disengage from visual attention and become more prone to stress. This enhanced sensitivity to threat is associated with underlying causes of anxiety disorders. Fox and others (2007) suggest children disposed to respond with fear and anxiety to novelty or uncertainty may have these tendencies further reinforced by influences in their immediate environments. Thus it appears that caregivers who continually highlight negative features in the child's environment in an effort to control behaviour may in fact be promoting attention bias in the child. Fox and others (2007) note that, not only does this deepen the immediate anxiety to environmental stress, but it also primes the child to respond with a similar behavioural repertoire in the future, developing avoidance strategies and maintaining anxious behaviour to threat and novelty into adulthood.

Rubin and others (2002) comment that certain parenting practices may exacerbate children's wariness and fearfulness. Thus, for example, parents' anxiety may often lead to protecting children from over-arousing situations, as evidenced through the 'discouragement of independent attempts to explore the unfamiliar, the direction and restriction of children's actions and activities (telling them what to do) and the intrusion on children's ongoing activities (stepping in to preclude the possibility of an accident)' (Rubin and others 2002: 485). They note that the result from these parenting styles may be to prevent children from engaging in necessary self-initiated coping techniques. Their longitudinal research of young children aged between two and four years old highlights that, where children who display early signs of attention bias and social reticence experience controlling caring styles, children's patterns of anxiety to novelty are increased. Similarly Kiel and Buss (2006) suggest that specific parenting styles that involve high levels of approach and inaccuracy in predicting children's distress in novel situations will have significant impact on children's future ability to respond to challenges.

Adult responses to children's risk-taking behaviour are evidenced by Smith and others' (2002) study of children's rough and tumble play forms of play fighting in school playgrounds. Their research notes that many teachers and midday supervisors tend to see play fighting in a negative way and over-estimate the number of play fights that turn into real fights.

Ball's (2004) analysis of the use of Impact Absorbing Surfaces (IAS) provides an example of the complex societal relationship between play and risk. Ball explains that the level of individual risk for a fatal accident in playgrounds falls comfortably inside the 'broadly acceptable' tier. Similarly, he reveals that the cases of injuries sustained by children during play on playgrounds amounts to two per cent of all Accident and Emergency attendances, again within tolerable limits of broadly acceptable risk. Yet there is continual pressure to invest further in safety measures in children's playgrounds, particularly through the introduction of Impact Absorbing Surfaces (IAS). Ball (2004: 664) notes:

> One should add that attempting to address risks as low as this is problematical – there is always the possibility that interventions will create new risks of their own which, especially if the target risk is small, could result in more harm, not less. There is much anecdotal evidence, for example, which suggests that both children and parents have changed their behaviour in response to greater perceived safety in playgrounds fitted with IAS.

Ball concludes that the benefits of using IAS do not support the imposition on play providers of the significant cost implications. The article raises a more serious concern about the approach to safety in children's play through questioning the basis for such a drive that is founded more on belief than any clear research and analysis.

Play and creativity

Much of the literature on play and creativity is situated within the dominant psychological framework and has largely been concerned with the 'supposedly serious functions of problem solving, learning and exploration, as well as quantifiable kinds of creativity' (Sutton-Smith 1997: 156). Smith (2005) gives a detailed analysis of the psychological approaches to studying social and pretend play. Yet, as Sutton-Smith (1997) suggests, play supports adaptive variability rather than logical and narrow responses. The key relationship between play and creativity exists in the flexibility of responses to the situation and the non-serious interpretation of disparate stimuli.

Creativity and brain development

Bateson (2005: 18) acknowledges that human play has acquired more complex cognitive forms through evolution, 'rearranging the world in ways that ultimately enhance understanding'. He asserts that play may be an effective mechanism for facilitating innovation, a playful rearrangement of disparate thoughts into novel, nonsense combinations, 'most of which turn out to be useless'. Siviy (1998: 236) also comments:

> Widespread activation of the brain would also tend to facilitate the formation of novel connections between brain areas that might not be connected, perhaps enhancing creativity.

'... there is a prevailing over-controlling and fearful attitude to forms of play that contain seemingly risky elements.'

Greenberg (2004) proposes that creativity is an adaptive biological trait, that is, creativity provides a demonstrable contribution to 'fitness':

> Creativity is a potent biological adaptation in that it catalyses or facilitates a regulatory or advantageous change in response to a real or perceived stress by an individual or group of individuals.

In exploring the neural circuitry of creativity, Greenberg cites the importance of the basal ganglia and the action of the neurotransmitter dopamine. The basal ganglia are a group of nuclei that have connections along the vertical axis to the cortex, thalamus and brain stem regions, and are associated with a variety of functions that include motor control, cognition and emotions. Many organisms actively seek out novelty, and the intrinsically motivating quality of novelty can evoke a sense of pleasure in the basal ganglia and the release of dopamine; but while rewarding stimuli can activate these structures, the activation becomes more intense when the reward is unexpected. This again connects with Spinka and others' (2001: 143) account of the ancestral function of play to provide 'training for the unexpected':

> In short, we propose that play (1) results in increased versatility of movements used to recover from sudden 'gravitational', 'kinematic' or 'positional' shocks such as losing ground underfoot, falling over, being knocked over, being pinned down or being shaken vigorously; and (2) enhances the ability of the animals to cope emotionally with unexpected situations. These may include both locomotor shocks as described above, and 'psychological' shocks such as suddenly being faced with frightening or dangerous stimuli, unexpectedly meeting a stranger or experiencing a sudden reversal in dominance.

The brain can conjure mental pictures through neuronal activity (Burghardt 2005; Decety and Grezes 2006). This adaptive strategy enables us to rehearse different actions and to select the most appropriate without having to undertake the actual behaviours: 'linking these mental rehearsals with possible outcomes is a hallmark of creativity, innovation, and social adeptness' (Burghardt 2005: 397).

Play and creativity

Russ' (2004) evidence review also suggests that pretend play has a vital role in the development of cognitive capabilities through problem solving and conflict resolution, approaching problems as something to be resolved and the ability to work things out. There is a body of evidence which demonstrates the effectiveness of play in promoting problem-solving abilities (Bergen 2002). Drawing on research, Bergen highlights the reciprocal relationship between pretend play and problem solving, noting that cooperative social play may have a more general influence on divergent problem solving, with thematic play having a more specific influence on semantic problem solving. Ahn and Filipenko (2007), undertaking narrative research with children from a kindergarten in Canada, highlight the way in which children explored their identity, negotiated roles and developed understandings about relationships. Much of the pretend play of young children drew on improvisational exchanges demonstrating a high level of linguistic skills (Bergen 2002).

Howard-Jones and others (2002) suggest that participation in unstructured play may lead to further creative approaches in subsequent activities; there is evidence of a 'trickle down' (Sutton Smith 2002) response from playing. Holmes and Geiger (2002), using a range of creative methods with preschool children, suggest that particular cognitive abilities may be enhanced through creative activities. Observations of children's playing with blocks indicate a positive relationship between construction and language ability; those children who displayed more diverse and elaborate approaches to block use had a more varied and expansive vocabulary. The authors suggest that this may also enhance divergent thinking skills in other cognitive domains.

The results from Mullineaux and DiLalla's (2006) longitudinal study of the connection between pretend play and creativity suggest that early pretend play behaviour is a significant predictor of later creativity in early adolescence. Overall, the research findings suggest that early pretend play behaviours may be utilising similar cognitive mechanisms or facilitating thought processes associated with creative thinking during adolescence.

Russ (2004) comments that there is a large body of studies which have found relations between play processes and creativity. Much of the research mentioned by Russ dates back to the 1980s and 1990s, and looks at the contribution of play to cognitive processes or the global effect of play on children's creativity. Russ's own research, and a smaller number of studies, has also found a positive relationship between affective processes in play and creativity. A summary of research leads Russ (2004: 25) to claim that pretend play may, over time help children to become more creative by enabling them to:

- practice with free flow of associations that is a part of divergent thinking
- practice with symbol substitution, recombining of ideas and manipulation of object representations, processes associated with insight and the ability to transform ideas
- express and experience positive affect, building intrinsic motivation
- express and think about positive and negative affect themes within the comparative safety of the play frame and, through this, build up a repertoire of associations to be used in problem solving
- develop cognitive structures that enable emotion regulation.

Trevlas and others' (2003) research with pre-school children in Greece explores the way in which children develop motor creativity through play. Trevlas and others explain that motor creativity may be seen as the combination of perceptions into new and fresh motor patterns that can be either a solution to a pre-established problem, or the expression of an idea or emotion by means of the human body. The results from their survey indicate that children who scored highly on the playfulness scale used in the research have a high predisposition for play, communication and joy and were:

> ... also physically creative, meaning fluency in novel and divergent movement patterns or in ideas production. He/she has, namely, a more developed ability in divergent movement, which is a product of creative and critical thinking.
> (Trevlas and others 2003: 540)

In summary, Trevlas and others acknowledge that children have a need for freedom in the selection and execution of different movements. In the same way, it is clear that children have to acquire a feeling of self-control. Through creative movement, children have the ability to express their feelings and their thoughts, and to act and communicate using their body. This expressiveness through the body manifests itself more prevalently than speech in the early years. The authors claim that play provides a framework in which children can develop and refine physical skills, try out new roles, experiment and explore and solve complex problems that cannot be solved in other ways.

Play and learning

Making the Case for Play (Cole-Hamilton and others 2002) highlights a relationship between play and learning. There is a close connection between this theme and the previous exploration of the relationship between play and 'creativity'. This has been a traditional approach to considering the benefits of play, intuitively expressed as play supporting the development of cognitive and problem-solving skills. Russ' (2004) review of research illustrates this by outlining the ways in which play enhances the cognitive processes of expanding vocabulary, developing logical time sequences in narratives, learning strategies for problem solving and developing divergent thinking ability.

However, as previously mentioned, Burghardt (2005) suggests that perhaps the primary benefits of play are found within the integration of motor, affective and reward systems rather than the higher cognitive aspects of brain development. This point is recognised by Russ (2004) who suggests that affective processes may account for the relationship between play, creativity and learning. Such a perspective has implications for the current adult focus on the content of playing as an indication of what might be learned from the experience, rather than on the emotional experience the process of playing affords.

Play in the classroom

The idea of learning through play has a long history. Play has been identified as essential for children's development and as a key element in effective learning (Christie 2001; Bergen 2002; Trageton 2005; Howard and others 2006; Gmitrova and Gmitrov 2004).

Bergen (2002) synthesises research, mainly from the US and from an early childhood perspective, which explores the role of play in cognitive competence, noting that many cognitive strategies are exhibited during pretend play. Equally, Gmitrova and Gmitrov (2004) suggest that there is a growing body of evidence which supports the positive relationship between cognitive skills and high quality play. They explain that pretend play requires the ability to transform objects and actions, contains interactive social communication and negotiation, and involves role-taking and improvisation. In maintaining the play, children use many cognitive strategies such as problem-solving, joint planning and negotiation. Bergen (2002) suggests that pretend play engages many areas of the brain because it involves emotion, cognition, language and sensorimotor actions and so 'it may promote the development of dense synaptic connections'. Bergen concludes her research review noting the growing body of evidence supporting the connection between high-quality pretend play and cognitive competence. The evidence highlighted in her report supports the necessity to ensure that children are given time and space for social pretend play experiences.

Yet, as Bergen comments, the current demands of educational testing may have reduced the time and emphasis given to supporting a play-based curriculum in the early and primary years. Given its fluidity, flexibility and unpredictability, play may be difficult to control and justify in the pursuit of the 'serious skills' for which teachers are held accountable. Time allocated to play, therefore, may be viewed as inefficient and better spent on more specific activities (for example focusing on literacy) where the educational benefits are scientifically clear (Zigler and others 2004).

This point is reinforced in Morgan and Kennewell's (2006) research which suggests that primary schools in England and Wales seem to have neglected the value of play over recent years, due largely to the considerable demands of the National Curriculum and the methods encouraged by the national strategies for literacy and numeracy. The place of play in schools is also explored in Chapter 5.

Attachment and the development of peer play culture

Attachment may be seen as a general descriptive term for the processes that maintain and regulate continuing social relationships (Hofer 2006). Over the past decade, numerous studies have emerged which consider the significance of the child's early attachment for healthy brain development (Schore 2001; Swain and others 2007; Hofer 2006). In humans and primates, disruption to the mother-infant bonding and attachment process has been correlated with impairment of socio-emotional and cognitive competence and with vulnerability to major psychiatric conditions (Bock and others 2005; Suomi 2006). Bock and others (2005) suggest that the synaptic circuits within the limbic area, which are pivotal in emotion regulation, learning and memory, are adapted to the animal's early experiences. These experiences shape the network capacities for behaviour in adolescent and adult animals. Balbernie (2001) concurs with this in recognising that a child's neural circuitry is shaped by the quality and content of their emotional surroundings. Different patterns of early infant interaction might shape the course of development for children (Hofer 2006).

The infant is a highly emotional being and can make sophisticated emotional choices, becoming attached to smells, tastes and sounds within their immediate environment (Panksepp 2001). Schore (2001) outlines a process of 'affect synchrony' in which, for example, the carer's emotionally expressive face leads to periods of mutual gazing, and the caregiver and child begin to attune responses. The carer's anticipation and response to a child's emotional needs establishes a 'positive informational matrix and a positive sense of intersubjectivity' (Panksepp 2001: 148).

Viewed as a formative experience for the development of the social brain, affect synchrony (the ability to mutually read and attune emotional responses) has an impact on the development of emotion regulation, language use, and empathy across childhood and adolescence (Feldman 2007). The simultaneous matching of affect increases the degree of engagement between the partners in a rapid coordinated response that would suggest a 'bond of unconscious communication' (Schore 2001: 303). Thus positive attachment, according to Schore, allows for an internal sense of security and resilience. The infant can unconsciously and non-verbally regulate and attune their emotions through increasing regulation of their own bodily emotional states in a secure relationship. Indeed, Panksepp (2001) maintains that this attuning of responses and early affective resonance plays an important role in shaping the internal affective landscape: where children can have a full and open expression of their emotions they are more likely to develop effective self-regulation mechanisms.

Shared play episodes between carer and infant, in which both contribute through a repertoire of interactive behaviour, involves a sharing of affect (Decety and Jackson 2005). From an early age, play becomes an important process for the development of self-other differentiation and attributing value to verbal and non-verbal communication. It is ultimately a prerequisite for the ability to understand the feelings of oneself and others (Mohaupt and others 2006). Following extensive research studying the play and laughter patterns of rats, Panksepp (2001) suggests that early play interactions with a carer establish a foundation for later more sophisticated forms of play. An initial delight in tickling and physical contact may pave the way for peek-a-boo type play, giving rise to wider forms of positive emotions:

> The anticipation of sudden social presence and absence can magnetize the delighted attentions of infants. These antecedents may pave the way for their eventual enjoyment of unpredictability in games, as well as mischievous pranks and practical jokes. (Panksepp 2001: 155)

Ginsberg (2007) notes that parents' observations and sharing of child-driven play experiences enable a mutual attunement and attention process that enables more effective communication with children. This also becomes a self-reinforcing process due to the positive affect generated from this attachment.

Peer friendships
People (including children) are embedded in a web, or 'personal community', of relationships within and between generations (Pahl and Spencer 2004). Relationships are important in the emotional and social development of the child during the early years of life. As Weller (2007a) comments, friendship plays an important role as a social asset and provides a valuable source of social capital for children. Children's friendships offer an entry into wider social networks. Research into children's social networks has also shown that they play a key role in strengthening local communities and neighbourhood safety. Parents say that they build local social networks more through their children than any other means (Weller 2007b). Equally, children themselves place high value on their friendships, as evidence to the current Good Childhood Inquiry (The Children's Society 2007a) suggests. Here children comment that they enjoy having time to play with friends.

Development is an ongoing process, and close, emotionally involving relationships are influential throughout the lifespan. The importance of childhood may be that the brain structures which mediate social and emotional functioning begin to develop during this time in a manner that appears to be dependent upon interpersonal experience (Siegel 2001).

From an early secure attachment, the child is able to use the carer as a 'secure base' (Burghardt 2005) for exploration and developing further relationships with others, including the establishment of relationships with peers. The role of out-of-family relationships and activities has received less research attention than parent-child attachment, but it is likely that the child's experience of attachment plays a role in determining the quality of his or her relationships with peers. Children with positive relationships and expectations are at an advantage in accessing and maintaining relationships outside the home (Atwool 2006). Booth-

'A range of longitudinal studies highlights the significance of peer friendships for children's well-being.'

Laforce and others (2005) suggest that there is a causal link between the nature of early attachments and children's quality of friendships in the middle years. However, they also note that strong peer friendships may also serve a compensatory function when family relations are unsupportive, providing a closeness and intimacy that may not be present in the family.

In the period of middle childhood, the role of peer friendships takes on more significance. Booth-Laforce and others (2005), summarising a number of research studies, say that having high quality friendships shows a positive correlation to peer-assessed sociability and provides a buffer to anxiety and stress. Relationships with peers help children feel safe, and this may also serve to enhance academic performance. Resources gained from close friendships may allow children to cope with a variety of community stressors (Ratner and others 2006).

Attree (2004), undertaking a systematic review of the literature on the impact of poverty into children's lives, highlights the significance of children's peer friendships and social networks outside the family as a health and psychosocial protective factor. A range of longitudinal studies highlights the significance of peer friendships for children's well-being (Dougherty 2006). Abou-ezzeddine and others' (2007) study of children's friendship and victimisation in South Korea and China notes the important protective effects offered by establishing positive relationships with at least a sub-group of peers. These protective effects may be related to a number of underlying processes. For example, positive peer relationships might encourage the development of adaptive social skills which are useful in dealing with approaches from aggressors. Also, friends may develop caring and supportive roles in looking after each other in situations of peer aggression. Their study concludes that, in line with other studies in Europe and the US, positive peer relationships moderate the association between behavioural and educational risk factors and peer victimisation. Sutton and others' (2007) research with children from two contrasting areas suggests that working class children valued their peer friendships for the protective features they offered within their estates. The children interviewed in the study talked of 'banding together' to provide help and support. Yet this distinctive feature of the peer culture is likely to attract attention and censure from those in authority.

Research findings suggest that having a strong mutual relationship with a peer and being popular and accepted within a peer group have independent effects on a child's feelings of self-worth (Qualter and Munn 2005). They note:

> Given ... that lonely children report a lack of emotional support provided within the family ... peer friendship may be a good, if not the only, source of emotional security for lonely children. Having someone with whom a child can either play or confide in may be crucial in determining how a lonely child copes with a particular stressor or with his or her loneliness in general. (Qualter and Munn 2005: 381)

From this, it may be seen that the presence of strong, emotionally supportive friendships may serve as a protective factor. Thus, while it is most desirable for the developing child to have secure relationships with one or more primary carers, it is important to realise that attachment relationships of lesser significance may still play an important protective role for a child (Gilligan 2000, as discussed in Chapter 2).

Attachment pathologies

Research suggests that various forms of attachment pathologies (understood as the breakdown or absence of secure attachments) will have harmful effects, manifested through empathy disorders and a limited ability to read the emotions of others (Schore 2001; Fonagy and others 2007). Accompanying this will be deficits in self-regulation of emotions with limited ability to modulate the intensity and duration of emotional states. Panksepp (2001: 152) asserts that it is reasonable to suppose that milder effects on brain systems could establish 'chronic shyness and introverted tendencies in children and perhaps lifelong tendencies towards submissive behaviours and feelings of defeat in adulthood'.

Recent research studies have increasingly focused on the role of emotion in children's friendship patterns. Dougherty's (2006) review of this research highlights the disruptive impact of negative emotions on friendships. This covers all types of negative emotions, for example, fear may predict low social status due to high behavioural inhibition and withdrawal from peer interactions, whereas anger may predict low social status due to an aggressive approach in seeking contact with others which may be perceived as threatening by peers.

A longitudinal study in the US (Rubin and others 2002) found that fifth-graders (children aged 10-11 years) without friends, compared to those with friends, had lower self-esteem and more psychopathological problems in adulthood. Rubin and others' (2002) research notes that fifth-grade children without friends were perceived by their peers as more aggressive, less popular and more victimised and rejected than children who possessed mutual best friendships.

Qualter and Munn's (2005) research into children's loneliness and play partners highlights two distinct forms of loneliness:

- **Social loneliness** refers to the physical absence of other people or social isolation and may relate to a lack of group acceptance.

- **Emotional loneliness** stems from the absence of a close attachment with 'best friends'.

Their observations of children at playtime showed that lonely or lonely/rejected children tended to choose each other as play partners and that their interactions were rated as positive by the observers. Qualter and Munn suggest that these may be 'opportunistic' meetings, where isolated children wander around looking for someone to play with and end up playing with other lonely children. The underlying theme of positive behaviour with each other in the play may be explained by the fact that the encounters are merely opportunistic and there is little emotional investment. The authors cite studies which suggest that arguments are the preserve of close friendships and children engage in more conflict within their friendships than outside these groups. This finds support from Goodwin's (2006: 33) analysis of the central role of dispute and conflict in the development of peer relationships:

> Dispute is an interactional accomplishment, and one of the most important loci for the development of friendships and peer relationships. Neither an aberration or something to be avoided at all costs, it is, rather, constitutive of children's dealings with one another, establishes group cohesiveness, and provides a primary way that activities are constituted.

Corsaro's (2003) ethnographic study of children's peer friendship also concurs with this analysis, noting that conflict is a natural element of children's culture and peer relations. Corsaro's (2003: 193) research, notes that children's conflicts and disputes are generally seen as negative and threatening by adults, who would prefer that children 'get along and play nicely'. Corsaro suggests that this response may have a sociocultural bias, noting that African-

American teachers and parents viewed children's peer conflicts as dramatic exchanges and responded to these with playful banter.

Play and friendships

Panksepp (2007: 6) notes that play is the mechanism through which young children 'learn about social dynamics in an affectively positive environment, and many behavioural and mental functions may be refined during play'. Moreover, through play experiences, the child learns about normative roles, rules, and how to negotiate his or her way through interpersonal dilemmas (Booth-Laforce and others 2005).

Activities with friends are an important part of the daily lives of children and adolescents. These activities provide children and young people with enjoyment, a sense of accomplishment and belonging, opportunities for informal learning, and a context in which to explore their social worlds. While engaged in activities, friends can get to know one anothers' likes and dislikes; disclose private thoughts; reveal their academic, social, and athletic competencies; and build shared social relationships (Mathur and Berndt 2006).

Mathur and Berndt's comparative study of child and adolescent friendships notes that children may develop stable friendships in play, and this is where they develop the social skills needed to maintain friendships. Time spent 'hanging out', socialising, sharing current media interests and informal activity contributes to friendship maintenance through building trust and intimacy. Mathur and Berndt highlight the importance of both the quality and quantity of opportunities for peer interaction: children and adolescents who have more opportunity for social contact and a diverse range of socialising activities perceived their friendships as being higher in quality.

74

Fantuzzo and others (2004) suggest that a key component of children's early peer competence is the establishment of positive interactions in play. They cite wide-ranging research which highlights that children, within their play friendships, develop the multiple skills necessary for effective peer relationships:

> … entering a peer play group and assessing other children's responses to play initiations, requires the acquisition of cognitive, linguistic, and socioemotional abilities. As children develop problem solving, reasoning, and perspective taking skills through peer play interactions, they are better able to cooperate, resolve conflicts, and develop empathy. (Fantuzzo and others 2004: 183)

Their own empirical research with children aged between three and seven years old in the US Headstart programme indicates that children exhibiting high levels of peer play interaction were found to demonstrate more competent emotion regulation, initiation, self-determination, and receptive vocabulary skills. Using a range of play assessment tools to explore play interaction, play disruption and play disconnection, the study concludes that positive play engagement was associated with lower levels of aggression, shyness and withdrawal behaviours. Also, successful interaction in peer play led to greater cognitive, social, and movement/coordination outcomes while disruptive and disconnected peer play behaviours were associated with negative emotional and behavioural outcomes (Fantuzzo and others 2004).

Colwell and Lindsey (2005) summarise research which indicates that both the amount and the type of children's play are linked with qualities of peer competence. Given the heterogeneous and complex nature of children's play and the multifaceted nature of children's friendship patterns it is not easy to establish direct cause-and-effect connections. As such, they assert that questions remain about the specific relationship between play and social competence.

Research into pretend play in early childhood (Andresen 2005) highlights the importance of playful interaction between preschool children in making a significant contribution to their ability to self-regulate, to explore and to follow rules. In addition, in the preschool years, role-play between children is accompanied by important changes in interaction and language use through their mutual engagement in the play process.

Goodwin's (2006) detailed ethnographic research into children's playground games of hopscotch and jump rope in a US elementary school provides many examples of the ways in which children contested and disputed play behaviours and actions of others. While the study primarily considered the social relationships developed in girls' groups, Goodwin suggests that the interactive practices are not unique to girls. The observations clearly illustrate a range of common strategies employed by children in developing and maintaining their play frames. Such disputes provide a way of playing with language, asserting one's position both verbally and physically, taking affective stances, challenging rule-breaking and rearranging the social structure of the group

Freeman and Brown (2004) describe the complex nature of children's rough and tumble play as a staging area for expressions of friendship and caring. The structure of rough and tumble play requires sophisticated interactions between experiences of being a caregiver as well as being cared for. Reed (2005) also outlines the considerable caring that takes place in rough and tumble play, with particular reference to a game called 'Smear', a high physical contact game observed in a youth centre by a group of boys aged between six and nine years. The observations and child interviews show clearly that there was a higher intensity of physical contact and the game was played for a longer period where the players were close friends. While other children were included, their participation lacked the intimate contact that friends displayed when playing. When, on rare occasions, children were injured in the game, there were a series of caring strategies employed by the other players to look after the injured child. As Reed (2005: 67) notes:

> R and T play is a staging area for friendships, for negotiations, problem solving, to fulfil their need and belong to a group, to have intimate caring relationships with friends, experience friendly competition, develop a sense of community somewhere between the warmth and closeness of family and isolation, and indifference of the adult masculine world.

Pellis and Pellis (2007) provide a valuable summary of their own, and other, research in studying rough and tumble play in animals and the possible parallels with human forms of this play type. They note that rough and tumble play is a recurring feature of childhood, and research indicates that it has a significant role in developing social competence. Drawing on the work of Burghardt (2005), Pellis and Pellis (2007) note the fundamental characteristics of this play form as being voluntary and associated with positive affect, which clearly distinguishes it from serious fighting. In looking at the developmental sequence of this play behaviour in rats, they note the sophisticated ways in which offensive and defensive roles are organised to decrease the control that the animals have over their own and their play partner's movements:

> This organisation results in more frequent role reversals and provides the juvenile rats with an increased opportunity to experience not only novel bodily movements but also continually changing bodily configurations with their partners. (Pellis and Pellis 2007: 97)

They highlight that, as in many complex behaviours, rough and tumble play involves many areas of the brain. The pattern of behaviour and movement originates in the limbic and paralimbic regions and is mediated by the cortex, which draws upon past experiences and an assessment of the current context to develop playful actions consistent with the event. This integration is accompanied by the release of brain chemicals that promote growth and development in these areas. Pellis and Pellis point out that one of the key areas involved is the orbitofrontal cortex (OFC), a part of the brain involved in social discrimination and decision-making. Their research indicates that rats that have experienced damage to the OFC fail to modify their behaviours appropriately with their social partners in both play and non-play contexts:

> Findings from several laboratories indicate that the juvenile typical pattern of play fighting produces experiences that provide feedback for some of the brain areas responsible for generating such play and so promotes development of those areas. That such feedback may actually lead to functional enhancement in the output of these brain areas as the rats mature is suggested by deficits seen in rats with OFC damage and those with intact brains that have been deprived of play-fighting

experiences as juveniles. Furthermore, these brain areas are many of the same areas that regulate social behaviour and cognition in general, and so improvements derived from play fighting may improve the capacity for more subtle social interactions. (Pellis and Pellis 2007: 97)

This complements evidence of the interrelationship between brain organisation and play discussed at the opening stages of this chapter. They conclude with a suggestion that, given the similarity in brain structure between rats, primates and humans, experience of play fighting in childhood is causally related to social competence.

What the evidence overwhelmingly suggests is that the relationships that children develop from birth are of significant importance throughout the period of childhood and into adulthood. The quality of early childhood relationships is likely to affect the development of the child's sense of self in relationship with others, developing a capacity for emotional coupling, self-other awareness and the ability to understand the perspectives of others.

The neural mechanisms that underpin this capability (limbic-cortical vertical integration) retains high plasticity throughout childhood, and while the initial attachment to a primary caregiver is vital, it is not the sole determinant of developing effective empathic responses and emotional self-regulation. In other words, as Bruer (1999: 188) comments, we should never lose sight of the fact that humans are highly adaptive and 'our children are remarkably resilient'.

Children's play culture

The literature on the nature of peer friendships and play reveals contrasting research approaches. There are instrumental studies which see play as a medium in which children learn and acquire the appropriate social and cognitive skills required to become a competent adult. In this context, culture is produced for children by adults (Mouritsen 1998). This is represented through the institutional world, which is perceived as 'quality culture'. This adult-derived culture is designed to socialise children in the qualities that are deemed to be socially desirable and prepares the child to become a competent adult. The nature of these instrumental studies draws on empirical testing methods, generally employing tools that include teacher, parent or observer assessment of children against a measurable scale, subjecting the results for statistical analysis to arrive at a measure of a child's social competence.

Whilst families and institutions do provide important contexts for socialisation, the perspective of developmental psychology has given little credit to the child's ability to form and shape their interactions away from adults (Goodwin 2006). Corsaro (2003) suggests that the developmental psychology approach is dominated by adult concerns that fail to see the child embedded in the context of peer culture:

> A big reason that developmental psychologists underestimate the friendship knowledge and skills of young children is that they focus on outcomes. That is, they identify and classify children at various stages in the acquisition of adult friendship knowledge in relation to their age or other developmental abilities. There is an assumption here that kids must acquire or internalize adult concepts of friendships before they can really have complex friendship relations. (Corsaro 2003: 67)

Play culture arises from within children's peer networks and develops unique forms of expression (Mouritsen 1998). Kalliala's (2006) observations of children's play suggest that children's play culture thrives where children are given space away from adults to create their own imagined worlds. Here, the child 'filters material for its own purposes from what is offered by the dominant culture' (Kalliala 2006: 29). Kalliala's observations of children's play highlight the subtlety and complexity of the emerging play culture, identifying four categories of playing (after Callois 1961):

Competition and games: Children mutually develop and follow their own seemingly arbitrary rules. Within this frame, children are expected to apply the rules and to participate actively, but the idea of winners and losers often gets lost within the play. The most important thing about these competitive play forms is being a member of the group. There are various degrees of performance within these games, with subtle interventions of 'dizzyness' (see below) to add to the play. The significant feature is that children are in control of this process.

Games of chance: Kalliala highlights the significant element of chance in children's play culture, typified by the use of rhymes to select and eliminate others in play situations. These forms represent a strong ritualistic element in play and can be used as a way of resolving conflict without resorting to power (even if some players successfully manipulate the result they desire). Kalliala comments that the use of power in play can sometimes be cruel and can exclude others from playing.

Make-believe: Kalliala's observations highlight a range of play forms that imitate real life, involve fantasy and imagination and so on – play based around the notion that the scenario is 'as if' rather than 'for real'. Kalliala distinguishes the domestic, reality-based pretend and role-play situations from scenarios that are about having adventures and fights. She describes the intricacies of children's 'real-life' pretend play, particularly the imitation of much of their daily family routines and exploration of domestic and gendered roles. In contrast, the fantasy and adventure type of pretend play features a more structured narrative that can be 'funny, full of surprises, exciting, big or small' (Kalliala 2006: 75). A common theme in children's adventures and fantasy play appears to be the battle between good and evil. In her observations of children's play, Kalliala suggests that this represents an important part of identity formation; in order to come to terms with a complex and nuanced sense of 'right' and 'wrong', children first need to play at fighting between clearly defined good and evil.

Dizzy play: The momentary need to turn the world upside down, to lose control in an attempt to regain equilibrium. Much of this play includes 'forbidden' elements, often associated with disgust, toilet humour or sex, along with a range of risk-taking physical actions. As Kalliala points out, these forms of play are situated in time and place, drawing on the dominant cultural themes that currently concern children. Here again, we may see connections with Sutton-Smith's (2003) analysis and the role of play in emotion regulation.

It is apparent that adults often perceive many of the expressions which children display while playing as trivial or undesirable. Adults generally perceive children's play from a purposeful and functional perspective and regard children's expressions as childish nonsense and perhaps as noisy and chaotic (Mouritsen 1998). Adults often misread the nature of children's play evidenced, for example, by Smith and others' (2002) research with teacher interpretations of children's rough and tumble play and their misperceptions of this form of play compared with children's own interpretations (Smith and others 2004).

'Play culture arises from within children's peer networks and develops unique forms of expression.'

While adults may perceive certain forms of children's play as threatening, disruptive or having no benefits (Smith and others 2002), children certainly do not perceive these as unimportant. As Sutton-Smith (2001: 43) suggests, 'while the adult group typically exercises much pressure to have children adhere to the culture's stereotypic belief systems, in many modern cases children's own imaginings far transgress the implications of these systems and pursue phantasmagorical routes of their own'.

Guss (2005), through her examination of children's narrative in a pretend play situation, indicates that children's pretence is not simply an imitation of the real world but is highly innovative. Thus, children's pretend play may be subversive rather than simply being socially integrative. Guss asserts that play has the potential for inverting the established order and creating new cultural norms. In this way play can be:

> … both generative and expressive of personality and culture. Generating and expressing personality and culture have to do with giving form to and forming individual and cultural identities. (Guss 2005:241)

Equally Pramling, Samuelsson and Johansson (2006), reviewing the literature on children's play and learning, note that in play children experience and create a world of meaning that contains it own values. Children share their life-worlds with other children; the maintenance of play requires continuous negotiation and renegotiation between children. As they explain:

> Since children interact on equal conditions while the situations and the participants often change, there is no absolute right or wrong in children's play worlds. Instead rules must constantly be defined and redefined. This makes play a perfect arena for children, in which they will develop communicative ability, an ability … fundamental for children's learning and creativity. In play, children learn to know others' perspectives and gradually learn to understand them. (Pramling, Samuelsson and Johansson 2006: 51)

Guss (2005: 233) reports that children, when left to their own devices, have 'serious fun' playing as 'they seek and construct form and meanings that have immediate significance for them'. Guss' (2005:242) critique of the instrumental perspective leads to an alternative approach which acknowledges that children, through their dramatic play, gain 'powerful tools for self-defining experiences of themselves and for forging enrichened identities' . Through their initiation and development of play, and in the privacy of their play culture:

> … children also have the cultural occasion, space and liberty to take control: to question, to speak for themselves, to represent, transform and define themselves, and to choose and to reach the aesthetic effect that satisfies their imaginations and complex wishes. In the cultural contexts of children's playing … the players can experiment with standpoints, redefine their identities and, thereby, take back their power of self-definition. (Guss 2005: 240)

The complexity of children's play cultures

Corsaro's (2003) exploration of children's friendships and peer cultures begins with an acknowledgement that children are active agents in their own socialisation and take information from the adult world to produce their own complex and dynamic childhood culture. Any attempt to understand the meanings of play must begin with the child's subjective experiences. A closer exploration of the complexity and dynamism may show that play is not simply about pleasurable experiences (although as previously discussed this does have a significant place in play) but will inevitably contain painful experiences, rejection, isolation, fear, cruelty and so on (Hughes 2006; Sutton-Smith 2003). Bailey (2002: 165) notes that children's social transactions are 'by turns co-operative, competitive and manipulative: networks of friendships are formed and reformed; compromises are made; plans are drawn, redrawn and withdrawn'.

A similar point is made by Lofdahl and Hagglund (2006), who note that a 'romantic' view of children's play does not reveal the complete nature of this form of behaviour; play is also a social arena for negative, difficult, and sometimes hurtful lessons and accompanying emotions. Using empirical data from a study of schoolchildren's play, Lofdahl and Hagglund demonstrate how children interpret adult determined rules within the setting to establish their own hierarchical and exclusionary play group. To legitimise exclusive practices, children manipulated school expectations, such as 'everyone can join in'. Through a highly complex process, children verbally and non-verbally participate in establishing common rules for inclusion and exclusion both within the play through the allocation of roles, and externally by 'inventing' rules of exclusion – 'you are too young', or changing selection rituals in turn-taking games. As the authors note:

> Over time, this kind of experience constitutes an important element in children's ongoing learning of basic conditions for being socially accepted and included. In a longer perspective we anticipate this to have bearing also for their insights of social participation and its cultural meanings and conditions in a more general sense.
> (Lofdahl and Hagglund 2006: 192)

In their observations, Lofdahl and Hagglund note that the intervention of a teacher to enforce the rule that every child can join in did little to support an excluded child. While complying with the teacher's request, the children allocated a lowly role in the play which meant that the child was physically included but no one need pay any attention to her.

Wohlwend's (2004) study of children in a school playground notes the complex ways in which children include and exclude each other in their social and play groupings and concludes that the solutions to these situations lay not so much with teacher initiated discussions but within the play process itself, and the dynamic nature of children's play groups created plentiful opportunity for strategies to change memberships or introduce innovation into the play to accommodate or exclude others.

Branco (2005) explores the nature of conflict in children's peer play and notes that research indicates the value of these experiences to questioning assumptions and attempting to see others' perspectives. Through this process, children increase their communication and meaning construction abilities. Where there are divergences in play, children may co-create and construct new meanings in order to keep the play flowing, which 'results in novel verbal and non-verbal elaborations that directly contribute to their linguistic abilities' (Branco 2005: 423).

Children's subjectivity and identity

De Castro (2004: 476), citing Alanen (2001a: 87), notes that through:

> ... participation in everyday social life, children ...gain a particular range of experiences and knowledge about the social relations within which they daily live, on the locations which are theirs. This knowledge, however, is normally not articulated and therefore remains hidden, implicit, unacknowledged. Beginning from where children stand and act, as subjects, in their everyday lives, an account of society from such a point – that is, from a children's standpoint – becomes conceivable.

The emerging disciplines of the sociology of childhood and children's social and cultural geographies have provided rich material which begins to consider the significance of children's peer friendships and relationships, largely from the subjective and situated experiences of children. From this perspective, it is acknowledged that children actively negotiate aspects of their identities as they align themselves with 'others' in places that hold multiple and shifting meanings (Vanderbeck and Dunkley 2003).

This emerging body of work perceives children not as a universal phenomenon, subject to a pervasive all-embracing theory (such as that of fixed ages and stages of development), but as producers of subjectivities that are uniquely intertwined with their material and discursive worlds. Each human being lives within a web of social relationships that make up their 'community', all the while developing a set of identities that influence and are in turn influenced by these networks.

Children's playful encounters may be seen as a vital element in the process of identity making; a significant process in which children continually construct their identities in a range of diverse social and physical landscapes (De Castro 2004; Goodwin 2006). The variability of places and people provides 'fluidity and plasticity in the process of engendering and reconstructing frontiers between one and the other' (De Castro 2004: 476). A vital link in this process is through the peer relationships that develop and fragment away from the gaze of adults. Valentine (2000) comments on the need for children and young people to learn how to articulate their individuality while at the same time fitting in with peer group identities. This delicate balancing act is 'complex and fragmentary' and requires constant 'maintenance work' on the self to manage the necessary choices that are made in differing contexts (Valentine 2000: 265).

A number of ethnographic studies have revealed the intricacies of this balancing act in the situated activities of children's lives, highlighting how children's peer friendships are arenas for the complex interplay of wider social processes. Children's lives vary according to a range of interconnected factors such as culture, class, gender, age, ethnicity, disability, religion and many other variables (Punch 2003). Equally Anthias and Yuval-Davis (1998) suggest that any exploration of the complex patterns associated with race, gender and class must be made in local and specific contexts, with close attention to how they are constructed within these specific sites.

Play and gender

The process of identity formation through peer friendships and play has perhaps been most apparent in studies of children's gender identity. As Aydt and Corsaro (2003: 1336) suggest, 'one of the most important identities that children learn to define themselves and others by is gender'.

The research into children's gendered play patterns reveals two basic and contrasting perspectives (Goodwin 2006). The first broad area suggests a binary or 'dual culture' approach to studying same-sex friendships and play behaviours. Based largely in the discipline of developmental psychology, this perspective suggests that boys and girls have distinctive cultures that manifest themselves in their play styles. These separate cultures provide the socialising influences for boys and girls as they grow older (Underwood 2007). Rose and Rudolph's (2006) critical review of research evidence concludes that there are some consistent differences in the styles and experiences of girls and boys with their same-sex peer groups. Girls engage in more prosocial interactions, evidenced in their conversations and self-disclosure. Also girls are more likely to focus on the importance of maintaining connections, are more sensitive to distress in others and to the status of their peer friendships, and display their emotions more openly. Rose and Rudolph (2006) suggest that boys, in contrast, interact in larger groups, engage in more rough and tumble and competitive play, emphasise dominance goals and self-interest, are more likely to experience direct physical and verbal victimisation and are more likely to use humour in response to stress.

Pellegrini and others' (2004) research into the gendered nature of children's play in school playgrounds in the UK and US reveals evidence of this 'two cultures' pattern. Their findings suggest that boys engaged in more games, in particular ball games, and chase games, than girls. Girls engaged in more jumping/verbal games, such as jump rope and clapping/chanting games. They suggest that these differences in play behaviours may be a reflection of the ways in which boys use the available space for their physical and competitive behaviours. Pellegrini and others suggest that girls are more sedentary and more verbally competent than boys. As such, girls preferred games in which these skills could be used. The research concludes that peer groups support gender role stereotypes; girls find the playground unpleasant, citing research from Blatchford (1998) which suggests that girls complain that their playtime is too long, and look for ways to opt out of going outside.

Jarvis' (2007) study of rough and tumble play with children in a primary school in the north of England suggests that boys engaged more frequently in rough and tumble play. Of the 33 observations of rough and tumble play behaviours, only four featured girls-only groups, while in contrast 15 boys-only episodes were observed. The boys displayed more physical confrontation and less complex narratives and language than were observed in the girl's-only episodes. However, there were 14 examples of mixed-gender rough and tumble play. The significant proportion were chasing games that were initiated by the girls. This generally involved girls seeking out a boy to offer an invitation, or 'play cue' (Sturrock and Else 1998) to chase them. The games developed with an underlying narrative that involved the boys pretending to be a frightening monster and the girls running away. Another chase game observed by Jarvis was the 'poison touch' game, where girls, once touched by a chasing boy had to lie down and 'play dead' until another girl's touch brought them back to life. Jarvis notes that a feature of the girls reactions to chasing games was to 'tell the teacher' when the boys' attention became too energetic, and the style of this 'telling' could evoke different responses from teachers. Girls' 'routine' complaints were often seen to be part of the fun for both girls and boys, and would result in a mild admonishment from the teacher that reinforced the boy's status as a good chaser. However, more serious transgressions would lead to more severe and less desirable admonishments. When they sensed that girls were going to tell and that the consequences might be severe, boys 'collaborated in an attempt to persuade the girls not to tell' (Jarvis 2007:185). This process of 'telling' signifies the exertion of a certain amount of power by the girls within the play. Jarvis notes that there is a complex web of inter- and intra-gender cooperation and competition within rough and tumble play that supports learning about 'complex physical and linguistic responses from other children of both genders, allowing the children concerned to create shared narratives through which they can practice independently controlled and motivated behaviour … within the peer group, whether they are male and female' (Jarvis 2007:186).

Aydt and Corsaro (2003) also comment that in research with young children in Italy, while there was evidence of traditional same sex-activities for boys (sports and superhero play) and girls (dolls), both girls and boys participated in role-playing games, in particular one game based on television game show in which both boys and girls took the role of the main character, a woman, demonstrating the flexible ways in which children can deal with gender issues in play. Their research into gender patterns across different cultures notes that:

> Examination of children's interactions across four different preschool settings demonstrates that although there are some similarities in cross-sex play, the salience of gender and the quality of interaction varies substantially from peer culture to peer culture. Although at least some level of gender segregation seems to be a universal feature in children's play, some peer cultures emphasize gender differences and ritualize cross-sex interactions and in other peer cultures, children do very little to enforce gender boundaries. (Aydt and Corsaro 2003: 1320)

These examples indicate a more complex pattern to children's gendered play than the 'two cultures' research suggests. Goodwin (2006) questions the perspective of the 'two cultures' approach and associated methodologies. The emphasis on experimental psychological studies rather than ethnographic accounts of children's situated relationships and activities has given rise to essentialist ideas. This is further reinforced by the fact that many studies are of white middle-class children which are then generalised to make universal claims about all children. The focus on difference in morality, emotionality and prosocial behaviour associated with the binary of male/female groups masks the multiple ways in which children negotiate the rules of behaviour within their peer societies and leaves little room to accommodate the changing power relations as they occur in time and space. Goodwin's detailed linguistic analysis of children's play in a US elementary school playground calls into question the notion that girls groups are prosocial, cooperative and polite. The girls in Goodwin's study displayed complex ways of delineating social difference within their groups and used subtle and more direct verbal and non-verbal directives to construct hierarchically organised relationships in both same-sex and in cross-sex play.

Swain (2005), citing the work of Thorne (1993), recognises that the binary language of 'boy' and 'girl' hides the fact that there is a greater variation within gender than across it. Boys and girls, at times, are separate (or are separated) within their groups, but they also come together to be part of the same world. One significant site for the separation and coming together of children is the school, an institution that generally features a dominant or exemplary form of masculinity (Swain 2005), often referred to as 'hegemonic masculinity'. The dominant masculine practices, norms and values that pervade these institutional spaces afford boys the opportunity to exert their influence – although as in previous discussion it should be recognised that this takes place within the context of the other intersecting features of class, ethnicity and so on. Swain's research in three contrasting primary schools highlights the ways in which boys draw significantly on their physicality and athleticism, inextricably linked to the body in forms of 'strength, toughness, power, skill, fitness, speed and so on' (Swain 2005: 77) as an expression of their masculinity. Masculinity is relationally produced and, as Swain comments, masculinity is always defined in relation to what is not masculine, namely, femininity.

The study notes that the nature of gendered relationships differed in each of the schools, but there were also a number of similarities, chief of which was that while children preferred to play in same-gender groups, these were generally not oppositional but complementary – boys did not generally need to resort to misogyny to reinforce their masculinity. What is apparent from the research is the dynamic, often subtle, and multiple ways in which children maintain and cross over gender divides. Swain cites an example from one school where boys and girls regularly played together in the playground, even in physical strength games. In the other schools, boys tended to dominate the use of playground space but this situation was contested by groups of girls who were able to deliberately exercise power over the boys.

Renold's (2004) study of how 'other' boys negotiate non-hegemonic masculinities in a primary school further extends the complexity of gender relationships. The choices for 'doing boy' are not simply about exercising personal preferences but must take into account the wider context; boys who move outside of the dominant masculine identity may place themselves in a position of powerlessness and exposure to ridicule and isolation. Renold highlights how the majority of boys interviewed expressed some concern over the pressures of hegemonic masculinity maintenance, and one third of the boys were 'struggling to do their gender in non-hegemonic ways' (Renold 2004: 261). In seeking to move away from a prevailing masculine hegemony, children would try out ('flirt') with non-hegemonic roles. To prevent sanction and ridicule from male peers, this flirting would still take place in a framework of dismissal of all things feminine. As Renold (2004: 261) notes, 'they had little awareness that investing in such discourses reinforced the very powers of hegemonic masculinities that they were trying to escape from'.

Epstein and others' (2001) ethnographic study of children's play in two primary schools notes different ways in which boys carry out the task of performing masculinity in their play. However, this is also informed by processes of ethnicity and sexuality. In one of the schools used in the study, playtime was dominated by the boys' football games, with the girls standing around the edges of the playing areas and framing the boys' games.

This observation is consistent with a number of other studies that have paid particular attention to the role of playground football in providing boys with a set of masculinising practices that are based almost entirely on physicality and embodied social action (see, for example, Smith 2007; Clark and Paechter 2007). The performance of 'football' offers a highly visible platform to display competence in an activity that personifies masculinity. Clark and Paechter's (2007) study of 10- to 11-year-olds' use of the school playground in two primary schools in London illustrates the ways in which boys' games of football lead to domination of the playground space and activity: 'gendered expectations about play and the use of the body serve actively to discourage girls whist consolidating male dominance of the game' (Clark and Paechter 2007: 262). A complex and interrelated series of behaviours and practices serve to exclude girls and marginalise non-footballing boys, including the legitimisation of this practice by teachers through 'cultural complicity' (Newman and others 2006; Smith 2007).

Epstein and others' (2001) study notes that girls spent much of their time appearing not to be interested in the boys, but talking about them, particularly in terms of their skills as footballers and their attractiveness. These discussions often spilled over into the skipping and clapping games played by the girls. The second school had a more identified space for playing football in the playground (the 'cage'), and the use of this space was prescribed by teachers with each year of the school allowed to use it on a separate day of the week, with one day being dedicated to girls only use. This not only established a pattern of girls playing football, which spilled over into girls playing in the 'cage' on their 'year days', but also created opportunities for play beyond football. The observations indicate that boys developed chasing and wrestling games, but also played with the girls in a largely girl-initiated and maintained role-play situation (significantly arising from the most popular girl and boy being 'boyfriend' and 'girlfriend' and wanting to play together, thus giving 'permission' for this form of behaviour to other boys). Epstein and others (2001: 170) conclude that:

> Children's enactments and embodiments of gendered, ethnicised, and sexualised subject positions are more fluid than commonly appears to be the case in school playgrounds ... Here we can see the possibilities of more fluid, hopeful, and less rigidly policed and disciplined masculinities and femininities that accrue from girls and boys having mixed friendship groups at this age.

Renold's (2007) research with 10- to 11-year-old children in a school in the east of England suggests that the dominant discourse of heterosexuality reinforces masculine hegemony. Her study shows how the 'heterosexual norms' associated with being boy and girl are continually negotiated, mainly through the practices of 'going out', 'dumping' and 'fancying'. These states rarely involved actual encounter or going anywhere as a couple but were positions playfully adopted to create subjects of 'boyfriend' and 'girlfriend'. Girls played a key role in developing and maintaining boyfriend/girlfriend cultures 'via complex interactive daily gossip networks, matchmakers and messengers' (Renold 2007: 282). The position of being a boyfriend was a key signifier of heterosexual masculinity while the performance of being a girlfriend was also a fundamental construction of what Renold refers to as 'proper' femininity.

While the process of having a girlfriend/being a boyfriend was valued as contributing to boys' masculinity, it paradoxically also created tension and anxiety by challenging other expressions of masculine hegemony created through an aversion to and disassociation from all things feminine. This tension often became apparent in the teasing patterns of behaviour that boys adopted when talking about girlfriends (largely oppressive and misogynistic). While most of the boyfriend/girlfriend relationships were ambiguous and fleeting, Renold develops a more detailed examination of the 'professional' boyfriend role – children who moved beyond the tension to adopt various ways of developing closer friendships with girls without loss of masculinity. This supports Epstein and others' (2001) observations of the modelling of boyfriend/girlfriend roles by popular and high status children which creates the opportunity for closer boy/girl friendships. This research highlights how the intersection of gender and sexuality gives rise to the highly complex and nuanced positions and behaviours that children adopt in their relationships.

83

Tellingly, most of the research on gendered relationships occurs in school settings, primarily in the playground. The separation of boys and girls tends to be greater in schools than in the neighbourhood, where children often play with anyone they can find and there is more chance to create spaces to play away from the sometimes admonishing observations of others (Swain 2005). James (1998) recalls an interview with a young child, Alice, who when asked the question 'Do you play with boys?' responded that she played with Bobby at home and on the way to school, but this friendship was put on hold at the school gate. On the journey home after school, the friendship was renewed. Equally, children's play relationships in their local neighbourhoods may differ significantly from those in school playgrounds. Meire (2007) cites the work of Ackerley (2003) who observes that the strict gender separation seen in school playgrounds was not replicated in children's other play spaces, for example, the home and the neighbourhood. Ackerly suggests that gender integration is more likely to occur without adult intervention, and thus in (rarely studied) settings like the street and the neighbourhood. This again highlights one of the key dilemmas in this research review and the relative paucity of research materials that explore children's play away from the school playground.

It should be acknowledged that gender, race and class intersect with space to produce patterns of territorial claims, as evidenced in the school playground research which illustrates the ways in which boys dominate the use of playground space. Morrow (2006) summarises the key findings from research which suggests that gender differences have a significant impact on children's use of space. Overall, research suggests that girls are more restricted than boys in where they can go.

Karsten's (2003) study of children's use of a neighbourhood playground in Amsterdam provides one of the few detailed ethnographic studies of children's play outside of the school playground. The starting point for the research is the recognition of the importance of 'access' to these informal sites of play. A child's ability to access these spaces will be a reflection of interest/ disinterest, their perception of the space and their ability to enter such sites. Karsten cites the work of Loflund (1985) who suggested that people living in cities try to reduce the complexities of living in a world of strangers. One method used to reduce this tension is to create 'home territories', a colonisation of the public spaces. Thomson (2005) notes that territorialisation is about possession of an area, and through this possession one is able to say to 'others' that 'this is our space, not yours'. This colonisation is achieved through getting to know the place and establishing 'residency', a situation in which children acquire sufficient knowledge about the social, physical and cultural characteristics of a place to change status from visitor to resident.

The notion of 'resident', according to Karsten, involves a number of key interrelated features. Thus, residents invest time in their places and as they spend time, they establish broad networks with other residents which become 'powerful resources that residents use to dictate the rules and defend their territory against outsiders' (Karsten 2003: 459). Residents also develop forms of communication that become exclusive; non-residents do not understand the language and rituals. Accompanying this, residents claim and assert 'property rights' over spaces and resources, simply justified by the fact that they are the residents in this space. Karsten (2003: 459) notes:

> Behaving like a resident would, of course, be impossible without at least tacit consent of the other visitors. In many cases, visitors take the colonizing behaviour for granted as long as they can use the place for a specific function. Thus children in the playground will tolerate the culture of the residents as long as they can play themselves. However, the kind of play may well be influenced by the behaviour of the residents. And the simple presence of a group of residents may prevent other children from visiting a playground.

Karsten's research identified some dominant themes of gendered access and participation in the residential play spaces, particularly across themes of presence, activity, space and time. The conclusion to the study highlighted the fact that in general girls are 'somewhat marginalized' within the residential play spaces.

> Boys outnumbered girls not only in frequency of participation but also in duration of time and in the size of the network and territory they controlled. This helped boys to obtain intimate knowledge of the playground which – in turn – reinforced their more frequent status as resident. Girls as a group were less visible, which made it more difficult for them to obtain this status.

While this was a general pattern, there was significant variety across space and time. Karsten notes that some girls with resident status were encountered in nearly every playground; and they used this position to dominate others and take a lead in organising games, allocating roles and manipulating rules and players to meet their own needs and to maintain status.

Beyond gender

In contrast to the considerable research into children's gender friendships and play, there is less research that pays direct attention to the influences of other sociocultural processes on children's play and identity. As Reay and Lucey (2000) comment, children's understandings of and relationships to local spaces are shaped by broader social relations in which class and race are just as potent as gender.

Meire (2007) notes play is valued differently among different cultures. Goncu and others (2000) comment that the prevailing developmental approach to the study of children's play in the Western world has led to an implicit presumption of universal patterns of play. Cross-cultural studies have questioned these assumptions and produced a growing body of evidence which suggests that communities vary in what they see as desirable and valuable for their children's development, what Sutton-Smith (1999) refers to as the adaptive dialectic of play. Gosso and others' (2007) study of children's pretend play across different cultures and locations in Brazil notes that the children from high and mixed socio-economic urban areas participated in pretend play more frequently than children from low socio-economic regions and a traditional Indian village. The study also reveals a difference in the content of children's make-believe play episodes, with children from mixed and high socio-economic status areas displaying more fantastic and media related themes, while children from other areas displayed themes that were more closely related to their everyday experiences.

Exploring children's play in four different communities (urban/rural, Western/non-Western) Goncu and others (2000) conclude that while there are similarities in the forms of play observed, there are also clear differences in the social play episodes and the number of children who engaged in these forms. Overall, Goncu and others' (2000:328) findings indicate that play will often reflect adults' beliefs about children's development and the social structures of the community in which children are located. They also comment on the importance of maintaining a cross cultural perspective and looking at children's play as part of the wider social and cultural networks within specific communities before proffering observations and conclusive statements about children's play patterns.

A number of studies have considered the influence of social class on children's play patterns (Lareau 2000; Tomanovic 2004; Ziviani and others 2007). Tomanovic's (2004) study of children and family life in Serbia adopts a 'lifestyle' framework in exploring the relationship between family socio-economic status and children's interactions within the home and in the wider neighbourhood. Tomanovic (2004: 343) explains that the family acts as 'one of the basic arenas of action for the child [and sets] the structural and interactional frames for the everyday practice of childhood'. The research compares family practices across working class and middle class families and notes the ways in which working class families organise practices centred on the home and family; leisure time was seen as informal, following routine patterns that chiefly concerned socialising with others. The middle class families produced highly structured use of family time, often spent in institutions and spaces that were regulated by adults, and consequently less time was available for free, self-initiated and self-organised activities. Tomanovic (2004: 354) concludes that the lives of the working class children in the study were orientated to 'a greater extent to family, the home, and the neighbourhood, with routine everyday schedules and social networks comprising family members, relatives, peers drawn from the neighbourhood and from school'. This contrasted with the middle class lifestyle in which children were orientated to spaces and institutions where time

'[There are] different patterns that middle class and working class families establish for the organisation of children's leisure time.'

was more organised and their social networks more diverse. Tomanovic asserts that the differing lifestyles established contrasting forms of social and cultural capital, which in turn constructed different childhood practices.

Lareau's (2000) ethnographic study in the US of white and African-American children aged between 7 and 10 years largely supports Tomanovic's observations of the different patterns that middle class and working class families establish for the organisation of children's leisure time, and notes that in terms of the structure of children's daily lives 'class appears to have a more dramatic impact than racialised ethnicity' (Lareau 2000: 156). Lareau's review of the research into children's daily experiences summarised the more adult structured and controlled activities associated with middle class children compared with less pressured and more relaxed patterns of working class children and raised the question about the acquisition of 'cultural capital' (Bourdieu 1984) through these differing childhood experiences.

> Compared with their working class counterparts, the middle-class children in this study have been in a wider variety of situations, often with more opportunities to perform and to gain experiences and expertise. It is possible that these differences in childhood experiences can provide different repertoires for them to draw on as they move into adulthood. (Lareau 2000: 169)

Both Tomanovic and Lareau adopt a macro, structural perspective to their research (that is, looking at the influences of broad social structures on children). Alternative studies have considered the ways in which children, as active agents, negotiate their ways through working class environments, often portrayed as 'ghettoes' and given other stereotypical descriptions by the media, compared with children from middle class areas.

Reay and Lucey (2000), in their study of the feelings of 9- to 11-year-old children about living on a large council estate, note that the responses of the children counter the perceptions of these sites as 'hopeless':

> The realities of children's lives on large council estates are far more complex and nuanced than ... media depictions suggest. Far from 'not caring', they have relationships to the places in which they live that are characterised by ambivalence and conflicting feelings of longing, belonging and abhorrence.

The research notes that children from working class families are knowledgeable agents with a rich store of real and mythic information about where they live. These 'topographies of the public and the private, the foreign and the familiar are powerfully classed, gendered and racialized' (Reay and Lucey 2002: 412). Interviews indicate that, in spite of the media portrayal of their neighbourhood, children devised tactics to preserve a self-image of decency and respectability and a denial of the fact that they may be poor, findings that were also evident in Sutton and others' (2007) research into children's views of social difference. Children's narratives in Reay and Lucey's study indicate a rather ambiguous relationship to their estate. Children generally viewed their estates as hostile social landscapes with the familiar patterns of alcohol and drug use, violence, vandalism and so on. In order to cope with this, children and families sometimes resorted to 'keeping to yourself' and avoidance strategies. Yet, as previously outlined, such strategies may not be effective in the development of resilience at a community level (Van der Hoek 2005). As Reay and Lucey (2000: 421) comment, children need a sense that the environment at some level can 'be a benign one, can "hold" us while we take the risks involved in growing up'. As an act of preserving their self-image of dignity and respectability, children referred to the process of 'being known': developing a personal knowledge of 'others' who live in the area in order to counteract stereotypes and generate feelings of safety when using public space. This 'being known' generated spaces and networks that were more trusted and established a feeling of 'belonging'. Reay and Lucey (2001: 424) conclude:

> Unlike the uniformly depressing, pathologising sentiments about 'sink' council estates and their tenants conveyed in both government documentation and media

reports on social exclusion, the children we interviewed communicated a far greater sense of both hope and survival. While prevailing dominant discourses tend to deny children and their families both agency and potential, the children themselves talked endlessly about hopes aspirations and desires. They also spoke of a need, not to find a better place, but to make the place they find themselves in better.

Sutton and others (2007), in their comparative study of children from a council estate and a middle class area, note the different ways children constructed their use of space and time. For many children from the middle class area, out of school activity, generally associated with 'education', was wider (both geographically and in terms of activities) and more expensive compared with children from the working class estate who reported spending more time 'hanging out' with friends in the neighbourhood rather than taking part in structured, adult organised activity. This concurs with Ziviani and others' (2007) research in Australia which notes that children from low socio-economic backgrounds spent significantly more time playing close to their homes than middle class children, who engaged in more structured and costly activities.

Sutton and others (2007) highlight the ways in which children's use of public space in the estate often consisted of playful activity – knock-a-door run, manhunt, kickstone – games that have a strong tradition and high value in children's play cultures. Yet their visibility in public space often created tension with neighbours and other adults, and they were often moved on by police if they assembled in groups. The loss of opportunity to meet with friends and 'become known' in public space drives children indoors, where there may be further tensions.

Children's play culture and technology

An example of the ways in which children appropriate and transform adult cultural forms may be seen through children's playful use of modern technology. Valentine and Holloway (2002) note that Information and Communication Technology (ICT) is bringing about, and will continue to bring about, widespread social, cultural, economic and political change in the 21st century. There are differences in interpreting the impact of this on children, ranging from concerns over the corruption of children and the loss of innocence (Postman 1983) to the positive and empowering role that technology has given to children (Tapscott 1996). Hsi (2007) comments that there is considerable societal concern about children's and young people's engagement with media technology, citing such issues as internet addiction, cyber bullying, gambling and exposure to pornography. Yet as Hsi comments, there has been no longitudinal study of children's cumulative experience of growing up with digital media. Livingstone (2007) draws attention to the lack of serious attention given to children's relationship with these media. The default position tends to be that children are particularly vulnerable to media influence and that the media harm some children in some ways under certain conditions. This marks a traditional response to the introduction of each new technological medium (from books to the cinema and rock 'n' roll). Livingstone criticises much of the research conducted in the field of children's relationship with media:

> Article after article published on media effects fails to acknowledge the familiar litany of problems, offering little justification for the supposed validity of a dependent measure, showing only short-term effects yet concluding in favour of long-term societal implications, or making no attempt to bring into the research design the many contextual, cultural factors that form part of the complex phenomena studied, factors that may even help explain the persistence of contradictory or null findings. (Livingstone 2007: 7)

Livingstone notes that the media and communications environment is diversifying rapidly, with global, personal, mobile and interactive media raising both old and new questions regarding media influence. In exploring this, it is important to consider the unique nature of individual children's use of technology, and the multiple factors that contribute to this, rather than rehearse a 'tired agenda' of media effect studies that make universal statements about the harm of new media technologies. In many ways, Livingstone's study parallels similar calls in relation to children's agency and subjective experiences.

Hsi (2007) reviews the impact of technology on children's daily lives and presents two vignettes based on observations of children, which explore the digital fluency of a 12-year-old boy and a 13-year-old girl in the US. Children use digital tools as part of their everyday routine activities and also to create and exchange messages and artefacts across social networks and online communities.

Sorensen and others' (2007) study of children's computer use in Denmark notes that to a large extent children have taught themselves to make use of the digital media, largely as a result of not being able to get help from other sources, mainly teachers and parents. As such, children have acquired skills through playing and supporting each other in discovering the potential applications of technology. As Sorensen and others (2007: 5) comment, children's use and exploration of the different digital media and communication systems enables them to develop 'new ways of putting the media to use and combining them, and in this context it is very much the case that they make use of new forms of collaboration, communication and learning'.

Children's use of the internet

The above introductory themes can be found particularly in relation to children's use of the internet. The discourses on children and ICT contain paradoxical representations of childhood (Holloway and Valentine 2002). These discourses see children on the one hand as technically competent in their use of ICT equipment and programmes, often much more so than adults, yet at the same time, these technical skills are seen to put children at risk through coming into contact with inappropriate materials or people.

In exploring these themes, Valentine and Holloway see a similar pattern in children's access to public space, where children are seen as being vulnerable and at risk, while at the same time their presence may constitute a risk to others. As such, efforts should be made to control and regulate children's access.

A key feature of children's and young people's use of the internet is for social networking, through the use of chat rooms, messenger services and personal pages on social networking websites. Valkenburg and others' (2005) study of 600 nine- to 18-year-olds explored the ways in which children and young people experimented with their identities online. They noted that internet communication has several qualities that lends itself to identity experimentation:

- It has less visual and auditory cues than face-to-face or telephone conversations, and this may encourage users to emphasise, change or hide aspects of their physical self.

- Internet communication is anonymous – particularly in the opening stages of entering a chat room – and this may enable people to feel less inhibited and to disclose certain information knowing that there is little chance of any connection with real life.

- Internet communication often happens in social communities that are isolated from those in real life.

Their study concluded that youngsters in early adolescence experiment with their identity significantly more than older adolescents. In general the younger group use the internet to engage with strangers and play with identity while the older group use it to communicate with their existing offline personal network. Boys and girls did not significantly differ in experimenting with identity but did differ in the strategies used for this. Girls pretended to be older than boys and to be beautiful, while boys adopted more 'macho' identities. The most important motive given by young people in internet-based identity experiments was 'self-exploration', followed by social compensation (to overcome shyness) and social facilitation (to make friends).

Huffaker and Calvert (2005) acknowledge that older children and young people spend a considerable amount of time using online settings such as multi-user domains, and these have been linked to ways of exploring and playing with identity. One of the newest venues for exploration is the 'blog', which is used in a variety of ways, but often as a personal journal or running commentary about oneself. Accompanying this trend is the emergence of online emotional expression through the language of 'emoticons' that help to form impressions of the author's mood and attitude. Interestingly, Huffaker and Calvert's research on the nature of blogs and identity construction notes that the sites created by males and females are more similar than contrasting. They suggest that the current generation of bloggers may be developing more androgynous styles in online communication and interaction. Kearney (2007) reviews the significant changes that digital technology may be making to traditional patterns of use of domestic spaces. Citing McRobbie and Garber's (1976: 213) analysis of girls' bedroom culture as spaces of 'experimenting with make-up, listening to records, reading the mags, sizing up the boyfriends, chatting, [and] jiving', Kearney suggests that digital technology enables girls to move from being consumers to producers and distributors of their identities, interests and needs:

> in other words, contemporary female youth are not retreating to private spaces; they are reconfiguring such sites to create new publics that can better serve their needs, interests and goals. (Kearney 2007: 138).

Social network sites (SNSs) such as such as MySpace and Facebook allow children and young people to present themselves, articulate their social networks, and establish or maintain connections with others (Ellison and others 2007; Hsi 2007). This growing trend has received little attention in research to date, but Ellison and others' research with college students in the US suggests that students' use of Facebook contributed to the maintenance and creation of social capital accompanied by student reports of well-being.

Valentine and Holloway (2002: 316), in the conclusion to their research, comment that use of an internet-connected computer is a different tool for different groups:

> For example, for some children it emerges as a tool to develop intimate on-line friendships, while for others it emerges as a tool of sociality that enhances and develops everyday off-line social networks; for some it emerges as an important tool for developing off-line hobbies, and for others as a casual tool for larking around … Our findings counter popular fears articulated by commentators … that ICT will impact on children's lives in either universally positive or universally negative ways.

89

'A key feature of children's and young people's use of the internet is for social networking, through the use of chat rooms, messenger services and personal pages on social networking websites.'

Children's game playing

Dovey (2007) draws a comparison between children's play in the 'mediasphere' and the human need to play in other forms of the environment. Children's play with computer games enables children to act out mediated fantasies through winning sports events, surviving against monsters, casting spells and so on. This acting out occurs within the zone of play that suspends the rules of everyday life 'in favour of creating a space that allows us to experience the taboo, the challenging, and the passionately desired' (Dovey 2007: 138). Such a media space offers the experience of a wide range of emotions found in other play forms. Taylor (2006) provides a detailed ethnographic account of the complex social landscapes created through multi-player online games, and notes how players negotiate and subvert a game's rules and representations, and collectively articulate and regulate – through on- and off-line play – the practices and protocols of their gaming communities.

Dovey also proposes that playing computer games becomes a learning process. As well as working out the basic game rules and objectives, children are also constantly figuring out how the game engine works, what it wants the player to do and how to test the limits of the game:

> … gameplay can be seen as a process of trying to understand, through our developing skill levels, the way that the game works. In this way it is argued that computer game play provides a crucial site for the development and education of our individual 'technicity' where this quality will be a significant part of our subjectivity in the 21st century. (Dovey 2007: 139)

Children's use of mobile phones

Another significant feature of the new technology is the use of mobile phones by children and teenagers. Campbell, writing in *The Observer* (2005), noted that a survey of children's use of mobile phones revealed that 24 per cent of seven- and eight-year-olds owned a mobile phone, as did 13 per cent of five- and six-year-olds. The survey indicates that the chief use of mobile phones is for texting.

Williams and Williams (2005) propose that the mobile phone affords teenagers increased leverage in bargaining with their parents for greater autonomy and, in doing so, often lifts these negotiations outside the spatial constraints of the household. Yet at the same time teenagers remain under control and surveillance by their parents who use this technology to enter their children's time and space and monitor their movements. As William and Williams (2005: 322) note:

> … the parents are able to socially influence the behaviour of their teenagers by potentially being at the end of the phone. Parents are able to keep in contact with their children and to a certain extent control them. Clearly the mobile phone is becoming central to the parent/teenager relationship because it facilitates negotiation and authority outside of the private sphere in a more public arena.

The teenagers studied in Williams and Williams' (2005) research accepted that by putting up with their parents' intrusion, they were in fact more empowered. They could have greater scope for the negotiation of movements, and families often developed an agreed set of rules for communicating individuals' whereabouts. The study concludes with an acknowledgement of the way in which mobile phones have become a vital component in relationships between children and parents.

Maybin (2003) explores the use of texting in young people's friendships. The style of communication between friends allows for a sense of privacy and intimacy. The language of texting is generally owned by young people, although increasingly adults are becoming more familiar with this format. The mobile phone provides children and young people with a cultural artefact that they own through their control over the interactive, flexible, sharing and communicative nature of this technology; they incorporate this into almost every aspect of their daily lives.

Jones and others (2003: 178) note the potential of further developments in mobile technology to both free and restrict children's movements and access to public space. On the positive side they note that the

> ... promise of these new technologies is their quintessentially spatial, mobile, outdoor capabilities. They may offer children ways of (re)occupying certain spaces in the city, offering a means of negotiating risk and fear, and of permeating adult-ordered geographies of the city.

Play and language

A key feature of children's play language is that it is often antithetical to the adult perspective of 'correct' language use. As Sutton-Smith (1999: 143) notes:

> ... the more players play together, the more elliptical and esoteric their dialogue tends to become. They develop their own peculiar argot, which would certainly not score very well on standard measures ... Play is itself a caricatural or schematic activity ... and when it moves verbally it breeds analogous and elliptic usages of language perhaps familiar only to those who are a part of the 'secret' community. Thus the ellipsis may serve to mask what is going on from those who are not members of the play group. Perhaps more important, the ellipsis helps to establish the players as a play community.

Goodwin's (2006) detailed analysis of children's linguistic strategies in peer play interactions highlights the complexity of language use as children become competent social actors. Cumming (2007), reviewing children's play language and the potential application to teaching poetry in the classroom, notes that the oral culture of play as shown in children's rhymes, chants, songs and riddles provides a significant part of friendships and peer interaction. Thomas (2004) presents a detailed analysis of the nature of children's playground poetry,[3] noting that this form of language resists and playfully engages the repressive elements of adult culture and it 'inspires children to construct their own tradition, to compose their own poetry,[3] to teach themselves' (Thomas 2004: 174). Given that the production of this form of poetry occurs away from adult authority figures, much of the material produced is often vulgar, disgusting, violent and funny. Thomas (2004: 155) notes that children's playground poetry:

91

> ... dismantles nostalgic notions of the innocent, obedient, and controllable child, and thus, in my experience, tends to disturb adults, as it implies sexualized, complicated child-agents able to control their world through linguistic play and sometimes violent, antiauthoritarian imagery.

Thomas explains that playground poetry is created and performed with the aim of generating a strong body reaction, often using the body as the subject of the poem. Delivery is intended to promote laughter, gasps, groans or more vigorous activity, as in the case of skipping (or 'jump') rope rhymes. Their subject matter perhaps challenges the mind/body dualism through providing a reminder that body and mind are intimately integrated.

Jones' (2004) painting in the Bethnal Green Museum of Childhood, London, and the forthcoming publication of the same name, *The Singing Playground*, shows how many playground songs and games are still a thriving part of playground culture. Some have died out, but others continue to flourish either in their original form or updated with contemporary references; the influences of immigration and ethnic diversity can also be seen, with songs in many languages and cultural fusions between themes and songs. The songs are 'rude, funny, silly, haunting, even surreal ... Silly frogs, boyfriends, marriage, babies, death, scary wolves, wee and farts all figure prominently, and knickers are practically inescapable' (Ward 2007).

Andresen's (2005) empirical investigations of children's role-play in early childhood show that language is a central means of creating pretence, noting that explicit metacommunication (talking and non-verbal language about the play) helps children to work together to establish

---

[3] Playground poetry refers more to the style and production of this play and language rather than the location of its use.

the central plot of the play, transform meanings and distinguish fiction from reality. Studies of children's rough and tumble play also highlight the significance of metacommunication to establish that the 'fighting' is in fact play and not real (Fry 2005).

Drawing on the work of Bateson (1955), Andresen highlights that play is accompanied by metacommunication because the players need to signal continuously to each other that what they are involved in is play. According to Bateson, metacommunication constructs a frame which characterises playing as play, and marks the boundary between behaviour within play and behaviour out of play. This process is essentially paradoxical because on the one hand it states that the behaviour is not serious, but on the other hand, children have to act as if the playful behaviour is real. In early childhood children use communication both implicitly within the play and explicitly by stepping out of the frame to reframe it ('we're only playing'). As children grow older, there tends to be a more complex implicit metacommunication pattern within the play; the language used while playing serves the purpose of keeping the play frame established. Andresen notes that this form is more demanding because children must hold in mind planning the plot, transforming, interpreting and communicating meanings, while at the same time carrying out the play. Branco (2005) comments that non-verbal gestures are of central importance in establishing the tone of the play frame and will at times serve to show agreement and affiliation, while at other times will display divergence, hostility and ambiguity. As Branco (2005: 419) notes:

> the quality of the frames co-constructed in social interactions are multiple and complex and contain ambivalence and ambiguity as children maintain the play through a range of smiles, frowns, gestures, grins, and an endless list of non-verbal and paralinguistic clues.

Andresen (2005) draws a clear distinction between adult–child and peer pretend play situations. In adult–child play it is invariably the adult who structures the interaction and constructs the play frame within which the child acts. In contrast to this, peer play involves a complex and continuous mutual interaction to negotiate and maintain the play frame and act co-jointly. A similar point is made by Brownell and others (2002) who note that the specific value of peer play resides in the fact that, when playing, children will talk more openly about shared emotions, intentions and inner states than they would with adults.

Sawyer (2003) highlights the many studies that demonstrate how children's metacommunicative skills develop rapidly during the preschool years, both through implicit and explicit means, and suggests that children's pretend play skills may provide an important context for developing general conversational skills. Similarly, Andresen (2005) sees pretend play as a key component in developing complex language and communication skills. Her research with children leads her to suggest that in role play children can transform the meanings of persons, objects and actions through language; this very action enables children to understand that words and symbols have many uses and contexts, 'a precondition for being able to use language flexibly without being bound to specific contexts' (Andresen 2005: 409).

Sinha (2005) through a detailed observation of a children's pretend play episode notes the ways in which the playful social interactions are developed through sharing symbolic meanings. The common meanings shared through this process enable the children to renegotiate roles, identity and narrative continually. Thus language serves as a valuable resource for the construction and exploration of self and identity in play.

Summary
This section has explored one of the primary adaptive systems for building resilience, namely, attachment and the development of mutually supportive relationships, both within the family and the wider context of children's peer friendships.

The research suggests that, from the first stages of growth through to adulthood, play has a central role in developing strong attachments. Play between caregiver and infant helps establish the neural pathways for developing wider attachments with other children and adults. The ability to establish friendships interconnects with other adaptive systems in highly complex feedback processes; playing with friends builds emotion regulation and, equally, emotion regulation is important to establishing friendships; playing with others is pleasurable and develops positive affect which broadens and builds flexible thinking, enables problem solving, promotes a sense of optimism which all feed back into establishing and enhancing strong friendships within children's peer play groups. The secure attachments within peer play groups afford opportunities to co-create situations of uncertainty and unbalance and work collectively to resolve these, developing flexible stress response systems. The dynamic process of playing with others requires constant maintenance, reading and mirroring the intentions of others and using language forms in highly complex and creative ways.

What this research highlights is that the nature of children's peer relationships and play culture is complex and dynamic. Play culture emerges when children find time and space to be away from adults; as such, this culture is inherently spatial. Yet even though children are away from adults, the influences of the adult world will still inevitably have significance for their relationships and play behaviours. Class, gender, disability, ethnicity and so on work in concert to influence the diverse ways in which children play or indeed are excluded from play, but the act of playing offers a potentiality to transform these wider social forces into new ways of being and construct new identities (Guss 2005). This process also incorporates adaptation and transformation of tools and symbols (technology and language) into new cultural forms and expressions.

The focus in this section has been to explore the nature of attachment and the importance of social relationships. However, as Meire (2007) observes, play does not occur in a vacuum but within a social and physical space. It is important to recognise that the context for children's peer interactions is situated, and the nature of the physical environment combines with the social to create localised spaces for play. Just as friendship and attachment with others support resilience, attachment to the places that children inhabit in their daily lives also allows for the creation of strong adaptive systems. It is this relationship that is explored in the next section of this review.

Children's play and place attachment

Active engagement with the outdoor environment presents great benefits. The world is perceived from different angles, giving differing perspectives. Such engagement helps to establish a working knowledge of the environment: recognising physical features and objects, knowing how things connect, realising interactional cause and effect, discovering things, learning what can and cannot be done with others and so on provides a repertoire of flexible responses to the immediate environment (Bateson 2005).

The discipline of environmental psychology is based upon an acceptance that environmental context has a critical role in behaviour and social attitudes (Clark and Uzzell 2006). Children's psychological health and well-being can be enhanced or impaired by the nature of the immediate neighbourhood (Percy-Smith 2002; Jutras and Lepage 2006). In reviewing the research literature into the relationship between brain development and the environment, Lewis (2004: 94) concludes that 'successful engagement with complex environments, particularly early in development, promises to have pervasive and significant effects on brain development and function'. The physical or built environment has come to the forefront of public health research, leading to a surge of research on environmental attributes and their connections with physical activity behaviours (Davison and Lawson 2006).

Dearing (2004), in a longitudinal study with school age children in the US, notes that neighbourhoods influence children through a number of interrelated processes including the range of community resources available (for example play spaces and community centres), social organisation features such as the level of social cohesion within the neighbourhood, and environmental conditions and 'contagions' (harmful or negative aspects).

Neighbourhood conditions are associated with child achievement and socio-emotional functioning. Research into this broad canvas of environment or 'neighbourhood' influence tends to fall into two themes: the first explores the potential harmful impact, or contagion, of negative forces within the neighbourhood, such as the impact of poverty and the socio-economic level of the neighbourhood, the presence of gangs, vandalism, and general dilapidation within the physical fabric of the neighbourhood. The second theme centres on the positive qualities of children's transactions within their immediate environments, and would suggest that children's well-being is supported by neighbourhoods in which children are able to play and range safely across different spaces, meet friends, observe the world and interact with nature (Chawla 2002). The connection between children and their outdoor neighbourhood places has been closely linked to ways in which children construct their identity (Percy-Smith 2002; Vanderbeck and Dunkley 2003; Wells and Leckies 2005; Matthews and Tucker 2006; Roe 2006). Vanderbeck and Dunkley (2003) highlight the importance of exploring children and young people's subjective accounts of their lives as a way of discovering how children construct their socio-spatial identities and make sense of their experiences as children in relation to the various public narratives that impact on this process.

Jutras and Lepage's (2006) study of parental perception of the local neighbourhood in Montreal indicates that parents placed high value on the child-friendliness of neighbourhoods, availability of playgrounds, the presence of other children to play with and the proximity of parks, playgrounds, school, recreation centres and homes of grandparents. Alongside this, parents valued cleanliness, tranquillity, attractive landscapes that facilitated ease of movement and so on. These values have also been commonly expressed by children and young people who tend to view the attractiveness of their local neighbourhoods in terms of what it affords for their activities, both as a physically attractive space and through the opportunity to be with friends (Percy-Smith 2002; Min and Lee 2006).

Research carried out for Playday 2006 notes that 80 per cent of children surveyed expressed a preference for playing outside but not all of them have the chance. Nearly three in four children would like to play out more often, and 82 per cent would rather play in natural spaces such as gardens, parks and local fields instead of places like streets or car parks. The survey also found that 86 per cent of children prefer outdoor activities, including playing out with their friends, building dens and getting muddy, to playing computer games.

Min and Lee's (2006) analysis of children's place transactions in Korea suggests that children form attachments to places in which they can carry out personally valued activities. In their daily neighbourhood experiences, children tend to focus on a few core qualities of a setting, such as being close to home, the availability of play materials and space, and close friends: 'it seems that the children focus on these environmental qualities because they are directly related to some core affordances needed for valued behaviours' (Min and Lee 2006: 69). Where children do not have access to these valued experiences, it is likely that they will place little value on their immediate neighbourhoods. Also, as Fuhrer (2004: 106) comments, children's place transactions will be different from adults', citing the example of a fence between gardens, intended as a barrier by adults but which, from children's perspective, afforded a major attraction and challenge for 'practicing and exhibiting all manner of athletic skills, experimenting with novel ways of transcending it, and of descending down into the landing area'.

Play in natural spaces

Lester and Maudsley (2006) provide a comprehensive review of research into the significance of children's playful encounter with natural spaces. The summary of their literature review concludes (Lester and Maudsley 2006: 4):

• Natural environments support a wide range of children's play. The diverse, dynamic and flexible features that can be found in natural spaces afford opportunities for extensive intentional play behaviours.

• Whilst children do not necessarily differentiate between natural and artificial elements in their play, predominantly natural outdoor settings are more likely to be perceived by children as free from adult agendas and thus more open to the possibilities of play.

• Playing in natural spaces offers possibilities for: control and mastery, construction of special spaces, manipulating loose parts, different ways of moving, risk-taking, etc. Childhood experiences of playing with nature also instil a sense of wonder, stimulating creativity, imagination and symbolic play.

• Children's opportunity to playfully access their immediate natural environments supports the development of a sense of place and attachment. Playing in natural spaces also supports a child's sense of self, allowing children to recognise their independence alongside an interdependence and connectedness with their ecological worlds.

• The powerful combination of a diversity of play experiences and direct contact with nature has direct benefits for children's physical, mental and emotional health. Free play opportunities in natural settings offer possibilities for restoration, and hence, well-being.

• Playful, experiential and interactive contact with nature in childhood is directly correlated with positive environmental sensibility and behaviour in later life.

There is significant research literature that clearly highlights the value children place on natural spaces (Taylor and Kuo 2006; Bingley and Milligan 2004). Evidence reviewed by Taylor and Kuo suggests that engagement with nearby natural places provides restoration from mental fatigue and support for more resilient and co-operative behaviour. Aspects of stronger community life are fostered by access to nature, suggesting that there are significant social as well as physical and psychological benefits from connection with the natural world (Barlett 2005). Kaplan and Kaplan (2005), continuing their extensive research into human connection with nature, suggest that connections to the natural world are restorative and help individuals become clear-headed, resilient and co-operative. This does not simply apply to large expanses of natural space but also to spaces of 'nearby nature' that exist in urban areas.

Taylor and Kuo's (2006) review of research findings also explores the relationship between green spaces and children's play and notes that children play in more creative ways in green space than in built spaces.

Research by Taylor and others (2001) highlights the potential benefits of playful contact with natural space for children with Attention Deficit Disorder (ADD). The research suggests that, compared with the after effects of play in paved outdoor areas, when playing in green spaces

'Research carried out for Playday 2006 notes that 80 per cent of children surveyed expressed a preference for playing outside but not all of them have the chance.'

children diagnosed with ADD were far more likely to be able to focus, concentrate and pay attention following the experience. The study indicates:

> Not only ... a strong nature–attention relationship, it also suggests a direction to that relationship. Because this study specifically focuses on attentional functioning after activities, it seems more plausible that participation in green activities causes improved attentional functioning than that improved attentional functioning causes participation in green activities. (Taylor and others 2001: 71)

While the study focused on children with ADD, as a general principle, it is likely that the nature–attention relationship would apply to all children. This gives further support to the considerable literature on the benefits of nature and encounter with the natural world for children.

Bingley and Milligan's (2004) research with a group of young people highlights the value that the group placed on their childhood natural play spaces. The study notes a positive correlation between where they played as children and the development of strategies for coping with their current issues and concerns. Bingley and Milligan (2004: 68) note that woodland spaces were considered to be of great benefit for many of the young people as they offered spaces of escape, restoration and support to mental health and well-being.

Lohr (2007: 83) suggests that the wealth of research material which addresses the positive benefits arising from nature are astounding; 'stress is lowered, social interactions are improved, recovery from illness is faster, mental fatigue is reduced, attention is increased, productivity is higher, and violence is reduced'.

Play, place making and place attachment

The creation of a sense of place 'is important in maintaining the quality of the environment as well as the integrity of human life within it' (Derr 2002: 126).

Chatterjee (2005) suggests that a child-friendly place is an environment that promotes exploration and actualisation of the potential within local communities for different activities and social interactions; one where there are opportunities for learning about the environment and developing competence through shaping the space by repeated use; and one that 'allows children to express themselves freely in creation and control of territories and special places; and protects the secrets and activities of children in these childhood places from harm' (Chatterjee 2005: 17). Chatterjee draws on research into the patterns and qualities of children's friendship and applies this to relationships with place, highlighting that many of the qualities and benefits associated with strong peer friendships (see previous section) may be evident in children's attachment to local places. Drawing on research from environmental psychology and environmental behaviour, Chatterjee suggests that children will feel 'friendship' for places that support mutual affection, shared interests and action, commitment, self-disclosure and mutual understanding and freedom of expression. Extending this, we may infer that a strong friendship with place will provide protective factors and support resilience in children.

Conversely, it could also be inferred that children who do not have contact with their immediate environment will acquire less local knowledge, giving rise to increased social fears and isolation. This is indeed borne out by Alton and others' (2007) research with children in Birmingham, which shows that those who walked more, rather than travelling by car, were less likely to be worried about strangers and less likely to report a lack of suitable spaces for playing. Chipuer's (2001) study of Australian adolescents and their relationship to local places suggests that individuals who do not have a 'sense of community' are at greater risk of feelings of social isolation and alienation, which may lead to experiencing loneliness. Chipuer cites a range of studies which indicate that children and adolescents who report higher levels of overall sense of community in both the neighbourhood and school, report lower perceptions of global loneliness and better psychological health. Chipuer's research concludes that higher levels of neighbourhood activity, friendships, and safety were associated with lower levels of neighbourhood loneliness. Opportunities to become involved with activities within the neighbourhood may provide children with exposure to others with whom they can develop friendships, as well as developing their own social skills. Engaging in neighbourhood activities can provide children with a supportive environment, with opportunities for social interaction outside the family unit. In turn, becoming involved within the neighbourhood contributes to the development of healthier communities.

Prezza and Picilli (2007), in interviews with Italian students recalling their experiences of playing, note that playing in public places exerts a direct influence on a sense of community:

> … more autonomy and play in the public areas during childhood influences more intense neighbourhood relations, a stronger sense of community and less fear of crime and, in turn, these latter variables consequently reduce feelings of loneliness during adolescence. (Prezza and Picilli 2007: 165)

The authors highlight the ways in which children may develop a sense of relationship with their immediate environment through access to the 'street' or informal play space (presence); the possibility of playing in this space (use and action); the sense that this space belongs to the child (appropriation) and the possibility that new children can join in and create their own spaces (disposition).

Derr (2002; 2006) provides a detailed analysis of the key components associated with children's emerging sense of place. Beginning with the recognition that children shape their own place experiences through ongoing interactions and transformations, Derr's research with 9-11-year-old children in New Mexico highlights the complexity of their relationship with their immediate environments as it occurs at multiple levels.

Derr's four themes are summarised below:

Theme	Description
Four wheelers, ramps and rites of passage	Children learn through adventure, risk-taking, exploration and self-created rites of passage. Experiential needs greater than place attachments.
The fort makers	Children experience imagination, escape, safety and creativity through active place-making and place attachment. Place and place-making integral to the experience.
Learning care	Children learn nurturance, companionship, respect, awe from animals, ethnobotany, gardening and place. Elements of nature help children to model care for larger scale.
The web	Experience of a cultural place, reasons to stay, reasons to go, rootedness and transience. Context for experience influences the meanings children attach to place.

Derr's analysis provides a useful framework for placing recent research into the significance of children's relationship with their local environments.

Four wheeler, ramps and rites of passage

At the micro level, the child-scale experience of place is developed through play activities and explorations with friends. Derr refers to this as a 'rites of passage' period in which children seek to develop mastery over their environment in order to become self-sufficient in using the available affordances. Exploration offers the chance to 'expand their view of the world, to test boundaries, and sometimes incorporate these physical experiences with place into their sense of identity' (Derr 2006: 110). Bell (2006) maintains that direct interaction afforded by local spaces is how children build mental representations of space. Cornell and others' (2001) study of children's wayfaring strategies suggests that the foundation for the development of complex cognitive skills is established in the relatively small scale of their neighbourhood play.

While parents or peers may initially introduce children into the local network, as children become older they extend their spatial knowledge through ranging further and also by wandering and exploring beyond the 'paths'. These extensions of range provide the 'motivation and proving grounds for way finding strategies' (Cornell and others 2001: 220). Cornell and Hill (2006) note that parents establish range boundaries for children, often reinforced by myths and stories that are designed to inhibit children from going beyond the set limits. However, research would suggest that children do not always follow these prescriptions and proscriptions, but develop a series of strategies both for extending the home range and for developing skills in negotiating their way around unfamiliar territory (Valentine 2004; Elsley 2004).

Roe's (2006) study of children's play patterns highlights the complexity of the process of establishing boundary definitions, a reflection of individual, familial and sociocultural factors influencing decisions. For the parents in her study, the key issue influencing ranging restrictions was concern over child safety.

In reviewing their research findings, Cornell and others (2001) highlight the significance of children's 'off-path' adventures for the development of problem solving strategies. Such adventures contain 'elements of risk, happenstance and wonder', and the challenge for children is to assess the new situation and develop successful responses. Wandering off the path means entering areas of uncertainty and the adventurer has to adopt an open-mind to planning and decision-making. The authors suggest that further exploration of these strategies may be useful:

> In adventure, adults and convention are not setting the goals and activities are unsupervised. These circumstances are different than arrangements for school curricula; studies of children responding to task demands in natural contexts may help us understand their strategic adjustments within arithmetic, spelling, and other formal problem domains. (Cornell and others 2001: 229)

A common theme to this playing and exploration was the seeking out of natural places, whether in remote wild spaces, in rural areas or close-to-home nature in urban areas.

Fort makers

In contrast to exploring and widening territorial range, another aspect of children's developing a sense of place relates to a more introspective process of creating special places. Derr's analysis of this feature finds support from European studies into its significance for children (Sobel 2002; Chawla 2002; Korpela and others 2002; Kylin 2003). In the New Mexico study, Derr remarks on the less than romantic construction of these places, often using found scrap resources and random materials, although these may frequently be decorated with natural elements, investing them with creativity and imagination.

Korpela and others (2002: 387) present the role of self-regulation as a process of maintaining balance between pleasant and unpleasant emotions, and a key part of this process is through environmental considerations:

> Environmental strategies of self-regulation involve the use of places and place cognitions and affects. Just as attachments to one's parents or friends represent social strategies of self-regulation … place attachments represent environmental strategies. Indeed a person may become attached to a place because it supports self-regulation, in part by enabling positive emotional changes and renewal of cognitive capacities needed to process events that challenge self-experience. Such changes characterise restorative experiences.

Kylin's (2003) study of den making in Sweden notes that the most interesting part of children's experiences and understandings of dens is the dual nature of the den as a social place and a secret place, where one does not exclude the other. The very notion of children creating special places raises a problem for planning of children's spaces. As Kylin comments, there may be some tension between what adults find desirable in outdoor public spaces, and children's needs. Many planners and other adults emphasise the visual aesthetic appearance, while the child places more value on what it affords for their play. It is reasonable to ask whether there is any point in 'planning' for children, as the results often run counter to children's play needs (see Chapter 5).

Roe's (2006) study of 6- to 10-year-old children's relationship with their local environment in a rural village in the north east of England highlights the significance of special areas for children's experiences. Roe notes that the need for children to find a place that was secret from adults, where they could simply 'hang-out', supports previous research by Korpela and others (2002). The absence of adult knowledge and intervention in the space was highly prized by the children. Roe (2006: 175) also comments that the special places:

> contained a number of attributes highly valued by children, and understood by parents, i.e. potential for danger, climbing, small spaces, potential for observation, out of bounds from parents, unmanaged by adults and 'untidy' or wild. In this study these places appeared often on the boundaries in 'in-between' spaces such as within hedgerows, or were in areas difficult to get to such as steep slopes or across the stream.

Learning care

The third theme associated with Derr's analysis of children's place-making relates to the caring connections that children establish with the environment, both through relationships with adults and directly with a sense of ownership and affiliation with their local spaces. Again, this theme would find support from other studies. Bixler and others (2002), in their study of children's play in wild areas, found that respondents who reported having played in wild environments had more positive perceptions of natural environments, outdoor recreation activities, and future indoor or outdoor occupational environments. Similarly Wells and Leckies' research (2006) concludes that childhood participation in activities in wild areas, along with 'caring' for nearby nature, have a positive relationship to adult environmental attitudes. Lohr (2007) suggests that childhood interactions with nature appear to correlate with a positive regard for the environment in later life. In general, this response is stronger if the interaction with nature in childhood is active rather than a passive appreciation of natural environments.

Thompson and others' (2008) research notes that childhood experience of playing out in natural space is a predictor of adult activity patterns of access to woodlands and green spaces. While this is a complex pattern, in general they assert that children's lack of green space experience may inhibit their motivation to visit green spaces as an adult. The research concludes that:

> People who often visited green places as children are more likely to associate natural areas with feeling energetic and more likely to visit green or wooded areas within walking distance of home, both of which suggest that habits of healthy outdoor exercise as adults are linked to patterns of use established in childhood. People who were frequent visitors as children are also more comfortable visiting woodlands and green places alone as adults and more likely to think green spaces can be magical places. It appears that such people have not just a physical relationship with green outdoor places but also an emotional one that influences how people feel about themselves and makes them more open to positive and elemental experiences in these places.

The research suggests that, given this possible connection between childhood activity in natural spaces and later adult access, it should be a matter of concern that current restrictions on children's access to natural spaces may be imposing limits to their future outdoor exercise as adults.

Cultural web

The final strand of Derr's analysis of children's relationship to place examines the cultural 'web' of experiences that children encounter in their daily interactions, the narratives and histories of others that add significance and meaning to place. As Derr (2006: 118) points out, 'the web consists of more than stories, it embodies an entire social relationship with extended family and community'.

Cornell and Hill (2006) comment that perhaps traditional narratives of witches, dragons and other mythical creatures associated with the outdoors have now been replaced by more scary stories of 'strangers'. The sense of fear that the modern outdoors generates may impact on children's freedom to establish strong connections and expand their social networks from the immediate family to peers and non-familial adults. Such restrictions may decrease children's sense of autonomy and their ability to develop solid, trusting relations with others (Spilsbury 2005).

Bixler and others (2002) highlight the significant influence of family and social relationships in developing and fostering positive or negative attitudes to the environment. Drawing on a number of research studies, they note there are many ways in which the values of parents or peers influence children's opportunity to play in natural space, for example, such as having parents with the interest and resources to buy a house near green space or a 'natural' park. They also suggest that even if there is no direct interest in the outdoors within the immediate family, a neighbourhood friendship may result in accessing and exploring natural spaces. Equally, the influence of the peer group may be significant in determining the value of such spaces.

> Not only are the values of the parent or peers important in access to wild play areas, the interpretation of the child's experiences by parents and peers may also be a factor in how children interpret their adventures in natural areas.
> (Bixler and others 2002:797)

Equally, as discussed in the section on children's identity and subjectivity, children's access to their local spaces will also be a feature of the wider social and cultural processes that impact on individual, family and the wider context. Thompson and others' (2008) review of the research suggests that there are gendered, class and ethnic forces which may restrict access. For example, they cite research findings from the UK and the US that minority ethnic groups' access to outdoor and natural environments is influenced by fear of racial attack and bullying.

Summary

The research presented in this section suggests that attachment and friendship involve an inextricable link between the social and the spatial. As Orr (1994: 147) comments:

> Knowledge of a place – where you are and where you come from – is intertwined with knowledge of who you are. Landscapes, in other words, shape mindscapes.

'... there may be some tension between what adults find desirable in outdoor public spaces, and children's needs.'

Children's places are not simply a physical space of size and landmarks, but places where they carry out everyday environmental transactions (Matthews and Tucker 2006); they are multi-layered and multi-faceted, what Hart (1979) in his ethnographic study of children's relationship to place refers to as 'phenomenal landscapes'. Children will seek to change and adapt their spaces to suit and accommodate their play needs and desires (Derr 2006). This will involve moving between the variety of spaces that the neighbourhood affords for play, developing strategies for finding one's way through the environment and developing coping mechanisms to respond to the novelty and uncertainty encountered. Similarly, at times of stress children will seek out their places of refuge and safety, often in natural sites, as indicated by the work of Korpela and others (2002). Yet this deliberate element is also subject to the wider pressures and influences at work within local places; children's relationship to place is related to the socio-political context of their lives. If children see spaces as 'no go areas', and there are clear public messages about the acceptable forms of behaviour in such spaces, then there will be an associated impact on children's emotional attachment to these places (Manzo 2003). This will be developed in Chapter Four with a further consideration of children's play patterns and contemporary issues that impact on children's transactional relationships with their immediate environments.

Factors that impinge upon playing

This chapter has, up to this point, considered the benefits of playing in terms of its capacity to promote systems that enable resilience. However, it cannot always be guaranteed that playing will produce the benefits we have so far seen from the evidence, since playing is one element in a range of factors that influence children's health, development and well-being (Sutton-Smith 2003). Indeed, Burghardt (2005) identifies forms of playing that may be considered to have a high, even unacceptable, cost attached (either to the player or, in the case of cruel play, to their victims), and that may be addictive or harmful. Yet there is also evidence that an inability to play will have a deleterious effect particularly on social and emotional health and development (for example, Panksepp 2007).

This section explores some of the literature on factors both within the child (endogenous) and external to the child (exogenous) which compromise (put at risk) the development of adaptive systems and resilience through playing. Once again, it should be stressed that internal and external factors are not separate but interrelated. This is not an exhaustive review, and medically diagnosed conditions such as Attention Deficit Hyperactivity Disorder (ADHD) and autism are included as illustrations only, showing how endogenous and exogenous factors can combine to have an influence on ability to play and therefore to realise any benefits for the development of adaptive systems that may accrue.

As previously noted in the introduction to the literature on resilience, Masten (2001) comments that this 'ordinary magic' is a commonplace strength of children that arises from a number of adaptive systems available to them during the period of childhood. Play operates across these adaptive systems, at different levels, to build and enhance resilience factors through developing flexible and responsive emotion regulation systems, promoting pleasure and enjoyment and a sense that life is worth living, enhancing stress response systems, developing creativity, and supporting strong attachment systems. Masten (2001) suggests that, where these systems are in good working order, development will be 'robust', even in the face of adversity and threat. However, if these systems are impaired then the likelihood of development problems is significantly increased, especially where the environmental hazards are profound and prolonged.

Throughout the review of play's relationship to this range of adaptive systems, evidence of the potential consequences of threats and compromises to these systems has also been noted. 'Threats' may operate in highly complex ways to destabilise these adaptive systems. This process of destabilisation, as Rutter (2006) indicates, operates in different ways in to each child and each situation, from its impact on the genes, on the cells in the body, and on brain development, right through to the impact of the wider physical and sociocultural environments that children inhabit.

The brain, as well as being enormously plastic, is also a self–organising system (Lewis 2005). That is, the relationship between brain, body and environmental experience helps shape the architecture of the brain. This shaping process establishes the ways in which the brain may respond to future experiences. Play, being flexible and open to novelty, supports the organisation of a highly responsive and finely tuned integration between the limbic and cortical regions, which, as Lewis (2005) suggests, acts as a powerful antidote to developing habitual patterns of appraisal and behaviour. This plasticity of the paralimbic system is the key to resilience.

However, where experiences are limited and threatening, the brain may develop adaptive neural connections that are likely to constrain flexibility and openness in both emotional and behavioural responses to situations (which suggests that adaptive systems may also be maladaptive). Children are 'responsive to environmental perturbations and adjust their behaviours in response to these changes' (Pellegrini and others 2007: 270). Thus, for example, Schore (2001) suggests that prolonged emotional stress in infancy may deactivate areas of the brain that are responsible for processing social information, and this 'loss of freedom' will impact on emotion regulation and response to novelty. As Lewis (2005) explains, this pattern of self-organisation may be the key to vulnerability to psychopathology.

Given that the brain organises itself in response to the pattern, nature and intensity of experiences, it is fairly evident that there are times when negative or depriving experiences are likely to have a serious and sustained impact on the development of the brain (Reid and Belsky 2002). Shore (2003) notes that trauma, neglect (emotional and physical), social deprivation and a chronic lack of appropriate stimulation are among the many factors identified as having a significant impact on development.

102

Children live within social, cultural and physical landscapes which are mutually connected and interactive. This environment has an effect on the playing child just as the child's biological systems inform their transactions with this environment: they mutually shape each other. Gendered, racial and class features intersect to create physical and sociocultural environments that at times may be oppressive and hostile. Children who have developed a playful, innovative response to their environments, with associated internal mechanisms of emotion regulation, strong attachment and social support mechanisms, and effective stress response systems, may adapt to these in flexible ways, displaying resilience.

'Children who have developed a playful innovative response to their environments ... may adapt to these in flexible ways, displaying resilience.'

However, this is a highly complex process and subject to multiple influences, as the literature on class differences in play discussed earlier showed. Children from both Reay and Lucey's (2000) and Sutton and other's (2007) studies demonstrated that their peer friendships, 'hanging out' and outdoor play behaviours represent a way for them to move beyond the security offered by staying in (and the avoidance of those who are seen as 'other') and afford the opportunity to know and be known by others in their neighbourhoods, building a sense of belonging and attachment. Yet this informal association may not currently be recognised or valued in key policy initiatives. In fact, as Sutton and others (2007) highlight, the interventions and guidance of young people into 'constructive activity' might penalise those very children and young people who might benefit from having a visible presence in public places. Play, for these children, takes the form of the things that help children to survive and thrive – a mixture of avoidance, connections, distaste and belonging (as experienced through the primary emotions) – and for the children living in these areas this represents a more coherent form of engagement than the middle class virtues that are often espoused through the social capital discourse as discussed in the next section of this chapter (Sutton and others 2007). Reay and Lucey (2000) also point out that attention needs to be given to working-class understandings of locality and place within the studies and research into children's connections with their local environments to 'counter the hegemony of middle-class versions … otherwise we will never be able to move very far from representations of deficit and pathology in relation to the urban poor' (Reay and Lucey 2000: 425).

Equally, Levinson's (2005) ethnographic study of Gypsy children's play in the UK raises some interesting and complex questions about the nature of play and cultural identity. Levinson's detailed longitudinal study highlights how play for Gypsy children may operate to maintain a separate identity and enforce boundaries. Yet this overtly aggressive and often destructive behaviour is perceived by many 'outsiders' as a barrier to participation in educational and social institutions. Children's play patterns are seen to differ from the 'norm' as Gypsy children attempt to 'fill a vacuum created by the erosion of traditional identity markers' (Levinson 2005: 500).

Stereotypies

Burghardt's (2005) study of animal play distinguishes between the characteristics of play behaviour and stereotypies, described as a repetitive aspect of behaviour that may have some similarity to play. Burghardt suggests that such behaviour develops during the animal's life and may be induced by poor or inadequate conditions. The development of stereotypies is generally considered to be pathological and harmful; it demonstrates inflexibility in response and narrowing of behaviour patterns. Yet as Burghardt claims, these behaviours may also provide adaptive benefits to psychological well-being. Thus, the times when boys 'do' being boys in their peer relationships may be a form of adaptive behaviour to the specific niche at that time, yet to an outsider it would appear to be oppressive or stereotypical behaviour.

As the research highlights, adopting and performing stereotypical roles may be one part of the nature of playful relationships between peers. Such positions may involve dispute and contest which, as Goodwin (2006) suggests, is a vital part of children's development of peer friendships and a primary way in which activity is constructed. This process also allows for the possibility of transforming these relationships and developing new ways of being (Guss 2005).

However, stereotypies may 'occur more frequently when the animal or person is under some stress or conflict' (Burghardt 2005: 63), and again is generally associated with poor or degraded environmental quality. Where this stress is prolonged, the behaviours are likely to become more stereotypical, limited and limiting. Nevertheless, as Burghardt comments, preventing the animal from performing the stereotypic act may actually cause further harm without removing the cause of the stress.

Given the complex environments that children inhabit, the relationship between brain, body and environment is likely to result in highly idiosyncratic features of organisation across these systems which reflect the nature of contemporary sociocultural environments. In the following sections, the literature on compromises to adaptive systems is explored, particularly studies on Attention Deficit Hyperactivity Disorder (ADHD), autism and play deprivation.

103

Attention Deficit Hyperactivity Disorder (ADHD)

The condition of ADHD is a disorder originating in childhood, normally characterised by overactive behaviour, impulse control, concentration and difficulty in paying attention (Brassett-Harknett and Butler 2007). Despite considerable research, there is longstanding controversy regarding the nature and validity of this condition (Stefanotos and Baron 2007). For example, a study by Banerjee and others (2007) suggests that, while a substantial fraction of the causes of ADHD may be due to genes, there are many environmental risks and potential gene-environment interactions that operate to increase the risk for this disorder. Banerjee and others highlight a range of potential risks including food additives, diet and lead contamination.

Although substantial evidence has accumulated to support the diagnostic validity of ADHD, some argue that ADHD symptoms may simply describe the exuberant behaviour of normal children. Others accept that some children with ADHD have a neurological disorder, but contend that weaknesses in the current diagnostic criteria cause some children to be diagnosed inappropriately (Markovitch 2004; Willcutt and Carlson 2005). Bassett-Harknett and Butler's (2007: 190) literature review into the causes and outcomes of ADHD notes:

> AD/HD can manifest itself in a variety of different ways and has a variety of causes, making it a very complex condition to understand. It is believed by some that AD/HD is located at the extreme end of a continuum with symptoms of inattention, hyperactivity and impulsivity being distributed continuously in the general population … What marks AD/HD apart is that the levels of activity, distractibility and impulsivity are considered developmentally inappropriate, cause impairment to normal functioning, and are evident in multiple settings, including home, school and in social relationships.

104

Rose (2005) notes that children diagnosed with ADHD are defined in relation to others, that is, in relation to what is expected from normal children by adults. Yet the cause of this aberrant behaviour is now unequivocally located inside the child's brain:

> This has led critics to describe ADHD not as a disorder but as a cultural construct, in a society that seeks to relocate problems from the social to the individual.
> (Rose 2005: 256)

Rose continues with a critique of many of the scientific claims made for a genetic origin of ADHD, noting that the child's behaviour is seen as an individual, medical problem, a deficit within the child, requiring a medical response. Timimi (2006) also suggests that the narrow medicalisation of ADHD may serve to obscure the diverse social, environmental and political causes of mental distress. Davis (2006) notes that the voices of children are rarely heard in the ADHD debate, and while recognising the biological influences, the study of this disorder needs to move from a medical model to one that locates ADHD within a disability perspective and considers the range of cultural and social influences that impact on children.

Prout (2005) seeks to resolve the social/biological binary: the ability to pay attention, maintain focus, sit still and so on will vary because of individual differences in brain functioning; these differences have no meaning in themselves but acquire meaning in the socio-cultural context. In other words, according to Prout, ADHD arises from a combination of biological difference and the needs of a mass schooling system which requires children to sit still, concentrate on tasks and achieve results. This system also measures the comparative success of students through continuous testing; those that are not up to the mark are seen as problematic. This is not an objective measurement, but is highly subjective based on the experiences of teachers, parents and other adults.

> Parents who feel their child is failing … seek remedies, often trying a number of different approaches before accepting the ADHD diagnosis. Other children, too, may find inattentive and impulsive behaviour disruptive of their schooling and children perceived as failing and/or problematic may come to experience themselves in these terms and want to find a solution. These different interests are drawn together, and allied to those of medical scientists, researchers, and pharmaceutical companies by groups such as Children and Adults with ADHD. (Prout 2005:139)

Given the increased pressure on education systems to deliver narrowly defined standards, and the accompanying rhetoric of the responsibility of parents for their children, it is understandable that all feel a sense of relief to know that the child has a medical condition; the label provides a legitimate justification to 'outsource' some of the responsibility for raising children (Cohen 2006). In looking at the arguments presented for the nature of ADHD we may see that both the genetic and the environmental proponents both downplay the societal and relational issues. Timimi (2006) comments that the gender gap in the distribution of ADHD (with a significantly higher proportion of boys diagnosed with the disorder) may be a reflection of the increasing feminisation of the space of childhood. While young males form the majority of those labelled, it is overwhelmingly adult females who make the first assessment that a child's behaviour is outside the 'normal' range. Singh (2002) also notes research that explores ADHD diagnosis as the medicalisation of 'normal' boys who are failing to achieve in a competitive social and educational environment. Citing the work of Hart and others (2006), Timimi (2006: 40) suggests that an ecological and cultural perspective on the nature of ADHD may be a barometer of social anxiety about children's (particularly sons') development, with stimulants being used as a tool for rearing and educating boys.

In many cases, diagnosis of ADHD will lead to medical treatment. Prout (2005) acknowledges that children in the US and Great Britain grow up in societies where drug use is accepted and pervasive. Given that ADHD is seen as a medical problem, then the expectation is that there is a medical treatment for this condition. The treatment developed has centred on a drug which enhances dopamine transmission – methylphenidate (best known by the trade name 'Ritalin'). The effect of this drug is similar to amphetamine, which has been widely used as a stimulant. It is proposed that by enhancing dopamine transmission, the connections between the limbic and prefrontal regions are improved, enabling the 'rational' brain to mediate the more emotional and impulsive areas, thus reducing the excesses of inattentive and impulsive behaviours. Rose (2005) comments that there is little scientific evidence to support these claims, and yet the drug does appear to work: medical treatment may indeed make a difficult life more comfortable for parents, teachers and for children themselves. Cohen (2006), looking at the figures for prescription of stimulants in England notes that there were 6,000 prescriptions in 1994. This figure rose to 186,2000 in 2,000, and by 2004 there were 458,000 prescriptions, a 7,600 per cent increase in a decade. Yet this figure is still five times lower per head of population than the US, which issued about 13 million prescriptions in 2003.

Cowgill and Marcovitch (2004) provide a useful summary of the key arguments for and against the administration of drugs. Marcovitch concludes the review with an acknowledgement that, while evidence suggests that prescriptions are safe in short term use, there is a lack of evidence that the right children are being treated.

In looking at the benefits of medical treatment of ADHD, Panksepp (1998; 2007) notes that short-term improvements in behaviour certainly occur. However, when treatment is withdrawn, there is every chance that the symptoms will reappear, which suggests that children are not learning to manage their lives any better. The administration of psycho-stimulants may have some harmful effects for children, along with an expression from some children that they do not like the feelings induced by these drugs, as this extract from Rose (2005: 259) indicates:

> Sometimes I like it but sometimes I don't … If I do take it when we didn't have school, I wouldn't want to go outside and play with my friends, or I would just want to stay in home by myself and read a book or watch television or something.

Panksepp (1998; 2007) also suggests that administration of psycho-stimulants may have a harmful impact on neural plasticity. A significant amount of brain plasticity is supported through the production of the neurotransmitter glutamate; in general the administration of psycho-stimulant may inhibit glutamate mediated neural transmission and decrease neural plasticity. While the research into the long-term effects of administering Ritalin and the newer medication Strattera, is unclear, it is important that 'we should always be entertaining environmental alternatives to deal with cultural problems' (Panksepp 1998: 95). Equally, Rose (2005) maintains that Ritalin does not 'cure' ADHD. The masking of the behaviours displayed may give some temporary and much needed respite for parents, the child and teachers, but this needs to be accompanied by attempts to resolve relational issues, to adjust society rather than simply numb the mind.

Armstrong (2006) suggests that a strong social undercurrent in relation to ADHD is the gradual decline in opportunities for free unstructured play for a variety of interconnected factors (discussed in more detail in Chapter Four). Panksepp (2002; 2007) notes that many of the symptoms associated with ADHD actually reflect playfulness and the medicines may be effective in that they reduce a child's playfulness and enable the child to adapt to a classroom environment:

> This idea also forces us to consider what types of beneficial effects for brain development might be advanced by allowing abundant natural play during childhood, and whether administration of play-reducing psychostimulants might reduce such benefits. (Panksepp 2002: 236)

Panksepp (2001) explains that the maturation of the cortical regions promotes and channels a child's ability to reflect on their situation, to plan for future actions, to share emotions with others and to 'confront the world with a creative and playful attitude' (Panksepp 2001: 157). This maturation is supported through the child's experiences within his or her environment (experience-dependent plasticity) which strengthen synaptic connections between the limbic and prefrontal cortex. Play, as discussed earlier in this chapter, may be the primary process for enhancing this connectivity. Panksepp asserts that there has been a neglect of some of the most simple and straightforward strategies for responding to the increase in the diagnosis of ADHD, and proposes that simply supporting children's rough and tumble forms of play may lead to the healthy maturation of children's brains. This would find support from many of the animal studies into rough and tumble play and the development of the 'social brain', for example, Pellis and Pellis (2007).

Alongside this, there may be other features within an environment that may strengthen connections between emotional-appraisal systems, as discussed in the section that looks at children's playful relationship to the outdoors, in particular access to natural space (Taylor and Kuo 2006) and access to modest environmental stressors (Yun and others 2005). Kuo and Taylor (2004) present research with children aged 7-12 years in the US which suggests that children identified with ADHD showed signs of reduced symptoms after participating in green space leisure activity.

> Results indicate that symptoms were better than usual after activities in relatively green settings. Moreover, the after effects of activities taking place in green outdoor settings were better than those of activities taking place either indoors or in relatively built outdoor settings, and the greener a child's typical play settings, the less severe his or her general symptoms. (Kuo and Taylor 2004:1581)

Following these initial studies, Kuo and Taylor undertook research with a broader sample across different regions and socio-economic conditions, which largely concurred with their initial research studies, concluding that access to natural settings for after-school and weekend activity may be widely effective in reducing the symptoms of ADHD. They argue that children's regular access to green space would enhance treatment for children currently receiving medication, allowing for a reduction in dosage and better self-management of attention. For those children not receiving medication, 'green time outdoors might offer the only relief for symptoms available' (Kuo and Taylor 2004: 1585). The research has attracted some critical commentary, for example, Canu and Gordon (2005) question the study design and the largely unproven conclusions drawn from a statistical analysis based on parent report. However, in response, Kuo and Taylor (2005) highlight the fact that while drawing on heterogeneous sources, the findings hold across a wide variety of activities, environments and children. They suggest that this raises exciting possibilities which are certainly worthy of continuing research.

Kaplan and Kaplan (2005) explore the concept of mental fatigue, arising from the overworked capacity of direct attention. Direct attention necessitates effort to get through a boring or difficult task and because it takes effort, it is susceptible to fatigue. The results of this fatigue may be evidenced through being readily distracted, having difficulty in planning, and an inclination to be impulsive and irritable.

An alternative form of attention may be found in 'fascination' – attention that is effortless, arises from excitement and interest and is less susceptible to tiredness. Kaplan and Kaplan's (2005: 277) attention restoration theory proposes that 'time spent in effortless pursuits and contexts is an important factor in the recovery of mental fatigue'. The review of research into the nature of fascination leads Kaplan and Kaplan to suggest that the natural environment has a strong restorative effect for many people.

Autism

Autism is considered to be the most severe of the childhood neuropsychiatric conditions. It is diagnosed on the basis of abnormal development of social behaviour, communication and imagination, often in the presence of marked obsessional, repetitive or ritualistic behaviour (Baron-Cohen 2003). Rose (2005) comments that whatever its genetic origins, autism is essentially a developmental defect which impacts on a child's ability to communicate, leading to a failure in attachment and bonding in the early years. Children and adults with autism have difficulties with everyday social interaction. Their ability to develop friendships is generally limited, as is their capacity to understand other people's emotional expression.

Recent research (Dapretto and others 2006) indicates that a dysfunctional mirror neuron system may underlie the social deficits observed in autism. Children with autism spectrum disorders (ASD), when given a face recognition task, may not engage a mirroring mechanism and thus must adopt an alternative strategy of increased visual and motor attention but without experiencing the emotional significance of the facial expression. Panksepp (2001) notes that some forms of early childhood autism may be due to brain abnormalities in systems that mediate emotions related to social attachments. One possible explanation may be found with the overproduction of brain-derived opioids – known to inhibit social motivation and causing social isolation and aloofness:

> Developmental changes in endogenous opioids may regulate feelings of social interest and independence. Because social aloofness is a common characteristic of autism, sustained overactivity of such brain systems could chronically change social motivation. (Panksepp 2001: 153)

However, as Panksepp (1997) observes, there is a general acceptance that autism is a multi-factorial disorder which is not the product of a single gene, brain chemical system or environmental insult, but is likely to be the result of many biological and environmental influences working in combination.

Rose (2005) provides a critical comment on the increasing diagnosis of autism, questioning whether it has become more common, better recognised or a 'currently fashionable label as part of the medicalisation of the human condition' (Rose 2005: 136). He observes that throughout history all cultures have recognised the existence of mental anguish and associated conditions of anxiety or distress, yet these forms of behaviour were accepted as being part of the diversity and 'rich tapestry' of the human condition. It is only in recent times that such behaviours are being classified as 'diseases'.

Autism and play

Libby and others (1998) comment that much controversy surrounds an understanding of the ability of children with autism to engage in spontaneous play. Traditional approaches have suggested that children with autism tend to produce highly rigid stereotypical behaviour towards toys and objects and do not engage in symbolic play. Libby and others (1998) question this stance, and their research with autistic children indicates that symbolic play skills were not totally absent.

Sherratt (2002) comments that children with autism may display a range of rigid and idiosyncratic play behaviours that indicate a delay or impairment in symbolic play, creativity and imagination. Sherratt's intervention study with children, in which a number of deliberate prompts were issued to support and guide symbolic play, notes the success of the intervention strategies in enabling children with autism to increase the amount and content of symbolic play episodes. Perhaps the most significant finding is that, not only did children demonstrate these new play 'skills' under guided conditions, but they 'ultimately used symbolic play spontaneously in unstructured settings' (Sherratt 2002: 177). Similarly, Field and others (2001) highlight the importance of early adult interventions to support the development of play in children with autism, particularly through adult imitation of children's behaviours.

Jarrold (2003) questions the reliability of some of the studies exploring the nature of pretend play in children with autism and notes that some individuals do appear to engage in pretend play, which suggests that children with autism may have an 'underlying capacity to pretend, but, for whatever reason, they fail to show this spontaneously' (Jarrold 2003: 382). In his review of the research, Jarrold concludes that judging whether a child is truly pretending is extremely difficult; we use actions to infer underlying intentions without any guarantee that one relates in any way to the other. In looking at the pretend play of children with autism, Jarrold acknowledges that, while it is apparent that children may have problems in pretend play, what is less clear is whether these problems reflect a basic inability to pretend or some other difficulty which affects the ease with which pretend play can be initiated. Drawing on research findings, Jarrold notes that children with autism may well understand the nature of pretend play, but the inability to produce pretend play forms may arise from the process of carrying out an act of pretence. This may suggest that children with autism can pretend, but 'tend not to do so because of some internal reluctance or lack of incentive to do so' (Jarrold 2003: 386). It may be that the preference for literal interpretations in their play and difficulties caused by having to make multiple interpretations in pretend play means that pretend play does not bring the same rewards as it does for the 'typical' child.

In their review of the literature on teaching children with autism spectrum disorders to play using behavioural techniques, Luckett and others (2007) question both the understanding of play used in the studies and also the motivation or purpose in teaching children to play in this way. They suggest that using external rewards and behavioural approaches in order to teach children to engage in symbolic play has raised concern that the children may not be playing in any genuine sense of the word. They note that the literature identifies two key reasons for encouraging playing in children with autism: firstly, the development potential and secondly the diversionary potential – diversion from other behaviours seen as unacceptable. Often, in behavioural studies, what was understood as 'inappropriate' play was replaced with 'appropriate' play through behavioural techniques. The authors cite Donnelly and Bovee (2003) who suggest that what in fact may have taken place was a replacement of play according to characteristics of choice, spontaneity, control and positive affect, with imitative behaviours that appear more socially acceptable:

> **There seems little doubt that people with autism often differ from the mainstream with regard to the activities that they find engaging, motivating, and enjoyable; their preferences demand consideration and respect. (Luckett and others 2007: 375)**

Generally, while changes could be seen in play behaviour, many of which could be generalised to situations beyond the training, there was little consistency in measuring the disposition towards the behaviour, and so the characteristics of playing could not be generalised from the studies reviewed.

The extensive research literature on the nature of play in children diagnosed with ASD largely considers the different interventions to increase or facilitate peer interactions in children's free play. Such studies tend to concentrate on the effectiveness of structured training initiatives and associated cognitive and social benefits from these interventions, There appear to be very few studies that consider the environmental influence on children's play patterns. However, recent work by Yuill and others (2007) does consider the ways in which children with ASD responded to a change in their outdoor playground. Working with an ASD unit for twelve 5- to 11-year-old children in West Sussex, the study explores how the introduction of a new playground influenced the level of social interaction and play behaviours of the children over time. Key features in the design were:

- the introduction of climbing walls, towers and slides that presented a challenge for children, in contrast to the old playground in which the equipment was well within all children's capabilities

- props for imaginative play that tended to remain constant in contrast to providing different toys and props on a daily basis in the old playground and thus not providing the opportunity to develop play routines

- the possibility of connecting pieces of equipment in flexible ways and through a circuit design so that movement over one piece of equipment would lead to the start of another, compared with a linear layout in the old playground

- observation points to enable children to have periods free from the need to interact with peers. The design features a lookout tower for a child to stand and observe play and other equipment.

Observations of children's use of this new space clearly indicated that group play was higher than in the old playground:

> Qualitative observation suggests that the layout of the playground was important in providing sufficient structure to guide children's activities together with an appropriate level of challenge and props to foster group and imaginative play. (Yuill and others 2007: 1195)

The research describes how children used the physical challenge presented in the environment to make comparisons of success over time, while the consistency of props enabled children to develop opportunities for imaginative play patterns to emerge, and the circuit structure of the playground components helped children to structure their play.

While this may inevitably be a feature of a novel environment, teacher observations report that the patterns established at the start of using the new space have continued over time. This study raises the potential value of considering the environmental features of outdoor play space for children with ASD and their affordance for play. In light of Luckett and others' (2007) review, such environmental interventions may hold a greater potential for children to develop their own play and peer interactions than structured intervention.

Play deprivation studies

If play is beneficial, then it would follow that depriving children of the opportunity to play would have harmful effects on their development and well-being (Bateson 2005). Siviy and others (2003) note that play behaviours are common across most mammalian species and in humans. The presence or absence of play may be useful as a diagnostic indicator of a child's overall state of well-being: 'Since playfulness is commonly thought to be an adaptive behaviour that is also associated with healthy development, the relative lack of play in an otherwise playful species could be indicative of some underlying pathology' (Siviy and others 2003: 293).

Hughes (2006: 79) provides a detailed discussion of the possible consequences of play deprivation, citing damage to children's 'identity, their social reference points, their neurological development, their search for homeostasis and even their potential to evolve'.

The factors that contribute to stress for children are highly complex, and research studies with children often do not allow the inference of causality that is evident in animal research because of the presence of so many uncontrolled and confounding variables (Hubbs-Tait 2006) in the human environment in contrast with the laboratory cage of a rat. Equally, isolation experiments with animals deprive the young not only of play but of other forms of contact and sensory stimulation from peers (Spinka and others 2001). However, the diverse range of animal studies that have explored the relationship between stress, environmental enrichment and play may allow the possibility of seeking general principles of operation and highlight neurological aspects of human brain/mind function which could not ethically or practically be approached with comparable rigour in the study of humans (Panksepp 2007).

Burghardt (2005) acknowledges there is little solid empirical evidence that play deprivation, as a single factor, has long lasting consequences for development. Indeed, it is very difficult to isolate play as a single feature of deprivation. Viera and others' (2005) study with hamsters suggests that, when the animals are deprived of play for short periods of time, there is a greater motivation for play following isolation, demonstrated through a 'play rebound'. Similar studies with rats (Holloway and Suter 2003) would confirm the existence of this phenomenon. Panksepp (2001) suggests that this 'play rebound' following a short period of play deprivation provides evidence of the importance of this form of behaviour for healthy brain and psychological maturation. Viera and others (2005) and Holloway and Suter (2003), along with numerous other studies, also show that prolonged play deprivation has a more profound and long lasting impact on behaviour.

Severe environmental stress has a deleterious impact on brain development (McEwen 2007). As Burghardt (2005) suggests, play takes place in a 'relaxed field' (that is, when there are no stresses or other constraints in the environment), and the lack of this relaxed field is likely to affect the potential for play to occur. Pellegrini and others (2007) also comment that play occurs in safe and familiar environments for children, and that where organisms are under stress, levels of play may be reduced or terminate completely. If, as Sutton-Smith (1997) asserts, play is central to maintaining plasticity, then the deprivation of play experiences is likely to have an impact on brain development and the loss of flexibility and integration across brain regions.

Animal based research has provided rich experimental data concerning the positive impact of environmental enrichment (for example, the provision of play materials) and the correspondingly negative impact of environmental deprivation on brain and behaviour. Research by Pellis and Pellis (2007) suggests that rats deprived of play are overly stressed by novel social encounters and are poor at developing strategies that can overcome these stressful situations. A key feature of play deprivation for rats appears to be damage to the orbito-frontal cortex, a key region of the brain involved in the mediation of emotions. Damasio (2003) highlights the fact that damage to this area has devastating consequences which result in inappropriate reactions to social situations and a 'skewed' concept of the social world (Roberts and others 2004).

Cui and others' (2006) research with rats notes that social and environmental stress in early life causes changes to the transmission of neurochemicals and/or cognitive defects which, in turn, may also increase susceptibility to depression in adult life. Arnold and Siviy (2002) explain that, although play is a relatively robust behaviour pattern, it can be disrupted by the presence of stressors or threats to the organism, citing research studies with animals which highlight the impact of fear, food deprivation and novelty on play behaviour. As well as the effects associated with these environmental stressors, early stress interventions have an influence on playfulness at a later stage in development.

Spinka and others (2001: 155) conclude that, on the whole, findings from animal research indicate that 'play deprivation results in increased fear and uncertainty in novel environments, and more escalated aggressive behaviour towards other animals in serious conflicts'.

Extreme deprivation

The question of the impact of early physical and social deprivation on human psychological development is obviously of great interest. However there are clear ethical and practical problems in being able to carry out detailed scientific research in this field. The severe and unusual set of circumstances generated by the fall of the Ceausescu regime in Romania at the end of the 1980s has provided an opportunity to examine the effects of extreme deprivation on a relatively large group of children.

Chugani and others' (2001) follow-up research with children from the Romanian orphanages adopted by families in the US comments on the rapid 'catch-up' made by children in their new homes but raises some issues about the impact of the early years stress on brain development. The study found that early and profound stress had affected the development of specific brain areas, in particular the limbic system, which has a significant role in emotions and behaviour, and that:

> … chronic stress endured in the Romanian orphanages during infancy in these children resulted in altered development of these limbic structures and that altered functional

connections in these circuits may represent the mechanism underlying persistent behavioural disturbances to the Romanian orphans. (Chugani and others 2001: 300)

Beckett and others (2006) report on the longitudinal study implemented with a number of Romanian children who were adopted by families in the UK. The studies use general cognitive testing methods, and previous studies have reported on the progress of these children at various ages through their childhood (Rutter and the English and Romanian Adoptee Study [ERA] 1998; Rutter, O'Connor and ERA 2004). Of particular interest is Kreppner and others' (1999) ERA study, which explores the impact of extreme and early deprivation on children's social play (in children aged 4 years). Using a control group of UK adoptees and two Romanian groups (early and later adoptees), their study indicates a general tendency for the UK group to engage in higher frequencies of pretend play and role-play, inferring different mental abilities from the Romanian groups. They suggest that deprivation has a striking impact on pretend and social role-play and that this may have serious implications for social relationships with other children. As Russ (2004) proposes, pretend play has a key role in children's emotion regulation and interpersonal processes and thus deprivation may have serious implications for young children's social and emotional development.

Beckett and others' (2006) study revisited the group at the age of 11 years and found that the effects of early institutional deprivation persisted despite the children having spent at least seven and a half years in their adoptive homes (although for the children identified with the lowest cognitive scores at the age of six there was some considerable improvement). The detailed research report considers some of the possible explanations of the impact of early deprivation, signposting the emerging field of gene-environment studies to suggest that part of the explanation for the diversity of results from the study may be attributable to genetically influenced variations in susceptibility to environmental hazards. In relation to the research's application to a wider examination of child development, the report concludes that any outcome of deprivation may vary according to the nature and timing of adverse experiences, and to the qualities of the environment to which children move when leaving the harmful situations.

Webb and Brown (2003) describe how playwork interventions with a group of children in a Romanian orphanage in Sighisoara promoted considerable recovery from many years of neglect and abuse:

> The findings suggest, above all else, that the Therapeutic Playwork project helped these children to become social beings, not isolated units. Every child began to form reciprocal relationships, which in turn led to a greater sense of self-worth.
> (Webb and Brown 2003: 175)

While specific research into the nature of play deprivation in humans is limited, there is a general acceptance that severe and prolonged stress will have a significant harmful impact on basic adaptive systems. The brain is pivotal in the response to stress as it determines what is threatening and potentially stressful, and what action to take in response to this.

Hughes (2006) notes that play deprivation, in its extreme form, leads to a detachment of the most fundamental sensory and emotional connections with the environment, citing Ogden's (2001) phrase, 'psychic disintegration', to describe the destructive cycle initiated by this impoverishment of experiences. Equally, Sturrock (2003) states that, where there is a disruption to play and the ludic ecology, there will inevitably be disturbances of the self.

McEwen (2007) comments that stress and the neurochemical response to it will produce both adaptive and maladaptive effects on the structure and shaping of the brain. Prolonged and severe stress will remodel key areas of the brain, which in turn will shape future behavioural and physiological responses. McEwen (2007: 873) also suggests that 'social and behavioural interventions such as regular physical activity and social support reduce the chronic stress burden and benefit brain and body health and resilience'.

Animal research has produced evidence of the importance of 'complex' or 'enriched' environments' in supporting healthy brain growth. For example, Benaroya-Milshtein and others'

(2004) research concluded that mice reared in an enriched environment displayed decreased anxiety-like behaviour and higher activity compared to standard mice, along with higher production of key cells involved in the immune system.

Cui and others (2006: 208) refer to environmental enrichment as a combination of 'complex inanimate objects and social stimulation'. Their research with rats noted that early life stress (repeated maternal separation, being reared in limited nesting, daily handling and so on) could be reversed by enriched environment experiences which trigger the release of nerve growth factors, activating neurotransmitter receptors or enhancing neurogenesis (the production of new neurons). In reviewing the research literature, Lewis (2004: 94) concludes that 'successful engagement with complex environments, particularly early in development, promises to have pervasive and significant effects on brain development and function'. However, while the laboratory experiments on animals can produce quite specific evidence, scientists are far from linking specific types or amounts of experience to the developing structure or neurochemistry of the brain. Lewis (2004) notes that little work has addressed the question of what key factors contribute to environmental complexity. A summary of the research leads Lewis (2004) to conclude that there are several commonalities, including increased spatial density, social density (in both cases, density is the interaction of two variables of individuals and amount of space) and novelty within the given environment.

The social environment for human development consists of: highly complex family resources and relationships; childcare and school quality and relationships; and neighborhood and community resources and relationships (Shonkoff and Phillips 2000). Although each of these components of social environments may exert a unique impact, they tend to be correlated. For example, children with fewer family resources also tend to experience lower quality schools, more frequent exposure to violence, and poorer neighbourhoods (Hubbs-Tait 2006).

This section has reviewed some of the literature on factors that impinge on the child's ability to play. It is evident from the literature that endogenous and exogenous factors are inextricably interrelated, and that any cause-and-effect relationship is complex. Children may have certain biological or neuropsychological traits which have an effect on their motivation or ability to engage in, or to regulate, the kind of spontaneous and unpredictable playing that is beneficial to adaptive systems; at the same time, their play expressions may not be supported by the environment, either because the environments do not provide appropriate support or because the behaviour is perceived as inappropriate. These two factors will influence each other by operating in a 'dynamic coupling' (Thompson and Varela 2001). Such an understanding points to the need to provide appropriate environments for children to play as a move towards an environmental response to complement, or as an alternative to, a medical model which perceives the 'problem' as a deficit within the child.

Play and well–being

The evidence presented to date would suggest that play operates across adaptive systems, enhancing and refining these systems and enabling children to adapt to their unique and complex environments. It represents the development of protective systems, not in a 'defensive' mode, but one that seeks to place children in better than neutral positions, that is, to enhance their current level of subjective well-being. Play as a broad and heterogeneous behaviour operates across systems through complex feedback processes at the levels of mind, body and environmental.

Reframing well–being

Throughout our lifetime, the body's primary purpose is to maintain the optimum state for survival. This requires knowledge about objects, people and situations in the external world as well as knowledge of our own biological systems (Damasio 2003). A biological need for maintaining life (known as 'homeostasis'[4]) drives organisms to seek a better than neutral

---

[4] Although as Rose (2005) highlights perhaps the notion of homeostasis is better represented by the phrase 'homeodynamics' which suggests that stability is achieved through dynamic processes and the ability to respond to continuously changing environmental conditions. McEwen (2000; 2007) suggests that the term 'allostasis' may be a better term for the process of keeping organisms alive and functioning through maintaining stability through change and promoting adaptation and coping.

state and to enhance their lives; this is what is known as 'well-being'. So a preferred state is one of joy and pleasure, which makes it easier to do things; the opposite of this, sadness and sorrow, means that organisms find it harder to do the things they need to do and this leads to depression (Damasio 2003).

The concept of well-being, recently gaining favour in public policy outcomes, is multi-dimensional and marks a shift in thinking from a medical model in which health and illness are seen as dimensionally different polarities (Almqvist and others 2006) to one in which individual health and well-being is seen as a product of social relationships, sometimes referred to as 'social capital' (Putnam 1995; Morrow 2004; Bassani 2007), a concept that is explored later in this section.

Prilleltensky (2005: 54) notes that well-being may be defined as a 'positive state of affairs in which the personal, relational, and collective needs and aspirations of individuals and communities are fulfilled'. From this, well-being becomes not simply an absence of disease, but an expression of the mutually influential qualities of the psychosocial, economic, political and physical environment. Also there are many aspects of well-being that reach far beyond health and into the realm of values, thriving, and spirituality.

Traditional approaches to studying well-being adopt an objective standpoint: external agencies measure and judge another person's life through the application of quantitative measures such as wealth or income, educational achievement, health status and so on (Fattore and others 2007). The limitations of this approach have led to an increasing focus on the ways in which individuals actually construct their own perspectives on well-being.

Keyes' (2006) review of the research suggests that subjective well-being is a key indicator of mental health and a fundamental component of 'quality of life'. A subjective perspective acknowledges that individuals evaluate the quality of their own lives. Research now supports the hypothesis that health is not merely the absence of illness, but is also the presence of higher levels of subjective well-being (Keyes 2006; Jutras and Lepage 2006).

Components of subjective well-being

Three broad themes emerge as components associated with an individual's own perception of well-being:

- **Hedonic or emotional well-being:** This consists of perceptions of avowed interest in life, happiness and satisfaction with life, and the balance of positive to negative affect. Jutras and Lepage (2006) note that this element is also associated with a realistic sense of personal power and a sense of one's own competence as well as the ability to cope with stress and frustration (also referred to as 'resilience').

- **Psychological well-being:** A positive evaluation of oneself and one's personal history, a sense of continued growth and development as a person, a belief that one's life is purposeful and meaningful, a sense of competence, and a sense of self-determination. In addition, Jutras and Lepage (2006) refer to the cognitive exercise of mental abilities: problem-solving and decision-making skills, creativity and involvement in personally meaningful activity.

- **Social well-being:** The perception of the quality of relationships with other people, their neighbourhoods and communities. Keyes (2006) asserts that social well-being is multi-dimensional and will include such concepts as social coherence, actualisation, belonging, acceptance, participation and contribution. In addition, Jutras and Lepage (2006) cite that quality of interpersonal relationships is evidenced through a range of supportive relationships, and the ability to empathise and co-operate with others.

The evidence presented to date through this chapter clearly illustrates how play might operate across these themes to promote well-being. Notions of well-being require the systematic examination of human behaviour to map the individual, environmental and transactional character of development across time, space, culture and circumstances (Jutras and Lepage 2006). This highly complex and dynamic web of actions and meanings provides the subjective experiences of daily lives.

Fattore and others (2007) make the point that an understanding of children's well-being should place children centrally and attempt to appreciate their perspectives and standpoints on well-being:

> Attempting to understand children's well-being from where they stand, starts from engaging with children as social actors and is driven by their experiences and opinions. (Fattore and others 2007: 6)

In their study of children's well-being in Australia, Fattore and others comment that recent approaches have seen a significant shift from a focus on survival and basic needs to 'beyond survival' and from focusing on childhood as preparation for adulthood (what Fattore and others refer to as 'well-becoming') to the present lives of, or 'well-being', of children in their childhoods. Yet it may be that the potential of subjective well-being which takes into account children's expressed experiences of their own lives is yet to be realised:

> ... it can also be argued that a failure to take into account children's perspectives on their well-being in their 'present(s)', as they are experiencing their lives as children, marginalises the importance of children's lives as experienced in the present, not just in the future. If well-being is defined as the successful attainment of developmental milestones, it is less important to take into account the way childhood is experienced by children in the 'here and now'. Standard measures on educational achievement, for instance, tell us little about children's own perceptions about the quality of their education or the processes by which they learn. Children are seen as objects of determinants, both internal and external, rather than as engaged social actors with varying levels of control over their social environments. The assumption is that children's social engagement is irrelevant, or that they lack agency. (Fattore and others 2007: 9)

However, there are several recent ethnographic studies that attempt to seek children's views about the quality of their daily experiences (see for example Morrow 2004; Rasmusssen and Smidt 2003). Gabhainn and Sixsmith's (2005) research with children exploring key aspects of their subjective well-being in Ireland highlights the value given to relationships and friendships and the activity-based nature of their relationships, in particular having fun and playing with friends. Of equal significance were children's expressions of the value attributed to the physical aspects of their neighbourhood, what is referred to as 'nature and geography' in the research study. These themes reappear frequently throughout this review.

The design features of play revisited

This brief framing of the use of the concept of 'well-being' provides a context for beginning to appreciate its connections with play. The evidence presented through this review suggests that the process of playing provides children and young people with the opportunity to adapt to and best fit their complex physical and social environments and to achieve a desirable state of well-being. But as Sutton-Smith (2003) warns, play is no guarantee of this. Indeed, as this review shows, children's position in society and lack of access to their immediate environments, and the poor quality of such environments, may present considerable barriers to being able to play and thus to actualise the potential that play can offer.

Burghardt suggests that play is largely about the development of connections between motivation, and emotional and reward systems of the brain. The question of motivation, once prominent in discussions about play, may have become less of an area of concern (Burghardt 2005). Yet it is a key defining aspect of the nature of play, often expressed as 'personally motivated behaviour'. Looking at animal play in general, Burghardt notes that a feature of play is the continuous and persistent seeking out of opportunities to play. An animal's relationship to its environment involves the seeking out of stimuli, and the perception of stimuli or cues initiates a further response, what Burghardt (2005: 136) refers to as an 'appetitive' stage in which 'most variation and openness exists' and where learning and adaptability results. It is within this appetitive stage that most play occurs.

'... children's position in society and lack of access to their immediate environments, and the poor quality of such environments, may present considerable barriers to being able to play ...'

This appreciation of play as a constant seeking out of stimuli that are personally relevant suggests that play is intrinsic, that is, it arises from motivations and urges to engage with the environment, an appetite for seeking out emotionally rewarding experiences. Such motivation will arise when the animal is placed in a 'relaxed field', free from stress and not under the influence of other basic motivational systems (Burghardt 2005). As previously discussed, the relaxed field of play may be a space of moderate stress and uncertainty, but this is initiated and valued by the animal, where virtual emotions are exercised to enhance the state of arousal (Sutton-Smith 2003).

It may be that play, or more accurately being playful, is a perceptual disposition towards the environment. Drawing on the work of Gibson (1986), Burghardt (2005) notes that play is facilitated by the presence and perception of specific stimuli in the environment. Kytta, (2004) extending the work of Gibson (1986) and Heft (1997), explains that each individual responds to specific stimuli within the environment in unique and idiosyncratic ways. Any environment offers, or affords, the potential for activity; the actualisation of these affordances is a reflection and interplay of the different characteristics of each individual and the features of the social and physical landscape at any given time.

Haglund and others (2007: 903) suggest that a well functioning system of reward pathways and response to attractive stimuli is a prerequisite for dealing with stress:

> The ability to respond appropriately to positive events and situations is vital to the preservation of reward expectation, optimism, and positive self-concept.

This process of motivation, perception and anticipation of reward is underpinned by the transmission of dopamine. Siviy (1998) suggests that dopamine plays a key role in the initiation of play through anticipating pleasure and reward. Through the increased release of dopamine, there is an increase in behaviours such as locomotor activity and systematic searching that improves the chance of actualising the affordances offered within the environment. This process is self-rewarding and reinforcing; 'play, in its various guises, makes life worth living' (Burghardt 2005: 393).

It is from this perspective that the significant value of play in supporting children's well-being becomes apparent. Such a perspective offers an alternative to the 'instrumental' viewpoint of play discussed in Chapter 1. Yet perhaps this reframing of play offers a far greater potential for responding to some of the current concerns about children and childhood.

Moving away from using play in a utilitarian and causal fashion as a tool to solve social problems towards a more holistic stance, which accepts play as a multifaceted behaviour in which children seek situations of arousal and uncertainty enables a shift from locating children as being at risk and having deficiencies and therefore in need of targeted interventions to one in which there is an acknowledgement that children are equipped with a range of adaptive systems, or 'ordinary magic' that will enable them to survive and thrive in the many localised environments they encounter in their daily lives. Attention then becomes focused on the nature of these environments to ensure that they can support the enhancement of adaptive systems. As Moss and Petrie (2002: 111) acknowledge in their outline of 'children's spaces':

> We are trying to suggest the importance we attach to: providing opportunities for excitement, wonder and the unexpected; children living childhoods not entirely ordered and determined for them by adults and their preoccupations; relationships and experiences that are not defined or legitimated only in terms of work and outcomes; the value of play and playfulness in its own right, and not just as a means to other ends.

The next section explores some of the implications of this for responding to current concerns about contemporary childhood and children's well-being.

Play and health

The state of children's health in the UK is a matter of considerable current concern. Trends towards an increase in numbers of obese children and declining levels of children's health and well-being (as previously described) have been observed in many western countries (Almqvist and others 2006; Alton 2007). Data from Chinn and Rona's (2001) longitudinal study of primary school children from three independent studies in the UK from 1974-1994 notes that overweight and obesity on the basis of body mass index (BMI) have increased noticeably since 1984. This trend has continued and given rise to growing concerns about the life expectancy of the current generation of children. Boseley (2005) reports that there are over one million obese children under 16 living in the UK, a third of the total in Europe. Some researchers predict that children of the current generation may die at an earlier age than their parents because of the health effects of inactivity, poor diet and obesity (Olshansky and others 2005). Most studies acknowledge that rising trends in children's obesity will almost certainly be represented in later trends in adult overweight and obesity and probably in an increase in associated adult morbidity (Chinn and Rona 2001). Alton and others (2007) estimate that 50 per cent of obese children become obese adults.

It is increasingly recognised that the phenomenon of childhood obesity is highly complex, with different interrelated genetic, metabolic, psychological, behavioural and environmental components, making causal pathways difficult to identify (Ells and others 2005). Given the tracking of obesity and the associated risk factors, it is apparent that the period of childhood is important for establishing preventative measures.

Diamond (2007) suggests that a full understanding of human development is influenced more and more by an appreciation of the multi-layered interrelations between cognitive abilities, emotions and motivations, perception, physiology, social relations and culture. From this perspective we may see that physical health and mental health are intimately interrelated. What we think and feel affects how our bodies function and how our brains develop. We are social beings and our physical and mental health can suffer if we do not have caring relationships and meaningful and reciprocal connections to others.

Equally, the health of our bodies affects how our brains work:

> Our thinking suffers, our brains atrophy and our vulnerability to disease increases if we are stressed, providing a powerful mechanism by which one's social situation, interpersonal interactions and emotions can affect one's cognitive performance, brain tissue and physical health. (Diamond 2007: 153)

Many of the policies aimed at improving the health of children and young people will have an impact on their mental as well as physical health; indeed, the BMA (2006) report highlights the fact that good physical health is dependent on emotional well-being. Good health is not merely the absence of illness. As Kaplan and Kaplan (2005) suggest, it seems inappropriate to consider people as healthy when they are irritable, feel frustrated in their ability to make plans and act in a competent manner and so on. They consider good health to be about feeling positive and effective, being clear-headed and resilient and that 'furthermore, health extends beyond personal well-being to community well-being' (Kaplan and Kaplan 2005: 272).

The interrelationship between physical and mental health may be illustrated by Bedimo-Rung and others (2005), who cite research indicating that exercise reduces depression symptoms; combining this with exercise in green spaces and parks brings an associated restoration effect from being in nature. Research by Pretty and others (2007) clearly indicates that both access to nature and physical activity improve mental health and psychological well-being over a short period. The authors also suggest that if the activity in green space is valued and enjoyable, it is likely to lead to further exposure to such experiences and continued health benefits.

Batch (2005) comments that physical exercise for children has many positive benefits and provides the opportunity for play activity and pleasure, allowing the child to explore their environment. Physical activity also facilitates the development of motor skills and increases energy expenditure. There is evidence that regular physical activity contributes to the primary and secondary prevention of several chronic diseases and is associated with a reduced risk of premature death (Alton 2007; Warburton and others 2006). Suandicani (2004) notes that regular physical activity has an impact on plasma lipids, circulatory functions, blood pressure and body mass index, leading to a better cardiovascular risk profile and lower risk of type II diabetes and ischaemic heart disease. Research by Saakslahti and others (2004) with children aged 4-7 years old in Finland suggest that levels of physical activity, particularly the amount of playing outdoors and the amount of 'high intensity' playing, correlates with coronary heart disease (CHD) risk factors and presents a protective factor in childhood.

Garcia and Baltodano (2005) summarise research findings which suggest physical activity relieves depression and anxiety by providing opportunities for social interaction, increased feelings of self-mastery and self-efficacy and stress relief. Equally, a research review undertaken by Ekeland and others (2005) clearly suggests that physical activity may be effective in improving self-esteem in children and young people, at least in the short term and for children and young people at risk. Given that all the research considered by Ekeland and others indicates many positive outcomes from physical activity and no negative impacts, they conclude that it is an important instrument in improving children's health. However, they do note that the specific forms of activity that best contribute to this are not apparent through the research review.

Engaging in physical activities that provide optimal amounts of enjoyment, challenge and self-direction, as opposed to stress, boredom and external direction, are important outcomes to measure when evaluating the positive benefits of different physical activity engagement experiences (Poulsen and Ziviani 2004). Where children are in a 'relaxed field' (meaning that their basic survival needs have been met) and have surplus energy resources available, they can respond to attractive and novel stimuli within the environment, and there is more opportunity for motivated reward seeking behaviours, namely play (Burghardt 2005).

Hume and others' (2005) research into children's activity patterns in Australia shows that children's perceptions of specific aspects of their home and neighbourhood correlate with their participation in different intensities of physical activity. The authors note the significance of the home for children, who described this as a site of safety. Studying children's reported value of this space, most of the children participated in sedentary activity, and few reported opportunities for physical activity. However, the report also notes that children who reported high levels of sedentary activity in the home also tended to report high levels of physical activity outside the home, leading to a questioning of perspectives that seek to place sedentary and physical activity as either/or factors in children's activity patterns; rather they co-exist as significant and valued aspects of children's daily lives. In their outdoor activities, the research indicates children's value of the school playground for play, and the social connections made at school also influence children's social interaction in the neighbourhood. Similarly, open areas and green space also appear in children's accounts and photographs as important features in the local environment for both physical and social activity. Hume and others (2005) highlight the importance of undertaking both qualitative and quantitative research to gain a fuller picture of children's activity patterns and the places and activities they value both at home and in their immediate neighbourhoods.

Mackett and Paskins' (2004) research emphasises that walking and playing away from the home can contribute significantly to children's health through physical activity. Their analysis of multiple factors associated with children's activity patterns clearly suggests that the place where children tend to be least active is in their own home. When they do go out, unstructured events (playing) tend to be more active than structured ones. The report indicates ways in which walking and playing will enhance health:

- they both have high intensities of physical activity compared with most events

- they tend to be mutually reinforcing: children tend to walk to unstructured activities, and children who walk to events tend to be more active when they arrive than those who go by car, and this includes playing.

The authors note that given the level of parental concern about decreasing physical activity levels of children and their health implications, their findings provide powerful arguments for the significance of the need for children to walk and play out. Brunton and others (2005), in their review of research into intervention programmes to support children's physical activity, comment that, to a large extent, children and parental views about activity are not given priority in developing health intervention schemes. The research review concludes that aiming to provide safer local environments in which children can actively travel and play with their friends may be an effective approach to supporting children's physical activity.

Almqvist and others (2006) comment on the importance of understanding and linking children's perception of health with designing activities and environments that support positive health behaviour. They note from their research with 4- to 5-year-old children that young children perceive health as a multi-dimensional construct formed around three key features of everyday functioning: healthy lifestyle, mental health (including a general sense of well-being) and the nature of social relationships. The analysis indicates that 'engagement' is an important factor in children's perception of health. In this sense, engagement seems to capture key elements of activity and participation:

> Children that interact with the environment and are encouraged to develop a higher level of engagement also develop a wider behavioural competence. Thus, young children understand that their role as active participants in their every-day context is important in relation to health. (Almqvist and others 2006: 282)

Children's responses in Almqvist and others' study indicate a series of variables connected with health, including: the possibility of performing different activities, the joy of sharing in activities with others, and a supportive environment. But as the authors suggest, the most salient responses relate to the possibility of playing. This implies that improvements of child engagement and ensuring opportunity to play should be emphasised in health promotion and to a greater extent be the central focus of health interventions for young children.

Mota and others' (2005) observations of activity in 8- to 10-year-old children during school recess time in Portugal, notes the significant contribution made by active free play to children's recommended period of daily moderate-to-vigorous activity. Burdette and Whitaker (2005) suggest that the focus on increasing children's physical exercise perhaps represents a narrow attempt to improve children's health and well-being. The research highlights, particularly in the early years, the need to change the language associated with preventative health care and move the focus from 'physical exercise' to 'play'.

Compared with adult activity, children at play have more spontaneity and less interest in sustaining a specific single activity. The level and patterns of physical activity of children change as they get older, with the physical activity patterns of children tending to be of short duration with high intensity. Play offers the opportunity for environmental interaction in response to the many stimuli that the environment (human and physical) offers. The range of choices, effort and persistence shown through playing are adaptive outcomes of activity engagement that are associated with increased intrinsic motivation and positive physical activity experiences (Poulsen and Ziviani 2004).

The current focus for responding to the obesity 'epidemic' relies on discussions of amounts of exercise and dietary habits. Burdette and Whitaker (2005) suggest that more emphasis should be placed on the three 'a's of physical health: attention, affiliation and affect.

- **Attention** Exploring issues of enriched environments and the improvement in cognitive skills (Wells 2000), Burdette and Whitaker highlight the significance of the 'enriched' (or natural) outdoors to support free play and opportunities for decision-making and problem solving. Alongside this, the outdoors generally provides a space in which there are fewer restrictions on physical movement and exploration (Lester and Maudsley 2006). Fjortoft's (2004) study with children aged between five and seven years in kindergarten in Telemark, Norway, shows that children who played in a natural environment made significant gains in physical motor fitness in comparison with a control group who played in their usual playgrounds featuring the same equipment (slides, sandpit, swings and so on) but without the natural elements presented to the experimental group. Fjortoft comments that natural environments afford more diverse play opportunities for children than traditional playgrounds; rough and uneven surfaces provide movement challenges, and landscape features and vegetation provide a diversity of different designs for playing and moving. The results of the study show that the experimental group displayed greater balance and co-ordination skills than the control group who played in a tradiitional playground. Fjortoft notes that these key abilities are components of all basic movements and are improved with diverse movement patterns. Spinka and others (2001) also suggest that animals tend to play more in new, rare, or more demanding local habitats. Equally, environmental change may stimulate play. Similarly Yun and others (2005) highlight the importance of engagement with diverse and challenging environmental cues to increase variable heart rates and retain flexibility in movement.

- **Affiliation** Play provides the opportunity for social interaction and the development of affiliations. The complex nature of social relationships developed through play may support and enhance the development of a range of social and emotional capabilities such as empathy, self- and other-awareness and self-regulation. Peer play culture thrives when children find time away from adult supervision.

- **Affect** Play is an enjoyable experience which promotes positive affect and reduces anxiety, depression and sleep problems. Williamson and others' (2001) study with 9- to 10-year-old children in the UK suggests that there is a significant increase in positive mood and significant decrease in negative mood following exercise. The results of the study by Penedo and Dahn (2005) add to a growing literature which suggests that exercise and physical activity have beneficial effects across several physical and mental health outcomes. Burdette and Whitaker suggest that gross motor play may be an important mechanism to reduce the physiological wear and tear on the body that results from the effort of responding to stress.

Recognising the significant contribution that play can make to children's health and well-being, Burdette and Whitaker suggest that attention should be given to ensuring that there are sufficient community resources to support children's play, through the provision of neighbourhood play spaces, traffic calming measures and creating stimulating streets and yards within local residential areas. The research concludes:

> We should promote it [free play] on its traditional merits – that play allows children to experience the joys of movement, creativity and friendship. Though it seems urgent to emphasise that play improves energy balance, we may get further in obesity prevention by realising that modern neurobiology supports grandmother's conventional wisdom that the brain will naturally reinforce behaviours that make it healthy. (Burdette and Whitaker 2005: 49)

Vaillant (2003) reviews the various attempts to define positive mental health and suggests a number of distinct approaches which include positive psychology, maturity (recognising that the human brain continues to grow throughout a lifetime), emotional intelligence, subjective well-being and resilience. In conclusion, Vaillant suggests that these are highly correlated with each other and provide multiple and interconnected ways to begin to appreciate the complexity of the qualities of positive mental health and well-being.

Play and social capital

Social capital is a somewhat elusive and mutifaceted concept (Leonard 2005) that has become increasing influential in framing social policy (Barnes and Prior 2007). A fundamental feature of social capital is the importance of social networks and trust in promoting a sense of belonging and well-being. Putnam (1995: 67) defines social capital as 'features of social organisation such as networks, norms and social trust that facilitate coordination and cooperation for mutual benefit'. Social capital is a resource that enables individuals or collectivities to act in certain ways and to do certain things they could not otherwise do. Putnam distinguishes between two forms of social capital:

Bonding: Bonding relationships refer to the social ties between people with similar identities and shared interests, enabling individuals to act together to achieve common goals. These relationships provide benefits of mutual support, care and protection, although such networks may also be exclusive, not extending their care and support to outsiders.

Bridging: Bridging relationships refer to the social ties between people with different identities and interests but some shared experiences, enabling dialogue between groups and agreement on joint action in pursuit of common goals. Here, norms of inclusivity, reciprocity and mutual understanding are significant, although for individuals such networks may not be able to offer strong sources of personal support (Barnes and Prior 2007).

Halpern's (2005) analysis of research data highlights a strong relationship between social capital and mental and physical health. However, simply knowing someone is not sufficient; the quality of the relationship is of prime importance. The most powerful and beneficial health aspects arise from positive and supportive relationships, what Halpern refers to as micro-level bonding capital.

Much of the empirical work underpinning the concept of social capital is based on studies of adult ties and connections, with scant attention to children and their networks and relationships (Leonard 2005; Morrow 2004). One of the key criticisms of Putnam's (1995) social capital model is that it is based on middle class norms and values. For example Boggs (2001: 284) suggests that the apparently arbitrary selection of indicators used by Putnam to measure decline in social capital is based on 'mostly safe, conformist, traditional community activities favoured by the older generations, and within these generations, by largely middle-class, or upper middle class strata'.

'Play provides the opportunity for social interaction and the development of affiliations.'

What Putnam's analysis fails to address is the contextual factors that play a role in determining what is of situated social value. As previously discussed, the research by Sutton and others (2007) would suggest that children's valued social capital of playing out in their local environments may not sit comfortably with middle class variables of social capital. When children are brought into the picture, it is often in a limited way, which places them as passive recipients of adult social capital. In this way, children's own social networks are largely rendered invisible (Holland and others 2007). Equally, Leonard (2005) suggests that social capital is viewed as a future orientated asset for children, something they will benefit from at a later stage in their development, again a reflection of the discourse of children as human becomings rather than human beings.

The realisation of social resources into social capital is 'not simple to delineate because humans are multidimensional and their behaviours are embedded within their unique cultural and historical contexts' (Bassani 2007: 24). Children's play could represent a biological, social and environmental resource which operates across basic adaptive systems, but the mobilisation of this into social capital and the well-being that arises from this process will be subject to highly complex and multifaceted factors.

A number of studies have recently sought to extend the potential of social capital theory by studying the nature of children's and young people's social networks.

Holland and others (2007) provide a review of three research projects that explore different transition contexts and the development of social capital: transitions from primary to secondary school, from youth to adulthood and the construction of identity for Caribbean youths in the UK. Applying Putnam's concept of bonding and bridging capital, their review notes the diverse ways in which children and young people draw on their peer social networks as positive resources to cope with the transition. For example, children who move to secondary school with an existing supportive peer group draw on the bonding capital that this offers to become familiar with the school and negotiate the novel rules (both formal and informal) and practices. This bonding capital also provides a secure base for a bridge into new relationships. Holland and others (2007: 113) comment:

> these young people are active agents in the production of social capital; they use social capital as a social resource to negotiate transitions in their lives and in the construction of identity. Social capital is differentiated according to its ability to establish bridging and bonding networks.

Goodwin and Armstrong-Esther's (2004) research into young people's health and well-being in rural Wales acknowledges the prime role of social contexts as key determinants of social capital with, in the case of children and young people, a complex and diverse range of networks that they encounter in their daily activities: family structure, schools and other institutions, peer groups and local communities. While having a primary health related focus, Goodwin and Armstrong-Esther's research (2004: 61) highlights the ability of children and young people to engage in peer support and participate in their own activities, and concludes that the 'children themselves are a key resource when examining and promoting health-enhancing behaviour'.

Offer and Schneider's (2007) US study of children's and young people's development of social capital explores the bi-directional nature of parents' and children's contribution to the production of social capital. Their research suggests that adolescents make a significant contribution to the development of family social capital. The strong networks that young people develop in their local communities offers the potential for parents to meet other parents. However, they note that low-income families living in poor quality neighbourhoods may be denied the opportunity to accrue this form of social capital by restricting their children's independent movements in the local community:

> In trying to protect their children, parents may distance themselves from other parents who may share similar values and norms. By distancing from these parents, they are also less likely to become involved in exchanges that could lead to social support. Considering the role social capital plays in educational and occupational success, the mechanism described in this study could yet be another source of inequality that should be tested in future research with more diverse populations. (Offer and Schneider 2007: 1138)

Morrow (2004) provides an example of how the concept of social capital may be applied in the study of children's subjective expressions of well-being. Morrow's research, carried out in two schools close to London with 12- to 15-year-olds, focused on some key issues in relation to children's valued experiences. Using a variety of qualitative research methods, Morrow's findings can be summarised under the following key themes:

- **The nature of children's social networks** The research reinforces the notion that children spend more time with their peers than with their families. Daily activities were often structured with friends, and children's expression of their feelings about where they lived often centred on the proximity of friends. Relationships with family were considered to be very important, playing an important role in a sense of well-being by being a source of emotional support. The research highlights the centrality of family and friends to establishing a sense of belonging rather than the presence of specific physical place features.

- **Attitudes to community resources and institutions** There were considerable differences in children's responses to questions about the neighbourhood and amenities based on gender, ethnicity and age. There was no clear consensus about neighbourhood safety within the research group: children from both schools expressed not feeling safe in local parks and on the street. There were some negative comments about neighbours as 'moany', although some of the group did express positive relationships, especially where they were long-standing neighbours. Traffic was seen as a problem for the younger children in the study. Both year groups mentioned not having enough to do in their neighbourhoods, with several younger children commenting on the lack of wild places to make dens. Also, children in one of the schools were not allowed to play football near their homes on communal green space.

- **Community and civic engagement** Participation in local communities was extremely limited and children did not seem to feel that they shared in community life, although the council had recently started a youth forum.

The study highlights how:

> ... a range of practical, environmental and economic constraints were experienced by this age group. These included not having safe spaces to play, not being able to cross the road because of the traffic, having no place to go except the shopping centre, but being regarded with suspicion because of lack of money. The extent to

which children moved around freely to participate in activities with their friends is likely to be constrained by the physical geography of the built environment, issues of community safety and traffic, parental norms about where children may go out, as well as access to financial resources. These issues are usually neglected in studies of children's health behaviours. (Morrow 2004: 222-223)

In conclusion, Morrow comments on the paradox that a focus on the here and now of children's lives rather than a future adult perspective would suggest that children are generally excluded from the social life of the community. Yet children also 'exist in the future and activities they undertake now for whatever reason have implications for their future wellbeing' (Morrow 2004: 223).

Play and learning: a critical perspective

Lofdahl (2005) notes that the ambiguity associated with play has led to different views of children's learning and the role of play. While there is an assumption that play has a functional relationship to learning, a deeper and broader appreciation of the nature of play is not fully explored and, as such, teachers are left in an ambiguous position themselves, uncertain about their own role in play as well as the nature and value of play within the curriculum.

Farne (2005) suggests that the interest of the educational field in the relationship between play and learning lies within a narrow instrumental approach through the design and management of playing experiences to meet clearly defined educational goals. Pramling Samuelsson and Johansson (2006: 49) cite De Jonghe (2001: 7) who, in her international review of the current state of research on children's play, notes:

> When educators speak about play, it is mostly in this instrumental sense of play: play as a means to reach a further goal or learning result, not the inherent value of play, is central in this vision.

This narrow discourse of learning through play is, according to de Jonghe, expressed in terms of learning-centred play, playful learning, pedagogical play, play-based learning, and so on.

This point is acknowledged by Lofdahl (2005) who highlights the attractiveness of the 'progressive' elements of play (the development of desirable cognitive and social capabilities), while at the same time, the less desirable elements, referred to in her work as 'chaotic play', cause great anxiety for teachers. Through her research with teachers, Lofdahl (2005: 197) asserts that these forms of play (for example play fighting, perceived violent play forms and 'dizzy' play) are not valued because they 'destroy our ideal picture of play'. Yet it is these forms of play that prove to be highly attractive to children. Citing the work of Bergstrom (1997), the study notes that play is seen as children's possibilities, and both structure and chaos feature in shifting patterns within the play, 'thanks to play, brain systems can develop when chaos is allowed to flow, therefore children should have the opportunity to play and to let all sides of play flow' (Lofdahl 2005: 197).

Following structured interviews with preschool and nursery teachers, Lofdahl discerns a number of themes in teacher's responses to children's chaotic play. A common feature in responses was a perception of the 'danger' involved in chaotic play, the play was noisy and messy, children could have hurt themselves and it was not 'real play'; as such it needed to be brought under control and substituted by more productive forms of play. A second theme that also emerged across responses was the need to 'supply meaning' to chaotic play when it emerged. Thus, teachers intervened to 'guide' the play as a way of controlling and re-establishing some adult order and direction to the play. Another approach to supplying meaning was also expressed through the provision of props and space for chaotic play to take place.

Lofdahl notes that few of the teachers expressed any sense of perceiving meaning from the children's chaotic play forms and feels that this is a significant dilemma. The traditional view of play and learning leaves little room for an appreciation and valuing of the nature of chaotic play. While the 'danger' and 'giving meaning' perspective are supported by an educational culture that justifies intervention to restore control and order, the acceptance of these play forms as significant in their own right places teachers in an ambiguous position. Lofdahl highlights the importance of teachers adopting a more reflective stance in working with these play forms, to follow the leads of children and to have a theoretical and practical knowledge base to support them in their interpretations of children's chaotic play behaviours.

Targeton (2005), commenting on the educational reforms in Norway, suggests that much of the research literature and training material for teachers is clearly targeted to early years provision and little is known about the nature of play and learning in the primary school context. For the reforms and the development of a play-based curriculum to be successful, all teachers must have a thorough training in play pedagogy (Targeton 2005).

The child's perspective

Howard and others (2006), through their research with 4- to 6-year-olds in Australia, highlight the importance of appreciating what children actually value in their play experiences in the classroom as a prerequisite for developing appropriate play and learning experiences for children. They note that much of the research literature considers play and learning from an adult perspective, and understanding children's play from the child's perspective should be the first step in designing a play-based curriculum. The research suggests that children can readily distinguish between play, non-play and work within the classroom, drawing on behavioural, social and environmental cues to inform their judgment of play and non-play situations. On this basis, Howard and others highlight research which suggests that children identify key cues that indicate they are playing, including: enjoyment of the task, the opportunity for pretence, the absence of predetermined goals and the amount of control held by the children in their play. Along with this, children are also sensitive to environmental and social cues, such as where the activity takes place and who is available to support the play.

The research concludes that appreciating the cues used by children to categorise their classroom activities assists understanding of the developmental potential of play; teachers may manipulate the environment to promote playful experiences.

Fitzsimmons and McKenzie (2003) highlight the role of humour in supporting the learning process. Their study indicates that 'humour as play' can:

- have a positive effect on the classroom atmosphere and culture, and the nature of interpersonal relationships

- provide an environment for developing and communicating ideas and feelings in a safe frame

- build a climate of empathic support in the classroom

- provide opportunities for children to understand the world, interact with each other, and express and develop their symbolic capabilities.

Fitzsimmons and McKenzie (2003) suggest that play should be an essential component of the curriculum. Similarly, Masselos (2003: 224) explores the development of humour in young children and indicates that early years educators should provide opportunities for children to have the freedom to 'appreciate, experience, enjoy, and engage in, as well as take risks in humorous situations and playful behaviours'. The conclusion to Masselos' observations of four-year-old children's play indoors and outside in a preschool highlights that with shared humorous experiences, children begin to fine tune their responses, develop creative expressions of their uses of humour, enjoy these occasions and use humour to relieve tensions that emerge in play.

Concluding remarks

This chapter has reviewed the literature on the importance of play in the lives of children, bringing in a number of alternative perspectives to the dominant paradigm of childhood as a period of preparation for adulthood and play as a way of rehearsing the skills needed in adult life. The findings show that play is an emotional endeavour, and that this is what shapes the architecture of the brain. These emotions provide both motivation and reward in a continuous cycle of emotional and bodily engagement with the social and physical environment.

'While there is an assumption that play has a functional relationship to learning, a deeper and broader appreciation of the value of play is not fully explored ...'

Reid and Belsky (2002: 584) comment that, as research into children and their environments continues, in all likelihood 'what will be discovered is that typical experiences provided on an everyday basis to most children in most families will be more than sufficient to foster normal brain development'. This section of the review has shown how play makes a significant contribution to these 'typical experiences'. However, taking things out of the environment is likely to have a deleterious impact on development (Smith 2002). The lesson for policy-makers here is that paying attention to children's environments and making them more 'playable' could produce significant rewards in terms of children's health and well-being.

What can be seen from this review of the literature on the importance of play in the lives of children is that it can make a significant contribution in broad, principled terms to the five outcomes of the Every Child Matters (ECM) agenda: be healthy, stay safe, achieve and enjoy, make a positive contribution and achieve economic well-being. However, an understanding of how play contributes to these outcomes needs to be grounded in the key messages from the research reviewed in this chapter. That is, that the characteristics of playing (for example, control, uncertainty, flexibility, novelty, routine, adaptiveness, non-productivity) are what give rise to pleasure and therefore further motivation to play, and in so doing help to shape and develop links between the regions of the brain involved in emotion, motivation and reward systems, supporting the vertical integration of brain regions, and refining coordination between perceptual, motor and thinking systems. Such an understanding of play allows those responsible for creating places for play to move beyond a focus on the content of playing as an indication of skills to be rehearsed for future adult life, towards an understanding of a more fundamental and emotional purpose for play. The chart on page 127 attempts to show how the research reviewed in this section can ultimately contribute to the five Every Child Matters outcomes.

Play, the five outcomes and the big picture

Everything is interconnected

The evidence presented in *Play for a Change* shows the interconnectedness of environment, health, well-being and development. The emerging brain sciences make it clear just how far genes, brain, body and environment interact continually in a lifelong developmental process. The brain is complex, a vast network of actual and possible synaptic connections. The continual interaction of genes and environment determines the growth of new synapses and which synaptic connections become actualised, thereby determining the architecture of the brain.

Playing and adaptability

Playing, with its unique characteristics of unpredictability, novelty, flexibility, personal control, imagination and 'as if' potential, has an impact on gene expression, brain connectivity and brain chemistry, which in turn influence the child's ability to adapt to, survive and thrive in her or his social and physical environments and to shape that environment. Although play can help to develop specific skills, its primary benefits are to do with emotions and motivation (Burghardt 2005), which underpin specific skills development and flexible behavioural responses as well as health and well-being.

Playing and resilience

In particular, play can help build resilience, the capacity for children to thrive despite adversity and stress in their lives. Key elements of resilience are the ability to regulate emotions, strong attachments and peer friendships, enjoyment and general positive and optimistic feelings, being able to cope with stress, being physically and mentally healthy. Play makes a fundamental contribution to all of these elements.

Resilience and social policy

The final report on the policy review on children and young people (HM Treasury and DfES 2007a), a part of the Comprehensive Spending Review, announces a new emphasis on building resilience, with a focus on three protective factors: high educational attainment, good social and emotional skills and positive parenting. The section on social and emotional skills highlights self-awareness, the ability to manage feelings, motivation and empathy. The evidence presented in *Play for a Change* shows how play is a highly effective mechanism for achieving this.

The spider's web diagram overleaf shows the interrelationship between play, resilience, social and emotional skills and the five outcomes, linking these to the resilience factors adapted from Masten and Obradovic (2006). Attempts at fitting the wide-ranging evidence generated from this review into discrete outcome boxes runs the risk of reducing this highly complex form of behaviour to simplistic linear and causal relationships, exactly the thing that current studies into the nature of resilience warn against (Rutter 2006). The key benefits of playing given on the following pages serve as an illustration of the complexity and interconnectivity of the relationship between play, well-being and the ECM outcomes.

Play in this context is flexible, unpredictable, imaginative, peer/self-directed, 'as-if' behaviour

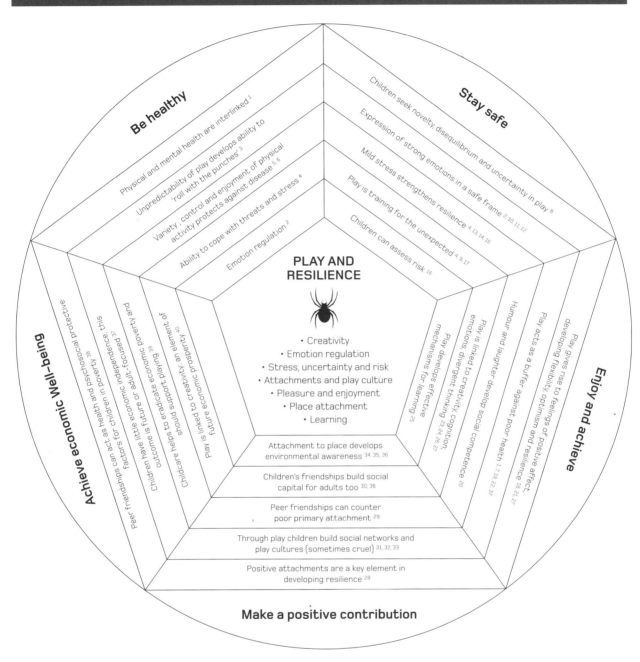

[These numbered points below relate to numbered points on the diagram]

1. Mental and physical health are interlinked (Diamond 2007).

2. Play provides a way of experiencing the primary emotions (anger, fear, sadness, happiness, disgust and shock) that are necessary for survival, at the same time keeping them in check through the rules and rituals of playing (Sutton-Smith 2003), thus helping to develop emotion regulation.

3. The unpredictability of play helps develop neural capacity to 'roll with the punches' of everyday social interactions (Siviy 1998).

4. Those who have not had exposure to novelty or the unexpected through play may pay more attention to potential threats and become more stressed by these threats (Fox and others 2007).

5. The enjoyment, challenge and self-direction of playing, as well as the range of motor actions, are more effective than externally directed exercise regimes that may be boring or stressful (Poulsen and Ziviani 2004).

6. Regular physical playing helps prevent chronic diseases (Alton and others 2007) and relieves depression and anxiety (Garcia and Baltodano 2005).

7. Enriched natural environments, strong social networks and enjoyment create the best opportunity for play and physical health (Burdette and Whitaker 2005).

8. Children seek novelty, disequilibrium and risk in their play (Spinka and others 2001; Kalliala 2006).

9. Play is 'training for the unexpected', both physical and emotional (Spinka and others 2001).

10. Play allows for the expression and experience of strong emotions within the safe frame (Sutton-Smith 2003).

11. Rough and tumble play is 'a sane and safe way of putting our vulnerabilities on the line' (Sheets-Johnstone 2003).

12. Risk-taking in play offers a way of being 'in control of being out of control and so enjoy a sense of both risk and mastery simultaneously' (Gordon and Esbjorn-Hargens 2007).

13. Mild stress is beneficial in terms of creating a variable heart rate (Yun and others 2005) and developing resilience (Rutter 2006).

14. Beneficial mild stress strengthens integration between emotional and executive functions in the brain (Panksepp 2001).

15. Play allows us to 'roll with the punches' associated with daily social interactions (Siviy 1998).

16. Children are capable of assessing risk (Levin and Hart 2003).

17. There is evidence that parents have become increasingly restrictive when it comes to unsupervised play and independent mobility. There is growing concern that there might be long-term costs to a generation of children that have had less opportunity to experience the world, make mistakes and learn from these experiences (CAPT 2002).

18. The enjoyment of playing leads to 'positive affect' (feeling good) and this has benefits for flexible thinking and problem solving, mastery and optimism and enhances performance (Isen and Reeve 2006; Pressman and Cohen 2005).

19. Positive emotions can be a buffer against maladaptive health outcomes (Tugade and others 2004).

20. Humour and laughter help develop social competence (Loizou 2005).

21. The enjoyment of playing promotes flexible thinking and facilitates the acquisition of personal resources that can be drawn on in times of need (Frederickson 2006).

22. Positive emotions generate psychological resources by promoting resilience, endurance and optimism (Salovey and others 2000).

23. Young children who are successful at playing with peers also show greater cognitive, social and physical abilities than those who are less skilled at playing (Fantuzzo and others 2004).

24. There is a positive relationship between cognitive skills and high quality play (Gmitrova and Gmitrov 2004).

25. Play helps to develop effective mechanisms for learning rather than specific learning (Burghardt 2005).

26. Pretend play engages many areas of the brain because it involves emotion, cognition, language and sensorimotor actions (Bergen 2002).

27. Play, particularly pretend play, is linked to creativity in the sense that it involves divergent thinking, symbol substitution, positive affect, problem solving skills and emotion regulation (Russ 2004).

28. Positive attachments are a key element in developing resilience, and begin with the primary carer but also develop through wider social networks as children grow (Hofer 2006).

29. Positive peer friendships may compensate for poor early attachment (Booth-Laforce and others 2005).

30. Children's friendships build social capital for both children and adults (Weller 2007b).

31. Pretend play, role play and rough and tumble play enable children to develop sophisticated attachments with peers (Andreson 2005; Freeman and Brown 2004; Reed 2005).

32. Through peer play children make positive contributions to their own social networks and to the development of play cultures (Corsaro 2003).

33. Play culture can be cruel (Hughes 2006) and can also evoke adult disapproval (Kalliala 2006; Ross 2004).

34. Children's outdoor play helps to build attachments to place; playing in the natural environment helps develop environmental awareness (Lester and Maudsley 2006).

35. Children and young people can make a positive contribution to the design, building and maintenance of public spaces (CabeSpace 2004; Brothwell 2006).

36. Children's play within their local communities enables children and young people to develop relationships with adults who are beyond the family and live in their neighbourhood. These forms of neighbourhood relations establish a strong sense of community and less fear of crime and, in turn, these later variables consequently reduce feelings of loneliness during adolescence (Prezza and Pacilli 2007).

37. As children have little economic independence, this outcome relates either to the current drive to eradicate child poverty, or to children's potential place in the employment market as adults.

38. Children's peer friendships can act as health and psychosocial protection factors for children living in poverty (Attree 2004).

39. The growth in out of school childcare is a key element of the government's drive to eradicate child poverty; however, children's ability to engage in free play varies across provision (Barker and others 2003).

40. Creativity is seen as an important element of education for future economic prosperity (NACCCE 1999); play is an important contributor to creativity (Russ 2004).

Chapter 4

Children's play patterns

Having considered the importance of play in children's lives from a benefits perspective, this chapter looks at where and how children actually play. It considers both playing out and playing in, bringing in studies of children at play in urban and rural areas, in the natural, the built and the home environment, as well as children's play with new technologies. It then considers constraints on children's play and concludes with a restatement of the importance of environments in which children can play.

Children's play patterns

Children's lives are complex, unique and inherently spatial, situated in time and place, and their spatial patterns will be a reflection of a web of factors including gender, ethnicity, family culture, and local and global factors as well as local place characteristics (O'Brien and others 2000; Spencer and Blades 2006). Their social and environmental transactions occur in the home, school, playground, street, shopping areas, natural spaces and all the places in between. Also children are increasingly developing virtual spaces and online identities through the use of media technology. Children are very good at circumventing adult expectations; they construct their own meanings and use of space, often without adult knowledge or involvement. Yet at the same time children are also subject to the prevailing sociocultural norms that influence their lives and their emerging identities.

This section will explore some of the general themes in children's play patterns, bearing in mind that the influence of the wider sociocultural processes of gender, ethnicity, family culture and so on will contribute to creating for each child a unique pattern of playful relationships with both the physical and social environment.

There is a lack of child-centred primary data when it comes to researching children's access to space and use of time (Mayhew and others 2004). Other than the 2002 UK Time Use Survey, there are no quantitative data sources that directly seek to explore where and how children spend their time.

Adult understandings of what children do in their free time are a mixture of personal memories and experiences, media reports, political rhetoric, limited research and anecdotal evidence. Collectively, this presents a picture where the environments in which children and young people currently live are markedly different from those of previous generations; the outdoors now generally presents a site of risk and danger. Any adult representation of childhood is embedded in a set of cultural values that distance us from the child's actual experiences. There may be a dissonance between our expectations of what children are doing and what children are actually doing (Aitken 2001). Philo (2003: 19) implores researchers of children's spatial experiences to 'try to re-envisage ourselves once again as children daydreaming about families and witches, friends and dinosaurs, local streets and distant space craft [in order that] we might end up writing more 'accurately' about children's geographies'.

Traditionally, children have been misunderstood and overlooked as reliable sources for understanding their own relationship with environments and communities (Burke 2005). However, in recent years there is increasing evidence of researching with rather than on

131

children and discovering in greater depth children's experiences of space and place (Roe 2006). The disciplines of children's geographies and environmental psychology have produced some detailed ethnographic studies of children's play lives. The classic works of Ward (1978; 1988), Hart (1979) and Moore (1986) have established benchmarks for approaches to working with children to discover the realities of their everyday encounters with their physical and social environments. As Ward (1978: 86) asserts 'children will play everywhere and with everything'.

More recent studies, and the development of a range of research tools to enhance an understanding of children's 'ways of seeing' (Burke 2005: 28) have enabled further detailed descriptions of the things children actually do and what they find of particular value in their immediate environments. As Fattore and others (2007) suggest, such evidence allows a greater appreciation of children's subjective well-being. Spencer and Blades (2006) in their introduction to a number of studies exploring children's relationship to their environments note that environmental psychology is one of the least neutral fields in the tradition of psychology, as it strives to work for better environments that support well-being. As a discipline, it acknowledges that places where children grow up, play and learn are generally designed by adults or are spaces 'left over' from the adult world.

Playing out

A range of studies has recently provided details of children's play patterns (Thompson and Philo 2004; Percy-Smith 2002; Rasmussen and Smidt 2003; Rasmussen 2004; Roe 2006; Armitage 2004; Burke 2005; Ross 2004; Matthews and Tucker 2006). Collectively, these studies explore both the formal and informal sites that children use in their daily play experiences. Formal sites are those planned spaces designed for use by children and young people; informal spaces are the spaces not specifically sanctioned by adult authority (Thompson and Philo 2004). These informal spaces are often the most attractive to children. Matthews and others (2000: 63) refer to these informal sites as 'the street':

> ... as a metaphor for all public outdoor places in which children are found, such as roads, cul-de-sacs, alleyways, walkways, shopping areas, car parks, vacant plots and derelict sites.

Thompson and Philo's (2004) study in Livingston, Scotland, using interview and mapping techniques with children, identifies the 'street' as a significant site for children's play. Children's maps and drawings produce a mixture of preferences for 'adult spaces' along with the 'informal' spaces that children carve out for themselves:

'It is interesting to note that the places that children value are the places for creating their myths, story telling, jokes and nonsense rhymes.'

> Because the children were as likely to draw a local shop as a leisure centre, a canal walkway as a local authority play space, a car park as a public park, the implication is that Livingston boasts a more chaotic social geography of play than might have been expected (at least by the policy makers). (Thompson and Philo 2004: 116)

When asked what things they played in these places, children's favoured responses were playing on bikes and rollerblading, playing in tree-houses and dens and playing in play parks. The second most favoured response was 'other', signifying those 'messing about', 'nothing doing' forms of play. It is interesting to note that the places that children value are the places for creating their myths, story telling, jokes and nonsense rhymes. As the seminal work of the Opies (1959) clearly shows, this form of playing is simply not intended for adult consumption and, indeed, an integral part of its attraction is that adults know nothing about it. If adults do discover it, they usually frown upon it and forbid it (which may indeed raise ethical issues for this field of research).

The research also examines the spatial boundaries set for children. For the most part children had a clear understanding of why such boundaries were set when playing out, although some admitted to testing these boundaries on occasions, with one particular child who confessed:

> I'm not allowed down at the burn (stream), in case I get wet, but I still go.
> (Thompson and Philo 2004: 119)

Children seemed aware that there were territories belonging to specific gangs, and that these were often sites of contest (raiding dens and tree houses). Thompson and Philo (2004: 121) note:

> It becomes apparent that there is here another layer of boundary constricting the movements of these children: one invisible from the adult gaze, one created by and for the young people on the street or in the woods, but also one that they are trying to conceal from both adults and other young people.

Roe's (2006) in-depth study with a small group of children in a village in County Durham highlights a complex pattern of relationships with the local environment. It is evident that the outdoors plays an important part in the lives of the children who recount significant valued aspects: trees for both an aesthetic and practical purpose, the river that runs through the village as both a site of fear of falling in and as an attractive play feature, and special places created in natural spaces (such as long grass or branches in trees). Natural environments represent different play opportunities for children. The rough surface provides movement challenges, and topography and vegetation provide a diversity of different designs for playing and moving (Fjortoft 2004).

Roe's (2006) study highlights the importance of diverse landscape elements and opportunities within children's immediate environments:

> There is a need to retain wild places at the borders of children's boundaries – particularly so that each child can create special places. This presents a considerable difficulty for landscape managers, indicating the need for less highly manicured areas, particularly the need for trees, large shrubs and long grass – exactly the kinds of areas that are often criticised as harbouring social dangers. (Roe 2006: 176)

Burke's (2005) study of children's play in east Leeds, using photo-diaries with children aged 6-11 years, notes that a large proportion of children's accounts of their play lives feature natural materials and environments. Her study revealed that 70 per cent of children's photographs were of outdoor spaces. Photographs of 'open' space were prominent in children's accounts, as one child explained: they represent 'lots of space ... there's space to be stupid' (Burke 2005: 43). Within these open spaces, local landmarks (street lamps and other prominent spots) had significance for social interactions as they often act as meeting places and talking with friends. Other features, apparently meaningless to an adult, acted as significant features to support play, such as kerbs or 'found' natural materials. As an example of this playful relationship with the outdoors, Burke explores the use of grass in children's play accounts:

133

> Young children appreciate grass, its aesthetic, its feel, smell, and function as a
> building material. They fight with grass and they mark out their boundaries with
> grass. Grass left after a mowing can transform a landscape into a new play
> opportunity. (Burke 2005: 46)

Rasmussen and Smidt's (2003) study of how children in Denmark perceive and use their environment provides further insight into the range of spaces and uses valued by children. Children's photographs of their favourite places depict a neighbourhood of a 'chaotic multitude of places, items and persons' (Rasmussen and Smidt 2003: 89). This includes a variety of places that are designed by adults (playgrounds and formal public places) and discovered and used by children for their own play needs (natural features such as trees, walls, shrubs; transitional spaces between the home and the more formal public areas). A significant feature of children's photographs is the different ways of moving between these sites, for example, on bikes, roller blades and home made go-carts, along with the more formal, accompanied forms of transport such as cars and buses.

Rasmussen and Smidt note that it is not surprising that children's photos included local playgrounds and when follow-up interviews were conducted with children there were two significant factors associated with these places:

• excitement factor – places of challenge and thrills;
• imaginative factor – the ability of the place to support fantasy, engage imagination and so on.

Rasmussen and Smidt (2003: 95) also detect the ability of the children to subvert adult designed spaces to their own needs and uses, particularly through the use of transitional niches to create their own dens and special places:

> There is an inherent latent conflict between, on the one hand, that which has been
> planned and organised by adults and, on the other hand, the children's recreation
> of public space and locations into their own territories. Only rarely are children
> allowed to take possession of essential parts of public places. It is for this reason
> that dens and secret places are found on the extremities of the recreational areas,
> in the country or in the transitional space between the landscaped areas and the
> overgrown areas.

In a later study Rasmussen (2004), again using photographic research with children, comments that children relate not only to the official places created for them by adults but establish their own informal 'children's places'. One particular set of photographs produced by a child shows a patch of rough land that children had reclaimed as a special place. Here they built their own 'houses' from mud with 'roads' and 'fields'; but to an adult, it appears as a seemingly random plot of ground. Reviewing another set of photographs taken by children living in urban areas, Rasmussen (2004) highlights the significance for children of a tree in a courtyard, 'the best tree for climbing' (Rasmussen 2004: 161); but children were prohibited from climbing on this tree and instead were expected to play on the adult designed swings and slides. Again, this denotes the contrast between a 'place for children' represented through adult design and 'children's places' in which children seek to claim space for their own play. The study describes a range of children's places – chalk drawings on the path, goal posts between bushes, a hole in a fence that offers a short cut; what Factor (2004) refers to as children's 'playlines'. These spaces are found close to where children live and can only be defined by children themselves. A place becomes a child's place after a child connects with it physically and experiences the physical sensations and emotional attachments from being in this place. Children's places are established in different contexts and will have individual and collective meanings for children. They can be short-lived or the relationship with a particular place may last for a long period of time. Also their use will be subject to a range of external conditions, in particular seasonal influences. However, to adults they often represent sites of 'disorder, mess, destruction and prohibited behaviour' (Rasmussen 2004: 162).

A study of children's play in urban and rural areas of Fife (Ross 2004) also highlights the significance of natural and unkempt environments. Ross notes the diverse ways in which children use natural features and resources in their play, citing examples of children using trees for climbing, hiding, den-making, swings, goals, and general meeting places and 'bases' for a range of games. Local woods provide attractive 'scary' places for children, simultaneously offering dark and mysterious sites that are appealing for risky and exciting play forms. The study also highlights children's ability to claim local unkempt places through play, using whatever materials were at hand within these spaces to develop impromptu play forms. Children's play in these sites often met with parental disapproval. As Ross notes, a part of the attraction of such sites is their marginal status; they have not been named and fixed by adults, and they are often ignored by adults as being of any significance.

Percy-Smith's (2002) study of children and young people's experiences in Northampton highlights the complexity of their daily interactions. The children and young people expressed the importance of being with friends, having fun, messing about, playing sports, and doing something different as central to their use of free time. From this, it is apparent that the expressed needs are dynamic and will change as children move through and grow up in their neighbourhoods. Elsley's (2004) research with children from an urban area in Scotland emphasises that children generally like where they live and appreciate the spaces that are designed for them, citing play parks and the all-weather football pitch as examples of valued places. However, at times their use of these facilities contravened adult intended use and as such was often a focus for tension. Alongside these formal spaces, children also expressed liking for a wide variety of informal spaces: the streets, shops and especially the local 'wild areas'.

In both Percy-Smith's and Elsley's studies, while children value the local parks and play places, they were critical of the poor conditions of many of these spaces and the inappropriateness of the equipment to support their changing needs. As Percy-Smith (2002) notes, the parks cannot satisfy all children's needs, and for many of those interviewed in the study a significant part of their outdoor activities did not involve predictable place behaviour. The research notes the ways in which children used discarded items (supermarket trolleys, rope, tyres) and street furniture for their play as well as adapting the environment itself to create their own special places:

> In their search for fun, excitement and new experiences young people often discover hidden corners of their environment, places abandoned by adults but invaded by children. (Percy-Smith 2002: 67)

135

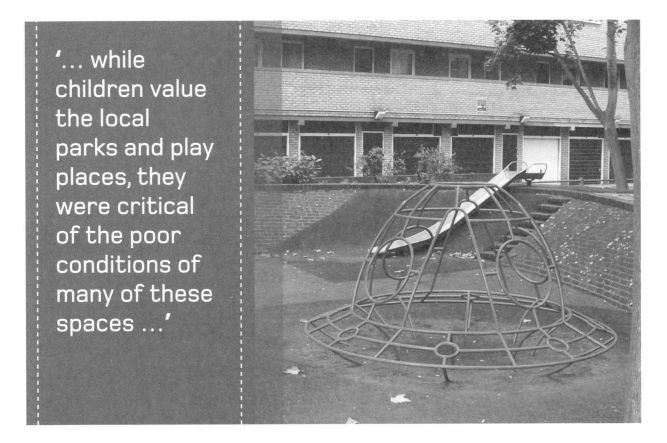

'... while children value the local parks and play places, they were critical of the poor conditions of many of these spaces ...'

Armitage (2004) suggests that there is a mismatch between the resources allocated to supporting children's supervised time and those dedicated to supporting children's free time. Armitage's research for the Hide and Seek project asserts that children manage to spend some significant time during the day away from adult supervision and in the company of other children. When asked about their preferences for this time, children report the significance of outdoor places and playing a variety of impromptu games with friends:

> ... the outdoor spaces that children of all ages choose to spend their time in have fuzzy boundaries: they seem to like wide open spaces for some of the time, and at other times prefer places with walls. On a different day they will seek out natural materials with trees, grasses, flowers and water, and on another will stick to the artificial world of the urban street. But one thing they will avoid when making their choice for the day will be fenced in areas. (Armitage 2004: 189)

This will be revisited later in this section when we explore the range of constraints that impact on children's opportunity to utilise outdoor spaces fully for their play needs.

Playing at home

While studies of children's spatial lives outdoors have attracted increasing interest it is also recognised that the home has become an increasingly significant element in the landscapes of children's play (Percy-Smith 2002; Valentine 2004; Nilsen and Rogers 2005; Karsten and van Vliet 2006b). There is widespread concern over the safety of children in the outdoors (see later in this section), and the spatial independence of children has become increasingly restricted as parents attempt to limit children's independent movements.

Karsten's (2005) study of children's play in the Netherlands notes that, whereas in the 1950s children's play meant playing outside, today many more play activities happen inside the home. This has led to a change in the ways in which children use the home through negotiating and contesting the available spaces. As Karsten and van Vliet (2006b) comment, the emergence of a category of indoor children who hardly ever go outside to play is a new phenomenon in Dutch history.

Harden (2000), in her study of children's perception of their public and private spaces, finds that children construct the home site as a place of safety and security and express concerns about their vulnerability in public space. Harden's research identifies that children see the public space as one of risk and threat, with expressed fears of getting lost, the nature and visual perception of the physical environment, and the people who may inhabit the public realm. Manzo (2003), reviewing the literature that explores children's place attachment, suggests that the use of 'home' acts as a powerful metaphor which attracts a wide set of associations, values and meanings. Home has become associated with the physical space of the 'house' (and often implicit images of safety, joy, comfort and so on) in comparison with the other sites encountered in daily interactions, the 'outdoors', which may increasingly be associated with less positive feelings. Such binary oppositions of indoors and outdoors may mask a whole series of complex issues, and Manzo highlights the importance of moving away from this to an appreciation of other places and experiences of 'residence', so we are better able to see the full range of places, feelings and experiences that combine to develop a sense of place.

Manzo's review reveals that attachment is largely viewed in terms of positive affect. However, it is clear that not all humans will have positive feelings about their local spaces, both indoors and outdoors. Citing the work of Giuliani and Feldman (1993) Manzo (2003: 50) notes:

> If we accept the prevalent definitions of place attachment ... that it is an affective bond to place, we need to consider whether or not to include ... a negative emotional relationship. To speak of negative attachment contrasts with the everyday meaning of the word.

We can see that for some children the residence may not be a place of safety but instead is a place of fear and violence. For others, given increasing time spent indoors, it can be a site for increasing tensions with parents over the use of space. Nilsen and Rogers' (2005) study of children in their homes in Norway acknowledges that each home is a unique social construction of cultural meanings and practices. Within these, the family meanings may be both shared and contested.

Equally, the traditional notion of the early stages of childhood being centred on the home may be changing due to increasing services that offer affordable collective childcare, often connected with other political and economic agendas such that 'children's place is no longer seen to be always in the home' (Holloway and Valentine 2000: 16).

Burke's (2005) study notes that indoor and outdoor play in 'closed' intimate spaces is an important theme in children's stated preferences. Children's photographs from Burke's research suggest that they value a sense of enclosure and privacy, as suggested by their photographs of gardens, bedroom, cupboard and car. Equally Rasmussen (2004) highlights the importance of gardens in the daily lives of children. Reviewing children's photographs of playing in their gardens, Rasmussen draws on a particular example of a garden swing. To the child, this represents a special place of physical activity, imagination, daydreaming and songs. Valentine (2004) comments that most outdoor play is now closely centred on the home and its immediate surroundings. Valentine's research suggests that around 40 per cent of parents who responded to a questionnaire survey indicate that children who have access to private gardens spend most of their outdoor leisure time there.

With the apparent shift from outdoors to indoors, the home provides children with a variety of resources for their own, often unsupervised, use, both alone and with friends. However, as Nilsen and Rogers (2005) suggest, this does not necessarily imply that children have independent control over this space.

Pahl (2006), in a detailed photographic study with children from three families in London, highlights the intricate relationship between children and their home spaces. Pahl's field visits to the family homes over a two-year period establishes an 'inventory' of the toys, programmes watched, games played, care of pets and other domestic routines in the lives of the children. Analysing children's photographs and narratives, Pahl comments on the visible ways in which adults and children represent themselves in the home space. The ways in which adults formally order the arrangements and displays of the home contrasts with children's temporary and transient use of this space. This is demonstrated by children's photographs of their bedrooms as play spaces, with toys scattered around the floor and a general expression of excitement about playing in this space along with a perception of this as a 'mess' by adults and constant instructions to tidy up. The more formal shared spaces of the home appear to have an influence on the ways in which children used these spaces for their play. For example, a child playing in the front room with a play mat conformed to the space limits presented by the mat, and play was contained to this area in a very formal manner.

The importance of the bedroom

The bedroom is particularly important in the home as a space children come to appropriate and claim as their own, especially as children get older (Mayhew and others 2004). Mitchell and Reid-Walsh (2002) note the shift in play patterns that has traditionally seen boys being allowed into public spaces, while the 'bedroom culture' offered girls an alternative cultural space, often arising from parental restrictions on girls' access to public space. With the apparent reduction in access to public spaces and the increasing proliferation of modern technologies, the bedroom culture is being transformed into a 'digital bedroom' – a private space for children's cyber play – which engages both boys and girls in a virtual space that is both private and public at the same time. However, Sutton and others (2007) note from their comparative study with children from working and middle class backgrounds that middle class children valued the home for its affordance of 'personal space', while the working class children rarely mentioned this as an important space, possibly attributable to the fact that many of the children shared a bedroom with their siblings. Similarly, the children from the working class area had less access to media resources.

137

For many older children and young people, the bedroom is converted to a private, personal space reflecting the child's individual tastes and interests (Livingstone and Bovill 2001). It becomes a place where friends are brought into and others excluded. This is the place where they can listen to their personal music choices, read magazines, play their games and unfold their private lives (Mayhew and others 2004). For most adolescents, the bedroom becomes a personal space in which they can express and experiment with their identity.

Livingstone and Bovill (2001) note that, even for younger children aged 6-7 years, just over 50 per cent do not have to share a bedroom. The figures for older children show an even higher proportion: 69 per cent of 9- to 10-year-olds, 77 per cent of 12- to 13-year-olds, and 82 per cent of 15- to 16-year-olds having their own bedroom.

Children's play and media technology

Accompanying this trend towards the home as preferred site, the advance of new technologies (computers, video games and other electronic media) adds to the attraction of spending time at home. This is not a universal pattern, and age, gender, socio-economic status and so on are highly influential in determining preferences and patterns of use (Livingstone 2006). Indeed, as Mayhew and others (2004) highlight, a common feature within the literature and in children's own narratives of cyberculture is that of 'difference': virtual space is more accessible to some children than others and it is accessed from different places in different ways. Research suggests 'new sites of social exclusion are emerging in the UK because of different patterns of children's access to virtual space' (Mayhew and others 2004: 32).

While initially the preserve of teenage children, computers and video games have become more widely designed for and available to younger children. Marsh and others' (2005) research in Sheffield notes that many young children's lives are 'media-rich' and children are developing a wide range of skills, knowledge and understanding of media from an early age. Parents interviewed in the study report that media technologies play an important but not overwhelming role in children's leisure activities. In addition, engagement with media technologies 'appears to be a primarily social, not individual, activity, taking place most often with other family members and in shared parts of living spaces' (Marsh and others 2005: 5).

Livingstone (2006) notes that in the UK 87 per cent of children have a computer at home (71 per cent with internet access), 62 per cent have digital television (17 per cent with internet access), 82 per cent have a games console (eight per cent with internet access), and 81 per cent have their own mobile phone. In addition, those who have internet access at home are also more likely to have these other technologies.

Research collected from the UK Children Go Online project (Livingstone and Bober 2003) indicates that only 16 per cent of children and young people interviewed who use the internet on a weekly basis make use of this for discovering basic information. A further 29 per cent use the internet for games and email; yet a further 27 per cent expand their peer-to-peer uses with instant messaging and music downloading; and the remaining 27 per cent make a broad use of the internet, taking up such opportunities as completing quizzes, creating websites, voting, contributing to message boards, offering advice, filling in forms and so on.

Children's and young people's use of media technologies represents complex and multiple contradictions for adults. On the one hand adults value the fact that their children are 'safe' indoors, yet at the same time there are anxieties and tensions about what children actually get up to. Adults rarely understand the fascination of gaming (often hidden away in bedrooms and concealed from the scrutiny of parents), dismissing it as frivolous or sometimes dangerous in its capacity to 'corrupt' vulnerable children (Crowe and Bradford 2006). Just as parents control children's access to outdoor space (Valentine 2004) and impose temporal regulations (Christensen 2002), parents may seek to limit children's access to virtual space.

Parents are often persuaded to buy computers and associated software for their children to assist with educational tasks, but research suggests that children actually spend most of their time playing games not associated with education and learning (Kerawalla and Crook

2002). Equally, while media technologies are attractive for children, and parents support this by buying televisions and games machines, there are increasing concerns and 'moral panics' about the health risks associated with watching television and playing games. The contradictions and confusions are compounded by conflicting results from studies into the harm or benefits of playing games.

Buckingham (2000) notes that the arguments presented about children's relationship with new media technology tend to adopt either/or positions, seeing it as either harmful or beneficial. Both positions take up deterministic and essentialist stances that fail to acknowledge the lived experiences of the children and the ways in which they 'do' technology. Many studies have highlighted the harmful impact of playing violent computer games, with increased levels of violence and aggression and decreases in academic and positive social behaviour (Gentile and others 2004). Similarly, playing video games and watching television are implicated in children's increasing sedentary lifestyle and associated health problems (Clements 2004). Jordan and others' (2006) study suggests that the amount of time children spend in front of the screen is an important predictor of cognitive, behavioural and physical outcomes, including bullying, attention, school performance and weight. This has led to a recommendation in the US that children should spend no more than two hours per day watching television. Whilst more and more parents are placing a television set in their children's bedrooms, parents' attitudes towards this rising phenomenon are mixed. Jordan and others' study suggests that any recommendations about television use are unlikely to be supported by parents who indicate that they: use television as a safe and affordable distraction for children; demonstrate personal heavy television viewing patterns themselves; feel that children's free time should be theirs to do as they please; and believe that the television plays a significant role in the day-to-day routines of the household.

139

Studies such as Clements' (2004) interviews with parents about their children's play patterns clearly implicates the rise in television watching and games playing with a general trend of sedentary and home-based play. Clements suggests that this has profound effects on children; they are overly passive, the development of perceptual abilities may suffer and they become isolated from their peer groups.

Yet other studies would suggest exactly the opposite. For example, Schott and Hodgetts (2006) note that online and offline game practices enable children and young people to

'... children value a diversity of spaces to support their everyday play lives, including indoor and outdoor space.'

establish strong peer communities. Playing computer games can become the basis for face-to-face discussions and play. Children who cannot participate in this may be excluded through not being able to contribute to the cultural references established in children's everyday talk. Equally, children's game playing can become a rich social event as children offer suggestions and prompts, and share 'tricks' and 'cheats'; such forms add to children's 'repertoire of collective activities' (Schott and Hodgetts 2006: 312).

Boyce (2007) comments that the relationships between sedentary behaviour and health cannot be explained by using single markers of inactivity, such as television viewing or video/computer game use. Few studies examine whether media use replaces time spent outdoors playing, and where research exists, only a weak relationship is proposed.

From another perspective, Buckingham (2006) criticises the prevailing psychological perspectives in research into media use and highlights the importance of exploring children's perspectives and analysing their interactions with media, on their own terms. This process:

> ... draws attention to children's competence as media users – their 'media literacy' – and the ways in which media use is embedded in the contexts and relationships of everyday life. However, it also recognises that children's dealings with media are framed by the operations of the media industries, and by the constraints exerted by textual meanings: children are by no means simply free to make their own meanings in any way they choose. (Buckingham 2006: 44)

Summary

Mayhew and others (2004) in their review of the experience of childhood in the UK note the heterogeneous nature of children's lives: children are subject to a range of unique socio-economic, cultural, geographical and demographic factors. Yet children are not passive in this process; they are resilient and creative 'in dealing with the problems and difficulties they encounter: there is a sense that children are adept at "finding ways round things", and this is very much in line with the notion of children as active agents' (Mayhew and others 2004: 450).

Blinkert (2004) outlines the importance of viewing local neighbourhoods as 'action spaces', a territory close to home which has a number of key features: accessibility, safety, flexibility and opportunity for interaction with other children. The research highlighted at this stage suggests that children value a diversity of spaces to support their everyday play lives, including indoor and outdoor space. The use of ethnographic methods to capture children's play lives portrays a complex picture of children's relationships with each other, adults and spaces within their local neighbourhoods. Understanding these patterns can help adults appreciate how best to design spaces to support children's play, or indeed to acknowledge the existence of such patterns and do little other than protect children's right to participate within their local environments.

Woolley (2006) notes that current trends and policy initiatives suggest an increasing emphasis from some quarters on improving children's opportunity to play in open spaces, citing the example of the work by the Children's Play Council. Evidence from recent research is feeding into policy and funding opportunities for play through the Big Lottery Fund. Woolley suggests that, if results from research and funding are used wisely and creatively, there is an opportunity during the forthcoming years to provide exciting and challenging play opportunities for children and young people in their immediate environments.

Ward's (1978) study of the child in the city suggests that some children can successfully negotiate their way through this complex landscape, finding and creating time and places to play and 'unfolding' as individuals; but other children never 'get a foot on the ladder' and are isolated and alienated from their neighbourhoods. The next section explores some of the issues that may be affecting children's opportunity to play out.

Constraints on children's play

Children's play is a heterogeneous form of behaviour that is expressed in diverse spatial contexts. While children will play anywhere, features in the contemporary environment have a significant impact on many children's ability to find time and places to play. There is no universal pattern and there are significant variations in children's spatial lives.

A number of studies (Morrow 2004; Thomas and Hocking 2003; Unicef 2007) raise serious questions about children's quality of life, not as a measure of economic and material wealth but as a 'balanced combination of complementary states in four core areas' (Thomas and Hocking 2003: 10) namely:

- individual standard of living
- shared resources
- happiness and emotional well-being
- trust and inclusion.

Thomas and Hocking's analysis of children's well-being against these indicators shows that the current response to supporting children is fragmented and confusing:

> The combined impact of this fragmentation is to foster deep contradictions and inconsistencies in children's lives and to neglect certain aspects of their quality of life. Children doing paid work is frowned upon, yet British children complete 35 million test papers every year. Corporations spend millions of pounds researching and perfecting the child appeal of products, while families struggle with both time and money. Parents are increasingly fearful of allowing their children to be unsupervised in public, but obesity goes effectively unchecked. (Thomas and Hocking 2003: 12)

141

These contradictions and inconsistencies are evident in the ways in which children experience their daily lives and in their relationships with others in the physical environments in which they live. This section will explore some of these contradictions and pressures.

Environmental stress

Evans' (2004) review of research into the effects of acute and chronic environmental stress highlights the cumulative effect of poor environments for children living in poverty. Family stresses, housing conditions and poorer social networks do not support playing, nor does the outdoor physical environment:

> Poor children reside in more polluted, unhealthy environments. They breathe air and drink water that are more polluted. Their households are more crowded, noisier, and more physically deteriorated, and they contain more safety hazards. Low-income neighbourhoods are more dangerous, have poorer services, and are more physically deteriorated. The neighbourhoods where poor children live are more hazardous (e.g., greater traffic volume, more crime, less playground safety) and less likely to contain elements of nature. (Evans 2004: 88)

Hubbs-Tait and others' (2005) review of the research on they effect of neurotoxicants (such as lead, mercury and cadmium), micronutrients and social environments on children's development shows that toxicants have a negative impact on social and cognitive development, including play behaviours. Their review of animal-based research suggests that the detrimental effects of neurotoxins can be reversed by environmental enrichment. Exposure to such toxicants is higher for children living in poorer neighbourhoods. In some instances this can be compensated through adult facilitation of playing.

The culture of fear and risk aversion

Hillman (2006) notes that, while children's material worlds have improved, there is a downside, citing contributing factors of a car-based culture and the precautions to limit the risk of injury that are a reflection of a 'culture of fear' and risk aversion. The UK has one of the lowest rates of child accidents in the industrialised world. This has been achieved partly through the advances in health and safety legislation but perhaps more significantly by placing the responsibility for keeping children accident free on parents (Penn 2005). Thus, for example, road traffic presents a considerable risk to children and protection against road accidents is seen as the responsibility of parents rather than a societal issue; little is done to control traffic and restrict car use.

Compared with their parents, and even more so with their grandparents, children's lives today are much more circumscribed. The Child Accident Prevention Trust (CAPT) (2002: 2) reports:

> Risky activity, and risk taking itself, is recognised as an essential part of growing up. Parents must balance their natural desire to protect their children with the knowledge that their children must be allowed to grow through experiencing the outside world. There is evidence that parents have become increasingly restrictive when it comes to unsupervised play and transport to and from school. Such strategies may help reduce the immediate risk of injury to children and young people in the short term. But there is growing concern that there might be long-term costs to a generation of children that have had less opportunity to experience the world, make mistakes – and learn by them.

Furedi (2002) asserts that we now live in a time when risk is seen as something to avoid at all costs. The word has negative connotations; if there is a risk, it must be unhealthy and we should do everything possible to remove this. We have lost sight of the fact that there might be such a thing as a good risk. Avoidance, prevention, removal, management and assessment are all positive actions that arise from this fear of risk. Furedi (2002: 1) says:

> Safety has become the fundamental value of our times. Passions that were once devoted to a struggle to change the world (or to keep it the same) are now invested in trying to ensure that we are safe. The label 'safe' gives new meaning to a wide range of human activities that are meant to merit our automatic approval.

Many parents still have positive childhood memories of playing outdoors and recognise the value of such experiences for their own children (Clements 2004; Jenkins 2006). Karsten and van Vliet's (2006b) research in the Netherlands notes that all parents value the relationship between their children's good health and playing outdoors. Often the adults recall their own enjoyable memories of outdoor play and want to give their children similar positive outdoor play experiences. The combination of societal fear and personal aspiration for their children creates a 'parent paradox' between what parents wish for their children and what they feel they should be doing to protect them (The Children's Society 2007).

Thomas and Hocking (2003), in their analysis of childhood in the UK, examine the significant impact that risk aversion has on children's lives, particularly where there is a growing privatisation of childhood in which the responsibility for looking after children clearly lies with the family, with an associated reduction in any form of community responsibility for children. Parents are susceptible to media warnings about the safety of children outside the home (Valentine 2004). Alongside this, the increasing privatisation of parenthood places a great emphasis on parents making judgements about risk and leads to a great deal of uncertainty and anxiety about the outside world. This emotional response, alongside a lack of trust in the community, leads to an emotive disposition towards increasing regulation of children's activity (Jenkins 2006).

Research by Veitch and others (2006) in Australia notes the significant influence that parents have on children's ability to play out. Parents' issues about the safety of their children playing in places other than their own yard were mostly influenced by concerns about strangers, teenagers/gangs, and road traffic en route to the place of play. These safety concerns seemed to limit the number of places available for children to play.

A study by The Children's Society (2007) notes that parental anxiety about children playing out unsupervised denies today's children the freedom to spend time with friends that they once enjoyed themselves. When asked the best age for children to be allowed out with friends unsupervised most respondents (43 per cent) said aged 14 or over, despite the fact that most of them had been allowed out without an adult at the much younger age of 10 or under. Respondents over the age of 60 went even further, with 22 per cent saying children should be over 16 before going out alone.

Jenkins' (2006) research with families in South Wales explores the nature of parental concerns over their children's safety and notes the ways in which parents actively attempt to balance the competing sets of cultural orientations regarding the health and well-being of their children. It should be noted that the sample chosen by Jenkins was based on children who had visited accident and emergency units at hospital as a result of injuries that occurred while 'playing out', and as such there is evidence of the existence of quite sophisticated and dynamic negotiation processes already in place within the family. Research indicates that children adopt a wide range of strategies to reassure parents of their competence to negotiate their immediate environments independently (Harden 2000; Valentine 2004). Jenkins' (2006) study highlights the ways in which parents continually seek to modulate their strong emotional fears about children being outside with lay knowledge based on the principle 'you can't wrap children up in cotton wool'.

This phrase encapsulates two key features:

1. It recognises the fact that exposure to a certain level of adversity is inevitable; safety cannot be guaranteed in any situation and 'accidents will happen'.

2. A second feature acknowledges that it is 'morally wrong to protect children from all forms of adversity as this is detrimental to their physical and social development' (Jenkins 2006: 385).

143

Gill (2007b: 76) suggests that there is a need to shift from a philosophy of protection towards a philosophy of resilience; a need to take a proportionate view of risks of harm and of 'minor public offences and skirmishes involving children' (Gill 2007b: 82). In balancing the fears with an acceptance of the importance for children to play out, parents report using a variety of techniques based upon giving freedom while putting into place strategies designed to reduce the risk of misadventures occurring. Backett-Milburn and Harden's (2004) detailed family case studies also highlight the complex and dynamic ways in which families construct and negotiate risk and safety. Their research concludes that, while each case study family developed a 'bottom line' for establishing boundaries and expectations to manage risk and maintain safety, many risk-related issues had to be discussed and renegotiated on a regular basis.

Jenkins' (2006) research suggests that children and young people show a serious response to the fears and guidance from parents but adopt a variety of techniques to demonstrate their competence in being able to deal with these. Common strategies include avoiding particular people and places where they might be, having a mobile phone, having a plan of action to deal with possible situations and going around in groups (CAPT 2002; Valentine 2004). What this suggests is that the children selected in Jenkins study were 'effectively equipped with an arsenal of negotiation techniques in order to gain greater access to the outside world' (Jenkins 2006: 391).

As well as parents being anxious about their children playing out, there is evidence that children themselves now see the outdoors as a dangerous place. O'Brien and others (2000) note that about one third of the children interviewed in their study expressed anxiety about unsafe places in their neighbourhood and slightly more were worried about unknown youths and adults. Similarly, research by Thomas and Thompson (2004) indicates that children place a high priority on assessing danger as they move around in the outdoors. Wells' (2005) research with children aged 9 and 10 years from a primary school in a predominantly working class and ethnically diverse neighbourhood in London notes the ways in which children construct the notion of 'stranger'. Following on from high profile campaigns and initiatives about 'stranger-danger', the majority of children interviewed expressed an understanding of strangers as all those people who were not formally incorporated into their social networks. This broad concept of stranger, 'a figure who is not simply unknown but also dangerous, renders public space as a space saturated with uncertainty and even terror' (Wells 2005: 505).

Children in the public realm

Vanderbeck and Dunkley (2004), in their introduction to a series of articles on exclusion and inclusion of young people, acknowledge that children are excluded from full participation in activities and spaces both through the legal frameworks and everyday practices that reinforce the natural authority of adults. They seek to clarify the use of the phrase 'social exclusion', shifting this from a codeword for poverty to a broader understanding, citing the work of Duffy (1995):

> Social exclusion is a broader concept than poverty, encompassing not only low material means but also the inability to participate effectively in economic, social, political, and cultural life, and, in some characterisations, alienation and distance from the mainstream society. (Duffy 1995: 5; cited in Vanderbeck and Dunkley 2004: 178)

From this perspective, Vanderbeck and Dunkley identify a number of areas from which children are excluded, through the regulation of young people in consumption and other public space, restrictions on independent mobility and the imposition of age-based curfews (see Collins and Kearns 2001).

The work of Valentine (2004) provides a comprehensive review of the current issues affecting children's use of outdoor (public) spaces, ranging from parental concerns about children's safety in public spaces, discourses on child rearing practices, children's competence and ability to contest parental and public controls and expectations, and the changing nature of children's access to public space.

A considerable amount of research over the past decade indicates that children's opportunity to range independently in many industrialised societies has significantly diminished (Kytta 2004; Karsten and Van Vliet 2006a; Spilsbury 2005; Hillman 2006; Rissotto and Giuliani 2006). Karsten (2005), using oral history, statistical and archive research, detects a new form of childhood that is evidenced through a decrease in playing outdoors and an increase in adult supervision. Rissotto and Giuliani (2006) note that research carried out over the last two decades in several European countries, the US and Australia clearly indicates a sharp decline in children's independent mobility. Veitch and others (2006) in their study of children's play sites in Australia conclude that the opportunities for children's independent mobility and free play may be limited for many children. They find the results alarming, 'as active free play is quite likely to be an important component of children's overall physical activity' (Veitch and others 2005: 9).

'... children's opportunity to range independently in many industrialised societies has significantly diminished.'

Kytta's (2004) research in Finland and Belarus provides a framework for appreciating the covariance of children's independent mobility with the actualisation of affordances within an environment. She suggests that there are three 'fields of action' that determine whether affordances are actualised through activity:

- the field of promoted action, where socially approved actions are prescribed across place, time and manner

- the field of constrained action, where actions are restricted either through the barrenness of the environment, or through being deemed socially unacceptable

- overlapping these two and in the space in between them is the field of free action, where children can actualise affordances, which includes actions that are both promoted (physically and socially) and socially constrained. Affordances that are socially constrained may be actualised both by chance (through independent discovery) and deliberately. This is what is sometimes understood to be anti-social behaviour.

In their play, children often move from one field of action to another, and they are also likely to try and enlarge the field of free action (Kytta 2004).

Prezza and Pacilli (2007) explore the relationship between Italian children's autonomous mobility and play, and perceptions about crime and loss of community. The authors cite research which shows that the reduction of children's opportunity to experience unsupervised play in public places is a feature across many countries in Europe. While for children living in poor and degraded neighbourhoods this might present a positive support to children's health, for those living in low risk areas the restriction of opportunities for unmediated play and mobility may have negative developmental consequences. Rissotto and Giuliani (2006) suggest that the restriction on mobility has an adverse effect on the development of spatial skills; children are denied the opportunity to develop skills of wayfaring and associated problem solving techniques. Children are also denied the opportunity to acquire sensorimotor information about their local places necessary to integrate internal and external spatial information. A number of research studies suggest that restricting children's mobility might also have a harmful impact on children's health (Mackett and Paskins 2004; Alton 2007; Hillman 2006).

In addition, Prezza and Pacilli (2007), through undertaking research with adolescents using a number of key instruments to explore ranging behaviours, sense of community and isolation, suggest that the more children are confined to their homes, the less opportunity they have to access community social resources and to establish strong friendships. This also becomes a self-reinforcing process: children need other children with whom they can play, and outdoor play is essentially social play. As more children remain indoors, there are fewer children playing out and so children are less likely to go out to find their friends (Karsten and van Vliet 2006). Prezza and Pacilli's study notes the importance of children and young people developing relationships with adults who are beyond the family and live in their neighbourhood. The findings suggest that these forms of neighbourhood relations have positive outcomes for the well-being of children. Their research notes that more 'autonomy and play in public areas during childhood influences more intense neighbourhood relations, a strong sense of community and less fear of crime and, in turn, these later variables consequently reduce feelings of loneliness during adolescence' (Prezza and Pacilli 2007: 165).

Timperio and others' (2005) Australian study concludes that parental perceptions of the local neighbourhood may influence the extent to which children use the environmental resources and so reap associated health benefits. Their research, while finding no evidence between perceptions of the neighbourhood and weight status among 6- to 7-year-olds, does indicate that perceptions of traffic on local streets and concerns about road safety may be indirect influences on overweight and obesity among 10- to 12-year-old children through making parents anxious about letting children play out independently.

Studies of children's play patterns discussed in the previous section suggest that there may be a discrepancy between some of the research studies and public opinion about children's outdoor play and what children actually do in their local environments. This finds a parallel with an oft-stated public expression that children don't know how to play any more. A closer examination of children's movement and use of their local environments suggests a more complex picture (Ross 2004; Thompson and Philo 2004; Armitage 2004; Burke 2005). Armitage's (2004) study clearly illustrates that children interviewed report few restrictions placed on their opportunity to play out. Similarly Burke (2005) notes that children's photographs and descriptions of their use of the local neighbourhood appear to defy conventional public opinion. Burke suggests that, in spite of the many barriers presented in the adult designed environment, children's play patterns probably closely resemble those of previous generations. Ross' (2004) detailed study of children's play also establishes a picture of children being able to negotiate their way around their local spaces. Ross notes that many of the parents interviewed place a high priority on children's independent use of the local neighbourhood, and this has significant consequences:

> … not only for children's play experiences, but also for their social relationships. In their use of the local area children encountered and built ties with each other and with adults living and working in the area. These informal contacts are important in creating a sense of security and allowing children to feel part of a place … Most children conveyed strong attachments to their local area, naming and describing many favourite places, relating a definite sense of belonging and an ability to make their own space. (Ross 2004: 3)

These contrasting studies perhaps indicate the complexity of this issue and the fact that children do actively negotiate their way through their local spaces. As Veitch and others (2006) note from studying children's activity patterns in Australia, children's motivation and opportunity to play out will be influenced by their friendship groups, the ability to access attractive and local spaces for play, parental perceptions of the safety and desirability of children playing out, gender and cultural factors and the local social policy. O'Brien and others' (2000) study with 10- to 14-year-olds in London and a nearby New Town observes that many of the children appear to 'make do' in finding time and space in their everyday lives. Only a small minority in the study lead highly restricted lives, for example only four per cent of 10- to 11-year-olds and one per cent of 13- to 14-year-olds report not being allowed to play outside without adult supervision. In contrast to this, 23 per cent of 10- to 11-year-olds express a high degree of freedom in playing out, walking to school unaccompanied and being left at home on their own.

Yet, this is by no means an even pattern of access to the outdoors. As O'Brien and others (2000) comment, locality, gender and ethnicity are key influences in children's freedom to move around their neighbourhoods:

> In general girls and children from minority ethnic communities appeared to be more restricted in their use of urban space. Boys had greater freedom to roam and play out more independently than girls at both the primary and secondary levels. For instance, the proportions of 10/11 year old boys who could play out alone in inner London, outer London and Newtown were 84%, 87% and 93% in comparison to 67%, 75% and 82% of girls respectively. (O'Brien and others 2000: 5)

The results from detailed studies of children's access to the outdoors demonstrate the importance of seeking children's own views and use patterns of their environments because they are 'first, diverse and not unitary and, second, challenge deterministic accounts of young people as automatically excluded from public space' (Nairn and others 2003: 37). From this perspective we may see that children's and young people's use of public space is a fragmented and ambiguous relationship which can sometimes be inclusive and sometimes exclusive, and shifts over time and different spaces. As Elsley (2004) comments, understanding the heterogenous nature of children's relationship to public space must be a prerequisite for those involved in planning and policy-making.

Children in rural areas

While most of the research into children's use of their local environments focuses on urban areas, there are equally worrying trends in rural communities. As Matthews and Tucker (2006) comment, the notion of a 'rural idyll' persists as a common picture of living in the countryside. Yet recent research into the lives of children living in rural areas questions this traditional perspective. (Matthews and others 2000; Panelli 2002: Tillberg Mattsson 2002; Vanderbeck and Dunkley 2003; Giddings and Yarwood 2005). These studies highlight the constant struggles of children and young people to achieve the 'rural dream'. Rye (2006) comments that for many young people the positive aspects of a rural life co-exist with more negative perceptions of the 'rural dull', represented through expressions of boredom, a state of being non-modern and lack of opportunities.

Matthews and Tucker (2006), in their studies in Northamptonshire, comment on the confrontation, contradiction and frustration felt by children and young people in their daily transactions within rural communities.

Smith and Barker's (2001) study of children's play in rural areas concludes that there are severe restrictions on children's independent mobility. Children's opportunities to play are limited through the geographical distance between friends, the privatisation of rural land and adult concerns over children's unsupervised use of public space (Giddings and Yarwood 2005). Tillberg Mattsson (2002) notes from research in Sweden that children in the countryside had less independent mobility than children living in towns. Beach (2003) also notes the decline in children's play experiences in a rural setting in the US, attributing this to key factors such as loss of common areas for play, reduction in pathways and shortcuts, and changing school patterns. Matthews and Tucker's (2006) summary of their investigations into young teenagers lives in a rural area in Northamptonshire notes:

... far from being pastoral paradises many rural villages are desolate places for young people, characterised more often by spatialities that exclude, marginalise and persecute ... typically what emerge in their narratives are feelings of frustration, alienation and anger that play up the negative psychic and emotional aspects of their rural experience. (Matthews and Tucker 2006: 172)

147

'... for many young people the positive aspects of a rural life co-exist with the more negative perceptions of the "rural dull"...'

Institutionalisation of childhood

A significant change to children's daily activity patterns can be found in the increasing colonisation of children's lives (Thomas and Hocking 2003; Rasmussen 2004). The prevailing fears for children's safety lead adults to seek to ensure children are supervised at all times. Ginsberg (2007) comments that parents receive messages from a range of sources which clearly imply that good parenting is about developing educational skills and aptitudes from the earliest ages. This pressure leads parents to organise a range of out-of-school and out-of-home structured activities.

What used to be the children's leisure time has been transformed into organised time dedicated to different activities outside the home that are rigidly planned and usually incur some financial costs (Tonucci 2005). This increasingly structured pattern to some children's lives means that children's time for their own autonomous play is reduced; yet it is this very feature that is significant about children's play:

> Ultimately, colonisation reduces the child's opportunities to control his or her own relationship with time and space. It is not just an issue of parents taking direct control over individual children, but also of other forces in the wider society exerting greater influence, intruding more directly into childhood experience.
> (Thomas and Hocking 2003: 23)

Tonucci's (2005) review of children's opportunity to play out in Italy declares that play is a welfare parameter for urban life. His study highlights that play means 'losing time'; or losing oneself in time and encountering the world in an 'exciting relationship, full of mystery, risk, adventure' (Tonucci 2005: 186). Yet the current supervision of children lowers the opportunity for children's independent access to their immediate environments. Tonucci claims that children need free time without adult imposed agendas. Alongside this, children need a 'spring to walk towards', an exploration or search across an unlimited space and not one that is bounded, impoverished or designed specifically for playing.

Tillberg Mattsson's (2002) study of children's (in)dependent mobility in rural areas of Sweden notes the present day norm of parental desires that children are engaged in purposeful and organised activities:

> Organised leisure activities are supposed to constitute a more suitable setting for the creative development of the individual child's talents than unsupervised play in the streets. (Tillberg Mattsson 2002: 444)

'... in the past, out-of-school time was children's own time, now it is filled with extra-curricular access, sports and art lessons ...'

Similarly, Childress' (2004) study of teenagers' use of public space in the US comments on the increasing 'quasi-voluntary' nature of young people's activities: whereas in the past, out-of-school time was children's own time, now it is filled with extra-curricular classes, sports and art lessons which are perceived as more constructive and safer by parents and other adults (Childress 2004: 202). In reviewing the generational change in children's outdoor play in New York, Wridt (2004) notes the general decline of children's access to public spaces. Key contributory factors to this pattern include the lack of investment in the public parks and the increasing privatisation of and commercialisation of play activities.

As Zeiher (2003: 66), exploring children's daily experiences in Berlin, notes:

> In our cities, children play ball games in sports clubs rather than on the streets and climb playground apparatus rather than trees. Where urban areas are formed by functional differentiation, particular opportunities for and constraints on the actions of individuals are spatially fixed in specialised centres.

Zeiher's study of children's mobility in Berlin highlights the increasing location of children's places (planned and designed places specifically for children) as 'islands' scattered through the fabric of the city. Zeiher explores how each child develops an 'individual temporalised life space', a unique pattern of activity undertaken by the children in different locations. Similarly, Karsten and van Vliet (2006b) refer to the ways in which children are engaged in 'island-hopping' as they travel from one institution to another in their free time.

This pattern results in 'insularisation', with children spending their time in planned institutes and places, places that are increasingly organised around speciality, leaving little time for playing in the immediate local area. Even if there was time, the chances are that there would be few children to play with because of their engagement in the structured child-specific institutions. This institutionalisation of children also restricts their access to natural, open space; they are sheltered, fenced in and generally kept away from the elements.

Rasmussen's (2004) analysis of children's daily lives in Denmark shows how children move between three basic sites that represent corners of an institutionalised triangle. Thus, children move between the home, school and after-school facility. Each of these spaces is:

> … to a high degree designed and designated by adults as 'places for children'. The places are institutionalised to the extent that architects and planners intend them to be 'special' places for children; children spend an increasing amount of time in them; they put children into contact with 'professional' adults – the pedagogues, social workers, teachers and psychologists who staff these institutions.

In terms of children's play, there is concern about the serious pressures on children's free play time (Ginsberg 2007). Christensen (2002) comments on the temporal regulation of children's lives and their lack of ability to have a say over their use of time. She highlights the tension between children's constructs and use of time and adult ideas about what children should be doing with their time. Christensen's study of children in an urban and a rural setting in the north of England highlights the problems encountered by children in determining their use of time. Christensen notes that 'everyday' time for children is busy, and children's own use of time is threatened by the many plans and commitments made on their behalf by others. Christensen goes on to give extracts of comments from children about the difficulties of 'own' time:

> 'I'd like to have more own time but I can't really. Because like on Mondays or Tuesdays we have to go over to one of my mum's friend's houses …Then I go and do my homework for an hour and then I'll go and speak to my dad and then I'll watch a bit of TV and then I like to do reading and play games and do drawings and stuff like that. But I can't really, 'cos my day's too packed' (Caroline). (Christensen 2002: 86)

Melman and others (2007), drawing on research by Doherty and Clarkson (2002) suggest that in the US the past 20 years has seen a decline of twelve hours per week in children's free time, including a 25 per cent decrease in play and a 50 per cent decrease in outdoor activities.

149

Citing the example of 'over-scheduling' as parents feel increasingly pressured to ensure their children achieve at school, Ginsberg (2007) indicates that some children are reacting to this with increasing signs of anxiety and stress. Melman and others (2007), in their study of adolescents and participation in planned activities in the US, cites research which suggests that many adolescents may be juggling the various, and often competing, demands to participate in adult-structured activities, social clubs, expectations about academic achievement and pressure from parents about contributing to the regular household maintenance. While participation in a moderate amount of extra-curricular planned activities is seen as beneficial and enjoyable, the summary of their research indicates that the greater the amount of time students reported participating in activities, the higher the self-reported levels of anxiety. The authors acknowledge that the picture of participation patterns is complex, but their findings lead them to raise the question:

> … are we stifling children and youth's creativity and self-motivation by involving them in so many structured activities, usually under the direction and control of an adult?…. Only time will tell if there will be long-term effects on the social, emotional, and behavioral functioning of these individuals in adulthood but the results of this study suggest that overscheduling is an area of possible concern that needs to be examined in greater depth. (Melman and others 2007: 26)

Conflicting space use

Percy-Smith's (2002) research into children's and young people's views and use of the local environment highlights some key concerns expressed by the children:

Inappropriate recreational provision: Much of the planned recreational provision was of poor quality and limited function for children and young people. The research notes that supporting children's environmental needs is not simply providing single use and token opportunities but providing a network of spaces 'in which young people are free to engage in a range of activities and place uses according to their own values, needs and creative potential' (Percy-Smith 2002: 63).

Limited options for meeting up and hanging out with friends: Children express dissatisfaction with the restrictions on their use of open and public space and the conflicts that arise when this space is contested. Percy-Smith comments that younger children have access to a range of support networks, such as after-school clubs, playgroups, parents and toddler groups. But as children grow older and can move about independently then this network is no longer appropriate and the children and young people are viewed in a different way, what they described as 'getting grief'. This 'grief' was perceived as being told off for behaviours that the young people felt were normal and reasonable, but which adults perceived as socially unacceptable. Percy-Smith records the sense of alienation many young people felt within their local communities arising from their exclusion from much of the public realm and the intolerance shown by adults.

Of the children and young people interviewed in the study, nine out of ten stated that they preferred to be outside if they could, recognising this as a place of freedom. The local provision for this age group was generally seen to be irrelevant to their needs, or had a reputation that made the place unattractive. Given this, the children and young people tended to meet on the street.

Several studies discuss the conflict between children's and adults' value of space, noting that the adult desire for safety, order and visibility contrasts markedly with a child's desire for disorder, cover and loose materials (Rasmussen 2004; Thompson and Philo 2004; Ross 2004; Hart 2002). Pyle (2002) explores the nature and value attributed to open ground in urban areas. To adults, this space may be seen as 'waste ground' or a 'vacant lot' and, as such, needs to be reclaimed and developed. For most children these sites represent anything but a vacant space. As Pyle comments, they are the spaces where children can imagine, carry out their adventures, construct dens, create intimate space, search for bugs and so on.

Hart (2002) makes the point that children wish to explore a wider range of settings and have experiences beyond what playgrounds offer. Yet the adult assumption of how children use place often fails to see beyond the provision of specific places and the design for specific activities.

'... the adult desire for safety, order and visibility contrasts markedly with a child's desire for disorder, cover and loose materials.'

A number of studies highlight the mismatch between an adult construct of children's play spaces and what children value and prefer to do in their own time (Rasmussen 2004; Worpole 2003; Hart 2002; Thompson and Philo 2004; Armitage 2004; Frost 2006). Rasmussen (2004) comments that adult planners of children's space have forgotten what their own childhood play lives were like. He notes that children, as social and cultural actors, create places that are symbolic and physical in the corners of adult-planned spaces, and calls attention to:

> ... the interfaces between adults' understanding of what one can and should do in a place for children and children's understanding of this matter. From the different understandings of place that emerge ... one could ask if adults become less tolerant and accepting vis-à-vis children's places as they encapsulate and design places for children? (Rasmussen 2004: 171)

Hart's (2002) study of planning for play in New York reveals that the history of designing children's play spaces represents an expressed need to contain children, to keep them off the streets, safe from traffic and unsavoury influences. This drive to remove children from these perceived places of danger represents both a fear for and a fear of children, and bears little relationship to children's preferences – a trend that children have tended to resist. Tellingly Hart (2002: 138) notes:

> To this day all over the world, the major rationale that politicians use for play and recreation programmes is that they prevent violence and crime among children and youth. Not surprisingly, government funding often comes after rioting occurs.

Hart's exploration of the current state of planned play spaces notes the limitations that playgrounds may impose on children's potential range of play behaviours, substituting a narrow range of physical movements – running, jumping, climbing, swinging – for the more diverse and spontaneous forms of play that children display in more open, natural environments. Adult designed playgrounds also tend to isolate children from the daily life of their neighbourhoods, often through 'fencing' in children in discrete sites. As Armitage's (2004) study notes, the one thing that children tend to avoid when making decisions about their play spaces is fenced in areas; 'they simply don't like them, and will often actively remove fencing – sometimes to gain easier access, sometimes to make easier escape' (Armitage 2004: 189). What is needed, argues Hart (2004: 135), is 'not more segregated playgrounds, but a greater attempt to make neighbourhoods safe and welcoming for children, responding to their own preferences for free play close to home'.

Warpole's (2003) study of children's play outdoors largely concurs with Hart's analysis. Citing the results from The Children's Society and Children's Play Council 2002 survey, Warpole notes that the majority of the 500 children surveyed described their local parks and playgrounds as 'boring'.

> Furthermore, 45% said they were not allowed to play with water; 36% not allowed to climb trees; 27% not allowed to play on climbing equipment and 23% disallowed from riding bikes or playing on skateboards. (Warpole 2003: 3)

Warpole (2003) highlights the dissatisfaction children feel with what they are offered in terms of their play spaces and notes that increasing preoccupation with risk and fear has served to diminish the quality of play provision. Frost (2006) also explores this from a US perspective, noting that litigation and threats of litigation have made a significant impact on playground design and led to standardised and approved playground equipment. The selection of uninspiring equipment is wasteful and expensive, becomes quickly redundant in terms of play value and ignores many important forms of children's play needs (Frost 2006). Blinkert's (2004) research in Germany demonstrates that children use traditional playgrounds for a very short period of time.

It is not just children who express dissatisfaction with the provision of local play spaces. Veitch and others' (2006) research in Australia notes that approximately half of the parents interviewed raised concerns about the playground equipment, with the most common complaint being that the design of play equipment was largely aimed at younger children, and that older children found the parks boring. This had an impact on families with more than one child, as parents reported they would only go to the park if all children were happy to do so.

Barraclough and others (2004) report on developing play spaces in New Deal for Communities (NDC) projects found that there was a legacy of poor quality children's play spaces in the NDC areas; indeed some localities did not have any play areas at all. Where play spaces did exist, residents stated that 'they were generally poorly-maintained, often vandalised, in poor locations, contained old and inadequate play equipment and did not meet the needs of children and younger people of different ages and abilities' (Barraclough and others 2004: 6).

In looking at children's play needs, Warpole (2003: 3) acknowledges that children need access to good quality public space and defines this as:

> That continuous network of pavements, streets, amenity land, parks, playing fields, town squares, forecourts and curtileges (e.g. railway station forecourts, or retail car parks) and other paved open spaces which children and young people use in the course of their daily lives, and which makes up that familiar territory of place and attachment so often beloved in the literature of nostalgia in every generation.

'... increasing preoccupation with risk and fear has served to diminish the quality of play provision.'

What is evident from the review of the research literature is the tension between adult designed spaces for children and what children actually value. As Armitage (2004) suggests, this is not to say that playgrounds are not important places, but the current focus for safe and adult accompanied use denies many children the rich experiences that such spaces could potentially offer. Research indicates that children, where possible, use the available space within their local neighbourhoods to meet their ever-changing play needs. But this might not sit comfortably with adult perceptions of what children should be doing in their free time:

> When [children] have the choice they spend it outdoors in their local neighbourhoods in the places that are right for them, doing the things that are right for them and their friends. But what turns out to be the right place for them is often the wrong place for adults. This produces conflict between what children do and what adults feel they should do and in such conflicts children invariably lose. (Armitage 2004: 190)

School playgrounds

School playgrounds have been traditionally associated with children's play experiences. Thomson (2005) questions the assumption of school playgrounds affording children a degree of autonomy for their play. Her research concludes with an assertion that school playgrounds are spaces that are designed by adults to contain children and that each playground examined in her study had clear prescriptions about their use. These prescriptions create tensions for children who have to be constantly alert in their play for fear of stepping over the boundaries. She notes:

> Adults and agencies delimit the activities of, and the access in the playground. Through their control of children's games and play in this space, they explicitly and implicitly use the space to mould children's behaviour, to teach them what is acceptable and what is deviant …Their slightest aberrant movements are supervised and disciplined. (Thomson 2005: 76)

Armitage (2005: 536) suggests that the nature of school playtime is currently an area of concern for adults connected with schools. There is a feeling 'that what children do during these self-directed periods between lessons has changed for the worse in recent times'. The chief issue appears to be around a reported increase in rough play and an apparent increase in aggressive and violent behaviour. The response to this situation is often to reduce playtime at school, or even remove it altogether. Armitage notes that it has been estimated that the amount of time given to playtime and lunchtime in primary schools may have reduced by as much as half since 1971. Jarrett and Duckett-Hedgebeth (2003), noting a similar pattern in the US, suggest the increasing trend to reduce the amount of recess time in school is likely to have a harmful impact on the acknowledged benefits as discussed earlier in this section. Armitage (2005) also comments that adults often express concern that 'children don't know how to play any more', and this stance has given rise to a number of schools intervening in play time to teach children traditional games. Penn (2005) suggests that despite all the contemporary pressures, children still have their own strong play cultures.

This, again, suggests concern over the apparent purposelessness of children's use of this time. However, as Armitage notes, to most adults involved in schools, what actually occurs during school playtime is probably a mystery to them:

> What children play at playtimes in the primary schools of England and Wales today has a historical explanation in a number of different ways: despite some changes in detail, children today play much the same games at playtime as school children have done for at least two hundred years, if not more; further, not only do today's children play similar games to those of their predecessors but they play these games in similar places. In fact, many of the games that modern children play at older-designed schools may be being played in exactly the same place as their predecessors played them. (Armitage 2005: 553)

Rasmussen's study of children's environmental experiences in Denmark reviews the significance and value of school playgrounds in children's photographs. Returning to the theme of children's places and places for children, Rasmussen notes that, in general, school playgrounds represent the latter in their design and execution. Children do seek to construct their own meaningful places (citing examples of certain playthings, the caretaker's cellar, a bird's nest in the bushes) but often these are sanctioned by adult rules and prohibitions: 'You are not allowed to go in the bushes'.

Children's play in school playgrounds is also explored from a practice perspective in Chapter 5.

Concluding remarks

Chawla's (2002) comparative analysis of children's sense of place from different communities across the world notes that expressions of happiness are a reflection of children feeling that they have strong and valued roles within the local community, a sense of connectedness, space to play and meet with friends and an interesting and vibrant street life. These social advantages appear to outweigh standard economic indicators. Several of the studies took place in areas that were considerably less affluent than those studied in Australia, England and the US. Yet it is these latter studies where children expressed the highest levels of alienation. Chawla feels that the prevailing global free market, marked by rising levels of disposable income and rising consumption of material goods is not an appropriate model for considering children's development in urban spaces, pointing to the congruence that exists between:

> … the values expressed by children in the Growing Up in Cities [a UNESCO Project] and the models of sustainable development that stress a fair provision of the basic needs for everyone; beyond this level of general health and welfare for all, there must be a focus on improving the social, cultural and environmental quality of life rather than increasing material consumption. (Chawla 2002: 231)

Woolley (2006) asserts that the New Labour commitment to reduce child poverty is radical in intention. But the warning is that it may not be sufficient to remove children from economic poverty; children also need to be removed from 'the poverty of not being able to experience good quality public open spaces in their daily environment' (Woolley 2006: 57).

Returning to the framing of the notion of well-being, children place great emphasis on their ability to play out with their friends in their immediate local neighbourhoods. Failure to support this will impact on children's subjective assessment of well-being, as perhaps evidenced by Percy-Smith's (2002) study and the recent report from Unicef (2007). Evans and Pinnock (2007), in their review of the impact of the Children's Fund, note the apparent tension between, on the one hand, the individual targeting of children and measuring outcomes against gaining the skills and capabilities needed to become an adult, and on the other the value and benefits that children participating the Children's Fund projects express, such as 'having fun' and making new friends in play and leisure activities that were not previously available in their local environments. Clearly children's focus is on their current subjective well-being and quality of life, highlighting the need for services to create spaces within neighbourhoods and communities for the active enjoyment of the period of childhood.

Currently, as Blinkert (2004: 100) acknowledges, children 'more and more are living in an environment that is dangerous or boring, or often both'. They are often restricted or excluded from public space and placed in 'caretaking' spaces, and look to the 'fictions and simulations of computer games' for their adventures, what Blinkert refers to as a sort of 'dramatised childhood'.

Moss and Petrie's (2002) argument for the need for a more critical perspective on approaches to children's services provides a framework for looking at the current and potential future provision of children's spaces. The authors call for a new paradigm for envisioning children and childhood that moves away from instrumental and controlling approaches of children's services to one of providing children's spaces:

> … for provocation and confrontation, dissensus and indocility, complexity and diversity, uncertainty and ambivalence. For adults and children they are places where meanings are kept open. (Moss and Petrie 2002: 110)

Such an approach sees a shift from a narrow development of purposeful places for children, usually single purpose, to a much wider appreciation of children as members of a local community and a recognition of their needs for a wide range of spaces; from 'lightly structured space for children's outdoor, unsupervised play, to the more structured institutions encountered by children in their daily lives' (Moss and Petrie 2002: 177).

> … there is scope for many innovations, in particular making far more use of outdoor environments to support outdoor play and play provisions. Here we are envisaging more physical spaces for children, but recognising that physical spaces are also social spaces — the location of social practices and relationships — and can be discursive spaces also. (Moss and Petrie 2002: 179)

This provides a bridge into the next section of this review, where we consider the current level and effectiveness of provision made for children's play.

Chapter 5

From policy and
theory into practice:
provision for play

Chapter 2 reviewed the literature on understandings of contemporary childhood and how these are reflected in policy, Chapter 3 considered what the literature says about the benefits of playing for children's development and well-being and Chapter 4 looked at the literature on children's play patterns. We move on now to see how these aspects are translated into practice. Inevitably, there will be some overlap of material, but the focus in this section is on the practice of making provision for children's play rather than policy or theory.

Gathering the evidence on play provision

This section reviews the literature pertaining to public provision for children's play. The authors acknowledge that there is much good practice that goes on quietly in local neighbourhoods which is perhaps published in local newsletters and on websites. The scope of this literature review has not allowed for any gathering and analysis of these data, and has focused on larger scale external evaluations and academic evaluation research as well as nationally published literature. We acknowledge that this makes for a gap in the representation of provision for children's play and recommend that research be undertaken on examples of local good practice.

There is a dearth of peer-reviewed academic writing on play provision and playwork and a parallel paucity of longitudinal evaluation and research into playwork practice and other aspects of play provision. Most academic studies and national evaluations are concerned with the wider aspects of children's services and, as such, focus on specific topics such as education, neighbourhood renewal or crime prevention. Any reference to play within these studies largely takes an instrumental view of how play helps to meet these policy aims, and will therefore be underpinned by a particular instrumental view of play rather than the understandings that can be drawn from the theories reviewed in Chapter 3. Most of the nationally published literature on play provision falls broadly into four categories: theorising; practical guidance; research into practice; and published evaluation reports. In this section we have drawn to some extent on the theorising and guidance to inform the discussion, but have focused largely on the research and evaluation.

In the current climate of evidence-based policy, the place of evaluation of practice remains contested. Roberts and Petticrew (2006) query whether policy is evidence-based, evidence-informed or evidence-aware. They also question what counts as evidence: is it research-based evidence or can 'consultations, anecdotes, observations, informal knowledge' (Roberts and Petticrew 2006: 20) play a part? They argue the case for a stronger role for research-based evidence, whilst not ignoring the voices of children and young people and other sources of evidence, highlighting the need to distinguish 'sound research from sound-bite research' (Roberts and Petticrew 2006: 22). Early intervention policies for children should be well evaluated in order to maximise benefit and minimise harm. Roberts and Petticrew cite the Sure Start programme as one which took account of evidence from the research and which was also extensively evaluated both locally and nationally, although they do point out the difficulties of highlighting problems and less successful aspects of programmes within evaluation reports in a way that ensures that they are heard and acted upon.

The use of evaluation reports in this literature review has presented some challenges. As Taylor and Balloch (2005: 1) assert, 'evaluation research should be understood as inherently political'. This is not to undermine its usefulness in informing policy, rather to place it realistically within context. Most evaluation research is commissioned with the task of determining how far the project or projects have met the stated objectives as agreed with funding agencies. In the case of public funding, these will be heavily linked to social policy aims, objectives and targets. Such a framework determines the design and the focus of the evaluation, and evaluators are always mindful of the commissioners' need to show the success of the projects in these terms. Independent academic research allows for rather more freedom of focus and conclusion (and indeed frequently provides useful critiques of policies and their implementation). Both, however, are subject to what Oakley (2000, cited in Taylor and Balloch 2005) calls 'paradigm wars'. One example pertinent to this section is the tension between what is often termed a 'positivist' and a 'constructionist' approach. As Robson (2002: 16) asks:

> When carrying out real world research involving people, can we, or should we, be scientific? This question raises a wide set of issues. What does 'being scientific' mean?

Robson (2002: 19) suggests that the 'standard view' of science is a positivist one, where the underlying principle is that an understanding of social phenomena is advanced through the development and testing of theories. A positivist adopts the natural science methodologies by explaining social life in the same way as natural scientists explain natural phenomena. A positivist produces 'laws' of human behaviour and attempts to generalise from the observations to the population at large. Thus a positivist explains behaviour as 'cause and effect' and data are collected to explain that cause and effect. Positivism is based on the premise that there are undisputed 'facts' to be gathered about the social world.

Constructionists, on the other hand, highlight the difficulty of objectivity and of cause and effect in studying social life. Researchers are themselves attempting to make meaning of what they see, and inevitably they will interpret according to their particular worldview. People do not merely react to things in a predictable manner; they act on the world around them in their own attempts to make meaning of their lives.

158

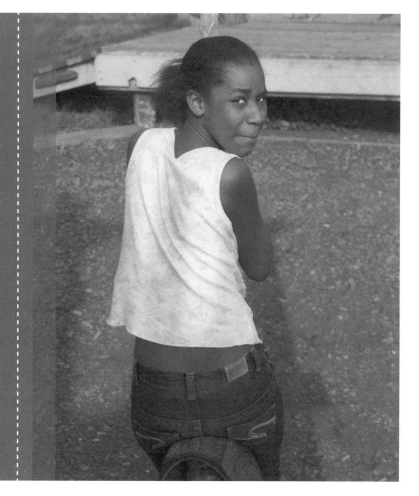

'Issues of timing and investment in valid and reliable evaluation have raised questions in the research community about "policy-based evidence" rather that "evidence-based policy".'

Evaluation of provision for play

These paradigm wars, together with the political nature of evaluation, raise questions for both evidence-based and outcomes-focused policy making, two key strands of the *Modernising Government* White Paper (Cabinet Office 1999; Bullock and others 2001). France and Utting (2005) stress the need for evaluation to be longitudinal, and even then it is difficult to attribute cause and effect, either to the programme as a whole or to components of it, and the issue of comparison with similar groups that were not subject to the interventions raises questions of ethics and reliability. There are also specific difficulties regarding public provision for children's play. If evidence from research shows particular benefits for children's play that are linked to the five Every Child Matters outcomes (DfES 2004), this may well lead to the design of specific interventions aimed at specific outcomes. These specific interventions run the risk of removing the key characteristics of play (for example, intrinsic motivation, personal control, unpredictability, spontaneity), thereby reducing the benefits that accrue from these very characteristics as outlined in Chapter 3.

Issues of timing and investment in valid and reliable evaluation have raised questions in the research community about 'policy-based evidence' rather than 'evidence-based policy' (France and Utting 2005). Mcneish and Gill (2006: 6) echo these concerns, highlighting the need for 'closer collaboration between researchers, policy-makers and practitioners to address the evidential needs of complex problems and interventions.' However, Prout (2002) points to specific influences that the ESRC Children 5-16 Programme had on policy development, whilst recognising that such direct and immediate links are rare and that the contribution of academic research is to the general discussion in which many participate.

Theoretical frameworks

The National Evaluation of the Children's Fund placed its evaluation within two theoretical frameworks: activity theory, used mainly for the case studies on partnership working, and theory of change, used as a way of evaluating the effectiveness of the programme in preventing social exclusion. Theory of change involves 'a systematic and cumulative study of the links between activities, outcomes and contexts of the initiative' (Connell and Kubisch 1998: 16, cited in Edwards and others 2006: 253).

This involves identifying short term changes which may indicate that the change programme is headed in the right direction and, in the absence of any comparative study groups, attempts to overcome the problems of attribution (in other words, how any change might be attributed to the intervention). Such an approach requires explicit articulation of how short-term changes can be linked to the long-term aims of the programme.

It is worth highlighting here the methodology employed by Creegan and others (2004) in their evaluation of the Tower Hamlets Community Play Programme. In common with the Better Play programme (see 'supervised play provision and playwork' below for an explanation of this and the Best Play objectives), this evaluation research drew on the *Best Play* (NPFA and others 2000) objectives, which acknowledge the intrinsic value of play and the characteristics of free play. The research placed a strong emphasis on the participative development of the evaluation framework with the projects being evaluated; in this way the evaluation process itself became developmental and formative as well as summative. Ten evaluation objectives were agreed upon and grouped into three categories (play provision, service delivery and children's well-being), with indicators being developed for each objective. The detail of the indicators reveals a stronger focus on organised activities rather than spontaneous play, although this is included, and the evaluation objective of children's ability to exercise choice has more indicators referring to choice between activities and involvement in planning than on flexible and spontaneous use of the environment and its resources.

> Many features of the lives of children are shaped by social policy and their futures are central to its concerns. (Fawcett and others 2004: 17)

Play provision is inextricably linked to social policy in the sense that it is a service or forms a part of a service. Banting (1979, cited in Levin 1997) suggests that services are one of the

159

three key mechanisms for implementing policy, the other two being income transfers (funding streams) and regulation (including monitoring and inspection). Whilst this conceptualisation is rather limited in its scope, neglecting broader influences such as social structures and power relations, it does provide a useful framework for analysis. However, as we have seen throughout this review, there is no overall coherent conception of children's play within social policy. This leads to a plurality of justifications for spending public money on play provision, with a parallel variance in how such services are monitored, evaluated and regulated. In addition, the risk and protection focused paradigm for policy discussed in Chapter 2 draws heavily from evidence of both effectiveness and cost-effectiveness of interventions, and is itself subject to 'stringent monitoring and, in many cases, large-scale national evaluations' (France and Utting 2005: 83).

Government initiatives such as Sure Start, the Children's Fund, On Track and New Deal for Communities have all been subject to this level of evaluation. However, long term evaluation is not always coterminous with party political drivers, and some programmes found themselves changing tack midway, thus causing confusion for the evaluation process (France and Utting 2005); similarly, local politics have a part to play particularly regarding the success or otherwise of partnership working where values and principles have to be renegotiated between agencies and sectors.

An outcomes focus

Mayall and Hood (2001) note the increasing scholarisation of children's lives in the UK, linking this with increased supervision, decreased self-determination and a particular understanding of learning. They highlight the:

> tension between the classic view that play – with its own rules, goals and activities – constitutes valuable use of time, as an enjoyable activity outside the normal constraints and concerns of daily life …, and, play as understood in the developmental paradigm, as a means of learning about the social order.
> (Mayall and Hood 2001: 78-79)

An approach to play provision which privileges the intrinsic value of playing is likely to fare poorly in an evidence-based, outcomes-focused policy and audit culture unless it can be fully understood. As we have seen, play's diversity and the difficulty in attributing direct and specific outcomes do not fit neatly within the compartmentalisation of the five Every Child Matters outcomes, particularly when the theme of enjoyment is conflated with, or rather subsumed under, achievement.

Hood (2004: 25) raises the difficulty of compartmentalisation in her discussion of the health outcome when she says:

> strategies to improve child health must adopt a broad approach which recognises that children's health is affected not only by the more traditional areas of health concern (usually physical health and social care services) but also by restricted activity, traffic danger, lack of access to appropriate play spaces, and by education policies which emphasise achievement at the expense of enjoyment.

Powell and Wellard (2008: 27) highlight the inconsistent understandings of play in their analysis of government documents that have an impact on children's play:

> The approach to delivering activities and descriptions of play appeared to rely upon the relevant departments' constructions of play (and childhoods) and their key policy drivers. For most this construction appeared to be instrumental, and so play was described as a vehicle for various outcomes. This was also the case for a range of activities (whether 'positive', 'enhancing' or 'enjoyable'). Few references stated or implied that provision for play opportunities would be made to fulfil children's right to play and / or that play means that the player has chosen and has power over the activity.

However, Clarke (2005: 31) suggests that 'even without headlining tightly defined positive outcomes, leisure and play for their own sake are important areas for children to express themselves and experience self-determination'. Very little of the evaluation literature that discusses play provision has drawn on the more recent theorising on play described in Chapters 3 and 4.

The New Economics Foundation's (2000) *Prove it!* approach to evaluation involves local people both in identifying indicators and in evaluating whether projects have met these indicators. It was developed specifically to measure the social, economic and environmental benefits of the Groundworks and Barclays SiteSavers projects, which aimed to transform derelict land into community leisure and recreation facilities, often including play areas. The approach to evaluation showed that the projects have had a measurable impact on local involvement, interaction, social capital and community safety.

The examples above can be characterised as approaches to (broadly) external evaluation of the effectiveness of interventions. Evaluation is closely linked to the planning process, particularly through audits of the quantity and quality of existing provision. Some of the tools that have been developed recently for this are discussed in the next section.

Planning for play

Making the Case for Play (Cole-Hamilton and Gill 2002) highlighted a lack of planning and strategic support for children's play at local authority level, and found that 'strategic development for play in England is inconsistent and frequently non-existent' (Cole-Hamilton and Gill 2002: 34), leading to the key recommendation that 'every local authority works with local partners to develop and promote a corporate play strategy' (Cole-Hamilton and Gill 2002: 48). Two years later, the report of the play review (DCMS 2004) recommended that the Big Lottery Fund's play programme should require local authorities to take a lead in planning for play.

PLAYLINK (2002: 13) warned against the dangers of too narrow a focus in planning for play:

> It is important that local authorities avoid the temptation to bracket off children's play into one or more forms of provision, or to represent play simply through a parks or playgrounds service-based approach.

There is some difficulty in adults planning for children's play, given the distance between adults' and children's perceptions of what makes a space a good play place, as Kylin (2003) notes:

> Adults, planners not excepted, describe and plan ... environments through an adult and professional perspective using cognitive and physical classifications. However, children mostly describe the same environment in terms of activity and meaning.

Given this, Kylin questions whether it is indeed possible to plan for children's play, since this requires more than just location, design and contents. Thompson and Philo (2004) and Ross (2004) talk of children using a range of places for their play, including those that incur adult disapproval or are away from the gaze of adults. Any planning for play needs to be informed by a recognition of this.

The Children's Play Council (CPC 2006a) produced guidance for local authorities and play partnerships in drawing up play strategies as the basis for portfolio bids to the Big Lottery Fund's Children's Play programme. The guidance encourages a holistic and partnership approach based on an assessment of need through audits and reference to children's own preferences. The Children's Play Information Service (CPIS 2007: 2) announced that, after the closing date for final applications to the Children's Play programme in September 2007, 'nearly all of the 355 local authorities in England now has a play strategy in their area, compared to less than 100 before the Big Lottery Fund's Children's Play programme was launched last year'.

The timing and scope of this review has not allowed for any scrutiny of play strategies (expected to be the focus of a separate review). Powell and Wellard (2008) included some analysis of Children and Young People's Plans (CYPPs) in their impact assessment of policies on children's play. They found an inconsistency across the plans in terms of whether play was

161

included or not, how play was understood and also how it helped to meet the five Every Child Matters outcomes. Payne and others (2006) undertook an analysis of 31 CYPPs to inform this report, cross-referencing this with the NfER (Lord and others 2006) analysis of 75 plans. They found that, whilst many of the plans acknowledged the importance of play and recreation in children's lives, there was wide variation in how play was interpreted, with sport, and structured and supervised activities predominating, and with little in the way of specific action plans, hard targets and measures to evaluate success in increasing access to opportunities to play. This focus on structured and supervised activities is at odds with the research on the benefits of play outlined in Chapter 3, which arise from flexibility and self- or peer-directed free play.

Non-statutory guidance on CYPPs (DfES 2005b) lists play and leisure services among the services to be included and also includes a paragraph on including housing authorities, specifically referring to 'the provision of quality open spaces for play and recreation, the safety of local streets and neighbourhood spaces' (DfES 2005b: 22). The guidance includes reference to play strategies in the list of plans linking to the CYPP. Consultation with children and young people, as a requirement of the development of CYPPs, varied. Approximately half of the plans reviewed by Payne and others (2006) included quotations from children and young people, and a considerable proportion of these related to play and informal recreation and issues of safety in relation to this. Payne and others note that this reflects other consultations with children and young people, specifically those carried out for the Youth Matters Green Paper, where issues of play and recreation consistently appeared as a top priority. They note the difficulty of assessing how far the views of children and young people, which tend to relate to specific wants, are translated into more general strategic policy documents.

162

Beyond consultation, the authors note the difficulty in judging how local authorities had assessed the local need for play and recreation. (For an exception, see Armstrong and others' (2005) evaluation of play provision and play needs in Redbridge below.) The authors found that only half of plans made any specific reference to play or informal recreation strategies, and several of these were described as 'in development' and several were limited in scope. Of the 31 plans, 22 made direct reference to Youth Matters, and the authors comment that this agenda places a duty on local authorities with budgets attached; 23 plans made specific reference to play and informal recreation as a specific objective or priority. Many plans make specific reference to access to play opportunities for marginalised or vulnerable groups of children. However, Contact a Family and others' (2006) analysis of 20 CYPPs found that plans for disabled children were 'vague' and had not involved disabled children and young people in the development of the plans. Finally, the report notes that, despite aspirational aims to improve access to play opportunities, there is little in the way of tangible targets or measures.

Cole-Hamilton (2006: 9) found 'widespread agreement in the play sector that if children are to have access to play provision in their own neighbourhoods and free of charge, these must be funded, at least in part, from both central and local government funds.' The planning process, therefore, needs to link to national and local policy priorities. *Strong and Prosperous Communities: The Local Government White Paper* (Communities and Local Government 2006) sets out changes to the local government planning process, with more emphasis on neighbourhoods and area-based planning. Local authorities will be required to develop Local Area Agreements (LAAs) based on four themes: children and young people; healthier communities and older people; economic development and the environment; and safer and stronger communities. There will be around 35 priorities with a single set of approximately 200 outcome-based indicators based on national priorities, a significant reduction in the current number of indicators. These outcome-based indicators will be informed by the Comprehensive Spending Review. They will be tied in to a new system of monitoring and assessment, a Comprehensive Area Assessment (CAA), which will replace the current Comprehensive Performance Assessment (CPA) (Communities and Local Government 2006).

Davis (2006a) gives guidance on how play can be incorporated into Local Area Agreements, citing evidence for how provision for play can help local authorities to meet the two themes of children and young people (linking to the five outcomes of the Every Child Matters agenda) and safer and stronger communities. An informal Children's Play Council survey (PlayToday 2007) found that local authority attitudes to planning for play had improved from the position reported in *Making the Case for Play* (Cole-Hamilton and others 2002), with one third of second round Local Area Agreements including indicators for improvements to play provision, parks and open spaces.

However, Hallsworth and Sutton's (2004) impact assessment of the changes in funding for holiday playscheme provision in a London borough found that the local authority's grant aid to community-run holiday playschemes had gradually declined to just over half over a five year period, and the authors found that children who could no longer access play provision of this nature were disproportionately from families newly arrived in the UK, Black and minority ethnic families or families where adults were unemployed. In addition, the social capital benefits of community provision were lost. They cite six shifts that have reshaped playscheme provision over the last decade, which are listed below. Some of these will be particular to the borough, but others may be applicable to other local authorities.

• The movement from open-access play to childcare.
• A movement from nominally charged-for universal services towards a market led model relying on parental fees to meet costs.
• A move from Council subsidising services towards government tax credits subsidising parents.
• A movement away from embedded community provision.
• The professionalisation of service delivery and service providers.
• A movement from universally available local services towards individually targeted provision. (Hallsworth and Sutton 2004: 5)

163

'... from the age of about eight years, children were critical of their environment, with ideas on how to improve it, voicing a desire for places to play where they felt safe ...'

Audit and assessment of need

Two key aspects of the planning process are highlighted in guidance on planning (for example Children's Play Council 2006a; Phillips 2006; PPG 17; DfES 2005b), namely the importance of an audit of existing provision and an assessment of need. There is emphasis on these being qualitative as well as quantitative and on the importance of involving children and young people in the planning process (see the section on 'participation and consultation' below). A number of tools have been developed, or are in the process of being developed, to help with audits and these tend to include some kind of performance indicators.

CABE Space (2007) has developed *Spaceshaper*, a process of gathering people's perceptions about a space across eight themes: access, use, other people, maintenance, environment, design and appearance, community, and you. Individuals complete a questionnaire, the responses are collated electronically and then there is facilitated dialogue using the results. The process aims to work with the differences in people's subjective ideas about public space rather than attempting to provide an objective assessment of the quality of the space.

Play England will be publishing local play indicators in autumn 2008 intended to assess a local authority's performance in terms of its support for children's and young people's play, either in their local neighbourhoods or in supervised settings. The indicators are:

> intended to capture the range, extent and quality of play provision and play opportunities across an area, and be practicable as both management tools and upward drivers of performance for the local authority and its partners in the delivery of 'the play offer'. (Play England, 2008)

The indicators aim to measure both quantitative (for example the time spent playing outside) and qualitative (satisfaction) aspects. There has been some concern voiced (for example PLAYLINK 2007) regarding the focus on objective measuring rather than recognising that assessing quality is necessarily a subjective process. The use of fixed scoring systems implies objective, quantitative measurements, whereas the extent to which a space is 'playable'[5] will depend on a number of variables, including social, cultural and temporal contexts. One example given is the presence of dogs, a factor that could make spaces more or less playable depending on each situation.

Armstrong and others (2005) carried out a major research project on existing play provision and play needs of children and young people in the London Borough of Redbridge, which gathered views of over 750 children and young people, 250 parents and 28 key staff, as a part of the Children's Fund requirement to gather views on services and to meet the borough's Children's Fund objective of improving access to better play and recreation opportunities. The research found that children valued and made use of a wide range of opportunities for playing, and most preferred to play outdoors but for some this was restricted by their parents, by fears or by having nothing to do outdoors. Muslim girls were most likely to play indoors. However, there were significant gaps in opportunities for play. There were needs: to increase the quantity and quality of outdoor play opportunities, particularly close to home, catering for a range of ages and needs; for organised provision run by playworkers, including adventure playgrounds, and also opportunities for less structured and supervised play; to improve access to play provision for particular marginalised groups, especially disabled children. Fears of bullying, racism, gangs and crime plus negative attitudes of adults towards children playing were key restricting factors. Play staff felt there was a lack of understanding about play and playwork and, as with other research, the tendency to conflate play with childcare, respite care or education was noted, as was the feeling among professionals that play was not valued by parents.

Camina (2004) carried out a Home Office commissioned study of four On Track areas. The study aimed to 'enhance understanding of deprived, high crime communities by exploring the perceptions of the local area of different groups living and working in the community: children,

---

[5] A term believed to be brought into current usage by Tim Gill, and used in David Lammy MP's (2007) article on the need to create playable cities (drawing on the work of the French philosopher Henri Lefebvre's concept of the ludic city).

parents, residents, local politicians and leaders, professionals and service providers.' (Camina 2004: iv). Whilst recognising the diversity of communities across factors such as income, gender and ethnicity, the research found that children were generally positive about their areas but aware of its bad reputation, which was often exacerbated by the media and by professionals working in the locality. From the age of about eight years, children were critical of their environment, with ideas on how to improve it, voicing a desire to have more places to play where they felt safe, possibly through some form of supervision. Children consistently asked for more places to play and things to do. Camina (2004: 22) notes that 'adults tend to forget just how important play spaces are to children' and observes that 'children's views are not accorded due weight in this democratic process' (Camina 2004: 43). Many playgrounds had closed, often because of health and safety concerns, and older people often did not want play areas reinstated. Local authorities were concerned about maintenance costs in the face of repeated vandalism, and Camina suggests this points to a need to take a holistic approach. Young people hanging out on the streets were seen as a problem, and the most often cited solution was to provide somewhere to go, something to do; however, in this research, though there were youth clubs available, they were seen as 'not cool', and young people preferred to hang out in places where they were in control. Camina (2004: 44) comments: 'There is a need to start from the perspective of the teenagers, to treat them as experts in their own lives, enable them to articulate their need and respond to them.'

Participation and consultation

A key focus of the Redbridge research (Armstrong and others 2005) and the On Track area study (Camina 2004) was hearing the voices of children and young people themselves. Armstrong and others used a number of methods to gather children's views, and the report recommended that these methods could be replicated elsewhere and that Redbridge Borough should continue to keep children 'in the loop' when reviewing its play services.

Chawla and Johnson (2004) identify the United Nations' adoption of the Convention on the Rights of the Child in 1989 as the watershed for children's participation. Cockburn (2005) notes that the commitment to listen to children and young people is a part of New Labour's social inclusion agenda. In 2001, the Children and Young People's Unit carried out a major consultation on a proposed strategy for children and young people (CYPU 2001a). In the same year they also published a document entitled *Learning to Listen: Core Principles for the Involvement of Children and Young People*, which gives advice to government departments on the participation of children and young people in the design and delivery of policies and services. This document also asks government departments to draw up action plans for involving children and young people in their work.

The Office of the Deputy Prime Minister (now the department for Communities and Local Government) published its action plan in July 2003, and this in turn encouraged local authorities to involve children and young people in the development and evaluation of Community Strategies, Local Strategic Partnerships, Best Value reviews and other aspects of local democracy. The action plan also included an endorsement of the National Youth Agency's *Hear by Right: Standards for the active involvement of children and young people* (Wade and Badham 2001).

Participation of children and young people has been given the status of a discrete section on the Every Child Matters website, and is a requirement in the development of Children and Young People's Plans and other areas of policy development (DfES 2005b). In 2003, the Department for Education and Skills published its handbook *Building a Culture of Participation: Involving children and young people in policy, service planning, delivery and evaluation* (DfES 2003d). It talks of a 'growing shift in UK policy requiring children and young people's participation in decisions' (Kirby and others 2003: 9). The government's views on children's participation are further embedded in policy with the Children Act 2004 and the establishment of a Children's Commissioner for England. The Act states that the Commissioner 'has the function of promoting awareness of the views and interests of children in England' (Children Act 2004, Chapter 31. Part 1: 2:1).

'When asked about their lives, children and young people consistently put play as a top priority ...'

Kirby and Bryson suggested in 2002 that more attention needed to be paid to evaluating and researching the effectiveness of participatory approaches across a number of themes, including: how children's and young people's views are used in final decision-making about policies and services; the benefits for the children, young people and adults involved; which children and young people become involved in participation and which do not; and children's and young people's competence in influencing policy-making and service delivery (Kirby and Bryson 2002).

When asked about their lives, children and young people consistently put play as a top priority and asked for more opportunities to play (for example CYPU 2002; Camina 2004; Elsley 2004 below; The Children's Society 2006) but these views are not always acted upon. This is reflected in the government's third report to the United Nations Committee on the Rights of the Child, as described in Chapter 2, where the report notes that, when asked about their lives, children say they want more opportunities to play, yet the report includes one paragraph on play in England in the main body, which refers to the DCMS publication of *Time for Play* and its support for national organisations (UK Government 2007).

A number of benefits arise from authentic and effective children's and young people's participation. Kirby and others (2003) found that acting on children's and young people's views brings benefits for services, for children's and young people's sense of citizenship and social inclusion, and in terms of personal development. Davies (2006) describes young people's participation, when carried out effectively, as a win-win situation with benefits for young people and adults alike. These include greater confidence, self-esteem and knowledge, forging of positive intergenerational relationships and challenging of stereotypes.

The Hear By Right project has developed a 'what's changed?' tool for reporting on the impact of consultation and participation, stating on the website that 'the success of participation activity must be measured by the changes that have resulted on specific issues and concerns raised by children and young people' (www.nya.org.uk).

Despite this, the 4Children Buzz Survey (4Children 2006: 4) found that

> Less than half the children (45 per cent) feel that adults listen to their opinions and views about what they want. 76 per cent think that it would make their lives better if they were treated with respect and 75 per cent if they were listened to as well. Children are still looking for more recognition and to be heard.

Elsley (2004) found that the majority of young people in her research felt that adults who were close to them did listen to them, but they unanimously said that outside their personal networks, adults did not listen to them. One respondent spoke of how she had talked several times of the need for more play facilities, complaining that the authorities often said they would provide more but then did not. Elsley cites research (Chawla and Malone 2003; DTLR

2002) which highlights the low priority given to children's and young people's stated leisure needs in regeneration plans. This is echoed by Camina (2004), who reports that adults give a low priority to children's requests for more places to play. Badham (2004) suggests that participation is not politically neutral. Whilst the rhetoric is of empowerment, such empowerment is only tolerated if it is expressed in ways acceptable to adults. Adults' attitudes to the authentic participation of children are subject to ambiguity towards children as being on the one hand separate from adults in spaces specially designed for children due to their need for protection and socialisation, and on the other as autonomous beings with rights to participation, expressing the tension between the dependent and the autonomous child (Jans 2004; Cockburn 2005). However, such ambivalence need not necessarily be problematic: children have themselves stated that they want to be both looked after and allowed some independence (Jans 2004; Madge 2006).

Much of the time, participation is about encouraging children and young people to engage in some form of democratic process, and is often underpinned in social policy by the stated desire of the government to encourage young people to take part in democratic political and civic life (CYPU 2001b). Cockburn (2005) suggests that, in reality, participation is often little more than a form of consumer survey, seeking children's and young people's views on services that they use, as Clark and Percy-Smith (2006) suggest, to give the illusion of children having a voice and to meet the requirements of social policy initiatives. Kelley (2006: 39-40) puts it more starkly:

> When we consult with children and young people, or indeed with any stakeholders, we are rarely participating in an open process of knowledge formation. Typically, we are seeking a response to or endorsement of an idea that already exists, one that we may be to a greater or lesser extent committed to.

Kelley's criticism is illustrated through the consultation process on Every Child Matters, which was dependent on children and young people firstly coming into contact with the opportunity to respond, and secondly being willing and able to read the paperwork. Opinions were sought on proposals and questions were phrased in a way which made any open discussion difficult and which required some in-depth knowledge of systems and procedures in order to give an informed response. Badham (2004) recognises the tension between this and genuinely devolving power to children and young people. Jans (2004) refers to this form of participation (for example, youth parliament, school councils, children's committees) as 'system participation': a model of democracy that has been transferred to children but with limited effectiveness because of the lack of political rights that children hold. Cockburn (2005: 114) states that membership of school councils 'tends to be by the usual selected students who are close in belief and attitudes to teachers'. Middleton (2006), writing of her experience as a member of several youth participation groups including the DfES Children and Youth Board, says that despite feelings on the part of some youth participants that the process lacks commitment and can be tokenistic, her overall view is that the trend should continue, with more emphasis on the quality of the participation methods and more involvement from children and young people themselves in designing the processes of participation, and she also calls on more young people to participate. Kelley (2006) suggests that it is worthwhile engaging children and young people in system participation, but that the discussion needs to begin earlier and be open and emergent, based on 'open knowledge' systems, which may yield a more authentic picture of children's views.

As an alternative to this systems model of participation, Jans (2004) proposes a life-world model. Key components of children's lives are being playful and making meaning of their worlds; these form the basis of their interactions with, and influences upon, their environments. Autonomy, power and control are key characteristics of free play, together with the necessity for cooperation in order to keep the play going. Jans suggests that children's playfulness is a 'child-sized' form of citizenship, it is children's way of engaging with their worlds and, for true participation of children, this needs to be recognised. Skivenes and Strandbu (2006: 13) make a useful distinction between 'child participation' and 'child perspective', commenting that there is a need for a clear understanding of what is meant by this in order to avoid what they term the 'benevolent child saver discourse' and recognise instead that 'children are seen as individuals, with opinions, interests, and viewpoints that they should be able to express' (Skivenes and Strandbu 2006: 12). This should involve recognising children as members of society in their own right, whilst accepting that special attention needs to be paid to their specific worldview and life experiences and also to understanding what children are communicating. This requires looking beyond the words spoken by children in order to try and understand the meanings of children's communicative attempts to express the world as they see it. Viewed in this manner, children's participation becomes much more than adults asking questions and recording children's answers.

When consulting children about play, a number of potential obstacles can be summarised and applied from the literature: our tendency to try and apply adult rationality as the benchmark of assessing competence (Archard 2004); our desire to maintain our power as adults (Badham 2004); the confusion of a civic engagement agenda with one of authentic participation (Badham 2004; Jans 2004); our lack of understanding of what children are saying because we are hearing it through adult ears (Skivenes and Strandbu 2006).

A number of playful ways of involving children in sharing their ideas about their play spaces have been developed. Devonplay's Playing for Real™ (Wood and Korndorfer 2005) involves a range of participatory techniques, particularly building models. Halden and Anastasiou (2007) describe the mixture of playful model building and parliamentary democracy that led to designs for adventure playgrounds where the children were involved in the fundraising, designing and building, using the company Design + Build Play. Clark and Moss (2004) have developed the Mosaic approach which combines traditional observation and interviewing with a range of child-centred participatory methods such as use of cameras, map-making and child-led tours. From their pilot study of involving three and four-year-olds in the process of changing their outdoor play space, Clark and Moss (2004: 1) identified three key elements to the success of this approach: 'the time and patience required to gather young children's perspectives, the value of group work, and the importance of making children's perspectives visible to adults with the power to bring about change'.

Burke (2005) also shows how it is possible to use visual techniques as an approach to developing an understanding of how children view their environments, which reflects children's own perspectives and allows for 'children's specific ways of seeing to be evidenced,' (Burke 2005: 28) and that 'recognises that young people are experts in their own worlds,' (Burke 2005: 30). The technique used by Burke and colleagues was to engage children (aged between seven and 11 years) as researchers rather than objects or subjects of research, giving them the autonomy to record their own lived experiences. Children were given cameras, were comprehensively briefed and asked to record where they played over the period of a week. The pictures were used in conjunction with conversations about their significance. Burke draws three key conclusions from the research. Firstly, children are capable of collecting and describing data that reveal their own lived experiences. Secondly, visual methods can engage children in talking about the meanings they attach to places and experiences. Thirdly, Burke (2005: 50) draws an interesting conclusion about the perception adults have of contemporary children's play:

> … this project presents a picture of urban childhood in the 21st century at odds with conventional adult popular opinion. In spite of enormous barriers posed by the adult-centred built environment, children will play in ways that resemble features of play known to past generations in the UK and to contemporaries in urban environments across the globe. This work challenges the popular opinion, voiced so often by parents, grandparents, teachers and other adults concerned about the condition of modern childhood, that 'children do not play like they used to'.

This would appear to present a picture of children's play patterns which is at odds with other forms of evidence (for example, Lacey 2007a; Lacey 2007b) that show a decline in children playing out. It is of course perfectly possible that children's outdoor play has declined but perhaps not to the extent or in the way that adults perceive it to have done. Details of children's play patterns are addressed in Chapter 4; the purpose of including this example here is that when children are given ways of researching their own lives, the results will often present a picture different from that expected by the adults (or from a picture derived from merely asking questions).

However, even these participative, child-led and playful ways of involving children can at times, whilst well intentioned, still be tokenistic. MacIntyre (2007: 27) offers a personal reflection 'of one playworker on how easy it is, despite the best of intentions, to get caught up in the heady world of adult agendas such as consultation, participation, targets and outputs'. Working with children to design and build playgrounds had seemed like a highly participatory and democratic process respecting children's right to have a say. Yet there were a number of contradictions between this approach and the principles of playwork. Asking children what they wanted had, at times, led to simplistic responses and the creation of facilities that the children ended up not using, preferring to play in more flexible ways elsewhere. MacIntyre suggests that playworkers need to understand about play and be able to talk about what is happening in the playground as well as asking children. Focusing on the end product of the creation of a playground could ride roughshod over the process of playing, and create fixed aspects of the environment over which children had little control once they were complete. Sometimes, the focus on fun and the pressure for fast results did not allow time for the development of a range of ideas. MacIntyre suggests that playworkers should use Hughes' (1996b) model of IMEE: using Intuition, Memories of our own playing, Experience of what works with children and Evidence from the research and literature to inform planning for play.

The themes of engagement and antisocial behaviour are addressed by Brothwell (2006), in her report of a project looking into the validity of youth shelters as a form of intervention. There was evidence to show that spaces for young people to congregate did have some value, although this was dependent on both social context and where the shelters were sited. The project then worked with groups of young people to design and construct youth spaces (a term that was felt to have more value than 'youth shelters'). The underpinning philosophy was of engagement in the creative process across a range of young people and professionals (architects, artists, youth workers and others) and of '"designing in" creativity to public space rather than … "designing out" crime' (Brothwell 2006: 26). The emphasis on creativity helped to generate a different relationship between the professional adults and the young people, one that was not always comfortable:

> Their creative dialogues were unrehearsed, allowing for the unexpected, and challenged perceptions of normality. They embroiled young people in a new pattern of 'anarchic' behaviour, not as perpetrators, but as creative co-conspirators.
> (Brothwell 2006: 26)

CABE Space (2004) also found benefits in involving young people in the design and care of public space. Through 14 case studies of involving children and young people in projects including public parks, adventure playgrounds, skate parks, gardens, wild space and 'slack space', CABE Space highlights the involvement of children and young people in public space as a right and as a benefit, both for children and young people themselves and for the wider community. Engaging children and young people in decision-making about public space helps to develop respect for different members of the community and for the opinions of others. It leads to 'buy-in', as young people have useful knowledge about how space is and could be used. The research showed that children and young people can be both keen and competent, that they 'can understand and discuss complex issues. They are capable of judging risks, taking decisions and making things happen. They are often concerned about local issues and the needs of other people, and are keen to do something to make a difference' (CABE Space 2004: 36). The skills and confidence gained in involvement in this process also help children and young people in other areas of public life.

Providing opportunities for play

Children play anywhere and everywhere, and public provision for children to play includes removing barriers to playing in public spaces, supporting play in children's services such as schools and hospitals, and unsupervised and supervised dedicated play settings. In their development of play indicators, Play England (2008) devised a framework for classifying play opportunities for children along two axes: unsupervised/supervised and dedicated/undedicated spaces for play. It needs to be recognised that these are not absolute categories: what constitutes supervision can range from no supervision at all, to informal supervision (for example, local houses overlooking a play area) to supervision by children's carers through to supervision by professional staff, all of these varying at different times of the day, week or year. Such levels of supervision can exist in places that are both dedicated to children's play or part of the general environment; spaces can have different uses at different times of the day or year. However, despite these blurred boundaries, this matrix provides a useful way of grouping the evidence from the literature on play provision.

(Largely) unsupervised places for play

Getting Serious About Play (DCMS 2004: 10) states that:

> most play does not take place on sites formally designated as play spaces ... The visible presence of children and young people making harmless and inoffensive use of public spaces is a sign of a healthy community.

Playing in the street

For many years the street was the place where children played, and many children still play in the street today, although it is almost certain that the numbers have declined (Gill 2007a). Research by The Children's Society and the Children's Play Council has shown that two thirds of children still like to play out on a daily basis with their friends, yet 80 per cent of children aged 7 to 16 have been told off for playing out, 50 per cent shouted at and 25 per cent of young people aged 11 to 16 have been threatened with violence. Nearly a third of children aged 7- to 11-years said that being told off stops them playing out (PlayToday 2003). More recently, further research as a part of the Good Childhood Inquiry found that 'children's freedom to play out with their friends is being curtailed by adult anxiety about the modern world' (The Children's Society 2007a). Research for Playday 2007 *Our Streets Too!* on street play found that '71 per cent of adults report to have played in the street or area near their home everyday when they were a child. This compares to only 21 per cent of children today' (Lacey 2007b). Whilst there is plenty of evidence to show a decline in children playing out in the street (outlined in Chapter 4), such a steep decline in numbers playing out is in contrast to ethnographic research using participatory methods that record children's lived experiences of playing out (for example, Ross 2004; Thompson and Philo 2004; Armitage 2004; Burke 2005). The discrepancy may be explained both by the different methods used to capture data (for example between what children and adults say happens and what actually happens) and also to the complexity of the nature of playing out.

The decline in street play can be attributed to a number of factors; Gill (2007) highlights two: the dominance of the car (both moving and parked) and adult permission and tolerance. The idea of home zones, developed from the Dutch 'woonerf' model, has been gaining in popularity for the last 10 years. It is based on the idea of the street as a social space, where 'design and other measures come together to create streetspace where social uses are primary and car uses secondary' (Gill 2007a: 8). As a result of the Children's Play Council and Transport 2000 campaign for home zones, together with legislation placing home zones on a legal footing and £30 million of government money through the Home Zones Challenge launched in 2001, it is estimated there are now approximately 100 completed schemes in the UK (Gill 2007a).

Research from home zones both in Northern Europe and in the UK has found the following benefits (Biddulph 2001): increased social activity; wider ranging activity and children's play;

more efficient use of carriageway space; a more attractive and visually diverse street scene; increasing levels of communication between drivers and pedestrians; reduced driving speeds; greater levels of safety.

The Home Zones Challenge Fund approved 61 applications across 57 local authorities (DfT 2005a). The final report (DfT 2005a) includes key lessons learned about the process, including the importance of building on what already exists, and ensuring maximum participation (not just consultation) from the wider community in scheme development. Gill's (2007) evaluation of the London Play Home Zones project found that the development process can be very slow: so slow, in fact, that the length of the project was not sufficient to establish Home Zones in all the chosen areas.

> The Challenge schemes are showing clear improvements in many of the social, crime and health aspects of residential areas that can provide incentives for other agencies to contribute to their development. (DfT 2005a: 24)

The Home Zones Challenge found that the main outcome of the successful home zones was a stronger community, that there was much more activity on the street and that people felt happier with their environment. Children were able to play in the street, whether formal play equipment was introduced or not, although there were some examples of where this caused tension, particularly as in some places there was a perception that the home zones attracted teenagers. Other benefits include a significant lowering of traffic speed and a reduction in crime. Longer-term benefits from these schemes have yet to be seen.

Gill (2007) asserts that home zones make a real difference to children's lives, although, as the DfT report also states, there will always be a minority of people who find children playing a nuisance. Sometimes this will have an effect on the final design and effectiveness of a home zone. In addition, 'retrofit' schemes (that is, adaptation of existing streets as opposed to new build) is very expensive, and although the government supports the concept, there is currently no further targeted funding for their development. The balance of cost, either for national or local government, against the numbers of people benefiting can appear unjustifiably high, especially as in some places the development of a home zone has added to prices of privately owned properties. Given this, the transport charity Sustrans has launched a 'DIY streets' project with funding from the Esmé Fairbairn Foundation to pilot much cheaper ways of redesigning streets in order to prioritise social over car use.

171

'... for many years the street was the place where children played, and many children still play in the street today, although it is almost certain that the numbers have declined.'

The relationship between deprivation and child pedestrian accidents has been shown (Grayling and others 2002): children from poorer families are four times more likely to be injured or killed on the roads than their better off peers. The same holds for children in rural areas from lower socio-economic groups (Christie and others 2002). There is evidence to show that the decrease in child pedestrian injuries and fatalities since 2000 is more likely to be due to 'withdrawing children from the … danger' rather than 'withdrawing danger from children' (Hillman 2006: 64). In other words, parents who own cars now chauffeur their children to school and to out of school activities, increasing road traffic volume in urban areas and placing poorer children at greater risk. In 2005 around 80 per cent of the average distance travelled by a child was by car, 10 per cent by bus, five per cent on foot and only one per cent by pedal cycle (DfT 2007). In urban areas at peak times, one in four cars is on the 'school run' (DfT 2005b). Grayling and others (2002) also suggest that the child pedestrian accident rate is disproportionately higher for children in deprived areas because they more often use the street as a playspace, not having access to gardens or safe play areas. They report that traffic calmed 20mph areas are very effective and have reduced child pedestrian accidents by 70 per cent.

Research by the DfT on attitudes to streetscapes and street use (DfT 2005c: 1) found that if streets could be redesigned, 'the three activities that most respondents thought should have priority were parking for residents, children playing and walking'.

Wheway (2007) also argues for a prioritising of children as users of residential streets. His research has shown that where traffic speeds are low, children play out. He suggests that the current strategies for tackling child obesity are based on a medical model, seeing the problem within the child and attempting to change children's behaviour: 'Obesity in children is not a disease, yet the government, doctors, drug companies and many therapists are treating it as if it is' (Wheway 2007: 26). An alternative environmental approach, through considering speed of traffic and street design, would be more in tune with children's desires to play out more and so regulate their own physical activity levels.

Appleyard (2005) reports on a project in California where cognitive mapping (Lynch 1980; Appleyard 1981) was used to assess children's connections to their local environment. Children were mostly chauffered to school and could identify few local features and expressed dislike and fear of their neighbourhoods. Following the introduction of new walkways and stop signs, the studies were repeated and the children's stories and pictures showed richer and more positive connections with and detailed knowledge about their neighbourhoods and communities.

Alton and others (2007) also found that children's perceptions of their environments differed according to whether they were 'high' (42 per cent of the sample of 9- to 11-year-olds in Birmingham) or 'low' (58 per cent) walkers. High walkers were more likely to perceive traffic as dangerous but were less likely to be worried about strangers and less likely to report a lack of parks or sports grounds to play in nearby. The research also found that children from ethnic minority backgrounds generally, and specifically Asian children, were less likely to walk than white children.

CABE Space (2004: 8) highlights how important public space generally is for children and young people:

> Parks, street corners, playgrounds, football pitches, pavements and open patches of grass and trees provide space for children to meet and play, to establish a world for themselves independent of their parents and to explore the natural and built environment around them and the people who live in it … It is not only parks and playgrounds that are important … Public space links together the space outside the front door with the playground around the corner or their friend's house across the road … These issues need to be considered at all stages of development.

Reay and Lucey (2000: 410) note that experience of public space is 'structured in all sorts of ways by broader social power relations, which include race, class and age as well as gender'.

In his consideration of the public policy implications for children's use of public space (streets and the wider public realm), the Rt Hon David Lammy MP (2007) identifies four benefits:

1. Being able to play freely and spontaneously in public spaces is what children want to be able to do. Creating playable public spaces is a highly effective way of increasing physical activity as a way of countering the rise of childhood obesity.

2. Playing out helps to create an 'encounter culture' where members of the community meet each other, with benefits for citizenship and community cohesion.

3. Contact with the natural outdoor environment has health benefits for children and also helps to develop respect for and an interest in the environment.

4. The enjoyment of playing out is of value in its own right.

Several local authorities run street play projects in school holidays where teams of playworkers organise street games sessions in residential areas; however, given the timing and scope of this review, direct contact with local authorities was not possible and so little documentary evidence was available. These projects often run in tandem with play sessions in parks and other public areas; the section below considers the work of these play rangers.

Playing in play areas, parks and other public places

Woolley (2006) notes that, following a period of neglect, there has been a revival of public policy interest in the importance and benefits of public open spaces in the last decade. Academic research on children's use of open space has been increasing in the last 40 years and is covered in Chapter 4. Kelley (2006) lists key documents that have informed policy-makers on children's use of open public space for their play (for example NPFA and others 2000; Cole-Hamilton and Gill 2002; Warpole 2003; Thomas and Thompson 2004), saying that these have helped to highlight the benefits of play for children and society and the importance of children being able to use public open space for their play and informal recreation. Woolley (2006: 49) sees this as cause for optimism, particularly in the light of funding for play provision through the Big Lottery Fund, and states:

> If such research and funding is used wisely and creatively there is the opportunity during the forthcoming years to provide exciting and challenging play opportunities for children and young people in our open spaces.

Much of the evaluation literature on play areas is concerned with the process of making improvements through neighbourhood initiatives. There is little on the use of these areas following improvements.

Barraclough and others (2004), in their evaluation of delivering improvements to play spaces in New Deal for Communities areas, found that poor public space, and lack of play space in particular, was a prominent issue for residents:

> The state of play spaces in many NDC areas is characterised by conditions such as poor maintenance, inadequate safety standards, poor provision for a range of different needs, inappropriate locations and problems associated with antisocial behaviour and crime. (Barraclough and others 2004: 1)

Although their study was small scale (eight NDC areas, with an in-depth case study of two areas), a number of generalisations were drawn in terms of the success or otherwise of play area improvement schemes. These included a recognition of the need for well-designed and well-maintained play spaces for a range of children and young people (including provision for disabled children); consultation needed to be specific rather than abstract, and to employ a range of approaches in order to engage a range of stakeholders, including older people; the relationship between engendering a sense of 'ownership' and lower levels of vandalism was unclear; a number of measures can be taken against antisocial behaviour including 'target hardening' (for example, locking gates in the evening to deter older children and young people from certain spaces), good maintenance to avoid further vandalism, appropriate location, robust equipment and use of neighbourhood wardens and community policing.

173

Similar themes emerged from Kapasi's (2006a) report of work with five community groups to pilot a guide and set of resources (the *Neighbourhood Play Toolkit*) to support the improvement of public neighbourhood play spaces and services for children and young people. A further aim of this project was to develop local community capacity and cohesion that could continue beyond the life of the project. Kapasi also reports the importance of taking a structured and flexible approach that can both stay focused and respond to unexpected events; the necessity of involving all stakeholders from the start; the need to keep consultations real and the benefits of having 'quick hit' results (for example, minor improvements, trips, play sessions) to maintain interest and morale. The project succeeded in terms of achieving 'new play areas, playschemes for older children, mobile play opportunities and funding for a new community centre' as well as other benefits: 'increased confidence in the individuals and groups who took part; greater cohesion in communities; less conflict, particularly between different generations; increased skills and knowledge in the groups; more partnerships between agencies' (Kapasi 2006: 22), although the report does not specify how these concepts were defined or measured. The report also notes that having a proactive approach and asking the question 'How can we increase play opportunities for children?' allowed groups to place children and their well-being at the centre of the process, rather than responding to children as being a nuisance or antisocial.

Children's access to the natural environment has been shown to have a number of benefits that are outlined in Chapters 3 and 4, although what constitutes 'natural' is open to question (Lester and Maudsley 2006). A growing awareness of the importance of access to the natural environment for children and young people is reflected in a number of projects. Ward Thompson and others (2006), in their report for Natural England, carried out an analysis of over 70 self-evaluated projects working with young people in wild places in both urban and rural contexts. Whilst noting the lack of robust evaluation of the benefits of these projects, most of which offered structured activities, the report notes that project managers identified a number of benefits, including personal development (for example increased self-confidence and independence), skill acquisition, development of social skills and team building, widening of horizons, environmental awareness, social tolerance and changes in behaviour.

As described in Chapter 4, Milligan and Bingley (2004) found young adults' ideas about woodlands varied from being spaces for adventure and refuge to places of fear. Young people sought safe outdoor places to relieve stress, and said that visiting woodlands can have therapeutic benefits, although use of woodland as a place of refuge in times of stress was dependent upon, inter alia, positive childhood play experiences in woodland. The report suggests

'Being able to play freely and spontaneously in public spaces is what children want to be able to do.'

that there is a role for adults in creating spaces to play in woodland where children feel safe. A number of projects that facilitate children's access to woodland are emerging, including the Growing Adventure project, the Woodland Playcentre and Forest Schools, with more projects focusing generally on children's play in the natural outdoor environment (such as Wild About Play, Wildplay, Wildwise); these vary regarding the focus on free play or environmental education.

Gill (2006) reports that the Forestry Commission supports children's play in a number of ways, for example through providing play spaces, trails and activities for children and families, as well as the opportunity for free play in woodland. The Forestry Commission's Growing Adventure project sought to offer 'ladders of engagement' providing graduated opportunities to stimulate and extend young visitors' self-directed interactions with woodlands' (Gill 2007a: 4) through focusing on three areas: nature play spaces; environmental play programmes; and independent play in woodlands. Recognising that not all children would be comfortable, or allowed, to play independently in woodlands, the Growing Adventure project sees more specific play provision such as play areas and supervised activities and playschemes as a stepping stone towards a culture that accepts children's independent playing in woodland.

Forest Schools have developed in Britain from a Scandinavian idea that sees contact with the natural environment as important from an early age. It is an educational approach aimed at whole child developmental and educational outcomes. The English network for Forest School describes it as 'an inspirational process that offers children, young people and adults regular opportunities to achieve, and develop confidence and self-esteem through hands-on learning experiences in a woodland environment' (Murray and O'Brien 2005: 11). The approach emphasises the importance of freedom to explore using multiple senses and so play features significantly, despite the educational underpinnings. As children become more familiar and confident with the woodland environment, they are supported in leading their own play and activities. The evaluation of Forest School across three counties of England (Murray and O'Brien 2005) found that the freedom, time and space to experiment in and play with the woodland environment contributed to a number of positive outcomes, including improved confidence, language and communication, motivation and concentration, knowledge and understanding, and new perspectives for both teachers and pupils.

The Wild About Play project in the south west of England was funded by the Better Play programme and ran from 2002-2005, aiming to support, develop and promote opportunities for children to play freely in and around wild spaces. The project carried out research into the children's experiences of and aspirations for environmental play, and also the experiences of adults working to support this. Findings from the children's survey showed that playing in woodland, fields, rivers or hills is relatively uncommon, with nearly three quarters of children saying they had never made or cooked on a fire and fewer than half saying they had built dens or climbed trees (Maudsley 2005). The survey of playworkers, and the work of the network itself, showed a genuine enthusiasm for working outdoors with children, with barriers being lack of access to wild places, health and safety concerns and lack of confidence; enablers were identified as training, information and support both for those working to support playing in wild places and for others such as parents, managers and funders. Maudsley (2005) highlights some examples of good practice across the south west of England, including the Wild and Away annual conference for playworkers.

Play rangers

Much of the time, play in parks and local play areas is unsupervised, other than by parents and carers, and informal levels of supervision. In the last decade there has been a growth in the number of 'detached' playworkers whose main aim is to support children in accessing their local parks and other open spaces, where fear of older children or other adults using the park, lack of parental permission, lack of will or other factors, have prevented this access. Both parents and children express high levels of fear of bullying in public parks and playgrounds (Bath and North East Somerset Council 2006). One example of such a service is the Community Play Ranger service in Bath and North East Somerset, whose main aims are defined as 'to encourage children to play outside and make more use of parks and open spaces all year round; to reduce children's fears of bullying; and to help children to feel that they have someone to listen to their needs and turn to for advice' (Rees-Jones 2007: 6). These aims draw directly from the top issues highlighted by children in a consultation carried out in 2002 by the local Children's Fund Board to find out what made children happy and what would improve their lives. Follett (2007) outlines the key philosophy behind the Community Play Rangers as being to work with communities to facilitate children's access to public open spaces, using both community work and playwork skills. Working all year round allows for more stable relationships to be built between playworkers and children than could take place within temporary playschemes and, in addition, the scheme responds to children's stated desire to play outside. The project began with funding from Better Play, grew with funding from the Children's Fund, and a discrete training course for Community Play Rangers is currently being developed by Playwork Partnerships (based at the University of Gloucestershire) and Wansdyke Play Association, the current managers of the Community Play Ranger Service in Bath and North East Somerset (Follett 2007).

Those responsible for public provision for play need to recognise children's desire and need to play anywhere and with everything (Ward 1978) and think beyond 'places for children' to 'children's places' (Rasmussen 2004). This may be little more than a question of attitude, as the case of the staff and management at Somerset House in London shows. As described in Melville (2004), 55 water jets (the Edmond J Saffra Fountain) were installed in the courtyard of these 18th century buildings. The jets rise and fall in computer-controlled patterns. The original intention was aesthetic but it has proved irresistible to children, young people and adults as a place to play. Melville (2004) says, 'Management is meticulous but unobtrusive … though children's free play in the water was an unintended consequence of installing the fountains, the Trustees now actively support it.'

This section has considered public provision for children's play in public places, both in dedicated play places and in parts of the general environment. As described in Chapter Four, children and young people use their local environments in a number of different ways, playing in both designated and general places, with varying levels of adult approval or disapproval. Melville (2004: 2) decries the tendency 'to circumscribe [children's] outdoor play with monotonously conceived, fenced "reservations" that are held to be safe. These reservations are to be found the length and breadth of the land, sad monuments to a widespread misunderstanding of what children want and need.' Gill (2007b) suggests that overprotection of children and the reframing of childhood and youthful boisterousness as antisocial or dangerous behaviour is harmful for children and presents obstacles to the development of resilience. He recognises that the culture of risk aversion is strong and well embedded, and that the move from a philosophy of protection towards a philosophy of resilience is not a simple one:

> Opening up the public realm for children requires strong leadership and a willingness to overcome other imperatives and confront powerful opposing interests. (Gill 2077b: 82)

Supervised play provision and playwork

Some 132,730 people are employed in the playwork sector in the UK (SkillsActive 2006a) across a number of roles (for example, face-to-face playwork, management, development, training) and a number of settings (breakfast clubs, after school clubs, holiday playschemes, play centres, adventure playgrounds, play buses, parks and open spaces, prisons, community and religious centres, family centres and more) (SkillsActive 2005; SkillsActive 2006b). The role of the playworker is generally accepted as facilitating play for children and young people aged 4- to 16-years-old in their out of school time (SkillsActive 2006a). What this means in practice is the subject of some debate within the sector, and varies depending on setting, although there are National Occupational Standards for playwork that are underpinned by a set of Playwork Principles (Playwork Principles Scrutiny Group 2005). These Principles replace the Assumptions and Values drawn up in the early 1990s to accompany the first set of National Occupational Standards. They are informed by a number of publications including *Best Play* (NPFA and others 2000) and *First Claim* (Play Wales 2001), based on Hughes' (2001) model of evolutionary playwork. The underpinning principle is that play that is freely chosen, intrinsically motivated and personally directed is of evolutionary significance and essential to children's well-being and healthy development. Given this, the role of the playworker is one of creating a physical and social environment where children can play freely rather than organising and directing activities aimed at particular instrumental ends.

This presents a number of tensions for playworkers, parallel to but distinct from the debate about play in early years settings (see below), particularly around the extent to which playworkers intervene in or direct children's play. The evaluation literature on playwork practice is often framed by the need to show how supervised play provision contributes towards social policy agendas (for example Manwaring and Taylor 2006), and *Planning for Play* (Children's Play Council 2006a) contains a section on how children's free play contributes towards the five outcomes of being healthy, staying safe, enjoying and achieving, making a positive contribution and achieving economic well-being (DfES 2004). Conway (2003: 103) suggests that playwork itself is an intervention aimed at compensating for the loss of play space in the general environment (through traffic, fear, agribusiness and other factors), yet is subject to being channelled into producing 'educational, social and ultimately economic outcomes in the wider interests of a complex and fast-moving society'. He recognises the difficulty of playwork trying to 'square the circle' of recognising play as being freely chosen and personally directed when the playwork offer is only available in designated spaces and designated times, and of the tendency of playworkers to see the equipment and the activities as the core of their work, rather than the playing of children. The core of professional practice should be 'the symbiotic relationship between [children's] play and the playwork culture, in which children's play shapes and drives the playwork response' (Conway 2003: 113).

Yet, as Russell (2006: 6) states:

> Supporting children's play is not straightforward. Our … tendency as adults
> is to protect, teach or socialise, and this construct of adult-child relations is
> deeply embedded in the current social policies relating to children and young
> people. In addition, children's play can elicit powerful feelings in us for a variety of
> reasons, which may in turn lead us to curb those play expressions that make us
> uncomfortable or anxious.

This can lead to a gap between theorising about playwork and the evidence base for these theories in practice, although there are signs that this is changing with some small-scale accounts of application emerging (see Russell 2006; Smith and Willans 2007; Hughes 2007 below and F Brown 2007). However, there is a need for more rigorous research into the relation between playwork theory and practice. Given this gap, it would seem appropriate to include in this section of the literature review, a brief overview of current theorising on playwork.

Three models of playwork are presented under the heading of 'theories of playwork' in Brown (2003): Brown's 'Compound Flexibility: the role of playwork in child development'; Hughes' 'Play deprivation, play bias and playwork practice'; and Sturrock's 'Towards a psycholudic definition of playwork'. Both Brown and Hughes take the line that playwork is a compensatory activity: opportunities for free play in the general environment are so restricted as to present a threat to children's healthy development, and sensitive playwork can help compensate for this lack. Brown's model of compound flexibility describes a virtuous circle (or, more accurately a spiral) of flexibility in the environment, stimulating opportunities for play and experimentation, leading to development of self-confidence and self-acceptance which, in turn, develops the child's adaptability and flexibility to respond to flexibility in the environment and so on. Play is a crucial element in this process. Playwork, therefore, should aim to create environments that are flexible enough to support this spiral of compound flexibility. Interventions are justified if they are at the request of the children: 'the first rule of playwork is to work to the child's agenda' (Brown 2003: 80). Drawing on previous research into play value, and the use of this research in therapeutic work with children in a Romanian orphanage (Webb and Brown 2003), Brown suggests 11 headings for assessing the play value of any setting: freedom; flexibility;

177

socialisation and social interaction; physical activity; intellectual stimulation; creativity and problem solving; emotional equilibrium; self-discovery; ethical stance; adult-child relationships; and general appeal.

Hughes (2003) suggests that playworkers can offer compensatory play experiences for children who experience play deprivation and play bias (a narrow band of play experiences resulting in a deprivation of other experiences). Such children may well display challenging behaviour, be withdrawn or engage in fantasy driven behaviour. Hughes proposes that a playwork response to this would be to offer play experiences that could balance the deficit, rather than more traditional behaviour management approaches. Hughes' ideas on evolutionary playwork (described in detail in Hughes 2001) are drawn from a belief that play is an evolutionary mechanism and that playwork based on ideas of socialisation and induction into adult society can be counterproductive and may be unethical. The ideal context for the expression of the child's biological drive to play is in adult-free environments; since these are increasingly restricted, evolutionary playwork seeks to support the play drive and to privilege this over societal agendas.

Sturrock (2003) also suggests that playwork can be healing, and draws on psychoanalytic theories to develop a particular understanding of the child at play and the playworker in service to the playing child. Children's playing can be seen as a form of free association, an expression of latent material. Successful playing out of internal fantasies can help prevent the development of neuroses. Playworkers should develop an appreciation of the impact that children's playing has on them, particularly in terms of their own unplayed out material. In understanding the deep symbolism of playing in this way, playworkers can engage with children to support the expression of this material, a process that can ultimately be healing (Sturrock and Else 2005). Earlier work by Sturrock and Else (1998) introduced the notion that play takes the form of a cycle with six component parts and that the enjoyment children derive from playing out the full cycle is crucial to healthy development. The cycle takes place both in the internal world (the mind) and the external world of the child. The starting point they term the 'metalude', and this is the moment of imagination or daydreaming in the child's mind which results in their issuing a 'play cue'. This cue can be verbal or non-verbal and is an invitation to another child or adult, or to an object or the environment. Play cues are issued with the expectation of some kind of response: if a positive 'return' is made (either in terms of a person joining in the play or in terms of sufficient flexibility or interest from an object or the environment) then a 'play frame' is created. The play frame forms a boundary that separates what takes place within (play) from what is outside, and can be created by physical boundaries, rules, rituals and narratives as well as play faces and body language (metacommunication) which tells the players that this is play and not for real. Once the cue and return have been established within the play frame, then 'play flow' takes place; this is where the players become engrossed in the content, narratives, themes or exchanges of the play frame. Sturrock and Else term the sixth and final element of the play cycle 'play annihilation', and this refers to the moment when the players decide to bring the cycle to an end. Often this moment is misunderstood by adults who may see it as destructive and attempt to maintain the playing. Sturrock and Else go on to explore how the playworker can support children in their play cycles and they identify four levels of intervention whose sole purpose is to maintain play frames as long as the players desire them to be maintained.

Sturrock and others (2004) acknowledge the tensions faced by playworkers both from their own values and beliefs and also from the expectations of other adults (for example funders, managers, parents) on what their role should be with respect to caring for children. There are times when intervention is necessary, either to prevent serious harm or injury or to support the play. Given this, they propose that playworkers find themselves operating on a continuum of responses to children ranging from, at one extreme a 'didactic' response which seeks to teach and direct, through to a 'chaotic' response, which is either negligent or privileges the play desires of the playworker over those of the children. Poised dynamically between these two extremes is a 'ludocentric' response: one that aims to support children's playing. These responses are behavioural; running in parallel to this behavioural continuum is an internal emotional continuum of responses.

'... playwork based on ideas of socialisation and induction into adult society can be counterproductive and may be unethical.'

Aspects of the work of Hughes and Sturrock and Else were applied in a study of how playworkers could work with children with challenging behaviour in two mainstream play settings (Russell 2006). In an action research project playworkers drew on a range of theories of children's play, specifically theories relating to power and identity (Sutton-Smith 1997), the therapeutic value of play (Sturrock and Else 1998) and emotional health (Sutton-Smith 2003), to explore the relationship between playing, behaviour and the role of the playworker. The playworkers used tools drawn from playwork theories (play types and play narratives: Hughes 2002; play cues and play frames: Sturrock and Else 1998) to draw up play profiles of seven children displaying challenging behaviour. In facilitated group meetings, this information was used to develop a discrete playwork analysis of the children's play and non-play behaviour, and to explore ways in which playworkers could support the play of these children rather than manage the behaviour. The playworkers reported that this allowed them to understand the behaviour that had been considered challenging in a new way, as part of a more holistic understanding of how each child plays. They then worked to develop ways of helping children to establish and maintain play frames where the desired narratives could be expressed in ways that did not disrupt the playing of others or threaten safety. Overwhelmingly, the playworkers felt more relaxed about the behaviour and, as a result, more able to respond 'ludocentrically'. This, in turn, had a positive impact on the general, playful atmosphere of the setting.

Similar tools were used in a case study described by Smith and Willans (2007). Layla, a 10-year-old girl with Athetoid Cerebral Palsy and dysarthia, was perceived by staff and other children as naughty and spiteful. Using concepts such as play cues and play types, together with an understanding of modes of communication, playworkers were able to understand how Layla wanted to play and to respond to this, and through this to find ways of reducing her spitefulness that could be understood as frustration at not being able to play in the way she wanted.

Hughes (2007) reports on a project with Islington Play Association exploring how far environmental modification to adventure playgrounds can lead to an increase in locomotor play. 'Dead space' on the playground sites was identified, and instruments developed to measure its use for locomotor play through video recordings. New play structures were designed and built, with the intensity of locomotor play being measured post-modification in the same way as prior to modification. At the time the report was written, the project was ongoing, but early indications showed an increase in locomotor play of between 30 and 50 per cent, although it is recognised that novelty plays a key role in use and therefore may not be sustained over time.

Best Play: What play provision should do for children (NPFA and others 2000) has proved to be a key publication in terms of balancing the need to show both the instrumental and intrinsic value of play provision. The seven objectives for play provision articulate the importance of choice and control, and acknowledge that children's play can sometimes be challenging and risky. The first four objectives can be more easily assessed than can the last three, which tend more towards outcomes than objectives (NPFA and others 2000: 8):

1. The provision extends the choice and control that children have over their play, the freedom they enjoy and the satisfaction they gain from it.

2. The provision recognises the child's need to test boundaries and responds positively to that need.

3. The provision manages the balance between the need to offer risk and the need to keep children safe from harm.

4. The provision maximises the range of play opportunities.

5. The provision fosters independence and self-esteem.

6. The provision fosters children's respect for others and offers opportunities for social interaction.

7. The provision fosters the child's well-being, healthy growth and development, knowledge and understanding, creativity and capacity to learn.

These objectives, together with the values of playwork from the same publication, and the quality areas listed in *Quality in Play* (Conway and Farley 2001), a quality assurance scheme for play settings, have provided the theoretical underpinning for a collection of stories about playwork in practice (Head 2001). The introduction states (Head 2001: 3) that 'the stories show the reasoning, beliefs, commitment and imagination that underpin the development of the play environment and the people within it.' The stories show the micro-detail of supporting play, which is sometimes lost in the grand theories, definitions and focus on outcomes.

The Better Play Programme, a four-year, £10.8 million programme delivered by Barnardo's and the Children's Play Council in partnership with the New Opportunities Fund, funded 225 projects over three rounds. The programme aimed to encourage communities to take part in providing play opportunities for children to play safely within their neighbourhoods, particularly those from disadvantaged areas. The evaluation of the programme (Youlden and Harrison 2006) was carried out against both the programme aims and the seven *Best Play* objectives (NPFA and others 2000). Although the evaluation found that the case study projects met the *Best Play* objectives, there were some provisos and recognition that the objectives are open to interpretation. For example, not all of the six case study projects worked to a definition of play as being freely chosen, personally directed and intrinsically motivated; in these projects freedom of choice was understood as choice between activities rather than self direction. Youlden and Harrison identified four levels of choice within these two points, and concluded that even in the projects where playful activities were mainly adult-led, the children enjoyed themselves, but in the projects where children's play was freely chosen, the children were more effectively supported in developing independence and the children themselves felt respected and valued. They found that the quality and experience of staff were important factors in the effectiveness of projects and that:

> the presence of skilled and experienced playworkers enhanced the range of choices children had and children were able to exert control [developed over time in many of the projects] through opportunities to state their preferences either through group consultation or through one-to-one communication with playworkers. (Youlden and Harrison 2006: 6)

Youlden and Harrison also developed a tool for evaluating how far projects had met the *Best Play* (NPFA and others 2000) objective five ('The project fosters independence and self esteem'), based on an adaptation of the Rosenberg (1965) Self-esteem Scale and parent questionnaires. This, together with their evaluation of the degree of choice and personal direction within each of the projects evaluated, contributed to the reliability of the findings, although the authors caution that the limitations of methods and data reduce the validity of any claims for cause and effect in terms of longer term benefit. Notwithstanding these limitations, the report found that although the six projects evaluated varied across four levels of choice and control (ranging from free play to adult controlled activities in which children were expected to participate), levels of satisfaction and development of independence and self-esteem were high, including in the projects catering for specific groups of children (for example, Traveller children, disabled children from Asian communities, and those affected by mental health issues or violence).

Creegan and others' (2004) evaluation of the community play programme in Tower Hamlets devised a detailed framework of indicators and gathered data from children and young people, staff and parents, using a number of methods. Again, the *Best Play* objectives, together with programme objectives, formed the framework for the indicators. The evaluation showed a high level of enthusiasm and enjoyment on the part of the children. Variety was important in sustaining this, and the space available had a big influence on what took place within it. The level of 'free play' (children directing their own spontaneous play) varied both among and within projects, and there was a sense of more structured projects moving towards more free play over the time of the project. The playworkers talked about a range of ways in which children tested physical, social and behavioural boundaries. Boundaries were in place in all projects in the form of both formal and informal rules, with varying degrees of understanding about how strictly these would be enforced. Risk was accepted as an important aspect of playing that could not be factored out but which needed to be assessed and managed within this understanding. Playworkers were concerned about the compensation culture, but parents generally understood about risk and their confidence was linked to their trust in the playworkers. Both parents and playworkers felt that children were safer at the project than on the street. Creegan and others were able to gather some data and draw some positive conclusions regarding concepts such as confidence, well-being and respect for others; however, these are presented in a tentative and cautionary manner, with the recommendation that long-term evaluation with multiple and measurable indicators needs to be carried out.

181

Community involvement in play provision was also the focus of the Equipe-funded Cornwall Neighbourhoods for Change (CN4C) Playschemes on Social Housing Estates project (Pearce 2006). The philosophy here was to work in partnership with others to engage communities in local play provision. Initially this meant working with local tenants and residents associations to put on one-day play promotion events and then supporting interested local parents, volunteers and professionals through development work and training to develop playschemes and other play provision. The evaluation found that running the one-day events over three years was successful in brokering sustainable local partnerships, enabling some continuation of community-based play provision in areas of social housing beyond the life of the project.

Hunt and Kapasi (2005) also highlight the reciprocal relationships that can be fostered through involving people in local communities in developing or improving play provision in their areas, and suggest that effective support for this can have long term benefits both for children's play provision and for community cohesion.

In Franklin's (2002: 32) study of children, staff and parents at adventure playgrounds across Lambeth, Southwark and Lewisham, most senior playworkers interviewed said that their role involved 'making sure they created a safe environment with stimulating activities'. Yet the meanings of the words 'safe' and 'activity' are contextually specific here. The children said that 'chatting and hanging around' was the most popular activity, closely followed by off-site activities and using the play structures. Activities that might be perceived as more specific, if not structured, such as formal sports and arts and crafts, scored the lowest. In this sense, the term 'activity' is understood by the young people as covering everything you do, rather than something that has to be planned or structured; however, creating an environment where children can mix structured and unstructured activities still has to be planned. In terms of safety, it was recognised that risk taking is an inherent part of playing and that the playworkers had a complex responsibility in making judgements regarding the design of the structures and the physical environment generally, and also in terms of the expectations of how young people behaved within the playground (the culture of the settings). For example, playworkers felt that many accidents occurred during children's first visit to the site, when they were unfamiliar with both the structures and the accepted ways of using them. The survey found that, generally speaking, the adventure playgrounds 'managed the balance between the need to offer risk and the need to keep children safe from harm' and that 'accidents, particularly serious accidents, were rare', although the need for greater consistency in recording accidents was noted (Franklin 2002: 36).

Manwaring (2006) gathered the views of children and young people aged 4 to 16 years who used supervised play provision (after school clubs, adventure playgrounds and holiday playschemes). Though urging caution due to an inevitable adult interpretation of children's own views, she extracts a number of key themes from the focus groups. In terms of what children want from a play setting, Manwaring (2006: 6) summarises the most important factors as:

> freedom, choice and control over what they chose to do, space to do their own thing and access to the outdoors, a variety of toys, equipment, trips and things to do, friendships with other children and their relationships with staff. In discussion, all the children across the different play settings agreed that they wanted freedom and choice and ultimately to play and have fun.

The Venture, an adventure playground in Wrexham set up in 1978, has managed to respond to social policy initiatives and still retain the central ethos of its core purpose as an adventure playground. Brown (2007) describes how the playground has, over its 30 years, received funding to run specific projects (for example, Intermediate Treatment, a mentoring programme, sports funding for a multi-use games area) alongside the core work of the adventure playground, including in their project funding bid a sum of money to pay towards the core. Such an approach works because of other factors, for example, the involvement of staff in local politics (as councillors and chairs of key committees), genuine involvement of children, and being rooted firmly in the local community. The Venture works with an explicit core philosophy:

'The children said that "chatting and hanging around" was the most popular activity, closely followed by off-site activities and using play structures.'

182

Give children a safe, staffed, open access play environment and they will not be able to resist the temptation to play. It is assumed at The Venture that children are biologically predisposed to playing, and once they start, their whole life is affected. The most fundamental lesson from practice is that play works.

For the staff at The Venture, play is the base from which their relationship with the child and the community starts. Even today, when the project has become multifaceted, play is still the core activity … Justifying this to external funding agencies can sometimes create problems, and it is tempting to take refuge in simplistic justifications such as crime reduction, social inclusion, educational attainment, etc. However that would undervalue something the staff regard as the focus of their work. (F Brown 2007: 24–25)

Brown (2007: 25) lists a number of values and principles underpinning the work of The Venture, including a fundamental child-centred approach which includes enabling children to create their own play space; being non-judgemental and non-stigmatising; avoiding 'adulteration' of play; working with and not giving up on the most challenging children and young people; employing home grown staff; community involvement; and reflective practice.

Out of school care

A recent survey of the playwork sector found that most respondents worked in settings 'either based on school premises or connected with schools in some way' (SkillsActive 2006b: 12), although the open-ended nature of responses made it difficult to give a precise figure. The assumption here is that these settings are childcare settings; the unprecedented growth in out of school childcare (Barker and others 2002) has taken place alongside a reduction in open access play provision (Head and Melville 2001; Hallsworth and Sutton 2004; Play England 2006). Barker and others (2003: 8) note that 'schools are becoming increasingly significant sites for the location of after school clubs'. Their research shows that relationships between out of school clubs and the school in which they are sited vary, with some clubs having separate accommodation, philosophy, staff and administration (and one where children changed out of their uniform) to others being fully integrated into the school, with curriculum-based activities and sometimes with children calling staff by their surname. This has an impact on the ethos of the club and particularly on children's relationship with staff. Where the out of school club had a different philosophy to the school, playworkers saw this as positive, as a break from the demands of academic achievement and a chance for free play. Some children found the switch from school to out of school difficult, particularly if some of the staff worked both in school and in the out of school club. Barker and others' assessment of the impact of out of school care is based on the social, educational and economic benefits and on barriers to accessing services. The impact was found to be generally positive (yet sounding a note of caution on the difficulties of attributing impact to the out of school club as distinct from other aspects of children's lives). Although it is acknowledged that children do play in out of school clubs, and that many value their out of school clubs because of this, no judgement is made in this report between the relative value of clubs that support free play and those that continue the school curriculum and a more formal academic ethos.

Earlier research by Smith and Barker (2000) highlights the role of out of school care in the increasing institutionalisation of childhood, and considers the power relations between playworkers and children in the negotiations of children's use of space and time within out of school clubs, finding that the wider school context has an influence on this. Although most children saw the out of school club as a place to play, most of the activities offered were planned and organised by the playworkers. Despite this, the research showed that the children found numerous ways to contest 'both the activities provided by adult staff and also adults' control over the way space was used and structured' (Smith and Barker 2000: 248). Examples given were the ways in which children would adapt planned activities for their own play, and also the popularity of dens as adult-free spaces. Playworkers' responses to this were dependent on the age and gender of the children: the efforts of younger children and girls to control their own play were generally seen as innocent, playful, or as examples of playing nicely, whereas similar attempts by older boys 'were treated as a hostile attempt to subvert the workings of the club' (Smith and Barker 2000: 249). Playworkers also found themselves imposing the boundaries for behaviour that were expected of the school as a wider institution, even if these did not match their own understandings of the role of playwork. In some cases, teachers would carry out both covert and overt supervision of the playworkers and at times would take charge if they felt the playworkers were not controlling the behaviour of the children adequately.

Similar issues of control of space and time in out of school care are discussed by Mayall and Hood (2001) through the lens of children's participation rights. In their case study out of school club, children and young people were involved in its development and in determining the ethos and activities of the service. Mayall and Hood emphasise the importance of the informality of the service, and suggest that youth workers and playworkers are better placed to work with children in this kind of setting than teachers. They note that the service also catered for drop-in use, as well as formally arranged childcare, and that the level of drop-in use showed that the service offered something that children chose to use.

The research on children's own views on out of school care consistently shows that they value being able to socialise with friends and having control and direction over their own playing, they want to be able to play outside, they want staff that are caring, friendly, helpful and playful, and they want to be treated with respect and to have a say about how the club is run (Mooney and Blackburn 2003).

Smith and Barker (2004: 3) cite international research sources that show the following possible benefits of out of school care as being:

> the opportunity to play and make new friends in a safe environment, the development of social skills and social competence, improved self-confidence, improved mental health outcomes, a reduction in problem behaviour in school, more positive relationships with schools and possible benefits in terms of raised educational attainment.

Yet they stress that the difficulties of showing any direct causality between these outcomes and out of school care itself in isolation from other aspects of children's lives. Their own small-scale qualitative research backs up the previous research in that it found that good quality out of school childcare 'provides a safe, dedicated and well-equipped space for children's free play' (Smith and Barker 2003: 7). Being with friends and making new friends was seen as important by children, and adults felt that this opportunity helped children to develop self-confidence and social skills.

The impact of out of school care on the economic status of families is clearer. The government's expansion of childcare is a key element of the commitment to eliminating child poverty. Smith and Barker (2004: 2) elaborate:

> In order to measure the success of this policy the government has set a number of key targets, including a 70 per cent employment rate for lone parents, a 12 per cent reduction in the number of children living in what are termed 'workless' households by 2006.

As a part of this strategy, funding was made available from the New Opportunities Fund for out of school clubs in the top 20 per cent most deprived wards in England (New Opportunities Fund 1999, cited in Smith and Barker 2004). Using a questionnaire with parents, interviews with playworkers and a range of child-centred qualitative methods with children across six case study clubs, the research found quality provision can have a positive impact, both economically and socially and also in terms of providing opportunities for playing that would not otherwise be available. The greatest potential was for benefiting children and families at risk of social exclusion; however, since provision is not universal, and since access is dependent upon parents' ability to pay, it is therefore not inclusive. The study found that those least likely to access the clubs were those living in deprivation and those from minority ethnic families generally, and, in these case studies, from Somali and Bangladeshi families in particular. For the children from minority ethnic families, barriers were cultural as well as economic. Playworkers spoke of the concern at having to survive purely on fees, since this excluded families who could not afford the fees and did not qualify for tax credits. The research sample was small and only involved families already using out of school care.

Play in schools

Some aspects of the literature review on play in schools can be found in Chapter 3, under the 'play and learning' heading, particularly literature on the relationship between play and learning. Sources included in this section pertain more to issues of policy implementation, service provision and professional practice.

Extended schools

Childcare is part of the core offer of the government's extended schools programme and the importance of children being able to play in these services is explicitly acknowledged (DfES 2005c). However, concerns have been expressed that the extended schools agenda has too heavy an educational focus (Barnardo's 2006). It is recognised that extra curricular activities such as study support, sport or music tuition can benefit some children, but those who have negative attitudes towards school, dislike teachers, or whose home life is not supportive of study are unlikely to engage with study support (Education Extra 2003, cited in Barnardo's 2006). Barnardo's small-scale research compared qualitative data from out of school care in rural, suburban and urban settings in Denmark and England. Although schools had many resources that were underused out of school time, shared use presented a number of challenges. Independent facilities helped children to view the out of school care scheme as separate from school and freed the service (both staff and children) from school norms and culture, making for a more play-friendly space. Children in Denmark had more access to challenging outdoor play spaces than their counterparts in England. The research also found that:

> good play opportunities in English schools often relied on one highly motivated, very energetic personality ... with a background in playwork. Where no such 'personality' was present, after school clubs tended to be less play focused and more controlled or 'school like', with fewer choices and fewer opportunities for children to control their play and activities. (Barnardo's 2006: 5)

The research concludes that if extended schools want to engage those who are alienated from mainstream school culture, more thought needs to be given to making extended school opportunities culturally distinct from the core school day.

Davis (2007) cites the Rt Hon Beverley Hughes MP, Minister for Children, Young People and Families, as emphasising the importance of play within this agenda:

> ... particularly but not exclusively for young children, play is a very important part of the concept of extended activities in schools. Indeed, the prospectus that we published made it clear that we want play to be an important aspect. Children should not just have study support and curriculum-focused activities at the end of the day; we want them to relax and unwind in a secure and stimulating environment. (Hansard, 27 April 2006)

Ofsted (2006, cited in Davis 2007) has recognised the importance of quality play provision within the extended schools agenda, of working with the play sector and employing qualified playworkers.

Pace (2006) carried out research with local authorities and key support organisations (4Children, ContinYou and the Training and Development Agency) across the south west of England, to make an early assessment of the potential for schools and partners to employ and train playworkers for appropriate extended school services such as out of school childcare. The findings include a shortage of playwork-qualified playworkers and possible recruitment difficulties, a need for transitional qualifications between early years and playwork, unclear funding sources for playwork training if outside of the Transformation Fund and unclear financial sustainability for out of school clubs.

'... playtimes and lunchtimes in primary schools in England and Wales have been reduced by as much as a half since 1971 ...'

Playtime and school playgrounds

Section 6 (1) of the Education and Inspections Act 2006 requires local authorities to ensure that primary and secondary education includes facilities for 'recreation and social and physical training' of children under 13 years of age. Concerns have been expressed for some time now regarding the tendency of schools to reduce children's time for free play in school playgrounds both during morning and afternoon breaks and at lunch time. Armitage (2005) estimates that playtimes and lunchtimes in primary schools in England and Wales have been reduced by as much as a half since 1971; surveys carried out in 1995 (Blatchford 1998) and again in 2006 (Blatchford and Baines 2006) show a continuing reduction in time for breaks and, in the 2006 survey, the virtual disappearance of an afternoon break at Key Stage 2 and secondary levels.

In their survey of children and adults for the Good Childhood Inquiry, The Children's Society (2007b) found that both children and adults felt that time to play with friends was important within the school day, and adults felt that there should be more time and less anxiety about children playing at school. Similar findings were also reported from the *Primary Review* (2007).

Research shows there are many benefits to playtime. Scott and Panksepp (2003) note from their study of children's rough and tumble play behaviours that after a period of high energy activity, the children appear to reach a point of satiety and this may be a precursor to other forms of social interaction. They also comment that, as this point is reached, the brain/mind may become more receptive for participating in less vigorous social and learning opportunities, and perhaps 'additional access to R&T play in young children at the beginning of a school day may have beneficial effects on behavioural inhibition and the ability of children to attend to lessons later in the day' (Scott and Panksepp 2003: 549).

A US study by Holmes and others (2006) into the relationship between school recess time and four-year-old children's attention in the classroom concludes that post-recess attention was greater following sustained outdoor play periods. Their findings support and parallel empirical findings with primary school children on the role of recess in children's cognitive performance, and the conclusion of the research suggests that it 'seems reasonable that outdoor recess breaks rejuvenate young children and help them attend to classroom tasks'. In making recommendations for policy, the authors suggest that brief, 20-minute periods of recess throughout the day are likely to provide the optimum benefit for maintaining classroom attention. Further support for Holmes and others (2006) is suggested by the findings of an international study of educational systems, which rank the Finnish schools as the world's best, based on students' test performance. Among several distinctive features of these schools is the requirement for a 15-minute recess every hour with play opportunities (Alvarez 2005).

Pellegrini and Bohn (2005) establish a clear and positive correlation between playtime and cognitive performance and adjustment to school. They suggest a 'cognitive immaturity hypothesis' to explain how children's tendency to believe themselves more able than they are (a belief that provides the motivation for learning) can become diminished during formal learning activity, and children's ability to maintain a focus on structured learning tasks is subject to 'interference'. Breaks during structured tasks can reduce cognitive interference and subsequently maximise learning achievements. Playtime enables children to regain a sense of control and mastery through their own self-directed and fantasy play, thus returning to school work with renewed attention and capacity for cognitive work. Pellegrini's and Bohn's empirical and longitudinal research shows that this is borne out in practice, in that children do return to work with increased attention following a break for unstructured play with peers. This bears a similarity with Kaplan and Kaplan's (2005) restoration theory in which their extensive research indicates that recovery from directed attention fatigue calls for different type of attention which requires no effort to sustain, namely activities that promote fascination and intriguing and meaningful action. Pellegrini and Bohn note that reduction of cognitive interference may require a substantial change in activity or stimulus materials before any benefits arise. Given this, instructional regimes or physical education programmes would not have the benefits associated with unstructured play opportunities.

Pellegrini and Bohn (2005) also highlight the importance of social exchanges between peers at playtime in making contributions to cognitive performance and a more general adjustment to school life. The qualities associated with establishing and maintaining successful peer relationships in play may buffer children from the stresses of early schooling. Longitudinal research carried out by Pellegrini and others (2004) demonstrates the importance of game playing in the playground in achieving and maintaining social competence with peers and adjusting to early schooling experiences.

Smith (2007) explores the key features valued by children in their school playgrounds. She notes that if the purpose of playtime is to provide an alternative to the teacher-directed regime of the classroom, children need to be self-determining in their activity, social contact and physical exercise; the play needs to stem from the children themselves and be under their control and for themselves. Any intervention by adults is counterproductive.

In the UK there is a tendency to restrict playtimes and to manage what time remains more directly, due to negative perceptions of playground behaviour (Blatchford 1998; Blatchford and Baines 2006). These perceptions include the rise in bullying and fighting in playgrounds, the potential for violent and racist incidents and general concern over behaviour in the playground that can spill over into school time (but see Smith and others 2002; and Armitage 2005 below). More recently, the notion that play is a distraction from the real work of schools has been expressed, most notably in the planned absence of a playground and time for play in the new Thomas Deacon City Academy (Hackett 2007), with the more familiar concerns over lack of control, bullying and truancy also being expressed. Adults also mourn the decline of children's traditional games, citing this as the reason for a decrease in co-operation and an increase in aggression, although this is disputed by Bishop and Curtis (2001: 181): 'detailed and extensive first hand ethnographic studies … have found a flourishing play culture despite dire warnings to the contrary'. However, a romantic notion of these games is unrealistic, and children are also just as likely as adults to be cruel and shocking in their play (Sutton-Smith 1997). Armitage (2005) cites evidence to show that adult concern over loss of traditional playground games and the rise in bullying and aggression is not a modern phenomenon but has been voiced for well over 100 years, with the cause being first school, then radio and cinema, and, more recently, television and computer games. He suggests that adults have a limited understanding of what actually takes place, and perceive playgrounds and play time as being 'anarchistic, difficult to control and a place of negative learning experience' (Armitage 2005: 538). Armitage illustrates how the architecture of playgrounds influences play in subtle ways, and how children are capable of self-organising so that specific areas of the space are allocated to particular forms of play. Adult observations that football dominates playgrounds pushing other forms of play to the boundaries may be only one way of seeing the self organisation of space and play forms.

Other studies have expressed the potential of the school playground to compensate for children's dwindling opportunity to play outdoors. Factor (2004) asserts that the school playground is more central to children's play lives than the street, park or adventure playground. It has assumed the role of a principal social centre for children's play cultures. Wilson (2001: 3) claims that for most young children the first public space that they encounter and develop intimate knowledge about is the school playground. However Thomas and Thompson (2004: 32) note that, although 63 per cent of the educational site is out of doors, it is estimated that school grounds are used to only 30 per cent of their potential.

Thomson (2005) researched the way that adults control both the playground space itself and movement in that space. Although the general perception is that the school playground is not an adult space, ultimately the design of the space and the rules as to what can happen within it are controlled by adults. Adults speak of this control in terms of the benefits for children, either in relation to the range of opportunities available, or to their health and safety. Thomson found three kinds of adult-controlled spaces within playgrounds: places that were out of bounds or off limits (such as school fields or areas designated for specific ages); privileged spaces (such as gardens and specially equipped areas, often place that the children had helped to raise funds for, design and build) and prescriptive spaces (designated for specific activities). Children were usually aware of the rules, although sometimes these were arbitrary and inconsistent. Often children would monitor the actions of others and remind their peers of the rules. Just as frequently, however, children resisted the rules and renegotiated territories within the playground, sometimes covertly, sometimes through ploys such as wayward balls that needed retrieving, and sometimes in direct and playful opposition. For example, at one school children would 'take great delight in taunting the supervisors by jumping on and off the edge of the field, or walking with one foot on the grass and one foot on the tarmacadam' (Thomson 2005: 75-76).

Smith and others (2002) also draw attention to the role that adult perception plays in understanding playground behaviour, particularly with reference to children's rough and tumble play. They cite research (Schäffer and Smith 1996) which found that playfighting occupies about 10 per cent of playground time, whereas real fighting is much less frequent, occupying about one per cent of playground time. However, teachers and playground supervisors tend to view playfighting negatively, overestimating the proportion that is real fighting. Pellegrini (2002: 223) suggests that perhaps one of the key reasons for adults not tolerating playfighting is that 'until rather recently, developmental psychologists have confused and conflated play fighting with aggression'. However, behavioural studies of animal and human young have shown that they are separate and that the key role of play fighting, in early and middle childhood and predominantly amongst boys, is in social competence and co-operative interaction rather than dominance. In adolescence there is a shift into its purpose in establishing and maintaining social dominance (Pellegrini 2002), together with the benefits for brain connectivity and chemistry outlined in Chapter 3. Teachers' concern with playfighting is that they feel it is likely to end up as a real fight. Yet Smith and others (2002: 187) state that observational research shows that 'for most children, only around one per cent of play fights turn into real fights.' However, children who are frequently rejected by social groups often have difficulty understanding the play signals accompanying play fighting and confuse the playful with the real; for this group of children, about a quarter of play fighting episodes turned into real fighting. In adolescence, the incidence of play fighting turning into real fighting is also increased (Smith and others 2002).

Blatchford (1998) acknowledges that some children are left out of group games, are not successful in finding play partners and can be subject to bullying and aggression. He suggests that the extremes of intervention and control on the one hand and non-intervention and respect for independence on the other both have their difficulties, and points to ways in which the physical environment can be adjusted and whole school approaches to behaviour can be introduced to reduce some of the more aggressive playground behaviours. Visser and Greenwood (2005) highlight the inadequacy of playground space and design and the withdrawal of government regulations for space and design of school playgrounds. They echo Blatchford's dilemma regarding how far adults should intervene. Their research was into the effects of a moderately interventionist approach which sought to change the playground ethos through the introduction of games requiring structured rules and turn taking, and they found that teachers perceived a significant improvement; there was a reduction in minor disputes but little change in severe disputes. The promotion of playground games by adults has become popular within primary schools and is supported by the government through the Healthy Schools agenda and also through Playground Fun (www.playgroundfun.org.uk), a website sponsored by the Department for Culture, Media and Sport's Culture Online initiative.

The Positive Playgrounds project in Northern Ireland (PlayBoard 2007, cited in Davis 2007) worked with lunchtime supervisors, teachers and children to enhance and support children's play. The project found that there was an increase in children's participation in playing and in activity levels; that bullying was reduced; and that attention in class increased.

Learning Through Landscapes (2006: 3) found that in a national survey of school grounds that had been redesigned, '73 per cent of schools who had improved their grounds reported that this had improved behaviour; 84 per cent that it had improved social interaction; and 64 per cent that it had reduced playtime incidents of bullying'. Common problems with school playgrounds were found to be too little space; domination of large, uniform, open spaces by groups of older boys (usually for football); and boring environments. Involving the whole school in the design of playgrounds, finding out key trouble spots for bullying, and finding out what children want to do (rather than what equipment they want) can help in effective playground design. Key features should be allowing for a range of active, imaginative, social and quiet space, as well as walkways that do not conflict with bigger games.

There is a renewed interest in school playgrounds, brought about through a number of initiatives including the Growing Schools programme, launched in 2001, the government's Learning Outside the Classroom (DfES 2006c), the Extended Schools agenda and the Building Schools for the Future programme, launched in 2005, which aims to rebuild or renew every secondary school over the next 50 years. In addition, *Schools for the Future, Designing School Grounds* (DfES 2006e, cited in Davis 2007) promotes the importance of play and physical activity both in the formal and informal curriculum:

> Schools should provide 'a variety of active play opportunity' and define the space for active play, using 'active features' such as traversing walls, playground markings, fixed play equipment, temporary play equipment, ball walls, balancing beams, fitness trails, logs and stepping stones. (Davis 2007: 7)

Coombes (2006) reports on a number of schools working with other organisations to develop 'natural, sustainable and fun play areas'.

Ridgers and others (2005a) researched into children's physical activity during playtime in school playgrounds. Using a uniaxial accelerometer, they measured the moderate, high and very high intensity physical activity of 116 boys and 112 girls aged between 6 and 10 years during the breaks in one day. Calculating the results, they conclude that playtime can contribute to 28 minutes of boys' recommended 60 minutes of moderate to vigorous physical activity a day and 21.5 minutes for girls. They recommend that interventions be considered to increase levels of physical activity. Ridgers and others (2005b) report on the Liverpool Sporting Playgrounds Project, part of a DfES and Nike partnership to invest £10 million into the development of sporting playgrounds across 600 primary schools in England. More than half of the schools involved did this through the Zoneparc playground (DfES 2006d). Playgrounds are zoned into red, blue and yellow areas designed to support particular activities: sport, activities and games, and chill-out zones respectively. Monitoring, observation and interviews with children generated data not only on the physical activity of the children but also on social behaviour, the range of playing, and attitudes towards their play. Data were gathered on activity levels for the

189

baseline, after six weeks, and then after six and 12 months. Variables notwithstanding, there was found to be a significant increase in physical activity, but for most children there was a fall off after about six months. Further research will look into ways of sustaining activity levels and also at the relationship between physical activity levels and play behaviours (Ridgers 2007).

There is a danger that redesigning playgrounds may unwittingly remove props for children's games that have been used for generations of children. Factor (2004) suggests that redesigning and landscaping of school playgrounds needs to be sensitive to the special places in playgrounds. She uses the concept of 'playlines', drawn from the Aboriginal concept of story and songlines: invisible traces that mark out historically significant places. Children have similar folklore and special places that have been used for generations of children in particular games and play forms, including in school playgrounds:

> Features of the playground never intended for play may be selected and stubbornly retained for a particular game, despite teachers' disapproval. Children were not supposed to play near school entrances, but metal poles supporting a covered walkway between buildings at Woodlands were both a meeting place and a site for swinging, hoppy and chasey games. (Factor 2004: 147)

Concerns for safety and litigation, together with fashions in the kinds of playing that adults find acceptable, have taken their toll on the resources available to children for their play in playgrounds. Armitage (2005) also identifies special elements of school playgrounds that have served particular functions in children's games for generations, for example the long black pipe used as a counting spot for chase games, that can often be unwittingly removed by adults in the name of playground improvements.

The National Union of Teachers (NUT 2007a; NUT 2007b) has published two documents under the heading *Time to Play*: a play policy and guidelines for implementation. The policy, which was developed following a debate at the NUT 2006 conference, recommends a review of the National

'Concerns for safety and litigation, together with fashions in the kinds of playing that adults find acceptable, have taken their toll on the resources available to children for their play ...'

Curriculum, in line with trends in Wales and Scotland, to incorporate play based approaches to learning and assessment. The policy also recommends that an audit of facilities for play, both inside school buildings and in school grounds, should be undertaken to inform the Building Schools for the Future initiative; that opportunities for informal play at breaks and lunch time should be enhanced; that local authorities should develop cross-departmental play policies; and that the government should fund an initiative to encourage imaginative play in education. With reference to the development of local play policies, the NUT (2007a: 14) recommends:

> In order for such policies to be effective, clearly designated and ring-fenced funding must be allocated by local authorities for the provision of qualified and skilled play advisers to work with schools and other educational and youth service settings to develop excellent play provision for all children and young people.

Play and creativity in the classroom

In 2000, the review of the National Curriculum emphasised the importance of creativity. The Qualifications and Curriculum Authority (QCA) was charged with investigating how schools could promote and support children's creativity. They carried out research abroad and at home into ways of nurturing creativity in the classroom, and have created a website for shared ideas and support for teachers (http://www.ncaction.org.uk/creativity/).

Creative Partnerships was set up in 2002 with funding from the DCMS and DfES and managed by Arts Council England. It aims to build partnerships between those in the creative industries and schools in disadvantaged areas to develop children's creativity and schools' approaches to creativity and partnership working. A survey of headteachers (Mackey and Ullman 2006) found that generally the involvement of Creative Partnerships in schools had improved pupils' confidence, communication skills, motivation and enjoyment of school and that it had helped teachers take a more creative approach to teaching.

Banaji and Burn (2006), in their review of the literature on creativity for Creative Partnerships, identified nine rhetorics (a term they use to describe discursive frameworks) of creativity including the creative genius (only a few talented people are truly creative), democratic and political creativity (creativity is present in popular culture and the cultures of resistance) and creativity as an economic imperative (innovation, risk and flexibility of thought and action are necessary to compete in the contemporary global economy). One of these rhetorics is play and creativity, a pedagogic focus highlighting the connections between play, creativity and learning. Although some aspects of this rhetoric draw on the recent research in the cognitive sciences as explored in Chapter 3, it is predominantly based in ideas of divergent thinking, and of childhood pretend play as the precursor to adult creativity and problem-solving. As well as these individual benefits, there are also social links between play and creativity. Symbolic play involves a process of developing shared meaning-making with others.

There are some questions, however, regarding the parallels of play and creativity. The first is that definitions of creativity usually involve a product: something that is created, whereas end product is not a necessary part of playing, as the emphasis is on process rather than product. The second is that creativity necessarily involves novel combinations, whereas some aspects of children's play cultures such as traditional games, emphasise continuity and repetition (Banaji and Burn 2006).

Howard and others' (2006) research on the importance of appreciating what children actually value in their play experiences in the classroom as a prerequisite for developing appropriate play and learning experiences for children is described in Chapter 3. This research also indicates that the role of the teacher is crucial. A key value attributed to children's perception of play in the classroom is the absence of the teacher from the activity. The involvement of the teacher in children's classroom play 'reduces the likelihood that children will perceive the activity as play' (Howard and others 2006: 392). This matches research by Gmitrova and Gmitrov (2004) who note the beneficial effects of engaging in pretend play in their study of children aged between 4- and 6-years-old, but the benefits are far greater when children are allowed to develop their own pretend play rather than participate in adult designed situations.

Cremin and others (2006) researched pedagogical approaches to supporting creativity in the early years in the UK, placing this within the broad policy context of fostering creativity in the curriculum. 'Possibility thinking' (imagining what might be) is at the core of creative learning. Characteristics of possibility thinking are defined as: posing questions, play, immersion and making connections, being imaginative, innovation, risk taking and self-determination. The parallels with the characteristics of play generally are of note here. In their research with three early years settings (an early childhood centre, and infants school and a junior school) they explored key elements of teachers' strategies for supporting creativity and possibility thinking. The results can be grouped into three elements: standing back (as a time for non-intervention and also of observation and noticing), profiling learner agency (supporting the children to take control of the activities, but also framing challenges) and creating time and space (not rushing or having a fixed end time, and making a wide range of resources available). Teachers would set up contexts and take the lead from the children, who showed high levels of self-organisation and engagement. Teachers would be available to support and extend, whilst not taking over.

There is currently a strong and perhaps at times confusing debate about the relationship between play, creativity and learning in the formal educational system. The UK government's 'cultural turn' (Buckingham and Jones 2001) reframed the promotion of creativity, which had been the central concern of the report of the National Advisory Committee on Creative and Cultural Education (NACCCE 1999). This report clearly outlines the importance of developing 'human resources' based on creativity, adaptability and better powers of communication. This entailed reviewing some of the basic assumptions that underpin the educational system. The report argues that new approaches are needed 'based on broader conceptions of young people's abilities, of how to promote their motivation and self-esteem, and of the skills and aptitudes they need' (NACCCE 1999: 9). At the heart of this shift lies creative and cultural education.

This has been further developed through *Excellence and Enjoyment* (DfES 2003c), yet alongside these announcements increasing emphasis on skills testing, targets and league tables appears to have constrained a more creative and innovative approach to education (Morgan and Kennewell 2006). However there are some signs that the rigidity associated with the national curriculum in England is also being relaxed. In the *Excellence and Enjoyment* strategy for primary schools there is recognition that 'primary education is about children experiencing the joy of discovery, solving problems, being creative in writing, art, music, developing their self-confidence as learners and maturing socially and emotionally' (Morgan and Kennewell, 2006: 308). Hartley (2006) questions the rhetoric of the *Excellence and Enjoyment* focus, stating that there is a fundamental contradiction between the two themes. Hartley notes the resurgence of 'creativity' · in the educational policy discourse. From its maligned position in education following the 1960s, creativity is now seen as a primary force through which the country will be able to maintain a competitive economic advantage. The key emphasis throughout the policy is the notion of creativity for future employability. Hartley also comments on the inclusion of enjoyment, noting that enjoyment is an emotion which appears to be grafted on to the discourse of standards and performance. This leads to a highly controlled curriculum in which the emphasis is on 'personalised standardisation: a personalised pick-and-mix of pedagogy and curriculum, but only from the standard menu, which is drawn up by the government' (Hartley 2006:13).

Thompson and others' (2006) report from a research project designed to explore the policy issues expressed in *Excellence and Enjoyment* notes a general change in attitudes to creativity within the school during the period of the project. Working with Creative Partnerships, the initial response from teaching staff in the primary school used in the research project was that their main priority lay with teaching the '3Rs'; the 'arts' were seen as marginal to classroom activity, although the teachers were reassured that there was an artist in residence within the school. The report highlights that the relationship between the school and visiting artists working with the children on a theme of identity and self-expression was restricted by the framing of this work as a 'project' with limited time/funding:

> A pedagogy, in which children's inherent competence and potential were taken as starting points, was continually compromised by the pressures of producing skills and

outputs. In addition, the project outcomes were not formally and rigorously assessed; they thus had little impact on the children's ongoing learning or the teaching that supported it. Products/performances were judged on their benefits for the school (assumed to be the same as for the child): they did not contribute to a formative understanding of the child's individual learning. (Thompson and others 2006: 6)

Witte-Townsend and Hill (2006), using narrative analysis based research, comment that an educational climate that supports teachers and children in the creative act of meaning making is a natural and important feature of classroom practice. However, they feel that the 'current prescriptive standards-conscious, numbers-driven practice that subjects young children to standardised testing also tends to insist that teachers follow only a few approved teaching methods and programmes' (Witte-Townsend and Hill 2006: 374). This inevitably constrains and limits teaching approaches to supporting creativity in the classroom through teachers being required to focus on pre-scripted materials that sit within very narrow guidelines.

Trageton (2005) reviews the changes to primary school education in Norway through the lowering of school entry age from seven years to six years, and the introduction of a national curriculum (1997). A key theme in the curriculum is the importance of children's free play for the entire primary school period. We can see a parallel here with much of the discourse about play and creativity expressed in other European countries (for example Lofdahl 2005). The educational policy changes in Norway are embedded in notions of the importance of both 'free play' and teacher designed structured play activities. Alongside this, staff are required to apply 'playful teaching' strategies. Within the revised curriculum, play is featured as a specific 'subject' to be included in daily teaching programmes.

The Primary Review

This independent review, supported by the Esmé Fairbairn Foundation and based at Cambridge University Faculty of Education, was launched in October 2006 and will run for two years. The review has three perspectives (children, the world in which they are growing up, and the education which mediates that world and prepares them for it) and 10 themes (six core themes of purposes and values; learning and teaching; curriculum and assessment; quality and standards; diversity and inclusion; settings and professionals; and four contingent themes of parenting, caring and education; beyond the school; structures and phases; and funding and governance). At the time of writing, the review is collecting evidence from academic research and from stakeholders.

Play England (Davis 2007) submitted evidence to the review which outlines the child's right to play and the importance of play in children's lives as well as the benefits of providing opportunities for play within schools, both within the core school day and the extended schools agenda. Davis cites research evidence showing how access to opportunities for playing can contribute towards all areas of school life and themes of the review. The response makes seven recommendations, including ensuring that play is considered in the Building Schools for the Future programme; that children can play out as much as possible; that play is integral to the extended services, including support for teams of playworkers to open up parks for children's free play as a part of extended services; and ensuring long-term revenue for play projects that offer children outdoor and physical play opportunities.

The first interim report, *Community Soundings* (Primary Review 2007) found widespread anxiety about pressures on children from testing and targets at school as well as from commercially-driven values in society generally. Children expressed concerns about the lack of safe play areas in their localities. Teachers felt that the curriculum was overstructured, rigid and overprescribed and that there was not enough time for play and creativity, and parents felt that at the start of primary schooling at least, there should be more time for play.

Play in early years settings

Some aspects of the literature review on play in early years settings can be found in Chapter 3 under the 'play and learning' heading, particularly literature on the relationship between play and learning. Sources included in this section pertain more to issues of policy implementation, service provision and professional practice.

Play England has published a literature review of free play in early childhood (Santer and others 2007). This section draws from and builds on this publication rather than replicating it. Santer and others highlight the lack of a coherent and well-defined understanding of play within current government legislation as well as a discrepancy between the ideology of the importance of play in the early years and actual practice, 'rhetoric and reality' (Santer and others 2007: 71), which is constrained by an emphasis on curriculum, attainment targets and testing. The focus of research and discussion on play in early years provision is predominantly on its relationship to learning and development, although within this there is an acknowledgement of the benefits for children's social relationships and well-being in the here and now (for example Corsaro 2003). Santer and others outline recent government initiatives concerning provision for early childhood, including the introduction of the Foundation Stage (three- to five-years) in 2000, together with curriculum guidance; the National Standards for Daycare and Childminding in 2001; the Birth to Three Matters Framework in 2003; as well as initiatives such as Early Excellence Centres (1997-2006), Sure Start (1999-2006), the Neighbourhood Nursery Initiative (2000-2006) and the current Children's Centres. Most recent is the introduction of the Early Years Foundation Stage (EYFS), which sets standards for the learning, development and care of children from birth to five years and will become mandatory in all schools and Ofsted registered settings catering for children under five (DfES 2007). The EYFS principles are grouped into four interrelated themes: a unique child, positive relationships, enabling environments, and learning and development (DfES 2007: 8). 'Play and exploration' sits under the theme of learning and development.

Santer and others (2007) summarise the literature on the role of play in children's development. If children's playing is allowed to develop, it becomes more complex and demanding cognitively and socially. Play is of particular benefit in emotional and cognitive development. A number of themes in play are explored: gender; children's own voices; cultural attitudes towards children and play; inclusion; play in children who are stressed, abused or ill; disabled children. Finally, the literature on the role of the adult in children's play is examined in terms of sensitivity and attachment; observation; interaction with children at play and creating an environment where children can play. Whilst free play does contribute to children's learning and development, the review also states that this is not the only way that children learn: there is also a place for adult-directed teaching activities in settings that have learning as a focus. Children also learn from those around them and from experiences that may not be play. The literature review highlights the tensions between different perspectives on play, both in academic research and in different areas of practice, as well as in differences of interpretation into early years practice. The review ends with a number of areas for consideration, including training early years staff in the benefits and support of free play; using practitioners as researchers; comparative studies of free play and adult-initiated play; and the need for a clearer understanding of terms used and the development of a coherent inter-professional approach to play.

Adams and others (2004) identify that, despite the recognition of the importance of play in the Foundation Stage, the pressures of the outcomes focus, the construct of children within the guidance, and a lack of strong understanding of the theoretical links between play and learning have led to a tension in practice between supporting (and justifying) children's play and teaching to curriculum outcomes. Rogers (2005), developing the concerns within the Adams and others report, found that pressure to meet curriculum targets meant that opportunities for pretend play, particularly outdoors, were limited in reception classes. Rogers noted gender differences: although both boys and girls liked to play and draw around similar themes (for example, castles), girls' play was mostly of domestic and nurturing roles, and the pictures were 'pretty', whereas boys played superhero and action roles and their drawing tended towards the more gory, despite teacher attempts to 'de-gender' play. Rogers emphasised that it was important to allow sustained periods of play without adult intervention so that complex themes and narratives can develop fully. The research identifies the need for teachers to develop a style of intervention that 'extends and rejuvenates play, rather than constrains and frustrates it' (Rogers 2005: 25).

Pramling Samuelsson and Johanssen (2006) suggest that the tendency to separate out play and learning is problematic for early years practice. Their study of playful interactions between teachers and children suggests that playing and learning are interconnected and interdependent. Although the theorising implies discrete characteristics of play and learning, many are experienced as in common, including 'joy, creativity, creation of meaning and possibilities to control and form goals' (Pramling Samuelsson and Johanssen 2006: 54). Teachers play a key role in their support for play, from helping to set the scene and create material and physical frames for the play, through to sensitive participation in the play. Much of this is through playful interactions that signal a respect for children's own playing.

Given the evidence of the value of play as a support for learning, the teacher must have an understanding of the play process and be confident in play as a teaching and learning medium:

> Rather than planning activities that look like play, identifying the cues used by children when making categorizations enables us to plan activities that are likely to encourage a playful approach. Knowledge of these cues facilitates research into the developmental potential of play that could help to elevate its status as a medium for learning. (Howard and others 2006: 392)

Pramling Samuelsson and Johansson (2006) agree with Howard and others about the sensitive nature of teaching and supporting children's play. They discuss the didactic aspects associated with the relationship between play and learning, and acknowledge that the influence of the teachers and the classroom environment can either promote or inhibit the integration between play and learning. In their review of early years education in Sweden, they note that play and learning may be different phenomena but that there may in fact be common attributes. Their research notes the potential benefits from teachers' 'genuine' participation in children's play within the classroom, as a positive message that play is important and valued and as a way of forming close and playful relationships with children. They illustrate this process in action through observation of child-teacher playful interactions and the reciprocal sense of joy and meaning making from these experiences. In developing this, the authors note the ways in which the intonations and gestures of the teachers maintain and value children's playful experiences. Similarly, Witte-Townsend and Hill (2006) note that becoming aware of and accepting children's invitations to engage in play enables teachers to move towards

195

'... rather than planning activities that look like play, identifying the cues used by children ... enables us to plan activities that are likely to encourage a playful approach.'

a pedagogical approach that allows for shifting frames and references to provide new opportunities for meaning making. They tellingly note:

> Children's light-ness of body and being and the sparkle of light in their eyes flourishes in classrooms where structure is generated for the sake of supporting meaningful engagement; depth emerges in relation to the opportunities an environment provides for engagement in an ongoing flow of life. When children ask questions like 'What would happen if …?', they remind us that while we respond to the current pressure to have them produce ever higher test scores, we must not abandon the spark of light in their eyes or the way that lightness moves through their bodies. (Witte-Townsend and Hill 2006: 375)

However, this may present a problem for teachers who feel under pressure from parents to show that children are acquiring basic skills through didactic teaching methods (Howard and others 2006).

Farne (2005: 173), exploring the relationship between play and learning, notes that an appreciation of children's play suggests that the more natural and unstructured the environment is, the 'richer children's play is as an educational activity'. From this, the teacher is not someone who makes a child play but the one who offers an environment, time, and resources that are largely free from adult intentions to enable children to apply their own active imaginations. But, as Farne notes, the idea of children playing in an unstructured manner in a classroom causes great concern; it implies a sense of 'emptiness' that needs to be filled. Yet to the child, this openness represents a space which offers possibilities.

> Released from all adult planning aimed at developing some specific playing opportunities, as well as managing them and controlling its outcomes, play expresses its most authentic educational dimension precisely when children can escape adult supervision and manage their own games following criteria based on freedom and negotiations established and shared within their own group. (Farne 2005: 176)

In looking at the use of play in the classroom, Farne suggests that play is the only field of experience in which children have the opportunity to be themselves and act accordingly, to make decisions and deal with uncertainty which may lead to conflict, controversial outcomes, interruptions and sudden shifts in action and emotion. Thus, it is not simply a matter of teachers using play in an instrumental form to meet some specific learning outcome but is more a matter of play being a 'category' or style; learning in the classroom becomes playful exploration, curiosity.

Guss (2005) comments that the drama performances of children's pretend play are not meant as a communication with anyone outside the child-cultural arena. Given this, Guss suggests that teachers study more closely what children perform when they are on their own. Given systematic aesthetic nourishment and models, and without direct adult intervention, some children can accomplish complex action and reflection.

David (2003), in a review of the research on approaches to teaching in early childhood, notes the shift from understanding child development theories as objective and universal, to an appreciation of socially constructed understandings of childhood that change over time and culture, and which therefore influence pedagogical theories and practice. She summarises studies of research into pedagogy at Foundation Stage and Key Stage 1, with the key findings relating to play being (David 2003: 8):

- Practitioners generally stressed their belief that play should be given a high priority but they have found this difficult to achieve in practice.

- Practitioners working at the Foundation Stage tended to lack the confidence, knowledge and training to teach aspects like literacy through play and they have been influenced by their fear of the assumed expectations of Ofsted inspectors.

- Adults enhanced children's learning through play when they helped them develop strategies for resolution of conflict.

- The most effective settings provided both teacher-initiated group work and freely chosen yet potentially instructive play activities.

- Settings rated as excellent tended to achieve an equal balance between adult-led and child-initiated interactions and activities.

- Children's learning and behaviour was enhanced in settings where practitioners modeled appropriate language, values and practices, praised encouraged and questioned, and where adults interacted verbally with children and encouraged socio-dramatic play.

David (2003) highlights the problematic nature of the relationship between play and learning in the early years, questioning some assumptions that learning will occur automatically through play. Citing the research of the Froebel Block Play Research Group (Gura 1992), she lists a number of conditions necessary to support high quality play, including: adult involvement; sharing the initiative between children and adults; enabling children to be playful and creative, and to take risks; creating an environment that maximises opportunities for learning; and observing and keeping records that can inform practice.

As they grow, children develop understandings of other children as intentional agents, and they begin to plan their play to take account of other children's intentions and needs in order to keep the playing going (Broadhead 2001). This raises the question of how adults support this peer process, which is often spontaneous and immediate. Effective interventions may be direct, such as participating in the play or designing tasks, and sometimes indirect, for example leaving play to develop and making flexible resources available to support this (as described in the Reggio Emilia approach, for example Abbott and Nutbrown 2001).

Walsh and others (2006) in their comparative study of early years education in Northern Ireland note that policy-makers have different views about how young children learn. Basically there is a divide between those who advocate a play-based approach until around the mid-primary school years and others who advocate a more formal approach, based on fostering academic skills from the outset of a child's education. Their research suggests that the traditional teacher-led curriculum, developed largely in response to concerns about standards and educational progress and achievement, does little to activate children's thinking and multiple skill acquisition. The more play-based, 'enriched curriculum' offered children a higher-quality learning experience than that of the more traditional Year 1 curriculum.

In their evaluation of the quality of early learning, play and childcare services in Sure Start Local Programmes, Anning and others (2005: 17) note that 'early childhood services are dominated by professional, white, middle class constructs of play'. Parents' play with their children reflects the norms of the home culture, and parents tend to view playing as recreational and may not subscribe to the educational value of play. This raises particular issues for working with parents within Sure Start Local Programmes, and the authors note that there is a paucity of previous research into these interrelationships that might inform any evaluation.

Play provision for all children: a closer look at particular groups and particular circumstances

It is useful to open this section with a note on terminology. As Kapasi (2002: 7) says, 'Language is a constant constraint when researching and writing about marginalised or minority groups.' The terms used to describe specific groups of children change over time and depending on the political stance taken by writers. In this section, the terms used are those that have been employed by the writers of the original research; in general sections, terminology reflects current usage in national policy documents.

Whilst broad generalisations can be made about childhood and the benefits of play, public provision for play needs to pay particular attention to specific groups of children and those living in specific circumstances. Childhood is not a singular, universal phenomenon experienced in the same way by all children. Age is only one mode of diversity or social division. Children are also boys or girls, they belong to a vast range of cultural and ethnic groups, they are born into a particular social class and lifestyle, and they may or may not be disabled in a variety of ways. Children may live in stable family homes, or with domestic violence, or in the care of the local authority. They may be socially or economically deprived, they may be in hospital or they may be newly arrived in this country as asylum seekers or refugees. None of these categories is either singly or statically experienced by children (Morrow and Connolly 2006), and although some generalisation can be made, children's own experiences of these social categories vary according to context. The very act of categorising in this manner runs the risk of generalising and stereotyping. The difficulty for those involved in working with children and young people is in recognising just how complex and diverse categories can be, to recognise the importance of children's own experiences of them and to acknowledge children's own competence in navigating them through their social relations as children. Failure to recognise these factors may mean that interventions intended to reduce the negative aspects of discrimination and stereotyping may indeed serve to further entrench attitudes and identities (Holland 2003; Bhavnani and others 2005; Brooker 2006; Morrow and Connolly 2006).

Anti-discriminatory methods of working, together with equal opportunities policies, have been a core aspect of working with children and young people for several decades, yet, as Brooker (2006: 118) states:

> Utopian beliefs that, in modern democracies, all children have equal life-chances, regardless of their social and cultural background and identity, have not been borne out by research evidence to date, although such beliefs persist as an underpinning strand of early childhood ideology.

Much of the practice research and evaluation of services for specific groups of children focuses on issues of access (both to and within provision or public space) and on the particular issues faced by these children. Exceptions to this (for example Ludvigsen and others 2005) also consider the quality of the play experiences of children attending projects. If the literature on play provision generally focuses on the instrumental rather than the intrinsic value of play (Powell and Wellard 2008), this focus is even stronger in the literature on services for specific groups of children.

It needs to be stated again that the authors are aware of much local provision for particular groups of children in particular circumstances, yet the scope and timing of the review has not allowed for the collection of local data.

This section reviews the literature and ends with a comment on its focus and its relation to the recent literature on play.

Social exclusion

'Social exclusion' is a relatively new term in contemporary UK social policy, although it has a longer history in Europe (Byrne 2005; Hobcraft 2007). The current Labour government has placed the concept at the heart of its approach to social welfare and social order, establishing a Social Exclusion Unit in 1997, which has since been replaced by a Social Exclusion Task Force. The concept of social exclusion includes, but is wider than, poverty and class, and generally recognises the dynamic and multidimensional nature of exclusion from social, economic, cultural and political systems (Byrne 2005). Buchanan and others (2004) note that the definitions of social exclusion usually relate to adults and particulary to those of working age; social exclusion from a child's perspective is likely to involve exclusion from 'the norms and customs of children's society' and to be experienced as feeling different and not being able to join in social and other activities (Ridge 2002, cited in Buchanan and others 2004: 19). Minority ethnic and disabled children are disproportionately likely to live in deprived areas and be socially excluded (Buchanan and others 2004).

The concepts of risk and protective factors and prevention in social policy discussed in Chapter 2 can be seen in initiatives such as Sure Start, On Track and the Children's Fund, which are targeted at children and families 'at risk' of social exclusion. Buchanan and others (2004) highlight the role of such initiatives in supporting the development of resilience as a protective factor, particularly through helping to build strong social networks, managed exposure to risk and acute (rather than chronic) stressors, and the opportunity to experience control, agency and mastery. Drawing on the evidence presented in Chapter 3, we may assume that these are aspects that can be effectively addressed through play provision.

The Children's Fund, launched in 2000, is a national preventative programme aimed at addressing risk and protective factors for children aged between 5 and 13 years and their families considered to be 'most at risk of social exclusion through poverty and disadvantage' (CYPU 2001, cited in Edwards and others 2006: iv). The programme was due to end in 2008, but in July 2007 the government announced that it would be extended until 2011.

The National Evaluation of the Children's Fund ran from January 2003 to March 2006. It found considerable diversity in the methods used by Children's Fund partnerships to identify which children and families should be targeted and also in the design of services to meet identified needs for this 'historically neglected age-group' (Edwards and others 2006: xvi). Some focused on particular groups of children (for example, young carers or Gypsy and Traveller children), others on particular problems (such as behaviour) and others on geographic areas with high deprivation. The evaluation report highlights the significant place of play provision within preventative services (Edwards and others 2006: 103):

> single services directly aimed at children in the initiative can be broadly categorised as follows: providing safe spaces through club provision, play or specialist activities; individual help through, for example, mentoring, counselling or therapeutic play; and enhancing local resources such as play areas.

The analysis of services provided through the Children's Fund shows 'club provision or playschemes' as the most numerous; however, 'club provision' included activity and homework clubs, so the proportion of these services that offered opportunities to play is unclear. The analysis of the benefits of these services focused on the value of safe space, with staff highlighting the need to be flexible and responsive, and parents highlighting the value of children being away from undesirable influences, developing skills and broadening horizons; children saw them as places to have fun and make friends across age ranges. Whilst play provision features frequently in the services discussed in the report, there is little discussion on how playing itself could contribute to developing resilience within these services.

The evaluation found that most projects focused on interventions at individual child and family level and did not address risk or protective factors at community or structural level, thereby focusing 'attention on individual children rather than on the processes by which they came to be excluded' (Barnes and Morris 2007: 194). Such a focus limited the opportunity to develop networks and social capital as key aspects of resilience, an approach that required recognition of children as social actors rather than individual socialisation projects. Edwards and others (2006: 103) note that parents 'located risk of exclusion in the social conditions of their children's development and often outside the family. These conditions included … poor local play and leisure facilities.' In this sense, play provision is seen as a universal rather than a targeted service, and one that is rooted in the community rather than working on the perceived deficits of individual children.

Inclusion and access: disabled children and young people

Ludvigsen and others (2005: 9) define inclusion as

> the process of conceiving, designing, planning and maintaining of all parts of the physical and cultural community to cater for the widest spectrum of ability and need.

Ward and others (2004: 5) offer this definition:

> Inclusion involves adaptation of all parts of the community – both people's attitudes and the physical environment – to cater for a wide spectrum of ability and need. This must be an ongoing process whose overall aim is to embrace diversity rather than simply tolerate differences.

The term is generally used to refer to the inclusion of disabled children into mainstream settings, or, less often, of non-disabled children into specialist provision for disabled children, rather than the inclusion of other groups of children likely to be excluded from provision because of their ethnicity, gender or other circumstance. However, disabled children and young people do not form a homogeneous group with uniform experiences, likes and dislikes. Not only is there an infinite variety and combination of impairments of physical, sensory and cognitive functioning, but disability is also experienced across gender, class, ethnicity, sexual orientation and so on.

McIntyre and Casey (2007: 2) found, in their review of the literature on inclusion for disabled children, that 'a sense of inclusion is more dependent on friendships and fun than simply being in the same location as others', and that inclusion not only meant removing barriers to participation but also promoting this sense of inclusion.

In almost all cases, the research reviewed in this section, and particularly that evaluating projects, states a commitment to practice founded on the social model of disability. This model sees the ways that society is arranged as being what disables people with impairments, rather than the individual or medical model, which sees the 'problem' of disability arising from the impairment (Oliver 1990). In addition, much of the research findings also take into account the views of disabled children and young people themselves, using a variety of methods to gather this data.

Sharma (2002: 5) reports that, despite the government's move to eradicate child poverty, 'many of Britain's 360,000 disabled children and young people and their families still live in poverty and are socially excluded from their communities.' Being able to access local play provision and other leisure facilities is an important aspect of participating in the local community (Clarke 2005).

The Disability Discrimination Act (DDA) 1995 requires service providers to make reasonable adjustments to their policy, practice and procedures and (since 2004) to make physical adjustments to their premises, in order to make their services accessible to disabled people; this includes play providers. The revised Act (2005) also requires public bodies and local authorities to promote disability equality.

The Audit Commission (2003) found a national shortage of play and leisure provision for disabled children and young people (both inclusive and specialist) across the public, private and voluntary sectors, although early indications of the impact of the DDA are that physical alterations to buildings are being made or planned, and disability awareness and inclusion training is being organised for staff. Sharma and Dowling (2004) report that approximately 10 per cent of families with a disabled child care for more than one disabled child, which brings particular demands on accessing appropriate play provision for each child. In addition, siblings of disabled children are often not eligible to use the specialist services, adding to organisational difficulties and preventing families from playing together. Petrie and others (2002, cited in Sharma and Dowling 2004) highlight the importance of reliable funding, good information for families and the importance of a policy basis for inclusion.

More recently four organisations working with disabled children and their families (Contact a Family, the Council for Disabled Children, Mencap and the Special Education Consortium) have established Every Disabled Child Matters (EDCM) as a campaigning group to advocate for disabled children, young people and their families within policy. The government announced in May 2007 that £340 million of new money would be committed to improve services for disabled children and their families over a three year period, as a part of the Comprehensive Spending Review, to include short breaks, increased access to childcare and participation (HM Treasury and DfES 2007b).

Barriers to access (and, therefore guidance for good practice) are identified as practical or environmental (such as physical access or transport to facilities), and attitudinal or social (Ludvigsen and others 2005). The importance of training for staff, in terms of disability awareness, meeting individual needs, and confidence building is seen as crucial for supervised provision (John and Wheway 2004; Ludvigsen and others 2005; Wilson and Gray 2006).

Round Three of the Better Play Programme, funded by the former New Opportunities Fund, focused on projects aiming to increase inclusive play provision. In their evaluation of this programme, Ludvigsen and others (2005) found a number of different interpretations of the concept of inclusion and, as a result, the adoption of different approaches. The evaluation found that projects fell largely into one of two approaches: offering provision for disabled and non-disabled children to play together, and offering separate provision, usually at separate times, for disabled and non-disabled children. Those that developed shared provision used a number of approaches, including working in partnership with other organisations, support workers working with specific children, setting up new sessions and developing inclusive play ranger services in parks. In a closer analysis of eight projects, the evaluation found that most children enjoyed the opportunities. All projects offered some choice and control but this did vary depending on the structure of sessions, the play environment and staff approaches to intervention. Those projects whose staff members were from an educational background tended to offer more structured activities whereas those staffed by playworkers offered more opportunity for free play. Projects that had additional resources specifically (although not exclusively) for disabled children were able to offer more choice. All projects were aware of health and safety issues and worked to minimise hazards and prevent accidents. Attitudes to risk-taking varied; sensitivity was needed with respect to the concerns of parents of disabled children, and it was important to build trust. Playworkers were more supportive of risk-taking and challenge than educational staff. Playing with friends was very important for children and the extent to which disabled and non-disabled children played together varied; the more flexible the projects were, the more likely it was that children would play together.

Ward and others (2004) report on work to develop inclusive provision in the north west of England and identified a number of determinants of success, including: supporting a shift in attitudes and assumptions on the part of staff, volunteers and parents; finding out what play and leisure opportunities exist, and discussing how inclusive they could become; meeting individual needs; addressing practical issues such as transport and change to routines; staff and volunteer resources both behind the scenes and face-to-face; acknowledging that change can take a long time; effective risk management and developing trust with children and families; and celebrating successes.

The extent to which disabled children were able to participate in playing in the school playground was the focus of Woolley and others' (2006a; 2006b) research into six primary schools across Yorkshire. Good practice and barriers were grouped under three headings: organisational, social and physical. Whilst identifying some barriers (for example, reduction in time for play in the school day – an aspect that affected all children; timing of care routines in some schools, but not all, meant that disabled children went out into the playground later that non-disabled children and after some games had started; lack of systematic auditing of the playgrounds for physical access; some level of over-protectiveness on the part of adults), the research generally found much to highlight as good practice, particularly regarding a recognition of the disabled children's own agency and skill in joining in and leading games, and the social benefit gained through use of their specialist equipment as play props. In some schools, support staff were well trained, valued and committed, this being reflected in their length of service and the relationships built up with children.

John and Wheway (2004: 11), in their study of disabled children's access to and use of outdoor playgrounds, note that whilst there is support for the principle of inclusion, many feel anxious about their own abilities to cope. Their research into disabled children's use of outdoor play spaces shows that this is less to do with the physical accessibility or suitability of equipment than with 'the attitudes of other children, the fears of the disabled children's parents and the belief of what is appropriate parenting'. They stress that any strategy for inclusion should consider this social aspect and not only the physical adjustments; it is impossible to make one playground accessible for all children given the range of impairments, needs and likes. Well-intentioned legislation and regulation requirements often disable rather than enable access to play provision. One of these is the tendency to be over-protective. The occasional bump and getting dirty should be seen as a normal part of playing, as much for disabled as for non-disabled children. Health and safety legislation is referred to as 'the polite discrimination', since it has been evoked to justify restrictions to play opportunities (John and Wheway 2004).

Dunn and others (2004), in their report on the research that underpinned the Office of the Deputy Prime Minister's (2003) *Developing Accessible Play Space: A good practice guide*, found that enabling disabled children and young people to play in the same public spaces with their siblings and other disabled and non-disabled children and young people has wider benefits for social inclusion, community building and networking. Design of the space is important, as is an understanding of what disabled children and young people want.

McIntyre and Casey (2007) report on two action research projects on inclusive play in supervised settings that extend the concept of inclusion beyond a focus on the provision itself to an emphasis on the importance of friendships and a sense of inclusion across a network of contexts and settings. Drawing on the theorising on play and playwork, the projects developed models of support for play (rather than access), through effective use of the environment, sensitive and responsive playworker involvement in play and observation-based reflections.

Smith and Willans (2007) also report on using playwork approaches, specifically identifying preferred play types (Hughes 2002) and understanding play cues (Sturrock and Else 1998) to support the playing of one disabled child whose behaviour had been interpreted as naughty and difficult. Once playworkers used these tools to understand how the child wanted to play, they could then respond in a play-centred way and thus reduce the difficult behaviour born out of frustration.

Ethnicity and racism

There is a strong tradition of anti-racist, anti-bias and multi-cultural practice amongst those working with children and young people, dating back to the early 1980s (Derman-Sparks 1989; Conway and others 2004; Brooker 2006) and continuing with explicit references in official standards documentation (for example DfES 2003a). The intention within these approaches is to challenge discrimination and stereotypes both directly and through offering a wide range of experiences intended to broaden understanding of other cultures. However, Mathers and others (2007) found in their study of the quality of childcare provision that the settings in their study were barely reaching minimal standards in the provision of resources and activities aimed at promoting awareness and understanding of racial and cultural diversity, and that many settings had not improved in this area since the previous assessment a decade before.

Smith and Barker (2000), in their research of children's experiences in more than 400 out of school clubs, found that children's ethnicity had a significant impact on their experiences at the clubs. At one club, where the majority of children were African-Caribbean, which had an abundance of African-Caribbean resources and promoted African-Caribbean cultures, the children spoke positively about this and had developed their own games and activities with the resources. However, in other clubs that were predominantly white and where the workers were also predominantly white, the researchers found that ethnic diversity was largely ignored, or treated as something exotic and foreign, for example:

> … well meaning but tokenistic attempts at serving food from around the world. These attempts were mostly done without context and children often constructed such activities as 'bizarre'. For children from ethnic minority groups the opportunity to contest such representations was limited by the fact that adult playworkers retained control over the food provided, the posters put on the walls and the resources bought for the clubs. Moreover, for a minority of children attending such clubs, the feeling that they as Black or Asian children were 'out of place' in these environments was exacerbated by these processes.

In such settings, attempts at increasing understanding and awareness may well serve to perpetuate stereotypes and exacerbate differences. The appropriateness of multicultural educational approaches in settings that aim to support free play has been questioned, in terms of its potential to direct children's play towards adult-determined ends (Hughes 2001), the potential for many adults' Eurocentric perspectives and values to ride roughshod over other cultural play expressions (Sturrock and Else 1998), and finally in terms of its effectiveness (Holland 2003; Connolly 2006; Brooker 2006). There is a need for more research into these issues.

Connolly (2006) shows how the identities of boys in primary schools were inextricably linked to their class and ethnicity and that practices within the school sometimes served to perpetuate stereotypes rather than challenge them (for example by seeing football as a way of engaging potentially disaffected Black boys in the life of the school).

Kapasi (2002), in her study of access to play provision by Black and minority children in London, found that the majority of users of play provision were white children and Black British children, although there are no data showing how this relates to the local population. Use of mainstream play provision by Asian and other minority children was limited, even when there was a large Asian population in the local area. Interviews with children, families and staff showed that:

> minority children preferred to attend community-led schemes where they felt at ease … The statistics showed that community-led schemes reached the most marginalised groups of children whilst mainstream providers consistently failed to do so. Yet these schemes seemed to remain under-funded, unrecognized and unsupported. (Kapasi 2002: 40)

Those children that did attend mainstream provision were most comfortable where they were in large numbers and had been attending over a long period of time; even so, children tended to play within cultural groups at the setting, rarely mixing, playing 'in parallel'. The report also found that, where projects employed Black or minority senior playworkers, they were more likely to attract Black and minority children. Kapasi (2002: 41) concludes that 'there was a lack of debate on the nature, manifestation and impact of institutional racism in mainstream provision.'

A later survey (Kapasi 2006b) focused on the employment of Black and minority playworkers and found varied levels of understanding about issues pertaining to ethnicity and racism among playworkers and play service managers, and varied levels of support for Black and minority playworkers, both in their current roles and for professional development. Most striking was a lack of engagement in any debate about the issues, and Kapasi (2006b: 26-27) concludes:

> It would appear that the more diverse London and the rest of the United Kingdom becomes, debates around race and racism are easier to avoid under concepts of 'diversity', 'culture', 'ethnicity' and 'inclusion'. Whilst identity continues to be a growing agenda in our society, all children on playgrounds and playcentres are also being affected by racist stereotyping, lack of role models and institutional racism.

Smith and Barker (2004) draw some of the same conclusions from their research into out of school clubs. Noting that out of school childcare is a key element of the government's aim to eradicate child poverty, they highlighted that some minority ethnic groups, particularly Somali and Bangladeshi families, although living within the community and using the school, did not attend the out of school club. They give two reasons for this, one being financial (many of the Somalis were refugees and, as such, not able to work, thus unable to afford or qualify for the childcare places), and the other cultural. The 2001 Childcare Workforce Survey (SQW and NOP 2002, cited in Smith and Barker 2004) showed that only 28 per cent of clubs across the UK employ minority ethnic staff. SkillsActive (2006b: 10), in their national survey of the playwork workforce, report that '5.3% of respondents indicated an ethnic origin other than white compared to 7% in the working population as a whole'. This figure rose to 12 per cent for holiday staff. In Smith and Barker's survey, half of the clubs employed staff from minority ethnic groups, encouraged playing together and undertook multicultural activities such as celebrating festivals, which were highly valued by children and parents. However, two of the clubs studied displayed a tokenistic attitude towards multiculturalism, despite having equal opportunities policies, and one club considered the issue irrelevant since only white children attended the club. Smith and Barker (2004: 14) conclude:

> Although this is a small sample, it raises serious doubts in many cases about the ability of the service to offer an inclusive environment attractive to families from minority ethnic groups.

Creegan and others (2004), in their evaluation of 10 Children's Fund projects in Tower Hamlets, found that inclusion and diversity varied depending on the local and cultural contexts. Some projects were used almost exclusively by particular groups such as Bengali or Somali children, while others were more mixed; in the mixed settings they observed the same playing in parallel reported by Kapasi (2002). Employing Bengali staff to attract Bengali children was effective, although this varied in terms of the gender both of the staff and the children, and how far this was supported by families. Playworkers sometimes reported ethnic tension between groups within projects and felt that although they could work to reduce this, such tensions continued outside of the project.

One of the indicators for Creegan and others' evaluation research was the extent to which children played together. At the majority of projects they found children of different ethnic groups playing together, although situations were observed where children played in small groups within the overall project that were not ethnically diverse; this was similar to Kapasi's (2002) finding of children playing 'in parallel'. Encouraging children of different ethnic groups to play together was seen as a positive step. The polarisation of communities was highlighted in research by the Community Cohesion Research Team following racial disturbances in Burnley and Oldham (Cantle 2001: 9):

> Separate educational arrangements, community and voluntary bodies, employment, places of worship, language, social and cultural networks, means that many communities operate on the basis of a series of parallel lives. These lives often do not seem to touch at any point, let alone overlap and promote any meaningful interchanges.

Yet a Home Office survey (Farmer 2005) found that nationally 64 per cent of children and young people surveyed had friends who were of a difference race or colour to them. Cantle (2001) notes that many of the well-intentioned projects and initiatives aimed at meeting the needs of different communities often served to institutionalise the very problems they were trying to solve, and to engender feelings of division and unfairness between groups. Projects that were working to break down divisions and build community cohesion were battling 'against the odds and with very limited and fragile resources … clinging on to the margins of anything that resembled a longer term strategy' (Cantle 2001: 9). The report concluded that there should be a proactive attempt to 'promote cross-cultural contact, … foster understanding and respect … [developing] a programme of myth-busting' (Cantle 2001: 11). Bhavnani and others (2005) found little evidence of the effectiveness of cohesion approaches. Bruegel (2006), however, in her research on friendships of primary school children and social capital, found that daily contact across ethnic and religious boundaries was the most effective way of breaking down barriers between communities rather than formal twinning or sporting arrangements between separate schools.

Maan (2005) recommends that community-led provision can play a part in the overall provision for play and that valuable lessons can be learned. She highlights the need to employ and support staff from Black and minority groups and also male playworkers. Play is valued differently in different communities and this needs to be addressed sensitively, recognising that some communities may have differing priorities that need addressing first.

Morris and others (2006) place their evaluation of preventative services to Black and minority ethnic children through the Children's Fund within the context of the Race Relations (Amendment) Act 2000, which places a duty on public bodies, amongst other things, to carry out a 'race equality audit of organisational systems, structures and practices' (Morris and others 2006: 10). However, evidence from the Audit Commission (2004) suggests that progress in implementing the Race Relations (Amendment) Act 2000 is slow. This evaluation focused on two case study areas and in both the emphasis was on addressing the link between the practices of mainstream education and poor educational outcome for this group of children and young people. Generally this was through supplementary informal educational activities delivered by community members, and in one case study this included after school clubs and holiday playschemes. The intention here was to develop shared cultural knowledge

'... although most organisations have equality and diversity policies and documentation, there is little research into evidence of what works.'

and increased self-esteem and confidence through culturally sensitive trips, activities and structured play. Practices that were seen as helpful included the flexibility of staff and their ability to engage with children and young people, and the importance of staff belonging to the same cultural group as the children and young people themselves. Although the key stated aim of these projects was to enhance learning, the children and young people themselves talked about their experiences as being fun, and of the value they placed on making friends with others in their community across generations. However, the report also notes that the focus of these services was more on change for the children and young people themselves rather than change within mainstream services, particularly education.

Bhavnani and others (2005) found that, although most organisations have equality and diversity policies and documentation, there is little research into evidence of what works. Tools such as ethnic monitoring can serve to entrench categories and therefore reproduce racism. Many interventions focus on local area working class racism rather than that emanating from the elite (such as politicians and the media). One of the problems in identifying success of strategies and interventions is how to measure this success. Bhavnani and others suggest that, rather than measuring impact in terms of access to opportunities, the measure should be of changes in attitudes and behaviour and in everyday racism. The most success, on this measure, was found to be from educational approaches aimed at improving understanding and communication, and which are strongly led. Open and honest approaches to confronting racism can heal rifts and promote reconciliation.

Much of the thinking about racism in the 1970s and 1980s was about the structure of society: how power worked within the system. Since then, issues of ethnicity and culture have become more complex. For example, many of the children attending play settings today are likely to be two, perhaps three generations away from the big wave of immigration in the 1950s from (post) colonial countries. Cross-cultural relationships have produced children and grandchildren whose ethnic heritage is multiple. In addition, the newer arrivals to Britain, economic migrants, refugees and asylum seekers, are from a far wider range of countries and cultures, including many African countries, Eastern and Central Europe, the former Soviet Union and the Middle East. Ideas about ethnicity and about religion have become both more integrated and more separate (Mac an Ghaill 1999).

Gypsy and Traveller children

One cultural group that is often omitted from discussions on racism are the Roma Gypsy and Traveller communities. A Mori poll (cited in Lawrence 2005) found that one in three respondents admitted to feelings of prejudice against Roma Gypsies and Travellers. Children often do not have access to services such as health care and education, partly because of fear of attack and also because often services are deemed inappropriate. Yet under the Race Relations (Amendment) Act 2000 public authorities have a statutory duty to promote race equality.

Roma Gypsies and Irish Travellers are recognised as a racial group for the purposes of the Act (Lawrence 2005). Mason and Broughton (2007) emphasise that 'Gypsy/Travellers' do not constitute a homogeneous group with shared values and culture (as well as Roma Gypsies and Irish Travellers there are also other mobile groups such as Fairground People and New Travellers), although they tend to be grouped together for the purposes of service provision.

Hester (2004, cited in Mason and Broughton 2007) identified that Gypsy and Traveller communities are amongst the most marginalised in the United Kingdom. Mason and Broughton report on a collaborative regional project to address the lack of play and leisure services for Gypsy/Traveller children through a consortium of Children's Fund Partnerships. The project aimed to make existing mainstream services accessible to Gypsy/Traveller children through support and training for staff, information and support to Gypsy/Traveller families to help access to service, direct support to the children and young people themselves and attempts to address discrimination within the settled community through other service providers in the area. However, a number of factors meant that a sustainable network beyond the life of the Children's Fund did not develop. The project focused largely on meeting the immediate play and leisure needs of the children, which left little time or capacity for developing more sustainable networks and access to services. In some cases, parents' fear and suspicion was a barrier to children accessing mainstream provision unless accompanied by project staff. Despite this, the project did succeed in supporting some mothers to access play provision with their children and to become involved in volunteering and developing further provision.

Refugee and asylum–seeking children

Refugee and asylum-seeking children arrive in the UK having fled from situations of conflict that they found so stressful as to be insupportable. Many have lost parents and have endured arduous and dangerous journeys (Hyder 2005). Although many families are interested in childcare services, as these are understood to help their children, there is a diversity of views on play. Often it is regarded as something that happens naturally without any support from adults. However, the isolation of families sometimes means that these opportunities no longer exist, and Hyder (2005) recommends that staff should be encouraged to convey the importance of play to parents, particularly as their children may benefit from the healing experience of play.

Those working in early years and play settings need to be aware of the role of play

> as a restorative and healing experience for young children. This is not just because play in itself is a formative experience for the child, but also because play is rooted in the experience and representation of events and objects within a family and a community. (Hyder 2005: 7)

Often, the mixture of supportive relationships, routine, and structured and free play is enough; others may need sensitive understanding of adults as they need to play out material that adults might find disturbing.

Nandy (2005) describes how policy does not always support the needs of asylum-seeking and refugee children: if immigration and asylum policies come into conflict with children's rights, the former take precedence. This is stated explicitly in the UK government's reservation lodged regarding the United Nations Convention on the Rights of the Child (UNCRC 1989) 'effectively creating a second class of children to whom the UNCRC does not equally apply' (Nandy 2005: 411).

Asylum-seeking and refugee children were a specific group targeted by the Children's Fund as being at risk of social exclusion. Beirens and others (2006) report that different services varied in their aims, which included dealing with trauma through therapeutic services, including play therapy, encouraging educational attainment and community cohesion. Therapeutic services needed to be culturally appropriate, so activity based therapies were felt to be more effective than counselling and other talking therapies. Informal after school and holiday projects provided support and space for children to make friends and play, improving their English language skills and their general emotional health and well-being accordingly. In one project, links were made between playworkers and play therapists.

Homeless children

Shelter (2006) estimates that 1.6 million children in Britain (1.4 million in England) live in bad housing (meaning they are homeless or in overcrowded or unfit accommodation). This amounts to one child in seven. These children are far more likely than those living in adequate accommodation to: miss school; leave school with no qualifications; be excluded from school; suffer from poor health, particularly respiratory and sleep problems; be depressed and have mothers who are depressed; be bullied; have nowhere to play; be in trouble with the police. The report states:

> Having friends over to play and playing independently or with siblings are vital to ensure a fun and stimulating childhood and healthy development both physical and emotional. Constant moving to new housing, long journeys to school, living in problem neighbourhoods, lack of space to play and cold, damp or infested conditions deny children living in bad housing this basic right. (Shelter 2006: 40)

Shatwell (2003) paints a similar story for homeless children in Leeds, saying that children, parents and staff all recognise the need for more opportunities for the children to play. The report identifies three examples of good practice (one local, the other two elsewhere in England). One project began by offering babysitting and childcare services and grew to taking children on trips and now has one flat operating as a play flat. Women's Aid refuges have a long history of providing children's workers and play provision. The draft *National Standards for Domestic and Sexual Violence* (Women's Aid Federation of England 2006) make explicit reference to the need to provide activities and play opportunities for children. This is understood both as an 'ordinary' need for children and also because children use play to help them come to terms with their experiences of domestic violence (this is discussed in more detail in the section on children and trauma).

Gender

The issues discussed in the literature relating to gender take a slightly different stance from those regarding disability and ethnicity, which tend to be focused on access and inclusion. It should not be forgotten that the categorisation of children in this way can sometimes mask the diversity of children's identities: both girls and boys will also have their own ethnicity and culture, family background and circumstance, experiences of disability and so on (James and Prout 1997). Furthermore, as discussed in Chapter 3, simplistic and binary categories of male/ female are not borne out in real life: there are more variations within than between genders (Browne 2004; Swain 2005).

Given this variation within gender, it is still largely apparent that adults' own expectations of and preferences for children's behaviour are clearly gendered. The workforce in early years and playwork is overwhelmingly female (Moss 2003; Rolfe and others 2003; SkillsActive 2006) and this has implications for attitudes towards the playing of boys and girls. In discussing play in such a gendered way, there is a tension between generalising about boys' and girls' play preferences on the one hand and perpetuating stereotypes on the other. As Morrow (2006: 93) warns:

> It is important to recognise that when talking about differences between children there is a danger of 'essentialising' — i.e. assuming that there are some universal characteristics that apply to all girls and all boys. Social differences do not operate in isolation, because social class, age, ethnicity, religion and location intersect to influence children's childhoods and their gender identities.

The expression of gender identities is also contextually-specific (Connolly 2006): children will behave in different ways according to the context, their ideas of the expectations of their peers as well as of adults, their desires to situate themselves within particular understandings of what it is to be a boy or a girl. There is no single universal or simple way to understand play and gender; yet often adults' expectations of behaviour and their perception of its acceptability are fundamentally based on stereotypical understandings of boys' and girls' play.

One example of this is Smith and others' (2002) comparison of teacher and pupil perceptions of play fighting in school playgrounds. Teachers tend to have a negative view of play fighting, seeing few benefits attached to it and expressing concern that it will turn into real fighting, which is not borne out by the research. The authors suggest that this may have something to do with the fact that most primary teachers are women and were less likely to engage in play fighting when they were children (or if they did play fight, may have forgotten what it felt like) and so may not appreciate the enjoyment derived from this way of playing.

Thomson (2005: 72) also found that midday supervisors, again mostly women, 'intensely disliked children playing football and pointed out to them any contravention of the football pitch space in an effort to contain and constrain the players'. Similar problematising of boys' more boisterous playing, and a corresponding positive attitude towards girls' more sedentary and social playing, by female early years practitioners and playworkers is reported by J Brown (2007b), Holland (2003) and Smith and Barker (2000). Smith and Barker (2000; 2004) report that boys in out of school clubs, particularly those over eight years of age, are aware of this and asked for more male playworkers because they felt that female playworkers did not understand their play preferences:

> Playworkers utilised adult discourses of equality of opportunity when they wanted to prevent what they saw as boys' subversive attempts to take over space, being used by girls, for football. The boys interpreted these adult attempts to limit football in terms of unequal gendered relations in clubs, primarily because most play workers were women. As one 10-year-old boy explained: 'They treat girls differently, and they treat boys like they are things that don't belong here'. (Smith and Barker 2000: 326)

Whilst recognising the need for more male playworkers, Smith and Barker (2003) say that there is also a need for playworkers to be made aware of these issues through training; a similar recommendation for midday supervisors and primary school teachers is made by Smith and others (2002). Rolfe and others (2003) and Rolfe (2006) identify potential benefits of more men in childcare and playwork as including the presence of role models, modelling equality between men and women and providing a balance of experience and approach. More research is needed into why men do not enter childcare, and although the low pay and conditions may be one factor, it may not be the overriding one, since men are still in the minority in this sector in Scandinavian countries where pay and conditions are good. The suggestion is that it may be because of the low status and the perception of working with children as being 'women's work', as well as the level of suspicion of men's motives for working with children.

Browne (2004) challenges the accepted concerns about the feminisation of the workforce and the value of male staff as positive role models. She suggests these concerns have their roots in anxiety about boys' underachievement in school, seen to be a result of 'feminine' approaches in schools to teaching and learning that favour girls. Such a perspective can be understood as blame, as one nursery teacher in her study said:

> I think we've been made to feel it's our fault because we're female and we can't cope with boys and therefore it would be better if there were more males in the profession. (Browne 2004: 125)

Browne cites suggestions (Mahoney and Hextall 2000; Haywood and Mac an Ghaill 2001) that the focus on tests, measurement, targets and key stages within the education system could be understood as a 'masculine' rationalisation of a service that is fundamentally about relationships and processes. However, the labels of 'feminisation' and 'masculinisation' perpetuate fixed and binary oppositions that are unhelpful in moving forward understandings of gender equity.

Such binary oppositions also lie at the root of Browne's challenges to the accepted notion of the value of men as positive role models in the children's workforce. Role modelling as a concept only has currency within an understanding of socialisation that sees children as passive recipients of adult norms and values rather than co-constructors of their own subjectivities and identities, as discussed in Chapter 3. In addition, if men are employed to be male role models, this implies that they have to conform to an ideal of what masculinity means, or, conversely, to be a living challenge to stereotypes, both of which perpetuate fixed oppositions of what it is to be masculine or feminine.

The dominant understanding of gender in childhood is still based in a developmental psychology ages and stages approach, although this has been criticised for not acknowledging children's own agency and competence and the complexity and diversity of children's experiences of gender. More recent sociological studies have addressed this, yet there is still a tendency to generalise, and these more recent theories have not yet been incorporated into the training of those working with children (Morrow 2006). This is borne out in Holland's (2003) research into early years practitioners' responses to gun and superhero play. Although the zero tolerance approach is based in feminist and pacifist thinking, Holland maintains that it is misguided in that the assumption is that such imaginative play has a relationship to aggression in later life. More recent understandings which show that this is not the case have been slow to permeate into practice, and Holland (2003: 15-16) warns:

> I believe our approach to gender relationships in early years settings over the past twenty years has served to harden rather than challenge stereotypical behaviour. This approach is characterised by the corrective and sometimes punitive form of response offered to active young boys in counterpoint to the celebratory response given to compliant and passive young girls playing in the home corner or at the writing table. Both of these responses should cause us equal concern … after twenty to thirty years of concerted attempts to promote equal opportunities between boys and girls one can look around most nursery classrooms and see the same gendered grouping of play preferences: girls in the home corner, boys on the construction carpet.

Browne (2004) suggests that tolerance of superhero and war play in boys in early years settings is a part of 'recuperative masculinity' strategies arising from concerns about boys' academic underachievement. She suggests that the new tolerance of this form of play rests on flawed 'scientific' and essentialist ideas of natural and biological differences between boys and girls and that 'such play may contribute to the maintenance of unequal gender power relations and "traditional" forms of "masculinity"' (Browne 2004: 121). The literature reviewed in Chapter 3 shows how many of those now working within the natural science fields recognise the interdependent relationship between biology and culture through the understanding that the brain is shaped as a result of interactions with the environment, leading to changes in behaviour and so on in a constant 'dynamic coupling' (Thompson and Varela 2001): the 'embodied brain embedded in the world'. Similarly, the ethnographic studies of children's play discussed in Chapter 4 show how children co-construct and reproduce gender identities in their play, and how difficult it is to cross gender boundaries. It may be that playing at gender in these frames allows an adaptation to the peer group that adults may understand as maladaptive and stereotypical.

Kalliala (2006) gives illustrations of common themes that exercise early years practitioners: the rough and tumble and war play of the boys and the sexualised play of girls with Barbie dolls. Whilst not banning such playing outright, the staff create strategies for easing their discomfort. With Barbie dolls, they solve the contradiction by framing an understanding of it as traditional doll play 'independent of Barbie's bust measurement' (Kalliala 2006: 123); often war play can be reframed as construction play (building the scene). With rough and tumble, they set boundaries by imposing rules. Kalliala (2006: 124) acknowledges:

> It is hard to mark off the boundary between positive and negative autonomy in children's play. There is a permanent tension between respect for children's intimacy and secrets, on the one hand, and control and enrichment of children's activities, on the other. Children need both sensitive supervision and stimulation and freedom when they develop their inner self, not either/or but both/and.

Adults' propensity to create understandings of playing that ease their own discomfort can also be seen in responses to children's sexual identities. The boyfriend-girlfriend play of children in the last year of junior school has generally been understood as innocent preparation for adult roles. Renold (2006) suggests, though, that this is more to do with gender performance in the here and now, and that children feel the need to conform to the heterosexual norms of this play narrative, with both boys and girls investing much time and emotional energy on getting together, dating, dumping, go-betweens and discussions about relationships. Any deviation from this norm is greeted with social punishment including exclusion and teasing. Only tomboys and the most popular and socially successful children can challenge these hegemonies without censure. This way of understanding the playground behaviour of primary school children challenges dominant thinking that children of this age are sexual innocents who play in single gender groups.

Brooker (2006) recognises the good intent of early childhood settings to challenge discrimination and inequality faced by some children, an approach based on offering a wide range of opportunities to children which extend their home experiences and challenge some of the stereotypes that may be encountered within the family. However, her research within a Korean kindergarten and UK reception class with a high proportion of Bangladeshi children questions the effectiveness of this approach and suggests that 'everyday life in educational settings, against the best intentions of educators, may serve to polarise children's identities along the gendered and ethnic lines, in ways which may further constrain their continuing development' (Brooker 2006: 117). In her observations she found that children in early childhood settings would actively reproduce a stereotypical version of their gender and ethnic identities that were far more complex, flexible and varied at home. This could have been due to the tendency to seek out other children 'like me' in unfamiliar contexts. Brooker suggests that in addition to this, the existence of play opportunities such as home corner, coupled with a support for children's freedom of choice, supported this tendency towards stereotypical behaviour that did not actually exist in the home. Conversation with the children about their own understandings of their play preferences and behaviour revealed a more complex approach than did the observations alone, and Brooker suggests that practitioners need to find out more about children's actual experiences and understandings rather than relying on adult interpretations of behaviour.

Newman and others (2006) gained an insight into the ways in which children position themselves physically in the playground in relation to their social popularity and positioning. A photography project aimed at encouraging children aged 10 to 11 years to question the 'reality' of photographs and to explore the stories that photographs can tell, revealed children's understandings of and feelings about their social status within their peer group, and this is paralleled through their choices of physical positioning in the playground. Much of this was gendered: confirming earlier studies, the research found that the largest amount of central space in the playground was occupied by the dominant boys playing football. Girls and the less 'masculine' boys occupied the spaces round the edge. Boys not fitting the traditional masculine stereotype of football playing could negotiate socially acceptable identities through humorous rule breaking and challenging of authority. One boy, who was perceived as effeminate and was bullied because of this, found places to hide during playtime. Staff, both male and female, suggested that he was at least partially to blame for the bullying as he did not fit into the hegemonic masculine identity. Similarly, a girl who stood up to her female bully using physical force, chose to do so away from adult eyes as she knew she would have been chided for not conforming to passive female roles.

These studies present a much more diverse and constellated view of children's active gender work through playing and raise questions for traditional approaches to anti-discriminatory practice.

Children in public care

Blower and others (2004), in their research on children in the care of one local authority, found that 56 per cent of the children interviewed were suffering from 'significant psychological morbidity', and that there was an urgent need to identify effective interventions. In a more wide-ranging survey for the Office of National Statistics, Meltzer and others (2003: 20) found that 'among young people, aged 5 – 17 years, looked after by local authorities, 45% were assessed as having a mental disorder: 37% had clinically significant conduct disorders; 12% were assessed as having emotional disorders – anxiety and depression – and 7% were rated as hyperactive.'

The Healthy Care Programme, developed by the National Children's Bureau and funded by the Department for Education and Skills, is 'a practical means of improving the health and well-being of looked after children and young people in line with the Department of Health guidance *Promoting the Health of Looked After Children* (2002) and the Change for Children Programme' (www.ncb.org.uk). The Healthy Care Standard developed through this project recognises the importance of play, and this is further supported through the Well-being, Creativity and Play project, which aims to 'increase awareness of the benefits of creative activities at a local level' (Chambers 2004: 2). Creativity and play can be particularly important for children in public care in terns of fostering resilience. Gilligan (2000: 37) describes a resilient child as 'one who bounces back having endured adversity, who continues to function reasonably well despite continued exposure to risk'. Chambers (2004) stresses the importance of play and creativity as part of the normal day-to-day experience rather than as acute play therapy services. Whilst those in care may require the help of professional therapists, carers can do much to support children to play in a very ordinary way, and this can in itself be a part of the healing process. The role of foster carers and residential staff is crucial in developing the attachments that can support playing and healing in this way. Database searches showed no results for evidence of supporting play for children in public care, while the focus of the government's *Care Matters* Green Paper (DfES 2006f) is on educational attainment.

Play in hospitals

The need for children who are visiting or staying in hospital to play is recognised in Standard 7 of the National Service Framework for Children, Young People and Maternity Services. Guidance on Standard 7 (DH 2003: 14) states:

> Children visiting or staying in hospital have a basic need for play and recreation that should be met routinely in all hospital departments providing a service to children. This applies equally to the siblings of patients, and so is also a consideration for neonatal units. Play may also be used for therapeutic purposes, as part of the child's care plan, and as a way of helping the child to: assimilate new information; adjust to and gain control over a potentially frightening environment; and prepare to cope with procedures and interventions. There is evidence that play hastens recovery, as well as reducing the need for interventions to be delivered under general anaesthesia.

Moore and Russ (2006) note that pretend play interventions with children are effective in both inpatient and outpatient settings for preventing and reducing anxiety and distress. Pretend play also has effects on reducing pain and adaptation to chronic illness.

Walker (2006) lists a number of reasons why children and young people in hospital should have the opportunity to play: as an essential ingredient of childhood and child development, the need to play continues during time in hospital; however, the unfamiliarity of the hospital context, the invasiveness of medical procedures and the sense of uncertainty regarding the outcomes of treatment are all factors likely to produce high levels of anxiety and stress at a time when children are most vulnerable because they are ill. Play can help mitigate all of these factors. The provision of play equipment sends messages that playing is welcome in the hospital, and the playing process can help in making the unfamiliar and unknown familiar and knowable. Play can also help aid physical recovery through encouraging movement, and it can also have a role in helping to heal trauma. Play specialists can help children to communicate their fears and needs as well as supporting the play process more generally. Walker draws a distinction between hospital play specialists and play therapists, whilst recognising the therapeutic benefits of play itself. Haiat and others (2003: 210) agree:

> Play is one of the most powerful and most effective tools used to reduce tension, anger, frustration, conflict, and anxiety, which are accompanied by the loss of control, and self-esteem. This can be said of all children in general, and especially of those who are hospitalised.

Play in prisons

The *Every Child Matters* (ECM) Green Paper (DfES 2003b: 43) states that 'seven per cent of children during their time at school experience the imprisonment of a father, while every year, approximately 150,000 children have a parent who enters custody'. The paper cites research showing that children usually want to keep in touch with their imprisoned parents but there are many obstacles, including visiting prisons. Efforts to establish and maintain support services are largely through the voluntary sector and dependent upon individual commitment. The paper seeks suggestions on the way forward but a search revealed no explicit reference to children visiting parents in prison in subsequent ECM documents.

The need for children visiting prisons to play is increasingly acknowledged, and although several projects were funded through the Children's Fund to develop support for children with family members in prison, a search revealed little in the way of systematic evaluation. Andrews (2005) reports on how having play facilities at prison visitor centres can help make visits easier for both children and mothers. Tamminen and Bailey (2001) use the experience of how the play facility at Wakefield Prison has a positive impact on the experiences of children visiting their fathers to develop guidelines for other prisons.

Children and trauma

Many of the groups of children considered in this section will have experienced, or still be experiencing, trauma. The healing effects of play have been recognised both in play therapy (for example Cattanach 2003) and in playwork approaches (Sturrock and Else 2005). The literature on this aspect of play is considerable and there has not been the opportunity within the scope of this review to look at it in any depth; however it is such an important aspect of playing that it needs to be included. Children who have experienced the trauma of natural disasters, terrorism or war will often play out the scenes they have witnessed (Sleek 1998; Howard 2007); this has been recognised as an element of children's play since the earlier documentations such as Ariès (1962, cited in Adams and Moyles 2005).

Adams and Moyles (2005) report the difficulty that early years practitioners have in knowing how to respond to children who have witnessed major events such as the attacks on the World Trade Centre in 2001, even if these events were witnessed at a distance. Many anecdotally report an increase in war play and also in tower building and destroying in children's play following the images of destruction seen on television screens. The sensitivities generated by differences of perspective on the reasons for and the responses to the attacks complicate the issue further. Reactions to children's playing out of scenes can range from discomfort through to offence. Adams and Moyles explore three interrelated themes of: images of violence in the media; practitioners' feelings and values regarding this and their emotional response to children's representations of violence in their play; and children's entitlement to express feelings of anger, frustration and anxiety in their playing. They suggest that talking with colleagues about these feelings may help work towards a response that supports the children in expressing these narratives rather than inhibiting them.

In their guidance on aid support for children in emergencies, developed in response to the Balkan conflict, Cuninghame and others (2001) devote a whole section to play. In it they promote the importance of 'ordinary' playing, both organised and spontaneous, as a part of children's routine and a way of helping them develop resilience to the emergency situations in which they find themselves. They advise that 'some activities may cause children to recall, and express, distressing memories (perhaps through drawings or make-believe play). This should be neither encouraged nor discouraged, but allowed and supported if initiated by the child' (Cuninghame and others 2001: 40).

Loughry and others (2006) carried out an empirical study of the impact of structured activities among Palestinian children from the West Bank and Gaza and found that this appeared to be helpful in improving children's emotional and behavioural well-being but not their hopefulness, and that it also helped to improve parental support. Structured activities were seen to:

'The starting point is the importance of recognising that all children need to play and that some children face greater barriers than others in accessing opportunities to play.'

213

provide a routine to counteract the chaos of the conflict; reduce the risks attached to children playing in unsafe ways and places; support children in expressing and playing out problems; and provide opportunities for children to develop attachments to other children and adults. In addition, parents could feel that their children were safe and could also benefit from participating alongside them.

Brown (2006b) reports on a playwork project with neglected and abused children in a paediatric hospital in Romania (Webb and Brown 2003; Brown and Webb 2005). Playworkers worked with the children to build relationships of trust and create opportunities for them to play, taking the child's own agenda as the starting point. A specifically designed play assessment tool was used to measure how the children's play developed. Significant improvements were observed in the children's play and development: 'in less than a year, these chronically abused and neglected children made the sort of progress that many experts assumed would be impossible' (Brown and Webb 2005: 155).

Sturrock and Else (2005) suggest that therapeutic approaches to playwork can be useful in less extreme situations. Playworkers need to recognise that children have issues and emotions that they need to express symbolically, and that such expressions may also provoke strong reactions in playworkers themselves. The role of the therapeutic playworker is to understand the elements of the play cycle (comprising play cues and returns, the establishment of play frames and loop and flow, and annihilation of the frame, as described earlier in this chapter under 'supervised play provision and playwork') and develop a repertoire of responses aimed at supporting the cycle.

Summary and comment

The nationally published literature on play provision for particular groups of children and those in particular circumstances shows a distance between on then one hand the assumptions underpinning practice and on the other the findings from the emerging geographies of childhood and the brain science research into play and peer friendships outlined in Chapters 3 and 4. The evaluation research shows a focus on access to provision, with less attention paid to supporting play, and with the beginnings of questioning current approaches to anti-discriminatory practice.

The starting point is the importance of recognising that all children need to play and that some children face greater barriers than others in accessing opportunities to play. Often, for children in extreme circumstances, immediate survival needs are addressed and play can sometimes be forgotten; where opportunities are created, benefits are tangible (for example Beirens and others 2006; Chambers 2004; Walker 2006; Shatwell 2003; Andrews 2005; Tamminen and Bailey 2001; Cuninghame and others 2001). There is a debate as to whether separate or inclusive provision is preferable. The importance of community-led provision for particular cultural or religious groups is acknowledged (Maan 2005); at the same time there is an underpinning assertion that playing together reduces ignorance and prejudice and therefore aids community cohesion (Cantle 2001), although this remains contested (Bhavnani and others 2005). Much of the literature reviewed here shows that children from different cultural groups, or disabled and non-disabled children, often play 'in parallel' and that this is a cause for concern. It may be that, given the lack of agreement on the benefits of being encouraged to play together, and the research showing the importance of children's own peer friendships (for example Booth-Laforce and others 2005; Qualter and Munn 2005), that further research in this area is warranted. In some cases, the culture of settings served to perpetuate stereotypes and entrench attitudes (Smith and Barker 2001; Holland 2003; Connolly 2006; Brooker 2006).

As the literature reviewed in Chapter 3 suggests, self- and peer-led playing can sometimes seem cruel, yet it is the creativity, flexibility, sense of control and 'as if' nature of play that are understood to aid development of such capacities as emotion regulation and affect synchrony. In addition, the research on resilience, risk and stress (Rutter 2006; Siviy 1998) shows that experience of mild stress or adversity has beneficial consequences for brain structure and neurochemistry, helping to develop coping strategies; Yun and others (2005) suggest that removal of mild stressors and the decrease in variety of environmental cues may have a negative impact on resistance to disease. Such research calls into question a 'zero tolerance' approach to bullying and other forms of teasing in children's play, as does research showing that children tend to argue more with close friends than with others outside their friendship groups (Qualter and Munn 2005). If adults who support play constantly interrupt these forms of playing with the well-intentioned aim of encouraging pro-social behaviour and preventing discrimination, could this be as counterproductive as attitudes towards play fighting (Smith and others 2002) and war play (Holland 2003) have been suggested to be?

Yet on the other hand there is a tendency to idealise play's intrinsic motivations and freedoms and assume that these will always be beneficial because they are somehow 'natural' (Sutton-Smith 1997; Browne 2004; Henricks 2006). The individualistic notion of personal control and freedom cannot relate absolutely to playing in groups: there has to be a level of negotiation and cooperation in order to agree how the play frame will progress. As Henricks (2006: 8) observes, 'play … exhibits social structures only somewhat dissimilar from those found in other parts of life'. Lofdahl and Hagglund (2006) show how power structures are played out and how more powerful children decide the roles within the play and who can or cannot join in. In some cases it may be that the challenges and stresses for the children with lesser status may be beneficial in the ways described by Rutter (2006) and Siviy (1998) above; for others, persistent or extreme exclusion may indeed be harmful.

Browne (2004: 2) highlights that 'many early years educators had become disheartened with their 'equal opportunities' strategies, not least because they felt that the strategies were simply not working'. These are challenging issues and there is a need to address them through further research.

Adult–child relations and adult involvement in play provision

Adults' involvement in children's play is not restricted to face-to-face work with children and young people but also includes those who develop and manage play provision and other settings where children and young people spend time as well as those who make decisions about the use of public space. However, this section focuses on the direct interface between adults and children at play.

> The workforce in early years and school-age childcare services is of central importance ... How good the services are depends on the people working in them. The workforce – how it is organised, how it is trained, its pay and other employment conditions, how gendered it is, how the work is understood – goes to the heart of policy ... The workforce – both its structure and conditions – has been neglected for decades. There has been little new thinking and no major reforms to produce a workforce for the 21st century. (Moss 2003: 1)

Moss' argument focuses on the gendered nature of the early years and childcare workforce and the need to reconsider work with children as 'women's work'. However, the sentiment can be extended to the quality of the work itself: there is a gap between the more recent theories about play, childhood, gender and ethnicity and the literature on practice. This is particularly true of playwork, less so of early years work. There are very few evaluations or studies of playwork practice that draw on recent theorising; and fewer still that employ rigorous methodologies.

The power relationships between adults and children need to be acknowledged in any professional or service-provider/client relationship. In most contexts, adult professionals are the experts; in any role of supporting play, Russell (2005) suggests that this expert/incompetent relationship becomes reversed. Adults have mostly forgotten what it feels like to play, and tend to view children's play as a hallmark of immaturity. Although adults still carry with them the adult responsibility for children's safety and well-being when in their care, the concept of play as child-led and very much of childhood, creates a contradiction for adults aiming to support play in any authentic way.

The literature on adult roles in supporting play within a framework of equality and anti-discriminatory practice has been reviewed in the previous section. This section looks at some of the other key contested areas of practice for those working with children and young people, namely: structure, direction and intervention; behaviour; and the importance of relationships.

Structure, direction and intervention

As we have seen throughout this report, evidence of the benefits of play, and particularly of play provision, is clouded by two areas of confusion: firstly, the lack of a consistent understanding of what is meant by play and secondly, directly following on from this, the level of direction and control by adults involved in such provision. The debates on the level and appropriateness of interventions are dependent upon the particular understanding of the purpose and function of play in any given setting, for example, whether it is valued for its own sake or whether it is a vehicle for learning, community cohesion or crime reduction.

In this section, intervention is understood as direct intervention in children's play episodes; although it is recognised that a broader understanding of intervention also exists which includes the creation and modification of the physical and social environment within which children play (for example, Hughes 1996b; Conway 2003).

Some of the literature on adult roles in relation to children's play in early years settings has already been discussed in the section on early years (for example, Rogers 2005; David 2003; Cremin and others 2006; Howard and others 2001).

Sandberg (2002) summarises the debates regarding teacher intervention in children's play in Swedish preschool and after school settings, from those who claim that intervention restricts children's ability to explore, take risks or engage in free play to those who assert that teacher participation shows adult acceptance of play, builds relationships and extends learning. It should be noted that the term 'teacher' here is possibly a translation from the Swedish 'pedagogue', a term used to refer to those who work with children in a range of settings from a shared value base (see Petrie and others 2005 below). Sandberg notes that: 'generally studies of play are based on adults' perspectives of a children's world which is "created" by adults' (Sandberg 2002: 18). Her research used observations of children (aged between five and nine years) at play, both with and without teacher involvement, followed by semi-structured interviews with the children to elicit their perceptions of teacher involvement in play. Her questions included 'Who should control play?', 'Can teachers play?', 'Can teachers contribute to play?' and 'How should teachers take part in play?' Generally, respondents felt that children should control their own play, and that if teachers took control, this was usually because of safety issues or because they preferred calm playing. The children thought that it was good to have teachers there to play with if there was no one else, and to call on if needed, but some of them felt teachers could not play 'because they cannot play pretend games, they guide the play, they interfere and change the play, and they nag at children in the play'. (Sandberg 2002: 20). Teachers could contribute to playing through helping to resolve conflicts, keeping track of the rules, and playing roles or parts no one else wanted. There were some forms of play to which teachers did not contribute, for example, as one boy said, 'the kissing-game'. This study shows that children's perception of teachers' involvement in play differs from adults' own perceptions: rather than the adult being a facilitator or playmate, or someone who can usefully extend play, children see them as often interfering, and useful in certain contexts only. Sandberg (2002: 21) concludes that 'teachers should be sensitive, observant and engaged, but should not control, decide or interrupt play'.

Petrie and others (2005) explore the notion of 'pedagogy' as an approach to working with children and young people which is common in many European countries. Pedagogues work with children and young people in a range of settings to support their holistic development rather than focusing on one aspect of professional intervention such as education or care. Pedagogues are usually trained to degree level and spend much of their education developing reflective practice drawing on knowledge of theories and of themselves. Petrie and others' research into models of pedagogy in five European countries found a number of common principles underpinning the work, including a focus on the child as a whole person; an understanding of relationship with children as co-constructed rather than hierarchical; an appreciation of children's rights; an emphasis on teamwork and also on practical skills such as arts, gardening, music, making meals with children; an acknowledgement of the children's social relationships with others in the group. Petrie and others (2005) suggest that the model could be usefully applied within the Every Child Matters agenda, and that training and education could be a starting place for change.

Creegan and others' (2004) evaluation of 10 community play projects found both structured and unstructured approaches to play. Some projects offered organised and timetabled activities and games, at others there was more of an emphasis on free play, with resources and activities being freely available for the children to choose as and when they wished. The report concludes (Creegan and others 2004: 52) 'The evidence underlines the importance of achieving a balance between free play and time, and organised activities and games, in order to secure and maintain the engagement of children'.

Feinstein and others' (2005) research into the recreational preferences of teenagers in the 1970 Cohort Study (described in more detail in Chapter 2) cautiously found an association between attendance at unstructured youth clubs and later social exclusion, either in terms of poor educational attainment or criminality. However, although they suggest that structured activities could benefit young people at risk of social exclusion, they recognise that such activities may not appeal.

Sturrock and others (2004) highlight the centrality of play in children's lives and suggest this could form the core of a shared approach to work with children and young people. Their continuum of responses to children that has a playful (ludocentric) response positioned dynamically between a didactic response and a chaotic one is explained in the section of the review on playwork theories. Within this framework, adult intervention is understood as behaviour intended to support children's play frames rather than meeting any other social agenda. In parallel to the principles of the pedagogic approach described above (Petrie and others 2005), this approach also pays attention to the subjective responses of the adult to children's play expressions, and requires a high level of self-awareness and self-knowledge.

Given the evidence outlined in Chapters 3 and 4 of this review, it should be clear that children's own control of their playing (in groups as well as individually) is part of its essence, as are its characteristics of flexibility, unpredictability, spontaneity and imagination. It is these characteristics that make play so effective in its role in brain structure and chemistry, with the attendant benefits of resilience, emotion regulation and enjoyment as well as the foundations for social competence and cognitive functioning. Given such a pedigree, it should be beyond doubt that adults who work with children at play should do their utmost to support this process.

Behaviour

Jane Brown (2007b) highlights the increased attention being given to 'problem behaviour' both in the media and in public policy. Policies are becoming increasingly interventionist and punitive; at the same time interventions are targeted at younger children, including Sure Start (which explicitly aims to identify early problem behaviour) and On Track (which works with children between 4 and 12 years who are identified as being at risk of antisocial behaviour in later life). Brown's small-scale study of the perceptions of staff and parents of children in preschool settings concluded that the institutionalisation of time and space through timetabling, zoning and expectations of behaviour, contributed to the perception of boys' boisterous colonisation of space as problematic, whilst girls' tendency to engage in quieter more sedentary activities led to the perception of their being well-behaved. Girls who did not fit this expectation were also considered to display problem behaviour. Flash points for 'problem behaviour' were times and spaces of transition – arriving and leaving the setting. In this way, the behaviour could be constructed as inappropriate within the limitations of the institution rather than any truly 'child-centred' provision that accommodated the need for boisterous, physical or superhero play.

Holland (2003) draws on social theory as well as developmental psychology theories and her own experiences to critique the 30-year-old zero tolerance approach to war, weapon and superhero play in early years settings. Recognising that the approach stemmed from feminist and pacifist concerns about male aggression (domestic, public and international), she could find little in the way of evidence to support a causal link between this kind of play and aggressive behaviours. She suggests that the discomfort is more about the needs and value base of practitioners (mostly female) than it is about supporting children. Early years practitioners were expending much time and energy imposing the ban on this kind of play seemingly to little effect, but developing quite negative relationships with (almost always) boys who persisted in this play. Holland makes connections between war, weapon and superhero play and imaginative play in general, and asks if the ban inhibits the development of imaginative play and therefore the development of skills in conflict resolution or emotional mediation. In her research, when the ban was lifted, and especially in cases where staff could support imaginative play, the weapon play would develop and incorporate other kinds of imaginative play, often girls would become involved, especially if staff joined in, and generally levels of real aggression fell. Once boys were allowed to develop this play, their play repertoires expanded and were less gender stereotypical, even border crossing. There was also concern that zero tolerance was harmful to these boys' self-concept and therefore self-esteem, especially if they were receiving different messages at home. Imaginative play helps to develop theory of mind and the capacity to understand that each person's mind is individual and therefore that other people experience things differently. Holland is not supportive of a straight laissez-faire approach that rests on a crude understanding of the concept of catharsis (getting it out of the system). Her thesis is that this is an entry into imaginative play and if it is blocked, this inhibits the development of imagination and all the benefits that accrue from that, particularly around deferred gratification, emotion regulation and theory of mind, leading to conflict resolution skills.

Thornton and Cox (2005) report on supporting and structuring the play of children with Autistic Spectrum Disorder (ASD) in order to reduce challenging behaviour and aid learning and development. Working with children in a residential setting, they drew on both current theories on the suppressed potential for play in children with ASD and earlier developmental theories (for example, Bruner's theory of scaffolding 1966; Vygotsky's Zone of Proximal Development 1933, cited in Thornton and Cox 2005) of the role of adults in extending children's play and learning experiences. Understanding the antecedents of displays of challenging behaviour (for example frustration and not being able to communicate desires or anxiety and not being able to meet demands) enabled the playworkers to identify ways of playing that could then be introduced at moments of stress to calm the challenging behaviour.

In an action research project with playworkers working with children identified as displaying challenging behaviour, Russell (2006) found that helping the playworkers to develop an understanding of the ways in which these children played, rather than focusing on unwanted behaviour, allowed them to develop more constructive relationship and for the children to play out narratives within a safer frame.

Millie and others (2005), in their discussion of strategies to address antisocial behaviour in the public realm (rather than in settings), identified three narratives of youth antisocial behaviour and three corresponding responses: those who understood antisocial behaviour as symptomatic of social and moral decline favoured a corrective and punitive approach to dealing with it; those who thought such behaviour was grounded in a disaffection with and disengagement from wider society, and in some cases their own families, favoured preventative approaches; those who thought that youth antisocial behaviour was part of being young ('kids will be kids'), the age old tendency for young people to test boundaries and challenge their elders, favoured diversionary approaches. Young people themselves cited boredom and material gain as the two key motivators for antisocial behaviour (Adamson 2003).

There have been a number of government initiatives aimed at reducing antisocial behaviour amongst young people, mostly framed within the risk and prevention paradigm for social policy explained in Chapter 2. Examples include the Children's Fund, On Track and Positive Activities for Young People. The On Track programme was aimed at children aged four to 12 who were deemed to be at risk of offending or antisocial behaviour, with a focus on minimising the risk factors and reinforcing protective factors. The national evaluation of On Track services and users (Dinos and others 2006) found that just over half of the services were described as universal and just under half as targeted, and just over half were housed within schools. Open access and drop-in after school clubs and playschemes are listed as forming a part of the

'A play-centred relationship with children has the potential to be highly beneficial for both children and adults.'

universal service portfolio. No further details are available at the time of writing on the role that play provision had in this programme. Similarly, the Positive Activities for Young People programme was used as a funding source for play projects, yet there is no explicit reference to their role in the final evaluation report (CRG 2006). Given the recent research pointing to a relationship between playing and resilience outlined in Chapter 3, particularly regarding emotion regulation, it would seem that there is an evidence base for including provision for children to engage in free play within these programmes.

The importance of relationships

Gilligan (2000: 45) highlights the role that key adults have in the development of resilience in children and young people:

> Caregivers, teachers and social workers should remember that the detail of what they do with children counts. The rituals, the smiles, the interest in little things, the daily routines, the talents they nurture, the interests they stimulate, the hobbies they encourage, the friendships they support, the sibling ties they preserve make a difference.

Manwaring's (2006) research into children's views of playworkers found that relationships with staff varied from child to child. Some liked the playworkers to join in, for others playworkers were insignificant to their play. Children valued the informality of their relationships with playworkers and the fact that they allowed them freedom to play in their own way. Key themes emerging from the discussions showed that children wanted their playworkers to be:

• nice, kind, caring and friendly

• good cooks (food was important to many)

• joining in (although children often wanted to be free from adult interruptions, they also at times wanted the playworkers to play with them)

• fairness (particularly in terms of preventing bullying or other children interrupting play: being good at telling off was seen as a positive quality)

• good fun and playful

• helpful

• not shouting.

The evaluation of London Street Games (Neighbourhood Renewal Unit 2004), a project to encourage young people's participation in sport, showed that the qualities of the coaches, who were working with young people in public open spaces and on estates often in informal ways to begin with, was a key pointer in the success of the project. Coaches came from similar backgrounds to the young people and gained their respect through being good at their jobs.

Furedi (2005) examines how adult-child relations are constructed. He suggests that the Criminal Records Bureau checking procedure for adults who work with children alters the relationship between staff, children and parents, as it is based on an assumption that adults in general are not to be trusted and are a potential threat to children. He cites the example of volunteer football coaches, stating that parents talk about them as if they are potential threats to their children rather than people who give up their free time to coach football. Whilst on a rational level, screening would seem justifiable if it prevents one abuser gaining access to children, the process has created a more general suspicion of adults that in turn affects how adults relate to children. Such a level of suspicion is problematic for adult-child relations. Nevertheless, Gilligan's (2000) research into the importance of everyday caring relationships can provide a counter perspective.

Much of the literature examined in this chapter has, either explicitly or implicitly, been about the role of adults in supporting children's play. A play-centred (ludocentric) relationship with children has the potential to be highly beneficial for both children and adults. It may be that there is a need to reconsider how adults work with children at play in the light of the research reviewed in Chapters 3 and 4.

Concluding remarks

This literature review has covered a broad span of research, policy documents, evaluation reports and academic papers on childhood and play. Current social policy is rooted in the risk-focused prevention paradigm, and the final report on the policy review on children and young people (HM Treasury and DfES 2007a), a part of the Comprehensive Spending Review, announces a new emphasis on building resilience. The emerging evidence from the brain sciences suggests that playing, as a spontaneous, flexible and goalless 'as if' behaviour, plays a significant role in the development of the brain's structure and chemistry, which gives rise to emotional and physical health, well-being and resilience, as well as laying the foundations for cognitive functioning and social competence. Given this weight of evidence, we should be ensuring that children can play, whether in their bedrooms, gardens, local neighbourhoods or dedicated children's settings.

The evidence also suggests that it is the very characteristics of personal direction, unpredictability, flexibility and so on that make play so special. So any public provision for play must recognise these characteristics and be planned, implemented and evaluated with this in mind. If the evidence for the significance of play for children's well-being and development is accepted, then provision should be judged on the outcome of whether children can play, not on any more instrumental outcome or direct link to any of the five Every Child Matters outcomes. There is no guarantee that play provides all these benefits; we can, however, be confident that these benefits are more likely to accrue than if children cannot play.

Such an understanding of play also relies on the other disciplines from which we have drawn evidence in this review, namely the sociologies and geographies of childhood. These studies have been amassing evidence that have challenged our understanding of childhood as a period of socialisation and preparation for adulthood during which children are weak and dependent. They have shown that children are competent social actors capable of negotiating complex social landscapes, building relationships through play, testing and contesting adult authority and power in direct and subtle ways. They have also shown that children have not forgotten how to play, rather that we as adults may have forgotten how to see how they are playing, or remember what it feels like. Such an understanding of children has a number of challenges for our relationships with them, especially if we are seeking to support their play.

The evidence presented here suggests that there is a need to rethink the knowledge that adults take with them into their work with children. The evidence from practice raises questions about, for example, the effectiveness of anti-discriminatory practices and approaches to challenging behaviour, as well as if, when and how to intervene in play. The scope of timing of the review has not allowed for any consideration of the current education and training landscape; however, the issue of training has been raised in a number of the sources reviewed. Given the significance of play in the lives of children, both from their own accounts and from the brain sciences, it would seem that it should as a minimum be a part of the common core of knowledge that every adult needs when working with children.

Appendix One: Sources used and search terms

Photograph: Play England/Alan Finlay

The literature search was carried out using a variety of techniques. The starting point was the authors' existing knowledge and research for writing distance learning materials for the University of Gloucestershire Playwork Degree course. This includes childhood and social policy, children's play and playwork, equality and diversity in playwork, the brain at play, children's play cultures and children's relationship to their local environment. This background provided a valuable starting point for the literature search.

Databases and search engines

Blackwell Science
Centre for Evidence-Based Social Services
ChildData
Children's Play Information Service
ESRC Network for Evidence Based Policy and Practice (Evidence Network)
Expanded Academic ASAP
Google Scholar
Health and Wellness Resource Centre
Ingenta
Joseph Rowntree Foundation
National Evaluation of the Children's Fund
National Statistics Online
Project Muse
Pub Med
Research In Practice
Sage Premier
Science Direct
SocINDEX
Social Policy Research Unit
Swetswise
Taylor and Francis
Wiley Interscience

Government websites

Department for Education and Skills (DfES) and Department for Children, Schools and Families
Every Child Matters (ECM)
Department of Health (DH)
Department for Transport (DfT)
Communities and Local Government (DCLG)
Home Office
Audit Office

Key academic journals included

Children's Environments Quarterly
Children's Geographies
Childhood and Society
Childhood
Children, Youth and Environments
Environment and Behaviour
Journal of Environmental Psychology
Social Indicators Research

Search terms

The list of search terms was potentially endless. Every theme and topic within the review will have been a search term at some point. Example terms included: child play and brain development; child affective play; child play and IT; child play and stress; child play and creativity; child play and identity; child play and culture; child play and mental health; child play and well-being; child play and risk; child play and friendships; child play and emotion regulation; play and resilience; play and gender; play and disability; play and prisons; locomotor play; rough and tumble play.

Limitations

The authors have extensive experience in playwork, but each would acknowledge their limitations when it comes to reading and interpreting complex scientific material. This perhaps suggests a need for greater interdisciplinary working to further develop an integrated perspective on the relationship between play, gene environment expression, behaviour and social policy implications.

There were limitations imposed by the time available for the research review and, as such, there are likely to be gaps in the evidence collected and reviewed.

In terms of the practice of providing for play, we acknowledge that there is much work currently taking place at local level that falls outside of this review. We have looked at the nationally published literature, rather than reviewing what actually goes on in terms of practice.

223

Glossary

Many of the definitions offered here are taken from workbooks for modules on the Playwork awards at the University of Gloucestershire or directly from sources in this literature review.

Adaptive systems	Systems that can adapt their behaviour according to changes in the environment or in parts of the system itself.
Adulteration	When used within the context of adult support for play provision, this term (Sturrock and Else 1998) refers to adult intervention that redirects or terminates playing in line with adult concerns rather than supporting children's own control over their playing.
Affect	Within psychology, affect is used to refer to emotions.
Affect synchrony	The 'tuning in' and matching of emotional behaviours between people, particularly between carer and infant.
Affordance	Within environmental psychology, this is understood to mean the dangers or opportunities that are perceived within a particular environment. Generally speaking, in terms of children and playing, the term is usually used to refer to opportunities rather than dangers.
Agency	The ability to take decisions and act upon them; this term also often implies that our actions have the ability and power to make a difference in the social world.
Amygdala	A collection of nuclei, part of the limbic system of the brain that has a role in affective behaviours.
Autotelic	Refers to an activity that is carried out for its own sake rather than for external reward or to avoid punishment.
Basal ganglia	A group of structures in the forebrain, located just beneath the neocortex with connections to the thalamus and to the midbrain; a key function is to coordinate movements of limbs and the body.
Behaviour	Any movement or pattern of movement produced by the nervous system.
Binary	See 'dualism'.
Brain plasticity	The ability of the brain to change its structure in response to experience, drugs, hormones or injury.
Brain sciences	The range of approaches to the scientific study of the brain including for example neuroscience, molecular neurobiology, artificial intelligence and the philosophy of the mind.
Brainstem	Central structures of the brain, including the thalamus, hypothalamus, midbrain and hindbrain.
Central nervous system	The part of the nervous system that consists of the brain and spinal cord.

Cerebral cortex	Layer of brain tissue, composed of neurons, which forms the surface of the brain.
Cognition	The act or process of knowing; in psychology it refers to the processes of thought.
Cognitive neuroscience	The study of the neural basis of thought or cognition.
Consciousness	Being aware of our thoughts and feelings, arguably what makes us human. Being able to understand, self-regulate and share one's own thoughts are at the core of consciousness.
Construct	A way of viewing something (for example, children) that is a product of culture and history but is accepted as reality. See 'social constructionism'.
Constructionism	See 'social constructionism'.
Cortex	Newest layer of the forebrain – also called the neocortex.
Cortisol	A hormone that helps the body deal with stress.
Critical period	A period in development in which an event has a long lasting influence on the brain; often referred to as a sensitive period.
Data	Factual information drawn from experiments or surveys, used as a basis to draw conclusions.
Deficit model of childhood	A way of understanding children as deficient in the skills and knowledge needed for adult life.
Dendrite	A branch of a neuron that consists of an extension of the cell body.
Dendritic spine	A protrusion of a dendrite that increases the area of a dendrite; the point of contact with axons.
Depression	An affective disorder marked by feelings of worthlessness and guilt.
Discourse	The way of communicating about a concept, including the specific language, icons, images and so on used to convey meaning. Sometimes used to refer to an institutionalised way of thinking and talking about particular concepts.
Dopamine	A chemical neurotransmitter released by dopamine neurons.
Dualism	The idea that two fundamental, usually opposing and fixed concepts exist, such as light/dark; adult/child; black/white; male/female; good/evil.
Drive	A state of arousal that motivates an organism to engage in a particular behaviour.
Emotion regulation	Maintaining a level of arousal that is both tolerable and flexible enough to support adaptive behaviour (Gayler and Evans 2001).
Epigenetics	The biological study of the causal interactions between genes and their products.
Essentialism	The belief that the essence of something, particularly group characteristics and traits, is biologically determined, fixed and unchanging.

Ethnography	The study of a group's way of life from their perspective.
Ethology	The biological study of the behaviour of animals, often in their natural habitat.
Frontal cortex	An area of the brain associated with higher order thinking.
Gene	The smallest hereditary unit. A gene is a section of DNA that encodes a protein, and proteins in turn contribute to the shaping of many aspects of an organism.
Gene expression	The manifestation of the effects of a gene, a 'switching on' of genes seen in the physical or physiological make up of an organism.
Genome	The full genetic make up of an organism.
Genotype	The genetic make up of an organism.
Glutamate	A neurotransmitter that excites neurons.
Hegemony	Control or dominating influence by one person or group over others; the process of domination in which one set of ideas subverts or co-opts another (from Greek hegemonia, 'leadership').
Heterogeneous	The opposite of 'homogeneous', this term is applied to an object, system or phenomenon when it comprises many different elements.
Homeostasis	A process of maintaining life, and regulating metabolic processes.
Hormone	A chemical that is released by a gland and circulates in the blood.
Hypothalamus	A part of the brain that contains many nuclei associated with temperature regulation, eating and drinking, and sexual behaviour.
Instrumental value	Where something is valued for the usefulness of the end product it creates.
Intrinsic value	Where something is valued for its own sake.
Limbic cortex	Cortical regions within the limbic systems; includes both the cingulated cortex and the cortex adjacent to the hippocampus.
Limbic system	Consists of structures that lie between the neocortex and the brainstem and form a hypothetical functional system which controls affective behaviour and certain forms of memory.
Linear causality	The belief that one thing/process/event directly, exclusively and consistently causes a particular outcome.
Metacommunication	Ways of communicating other than direct speech, including body language, tone or pitch of voice, facial expressions etc. In play, children use metacommunication to communicate the message 'this is play' (Bateson 1955).
Mirror neuron	A neuron that fires in response to the observation of a specific action in others.
Natural science	The branch of science that deals with the physical world. See also 'social science'.

Neocortex	Newest layer of the forebrain, composed of about six layers of grey matter.
Neonate	Newly born.
Nerve Growth Factor (NGF)	A neurotrophic factor that acts to keep neurons alive and to stimulate differentiation of some types of neurons; maintains neural plasticity.
Neurons	A nerve cell that transmits nerve impulses.
Neurogenesis	The creation of neurons.
Nervous system	Collective name for all the neurons in the body.
Neuroscience	The scientific study of the brain and the nervous system.
Ontogeny	The sequence of events involved in individual development (see phylogeny).
Orbitofrontal cortex	A region of the frontal cortex that is involved in motor function and communicates with the basal ganglia as well as other limbic structures.
Paradigm	The belief and/or value system that underpins the way people make sense of the world.
Phenomenon	Something that can be perceived or experienced by the senses; often used to refer to seemingly inexplicable phenomena, in the sciences this meaning is not necessarily implied.
Phenotype	Behavioural and physical traits of an organism.
Phylogeny	The sequence of events involved in the evolution of a species (see ontogeny).
Plasticity	Generally refers to flexibility or adaptability; specifically, in neuroscience, it is the brain's capacity for shaping itself in response to experience, including after damage.
Play frame	A psychological frame that bounds playing, where the players understand, through metacommunication, that everything that takes place within the frame is playing (and therefore set apart from that which happens outside the frame).
Positive affect	Positive emotions.
Prefrontal cortex	The cortex lying in front of the motor and premotor cortices of the frontal lobe, particularly large in the human brain; involved in the sensory guidance of movement.
Preventative policies	Prevention within social policy refers to ways of preventing poor outcomes for children and young people at risk of social exclusion. It involves the identification of risk and protective factors and interventions to reduce the former and increase the latter.
Primary emotions	The ancient, reflex emotions aimed at survival, often identified as fear, anger, surprise, disgust, happiness and sadness (Damasio 2003).

Progress rhetoric	One of seven 'rhetorics' of play identified by Sutton-Smith (1997), referring to the modern notion that children learn and develop through playing.
Prosody	Melody or tone of voice.
Resilience	The capacity to thrive despite adversity, to bounce back from and adapt to stressful or harmful events or environments. Within preventative social policy, resilience is a major protective factor.
Rhetoric	A way of understanding and discussing a particular phenomenon.
Secondary emotions	The newer, social emotions such as pride, sympathy, jealousy, shame.
Serotonin	The oldest neurotransmitter in the brain, important for emotional processing and sleep.
Social capital	The social networks, systems of reciprocal relations, norms and trust within a group or community.
Social constructionism	The concept that our understanding of the world is a product of our culture and history, rather than of objective fact. The idea of childhood as a social construction allows us to appreciate that there are many different ways to view children, none of them exclusively factual, all of them socially constructed.
Social exclusion	Refers to the exclusion from social, political, economic and cultural activities for a number of reasons, including poverty, alienation or discrimination.
Social science	The branch of science that deals with the social world. See also 'natural science'.
Socialisation	The social processes through which children develop an awareness of social norms and values, and achieve a distinct sense of self (Giddens 2002: 699).
Stress	Events or drugs that produce arousal, excite the fight-or-flight response and release cortisol from the adrenal gland; events that threaten homeostasis.
Stress hormone	A hormone, such as cortisol, which is activated by stress.
Subcortical regions	All the regions in the brain that lie beneath the neocortex.
Synapse	The connection between one neuron and another, usually between an end foot of an axon and the dendritic spine of another neuron.
Systems thinking	An approach that recognises the interconnectedness of component parts of a system and its environment.
Thalamus	A part of the brain through which all the sensory systems project to reach the neocortex and then project on to other brain regions.
Utilitarian value	See 'intrinsic and instrumental value'.
Vertical integration of brain systems	The bottom-up and top-down integration of different systems of the brain in an interconnected feedback loop.

229

References

4Children (2006) *Buzz Survey 2006 Report: 4Children's Annual National Survey on Children's Views and Aspirations: Summary of findings*. London: 4Children.

Abbott, L and Nutbrown, C (eds) (2001) *Experiencing Reggio Emilia*. Buckingham: Open University Press.

Abou-ezzeddine T, Schwartz, D, Chang, L, Lee-Shin, Y, Farver, J and Xu, Y (2007) 'Positive Peer Relationships and Risk of Victimization in Chinese and South Korean Children's Peer Groups', *Social Development*, 16(1): 106-127.

Ackerley, J (2003) 'Gender differences in the folklore play of children in primary school playgrounds', *Play and Folklore*, 44: 2-15. Cited in Meire, J (2007) *Qualitative Research on Children's Play: A review of recent literature. Belgium*: Childhood and Society Research Centre.

Adams, S, Alexander, E, Drummond, MJ and Moyles, J (2004) *Inside the Foundation Stage: Recreating the reception year*. London: Association of Teachers and Lecturers.

Adams, S and Moyles, J (2005) *Images of Violence: Responding to children's representations of the violence they see*. Lutterworth: Featherstone Education.

Adamson, S (2003) *Youth Crime: Diversionary approaches to reduction. Research Report 5*. Sheffield: New Deal for Communities National Evaluation, Sheffield Hallam University.

Ahn, J and Filipenko, M (2007) 'Narrative, Imaginary Play, Art, and Self: Intersecting Worlds', *Early Childhood Education Journal*, 34(4): 279-289.

Aitken, S (2001) *Geographies of Young People*. London: Routledge.

Alanen, L (2001a) 'Estudos feministas/ estudos da infância: paralelos, ligações e perspectivas', in de Castro, LR (ed)

Crianças e Jovens na Construção da Cultura, 69–92. Rio de Janeiro: Nau/ Faperj. Cited in de Castro, L (2004) 'Otherness in Me, Otherness in Others', *Childhood*, 11(4): 469-493.

Alanen, L (2001b) 'Explorations in Generational Analysis' in L Alanen and B Mayall (eds) *Conceptualizing Adult-Child Relations*. London: RoutledgeFalmer.

Almqvist, L, Hellnas, P, Stefansson, M and Granlund, M (2006) '"I can play!" Young children's perceptions of health', *Pediatric Rehabilitation*, 9(3): 275-284.

Alton, D, Adab, P and Barrett, T (2007) 'Relationship between walking levels and perceptions of the local neighbourhood environment', *Archives of Diseases in Childhood*, 92: 29-33.

Alvarez, L (2005) 'Educators flocking to Finland, land of literate children', New York Times, 9 April 2005. Cited in Singer, J (2006) 'Epilogue: Learning to play and learning through play', in Singer, D, Golinkoff, R and Hirsh-Pasek, K (eds) *Play=Learning: How play motivates and enhances children's cognitive and social-emotional growth*. New York, NY: Oxford University Press.

Andersen, L, Harro, M, Sardinha, L, Froberg, K, Ekelund, U, Brage, S and Anderssen, S (2006) 'Physical activity and clustered cardiovascular risk in children: A cross-sectional study (The European Youth Heart Study), *Lancet*, 368: 299-304.

Anderson, S and Teicher, M (2004) 'Delayed Effects of Early Stress on Hippocampal Development', *Neuropsychopharmacology*, 29: 1988-1993.

Andresen, H (2005) 'Role play and Language Development in the Preschool Years', *Culture and Psychology*, 11(4): 387-414.

Andrews, C (2005) 'Children Visiting Prison: Can it be made any easier?' *The Friend*, 20 May 2005.

231

Anning, A, Chesworth, E, Spurling, L and Partinoudi, KD (2005) *The Quality of Early Learning, Play and Childcare Services in Sure Start Local Programmes.* Nottingham: DfES.

Anthias, F (1998) 'Rethinking social divisions: Some notes towards a theoretical framework', *The Sociological Review*, 46(3): 505-535.

Appleyard, BS (2005) *Livable Streets for School Children: How safe routes to school programs can improve street and community livability for children.* NCBW Forum, March 2005. Available online at www.bikewalk.org/forunnewart.php (date accessed June 2008).

Appleyard, D (1981) *Livable Streets.* Berkeley: University of California Press.

Archard, D (2004) *Children, Rights and Childhood, 2nd edition.* London: Routledge.

Arco, A, Segovia, G, Garrido, P, de Blas, M and Mora, F (2007) 'Stress, Prefrontal Cortex and Environment Enrichment: Studies on dopamine and acetylcholine release and working memory performance in rats', *Behavioural Brain Research*, 176: 267-273.

Ariel, S (2002) *Children's Imaginative Play. A visit to wonderland.* Westport: Praeger.

Ariès, P (1962) translated by R Baldrick. *Centuries of Childhood: A social history of family life.* New York: Vintage Books.

Armitage, M (2004) 'Hide and Seek – Where do children spend their time after school', A paper for the Child in the City Conference, London.

Armitage, M (2005) 'The Influence of School Architecture and Design on the Outdoor Play Experience within the Primary School', *Paedogogica Historica*, 41(4&5): 535-553.

Armstrong, SC, Barker, D, Davey, R, Diosi, M, Horton, J, Kraftl, P, Lumsden, E,

Marandet, E, Matthews, H, Murray, J, Pyer, M and Smith F (2005) *Evaluation of Play Provision and Play Needs in the London Borough of Redbridge.* Northampton: Centre for Children and Youth.

Armstrong, T (2006) 'Canaries in the Coalmine. The symptoms of children labelled ADHD as biocultural feedback', in Lloyd, G, Stead, J and Cohen, C (eds) *Critical New Perspectives on ADHD.* London: Routledge.

Arnold, J and Siviy, S (2002) 'Effects of Neonatal Handling and Maternal Separation on Rough-and-Tumble Play in the Rat', *Developmental Psychobiology*, 41: 205-215.

Association of Teachers and Lecturers (2007) *Cyberbullying Survey.* London: ATL.

Attree, P (2004) 'Growing Up in Disadvantage: A systematic review of the qualitative evidence', *Child: Care, Health and Development* 30(6): 679–689.

Atwool, N (2006) 'Attachment and Resilience: Implications for children in care', *Child Care in Practice*, 12(4): 315-330.

Audit Commission (2003) *Services for Disabled Children: A review of services for disabled children and their families.* London: Audit Commission.

Audit Commission (2006) *Assessment of Local Services Beyond 2008.* Wetherby: Audit Commission.

Audit Commission (2007) *The Evolution of Regulation: Comprehensive Area Assessment and the changing face of public service improvement.* Wetherby: Audit Commission.

Aydt, H and Corsaro, W (2003) 'Differences in Children's Construction of Gender Across Culture', *American Behavioural Scientist*, 46(10): 1306-1325.

Backett-Milburn, K and Harden, J (2004) 'How Children and Their Families Construct and Negotiate Risk, Safety and Danger', *Childhood*, 11(4): 429–447.

Badham, B (2004) 'Participation – for a Change: Disabled young people lead the way', *Children and Society*, 11: 143-154.

Bailey, R (2002) 'Playing Social Chess: Children's play and social intelligence', *Early Years*, 22(2): 163-173.

Balbernie, R (2001) 'Circuits and circumstances: The neurobiological consequences of early relationship experiences and how they shape later behaviour', *Journal of Child Psychotherapy*, 27(3): 237-255.

Ball, D (2002) *Playgrounds: Risks, Benefits and Choices*. Sudbury: HSE.

Ball, D (2004) 'Policy Issues and Risk-Benefit Trade-offs of "Safer Surfacing" for Children's Playgrounds,' *Accident Analysis and Prevention* 36: 661-670.

Banaji, S and Burn, A with Buckingham, D (2006) *The Rhetorics of Creativity: A review of the literature*. London: Arts Council England.

Banerjee, T, Middleton, F and Faraone, S (2007) 'Environmental Risk Factors for Attention-Deficit Hyperactive Disorder', *Acta Paediatrica*, 96(9): 1269-1274.

Banting, K (1979) *Poverty, Politics and Policy*. London: Macmillan, cited in Levin (1979).

Bar-Haim, Y and Bart, O (2006) 'Motor Function and Social Participation in Kindergarten Children', *Social Development*, 15(2): 296-310.

Barker, J, Smith F, Morrow, V, Weller, S, Hey, V and Garwin, J (2003) *The Impact of Out of School Care: A qualitative study examining the views of children, families and playworkers. DfES Research Report RR446*. London: DfES.

Barlett, P (ed) (2005) *Urban Place: Reconnecting with the Natural World*. Cambridge MA: MIT Press.

Barnardo's (2006) *More School Less Play: The role of play in the extended school in Denmark and England*. Ilford: Barnardo's.

Barnes, M, Evans, R, Plumridge, G and McCabe, A (2006) *Preventative Services for Disabled Children: A final report from the National Evaluation of the Children's Fund*. London: DfES.

Barnes, M and Morris, K (2007) 'Networks, Connectedness and Resilience: Learning from the Children's Fund in context', *Social Policy and Society*, 6(2): 193-197.

Barnes, M and Prior, D (2007), 'Conceptualising Connectedness: Implications for policy and practice', *Social Policy and Society*, 6(2): 199-208.

Baron-Cohen, S (2003) *The Essential Difference: Men, women and the extreme male brain*. London: Penguin.

Barraclough, N, Bennington, J and Green, S (2004) *Delivering Play Spaces in NDC Areas: Research Report 38, New Deal for Communities National Evaluation*. Sheffield: Centre for Regional Economic and Social Research, Sheffield Hallam University.

Bassani, C (2007) 'Five Dimensions of Social Capital Theory as They Pertain to Youth Studies', *Journal of Youth Studies*, 10(1): 17-34.

Batch, J (2005) 'Benefits of Physical Activity in Obese Adolescents and Children', *Internal Medicine Journal*, 35: 446.

Bateson, G (1955) 'A Theory of Play and Fantasy: A report on theoretical aspects of the project for study of the role of paradoxes of abstraction in communication', *Approaches to the Study of Human Personality: American Psychiatric Association Psychiatric Research Reports*, 2: 39–51. Cited in Andresen (2005) 'Role play and Language Development in the Preschool Years', *Culture and Psychology*, 11(4): 387-414.

Bateson, P (2005) 'The Role of Play in the Evolution of Great Apes and Humans', in Pellegrini, A and Smith, P (eds) *The Nature of Play. Great Apes and Humans*. London: Guildford Press.

Bateson, P and Martin, P (1999) *Design for a Life*. London: Jonathon Cape.

Bath and North East Somerset Council (2006) *Bath and North East Somerset Play Strategy*.

BBC News (2007) Hand-built Skate Park Cuts Crime. BBC, 27 April.

Beckett, C, Maughan, B, Rutter, M, Castle, J, Colvert, E, Groothnes, C, Keppner, J, Stevens, S, O'Connor, T and Sonuga-Barke, E (2006) 'Do the Effects of Early Severe Deprivation on Cognition Persist Into Early Adolescence? Findings From the English and Romanian Adoptees Study', *Child Development*, 77(1): 696-711.

Bedimo-Rung, A, Mowen, A and Cohen, D (2005) 'The Significance of Parks to Physical Activity and Public Health: A conceptual model', *American Journal of Preventative Medicine*, 28(252): 159-168.

Beirens, H, Mason, P, Spicer, N, Hughes, N and Hek, R (2006) *Preventative Services for Refugee and Asylum Seeking Children. A final report from the National Evaluation of the Children's Fund*. Nottingham: DfES.

Bekoff, M and Byers, J (eds) (1998) *Animal Play: Evolutionary, comparative and ecological perspectives*. Cambridge: Cambridge University Press.

Benaroya-Milshtein, N, Hollander, N, Apter, A, Kukulansky, T, Raz, N, Wilf, A, Yaniv, I and Pick, C (2004) 'Environmental Enrichment in Mice Decreases Anxiety, Attenuates Stress Responses and Enhances Natural Killer Cell Activity', *European Journal of Neuroscience*, 20 (5): 1341-1347.

Bergen, D (2002) 'The Role of Pretend Play in Children's Cognitive Development', *Early Childhood Research and Practice*, 4(1).

Bergstrom, M (1997) Svarta och vita lekar. Stockholm: Wahlstrom and Widstrand, cited in Lofdahl, A (2005) 'Preschool Teachers' Conceptions of Children's "Chaotic Play"', in McMahon, F, Lytle, D and Sutton-Smith, B (eds) *Play: An Interdisciplinary Synthesis*. Maryland: University Press of America.

Berk, L, Mann, T and Ogan, T (2006) 'Make-Believe Play: Wellspring for Development of Self-Regulation', in Singer, D, Golinkoff, R and Hirsh-Pasek, K (eds) *Play=Learning: How play motivates and enhances children's cognitive and social-emotional growth*. New York, NY: Oxford University Press.

Bhavnani, R, Mirza, HS and Meetoo, V (2005) *Tackling the Roots of Racism: Lessons for success*. Bristol: The Policy Press.

Biddulph, M (2001) *Home Zones: A planning and design handbook*. Bristol: Policy Press.

Bishop, JC and Curtis, M (2001) 'The Importance of Play for Today', in Bishop, JC and Curtis, M (eds) *Play Today in the School Playground*. Buckingham: Open University Press.

Bixler, R, Floyd, M and Hammitt, W (2002) 'Environmental Socialization: Quantitative Tests of the Childhood Play Hypothesis', *Environment and Behaviour* 34(6): 795-818.

Bjorklund, D (2006) 'Mother Knows Best: Epigenetic inheritance, maternal effects, and the evolution of human intelligence', *Developmental Review*, 26: 213–242.

Black, J (1998) 'How a Child Builds its Brains: Some lessons from animal studies of neural plasticity', *Preventative Medicine*, 27: 168-171.

Blakemore, S and Frith, C (2003) 'Self-awareness and Action', *Current Opinions in Neurobiology*, 13: 219-224.

Blatchford, P (1998) 'The State of Play in Schools', *Child Psychology and Psychiatry Review*. 3(2): 58-67.

Blatchford, P and Baines, E (2006) *A Follow-Up National Survey of Breaktimes in Primary and Secondary Schools: Report to the Nuffield Foundation.* London: Institute of Education and Nuffield Foundation.

Blinkert, B (2004) 'Quality of the City for Children: Chaos and order', *Children, Youth and Environments*, 14(2): 99-112.

Blower, A, Addo, A, Hidgson, J, Lamington, L and Towlson, K (2004) 'Mental Health of "Looked after" Children: A Needs Assessment', *Clinical Child Psychology and Psychiatry* 9(1): 117-129.

Bock, J, Gruss, M, Becker, S and Braun, K (2005) 'Experience Induced Changes of Dendritic Spine Densities in the Prefrontal and Sensory Cortex: Correlation with developmental time windows', *Cerebral Cortex*, 15: 802-808.

Boggs, C (2001) 'Social Capital and Political Fantasy: Robert Putnam's "Bowling Alone"', *Theory and Society*, 30: 281-297.

Booth-LaForce, C, Rubin, K, Rose-Krasnor, L and Burgess, K (2005) 'Attachment and Friendship Predictors of Psychosocial Functioning in Middle Childhood and the Mediating Roles of Social Support and Self-worth', in Kerns, KA and Richardson, RA (eds) *Attachment in Middle Childhood.* New York: The Guilford Press.

Boseley, S (2005) 'Doctors urge action "diabesity"' *The Guardian*, 23 July 2005.

Boyce, T (2007) 'The Media and Obesity', *Obesity Reviews*, 8(1): 201-205.

Boyd, B (2004) 'Laughter and Literature: A play theory of humour', *Philosophy and Literature*, 28: 1-22.

Bradshaw, J Hoelscher, P and Richardson, D (2006) 'An Index of Child Well-being in the European Union', *Social Indicators Research*, USA: Springer.

Bradshaw, J, Hoelscher, P and Richardson, D (2007) 'Comparing Child Well-being in OECD Countries: Concepts and methods', *Innocenti Working Paper No 2006-03.* Florence: Unicef Innocenti Research Centre.

Bradshaw, J and Mayhew, E (eds) (2005) *The Well-being of Children in the UK.* London: Save the Children.

Branco, A (2005) 'Peer Interactions, Language Development and Metacommunication', *Culture and Psychology*, 11(4): 415-429.

Brassett-Harknett, A and Butler, N (2007) 'Attention-Deficit Hyperactive Disorder: An overview of the etiology and a review of the literature relating to the correlates and lifecourse outcomes for men and women', *Clinical Psychology Review*, 27: 188-210.

British Medical Association (BMA) (2005) *Preventing Childhood Obesity.* London: BMA.

British Medical Association (2006) *Child and Adolescent Mental Health: A guide for healthcare professionals.* London: BMA.

Broadhead, P (2001) 'Investigating Sociability and Cooperation in Four- and Five-year-olds in Reception Class Settings', *International Journal of Early Years Education*, 9(1): 23-35.

Bronwell, C, Zerwas, S and Balaram, G (2002) 'Peers, Cooperative Play, and the Development of Empathy in Children', *Behavioural and Brain Sciences*, 25(1): 28-29.

Brooker, L (2006) 'From Home to Home Corner: Observing children's identity maintenance in early childhood settings', *Children and Society*, 20(2): 116-127.

Brothwell, V (2006) 'A Place of Their Own', *Spaces and Places*, 23: 24-27, October 2006.

Brown, F (2003) 'Compound Flexibility: The role of playwork in child development', in Brown, F (ed) *Playwork Theory and Practice.* Buckingham: Open University Press.

Brown, F (2006a) Play Theories and the Value of Play, *Highlight No 223*. London: National Children's Bureau.

Brown, F (2006b) 'The Impact of a Playwork Project on a Group of Children in a Romanian Paediatric Hospital', paper delivered to TASP conference, May 2006.

Brown, F (2007) *The Venture: A case study of an adventure playground*. Cardiff: Play Wales.

Brown, F and Webb, S (2005) 'Children Without Play', *Journal of Education*, 35: 139-158.

Brown, J (2007a) 'Britain's children: Unhappy, neglected and poorly educated,' *The Independent*, 14 February 2007.

Brown, J (2007b) 'Time, Space and Gender: Understanding "problem" behaviour in young children', *Children and Society*, 21: 98-110.

Browne, N (2004) *Gender Equity in the Early Years*. Maidenhead: Open University Press.

Brownell, C, Zerwas, S and Balaram, G (2002) 'Peers, Cooperative Play, and the Development of Empathy in Children', *Behavioural and Brain Sciences*, 25(1): 28-29.

Bruegel, I (2006) *Social Capital, Diversity and Education Policy*. London: Families and Social Capital ESRC Research group, London South Bank University.

Bruer, J (1999) *The Myth of the First Three years: A new understanding of early brain development and lifelong learning*. New York: The Free Press.

Brunton, G, Thomas, J, Harden, H, Rees, R, Kavanagh, J, Oliver, S, Shepherd, J and Oakley, A (2005) 'Promoting Physical Activity of Children Outside of Physical Education Classes: A systematic review integrating intervention studies and qualitative studies', *Health Education Journal*, 64(4): 323-338.

Buchanan, A, Bennett, F, Ritchie, C, Smith, T, Smith, G, Harker, L and Vitali-Ebers, S (2004) *The impact of Government Policy on Social Exclusion Among Children Aged 0-13 and their Families: A review of the literature for the Social Exclusion Unit in the Breaking the Cycle series*. London: ODPM.

Buckingham, D (2000) *After the Death of Childhood: Growing up in the age of electronic media*. Cambridge: Polity Press.

Buckingham, D (2007) 'Childhood in the Age of Global Media', *Children's Geographies*, 5(1-2): 43–54.

Buckingham, D, and Jones, K (2001) 'New Labour's Cultural Turn: Some tensions in contemporary educational and cultural policy', *Journal of Education Policy*, 16(1): 1-14.

Bullock, H, Mountford J and Stanley, R (2001) *Better Policy Making*. London: Centre for Management and Policy Studies, Cabinet Office.

Burdette, H and Whitaker, R (2005) 'Resurrecting Free Play in Young Children: Looking beyond fitness and fatness to attention, affiliation, and affect', *Archives of Pediatric Adolescent Medicine*, 159: 46-50.

Burghardt, GM (2005) *The Genesis of Animal Play: Testing the limits*. Cambridge, MA: The MIT Press.

Burke, C (2005) '"Play in Focus": Children researching their own spaces and places for play', *Children, Youth and Environments*, 15(1): 27-53.

Byrne, D (2005) *Social Exclusion, 2nd edition*. Maidenhead: Open University Press.

CABE Space (2004) *What Would You Do with This Space? Involving young people in the design and care of urban spaces*. London: CABE Space.

CABE Space (2007) *Spaceshaper: A user's guide*. London: CABE.

Cabinet Office (1999) *Modernising Government*. London: HMSO.

CACHE (2006) *Level 3 Award in Playwork for Early Years and Child Care Workers and Level 3 Award in Early Years and Child Care for Playworkers*. St Alban's: CACHE.

Caillois, R ([1961] 2001) *Man, Play and Games, translated by Meyer Barash*. Urbana and Chicago: University of Illinois Press.

Cantle, T (2001) *Community Cohesion*, December 2001. London: Home Office.

Camina, M (2004) *Understanding and Engaging Deprived Communities: Home Office Online Report 07/04*. London: Home Office.

Campbell, D (2005) 'Mobiles, MP3s, DVDs: Raising a generation of techno-kids', *The Observer*, 13 February 2005.

Campos, J, Frankel, C and Camras, L (2004) 'On the Nature of Emotion Regulation', *Child Development*, 75(2) 377-394.

Canu, W and Gordon, M (2005) 'Mother Nature as Treatment for ADHD. Overstating the benefits of green', *American Journal of Public Health*, 95(3): 371.

Cattanach, A (2003) *Introduction to play therapy*. Hove: Brunner-Routledge.

Cekaite, A and Aronsson, K (2005) 'Language Play, a Collaborative Resource in Children's L2 Learning', *Applied Linguistics*, 26(2): 169-191.

Chambers, H (2004) Creative arts and play for the well-being of looked after children, *Highlight No 212*. London: National Children's Bureau.

Chapillon, P, Patin, V, Roy, V, Vincent, A and Caston, J (2002) 'Effects of Pre- and Postnatal Stimulation on Developmental, Emotional, and Cognitive Aspects in Rodents: A review', *Developmental Psychobiology*, 41(4): 373-387.

Chatterjee, S (2005) 'Children's Friendship with Place: A conceptual inquiry', *Children, Youth and Environments*, 15(1): 1 – 26.

Chawla, L (Ed) (2002) *Growing Up in an Urbanising World*. London: Earthscan.

Chawla, L and Malone, K (2003) 'Neighbourhood Quality in Children's Eyes', in Christensen, P and O'Brien, M (eds) *Children in the City: Home, neighbourhood and community*. London: RoutledgeFalmer.

Chawla, L and Johnson, V (2004) 'Not For Children Only: Lessons learnt from young people's participation', *Participatory Learning in Action*, 50: 63-72.

Child Accident Prevention Trust (CAPT) (2002) *Taking Chances: The lifestyles, leisure worlds and leisure risks of young people project summary*. London: CAPT.

Children and Young People's Unit (2001a) *Building a Strategy for Children and Young People Consultation Document*. London: HMSO.

Children and Young People's Unit (2001b) *Learning to Listen: Core principles for the involvement of children and young people*. London: HSMO.

Children and Young People's Unit (2002) *Reports on the Consultation for Building a Strategy for Children and Young People* (various). London: DfES.

Children's Play Council (2006a) *Planning for Play: Guidance on the development and implementation of a local play strategy*. London: National Children's Bureau and Big Lottery Fund.

Children's Play Council (2006b) Playday Survey. Summary of results available on-line at: www.playday.org.uk/Upload/2121522_play-survey-summary-playday-2006.pdf [accessed 19 April 2007].

Children's Play Council (2006c) *Neighbourhood Play Toolkit CD-ROM Create, Organise, Sustain*. London: National Children's Bureau.

Children's Play Information Service (2007) 'Play Strategies in Nearly Every Local Authority in England', *Children's Pay Update*, October 2007.

Children's Play Safety Forum (2002) *Managing Risk in Play Provision: A position statement*. London: National Children's Bureau.

Childress, H (2004) 'Teenagers, Territory and the Appropriation of Space', *Childhood 11*(2): 195-205.

Chinn, S and Rona, R (2001) 'Prevalence and Trends in Overweight and Obesity in Three Cross Sectional Studies of British Children, 1974-94', *British Medical Journal*, 322: 24-26.

Chipuer, H (2001) 'Dyadic Attachments and Community Connectedness: Links with youths' loneliness experiences', *Journal of Community Psychology*, 29(4): 429–446.

Christensen, P (2002) 'Why More "Quality Time" is Not on the Top of Children's Lists: The "qualities of time" for children', *Children and Society*, 16: 77-88.

Christie, J (2001) 'Play as a Learning Medium', in Reifel, S (Ed) *Theory in Context and Out: Play and Culture Studies*, 3. Westport: Ablex Publishing.

Christie, N, Dale, M, and Lowe, C (2002) *Road Safety Research Report No 32: Child Road Safety in Rural Areas – A critical review of the literature and commentary*. London: DfT.

Chugani, H, Behan, H, Muzik, O, Juhasz, C, Nagy, F and Chugani, C (2001) 'Local Brain Functional Activity Following Early Deprivation: A study of postinstitutionalized Romanian Orphans', *Neuroimage*, 14: 1290-1301.

Cicchetti, D and Blender, J (2006) 'A Multiple-Levels-of-Analysis Perspective on Resilience. Implications for the developing brain, neural plasticity, and preventive interventions', *Annals of the New York Academy of Science*, 1094: 248-258.

Clark, A and Moss, P (2004) *Young Children's Participation: Spaces to Play*. London: Thomas Coram Research Unit and Learning through Landscapes London.

Clark, A and Percy-Smith, B (2006) 'Beyond Consultation: Participatory practices in everyday spaces'. *Children, Youth and Environments*, 16(2): 1-9.

Clark, C and Uzell, D (2006) 'The Socio-environmental Affordances of Adolescents' Environments', in Spencer, C and Blades, M (eds) *Children and Their Environments*. Cambridge: Cambridge University Press.

Clark, S and Paechter, C (2007) '"Why can't girls play football?" Gender dynamics in the playground', *Sports, Education and Society*, 12(3): 261-276.

Clarke, H (2005) *Preventing Social Exclusion of Disabled Children and Their Families: Literature review paper produced for the National Evaluation of the Children's Fund*. Birmingham: Institute of Applied Social Studies, Birmingham University.

Clements, R (2004) 'An Investigation of the State of Outdoor Play', *Contemporary Issues in Early Childhood*, 5(1): 68-80.

Cloke, P and Jones, O (2005) '"Unclaimed Territory": Childhood and disordered space(s)', *Social and Cultural Geography*, 6(3): 311-323.

Coates, J (2007) 'Talk in a Play Frame: More on laughter and intimacy', *Journal of Pragmatics*, 39: 29-49.

Cockburn, T (2005b) 'Children's Participation in Social Policy: Inclusion, chimera or authenticity?' *Social Policy and Society*, 4(2): 109–119.

Cohen, D (2006) 'Critiques of the ADHD Enterprise' in Lloyd, G, Stead, J and Cohen, C (eds) *Critical New Perspectives on ADHD*. London: Routledge.

Cole, M, Martin, SE and Dennis, TA (2004) 'Emotion Regulation as a Scientific Construct: Methodological challenges and directions for child development research', *Child Development*, 75 (2): 317-333.

Cole-Hamilton, I and Gill, T (2002) *Making the Case for Play: Building policies and strategies for school-aged children*. London: National Children's Bureau.

Cole-Hamilton, I, Harrop, A and Street, C (2002) *Making the Case for Play: Gathering the evidence*. London: Children's Play Council, New Policy Institute and National Children's Bureau.

Cole-Hamilton, I (2006) *Playing On: Sustaining play provision in changing times*. London: National Children's Bureau.

Collins, D and Kearns, R (2001) 'Under Curfew and under Siege? Legal geographies of young people', *Geoforum*, 32: 389-403.

Collishaw, S, Maughan, B, Goodman, R and Pickles, A (2004) 'Time Trends in Adolescent Mental Health', *Journal of Child Psychology and Psychiatry*, 8: 1350-1363.

Colwell, M and Lindsey, E (2005) 'Preschool Children's Pretend and Physical Play and Sex of Play Partner: Connections to peer competence', *Sex Roles*, 52(7/8): 497-509.

Communities and Local Government (2006) *Strong and Prosperous Communities: The Local Government White Paper*. Wetherby: Communities and Local Government Publications.

Comptroller and Auditor General (2006) *Tackling Obesity – First Steps*. London: National Audit Office, Healthcare Commission and Audit Commission.

Connell, JP and Kubisch, AC (1998) 'Applying a Theory of Change Approach to the Evaluation of Comprehensive Community Initiatives: Progress, prospects, and problems' in Fulbright-

Anderson, K, Kubisch, AC and Connell, JP (eds) *New Approaches to Evaluating Community Initiatives Volume 2: Theory, Measurement and Analysis*. Washington DC: The Aspen Institute,

Connolly, P (2006) 'The Masculine Habitus as "Distributed Cognition": A case study of 5- to 6-year-old boys in an English inner-city, multi-ethnic primary school', *Children and Society*, 20: 140-152.

Conway, M (2003) 'Professional Playwork Practice', in Brown, F (ed) *Playwork Theory and Practice*. Buckingham: Open University Press.

Contact a Family, Council for Disabled Children, Mencap and Special Education Consortium (2006) *Off the Radar: How local authority plans fail disabled children*. London: Every Disabled Child Matters.

Conway, M and Farley, T (2001) *Quality in Play*. London: London Play.

Conway, M, Hughes, B and Sturrock, G (2004) *A Personal List of Events and Evolving Understanding that Have Led Playwork to Where it is Today*. Cardiff: Play Wales.

Coombes, R (2006) 'Playgrounds: Play school', *Children Now*, 3 May 2006.

Cornell, E, Hadley, D, Sterling, T, Chan, M and Boechler, P (2001) 'Adventure as a Stimulus for Cognitive Development', *Journal of Environmental Psychology*, 21: 219-231.

Cornell, E and Hill, K (2006) 'The problem of lost children', in Spencer, C and Blades, M (eds) *Children and Their Environments*. Cambridge: Cambridge University Press.

Corsaro, WA (2003) *We're Friends Right? Inside kids' cultures*. Washington DC: Joseph Henry Press.

Cowgill, D and Morcovitch, H (2004) 'Use of Stimulants for Attention Deficit Hyperactivy Disorder', *British Medical Journal*, 329: 907-909.

CRG Research Ltd (2006) *Positive Activities for Young People: National Evaluation.* Sheffield: DfES.

Creegan, C, Ludvigsen, A and Scott, S (2004) *Evaluation of the Tower Hamlets Community Play Programme.* Ilford: Barnardo's.

Cremin, T, Burnard, P and Craft, A (2006) 'Pedagogy and Possibility Thinking in the Early Years,' *Thinking Skills and Creativity*, 1: 108-119.

Crowe, N and Bradford, S (2006) '"Hanging out in Runescape": Identity, work and leisure in the virtual playground,' *Children's Geographies*, 4(3): 331–346.

Cui, M, Yangb, Y, Yang, J, Zhang, J, Hanb, H, Mab, W, Li, H, Maob, R, Xua, L, Haoa, W and Caob, J (2006) 'Enriched Environment Experience Overcomes the Memory Deficits and Depressive-like Behavior Induced by Early Life Stress', *Neuroscience Letters*, 404: 208–212.

Cumming, R (2007) 'Language Play in the Cassroom: Encouraging children's intuitive creativity with words through poetry', *Literacy*, 41(2): 93-101.

Cuninghame, C, Hyder, T and Kesler, D (2001) ECD *Guidelines for Emergencies: The Balkans.* London: Save the Children.

Cunningham, H (2006) *The Invention of Childhood.* London: BBC Books.

Daily Telegraph (2006) 'Daily Telegraph Campaign to Halt "Death of Childhood", [online]*Telegraph Speaker's Corner*, 13 September 2006.

Damasio, A (1994) *Descartes' Error.* New York: Harper Collins.

Damasio, A (1999) *The Feeling of What Happens.* London: Vintage.

Damasio, A (2003) *Looking for Spinoza.* London: Heinemann.

Dapretto, M, Davies, M, Pfeifer, J, Scott, A, Sigman, M, Bookheimer, S and Iacoboni, M (2006) 'Understanding Emotions in Others: Mirror neuron dysfunction in children with autism spectrum disorders', *Nature Neuroscience*, 9 (1): 28-30.

Darbyshire, P (2007) '"Childhood": Are Reports of its death greatly exaggerated?' *Journal of Child Health Care*, 11 (2): 85-97.

David, T (2003) *What Do We Know about Teaching Young Children? A professional user review of research based on the BERA academic review 'Early Years Research: Pedagogy, curriculum, adult roles, training and professionalism (2003).* Macclesfield: BERA.

Davies, B (2006) *Getting Involved: The pay off for young people and adults, in Groundwork UK Play, participation and potential. Putting young people at the heart of communities.* Birmingham: Groundwork UK.

Davis, J (2006) 'Disability, Childhood Studies, and the Construction of Medical Discourses. Questioning attention deficit hyperactivity disorder: a theoretical perspective', in Lloyd, G, Stead, J and Cohen, C (eds) *Critical New Perspectives on ADHD.* London: Routledge.

Davis, L (2006a) *Play: An essential part of your Local Area Agreement. Play Sector Briefing.* London: Play England/National Children's Bureau.

Davis, L (2006b) 'Time for Play: Encouraging greater play opportunities for children and young people?' *PlayToday*, 54, September 2006. London: National Children's Bureau.

Davis, L (2007) *The Primary Review: Response from Play England.* London: Play England/National Children's Bureau.

Davison, K and Lawson, C (2006) 'Do Attributes in the Physical Environment Influence Children's Physical Activity? A review of the literature', *International Journal of Behavioral Nutrition and Physical Activity*. 3(19): 1-17.

De Castro, L (2004) 'Otherness in Me, Otherness in Others', *Childhood*, 11(4): 469-493.

Dearing, E (2004) 'The Developmental Implications of Restrictive and Supportive Parenting Across Neighbourhoods and Ethnicities: Exceptions are the rule', *Applied Developmental Psychology*, 25: 555-575.

Decety, J and Jackson, P (2004) 'The Functional Architecture of Human Empathy', *Behavioural and Cognitive Neuroscience Review*, 3 (2); 71-100.

Decety, J and Grezes, J (2006) 'The Power of Simulation: Imagining one's own and other's behaviour', *Brain Research*, 1079: 4-14.

Decety, J and Jackson, P (2006) 'A Social-Neuroscience Perspective on Empathy', *Current Directions in Psychological Science*, 15(2): 54-58.

Department for Children, Schools and Families (2007) *The Children's Plan: Building brighter futures*. London: DCSF.

Department for Children, Schools and Families (2008) *Fair Play: A consultation on the play strategy*. London: DCSF.

Department for Culture, Media and Sport (2004) *Getting Serious about Play: A review of children's play*. London: DCMS.

Department for Culture, Media and Sport (2006a) *Time for Play: Encouraging greater play opportunities for children and young people*. London: DCMS.

Department for Culture, Media and Sport (2006b) *Nurturing Creativity in Children and Young People*. London: DCMS.

Department for Education and Skills (2003a) *National Standards for Daycare and Childminding*. Nottingham: DfES.

Department for Education and Skills (2003b) *Every Child Matters*. London: DfES.

Department for Education and Skills (2003c) *Excellence and Enjoyment: A strategy for primary schools*. Nottingham: DfES.

Department for Education and Skills (2003d) *Building a Culture of Participation: Involving children and young people in policy, service planning, delivery and evaluation*. London: DfES.

Department for Education and Skills (2004) *Every Child Matters: Change for children*. London: DfES.

Department for Education and Skills (2005a) *Common Core of Skills and Knowledge for the Children's Workforce*. Nottingham: DfES.

Department for Education and Skills (2005b) *Guidance on the Children and Young People's Plan*. Nottingham: DfES.

Department for Education and Skills (2005c) *Extended Schools: Access to opportunities and services for all: a prospectus*. Nottingham: DfES.

Department for Education and Skills (2006a) *Positive Activities for Young People National Evaluation: final report*. London: DfES.

Department for Education and Skills (2006b) *Youth Matters: Next steps*. Nottingham: DfES.

Department for Education and Skills (2006c) *Learning Outside the Classroom Manifesto*. Nottingham: DfES.

Department for Education and Skills (2006d) *Primary Playground Development*. London: DfES.

Department for Education and Skills (2006e) *Schools for the Future, Designing school grounds*. London: DfES.

Department for Education and Skills (2006f) *Care Matters: Transforming the lives of children and young people in care*. London: DfES.

Department for Education and Skills (2007) *Statutory Framework for the Early Years Foundation Stage*. Nottingham: DfES.

Department for Transport (2005a) *Home Zones: Challenging the future of our streets*. London: DfT.

Department for Transport (2005b) *National Travel Survey 2004*. London: DfT.

Department for Transport (2005c) *Attitudes to Streetscape and Street Uses*. London: DfT.

Department for Transport (2007) *DfT Child Road Safety Strategy*. London: DfT.

Department for Transport, Local Government and the Regions (2002) *Green Spaces, Better Places: Final Report of The Urban Green Spaces Taskforce*. London: DTLR.

Department for Work and Pensions (2007) *Working for Children*. London: The Stationery Office.

Department of Health (2002) *Promoting the Health of Looked After Children*. London: DH.

Department of Health (2003) *Getting the Right Start: National Service Framework for Children Standard for Hospital Services*. London: DH.

Department of Health (2004a) *At Least Five a Week: Evidence on the impact of physical activity and its relationship to health, a report from the Chief Medical Officer*. London: DH.

Department of Health (2004b) *Choosing Health: Making healthy choices easier*. London: DH.

Department of Health (2005) *Choosing Activity: A physical activity action plan* London: DH.

Derman-Sparks L (1989) *Anti Bias Curriculum: Tools for Empowering Young Children*. Washington, DC: NAEYC.

Derr, T (2002) 'Children's Sense of Place in Northern New Mexico', *Journal of Environmental Psychology*, 22: 125-137.

Derr, T (2006) '"Sometimes birds sound like fish": Perspectives on children's place experiences', in Spencer, C and Blades, M (eds) *Children and Their Environments*. Cambridge: Cambridge University Press.

Diamond, A (2007) 'Interrelated and Interdependent', *Developmental Science*, 10(1): 152-158.

Diamond, L and Aspinwall, L (2003) 'Emotion Regulation Across the Life Span: An integrative perspective emphasizing self-regulation, positive affect, and dyadic processes', *Motivation and Emotion*, 27(2): 125-156.

Dietz, WH (2001) `The obesity epidemic in young children', *British Medical Journal*, 322: 313-314.

Dinos, S, Tian, Y, Solanki, A-R and Hauari, H (2006) *National Evaluation of On Track Phase Two, Tracking Services and Users: On Track in practice*. Nottingham: DfES.

Dougherty, L (2006) 'Emotionality and Social Status: A meta-analytical review', *Social Development*, 15(3): 394-417.

Douglas, I (2005) 'Urban Greenspace and Mental Health', review paper prepared for UK MAB Urban Forum.

Douglas, N (1916, 1931) *London Street Games*. London: Chatto and Windus.

Dovey, J (2007) 'How do you play? Identity, technology and ludic culture', *Digital Creativity*, 17(3): 135-139.

Duckworth, A, Steen, T and Seligman, M (2005) 'Positive Psychology in Clinical Practice', *Annual Review of Clinical Psychology*, 1: 629-651.

Dunn, K, Moore, M and Murray, P (2004) *Research on Developing Accessible Play Space – Final Report.* London: ODPM.

Edelman, G (1992) *Bright Air, Brilliant Fire.* London: Penguin.

Edelman, G (2006) *Second Nature: Brain science and human knowledge.* New Haven: Yale University Press.

Edwards, A, Barnes, M, Plewis, I and Morris, K, and others (2006) *Working to Prevent the Social Exclusion of Children and Young People: Final lessons from the National Evaluation of the Children's Fund, Research Report 734.* London: DfES.

Edwards, A (2007) 'Working Collaboratively to Build Resilience: A CHAT approach', *Social Policy and Society*, 6(2): 255-264.

Egenfeldt-Nielsen, S and Smith, J (2003) *Playing With Fire: How do computer games affect the player? Report for The Media Council for Children and Young People.* Copenhagen: Game-Research.

Ekeland, E, Heian, F and Hagen, K (2005) 'Can Exercise Improve Self Esteem in Children and Young People? A systematic review of randomised controlled trials', *British Journal of Sports Medicine*, 39: 792–798.

Ellis, B, Jackson, J and Boyce, W (2006) 'The Stress Response Systems: Universality and adaptive individual differences', *Developmental Review*, 26: 175–212.

Ells, L, Campbell, K, Lidstone, J, Kelly, S, Lang, R and Summerbell, C (2005) 'Prevention of childhood obesity', *Best Practice & Research Clinical Endocrinology & Metabolism*, 19(3): 441–454.

Ellison, N, Steinfield, C and Lampe, C (2007) 'The Benefits of Facebook "friends": Social capital and college students use of online social network sites', *Journal of Computer Mediated Communication*, 12: 1146-1168.

Elsley, S (2004) 'Children's Experience of Public Space', *Children and Society*, 18: 155-164.

Epstein, D, Kehily, M, Mac an Ghaill, M and Redman, P (2001) 'Boys and Girls Come Out to Play', *Men and Masculinities*, 4(2): 158-172.

Evans, G (2004) 'The Environment of Childhood Poverty', *Amercian Psychologist*, 59(2): 77-92.

Evans, R and Pinnock, K (2007) 'Promoting Resilience and Protective Factors in the Children's Fund: Supporting children's and young people's pathways towards social inclusion?' *Journal of Children and Poverty*, 13(1): 21-36.

Factor, J (2004) 'Tree Stumps, Manhole Covers and Rubbish Tins: The invisible play-lines of a primary school playground', *Childhood*, 22(2): 142-154.

Fantuzzo, J, Sekino, Y and Cohen, H (2004) 'An Examination of the Contributions of Interactive Peer Play to Salient Classroom Competencies for Urban Head Start Children', *Psychology in the Schools*, 41(3): 323-336.

Farmer, C (2005) *2003 Home Office Citizenship Survey: Top-level findings from the children and young people's survey.* London: Home Office and DfES.

Farne, R (2005) 'Pedagogy of Play', *Topoi*, 24: 169-181.

Farrington D (2000) 'Explaining and Preventing Crime: The globalisation of knowledge', keynote address to the American Society for Criminology, 1999', *Criminology* 38(1): 1–24, cited in France, A and Utting, D (2005) 'The Paradigm of "Risk and Protection-Focused Prevention" and its Impact on Services for Children and Families', *Children and Society*, 19: 77-90.

Fattore, T, Mason, J and Watson, E (2007) 'Children's Conceptualisations of Their Well-being', *Social Indicators Research*, 80: 5-29.

Fawcett, B, Featherstone, B and Goddard, J (2004) *Contemporary Child Care Policy and Practice*. Basingstoke: Palgrave Macmillan.

Feinstein, L, Bynner, J and Duckworth, K (2005) *Leisure Contexts in Adolescence and their Effects on Adult Outcomes*. London: Centre for Research on the Wider Benefits of Learning.

Feinstein, L and Sabates, R (2006) *Predicting Adult Life Outcomes from Earlier Signals: Identifying those at risk. Report for the Prime Minister's Strategy Unit*. London: Centre for Research on the Wider Benefits of Learning, Institute of Education.

Feldman, R (2007) 'Parent–infant Synchrony and the Construction of Shared Timing: Physiological precursors, developmental outcomes, and risk conditions', *Journal of Child Psychology and Psychiatry*, 48(3/4): 329-354.

Fitzsimmons, P and McKenzie, B (2003) 'Play on Words: Humour as the means of developing authentic learning', in Lytle, D (Ed) *Play and Educational Theory and Practice. Play and Culture Studies, 5*. Westport: Praeger.

Fjortoft, I (2004) 'Landscape and Play: The effects of natural environments on children's play and motor development', *Children, Youth and Environments*, 14(2): 21-44.

Flinn, M (2006) 'Evolution and Ontogeny of Stress Response to Social Challenges in the Human Child', *Developmental Review*, 26: 138-174.

Follett, M (2007) 'The Emergence of the Play Ranger', *PlayToday*, No 57, April 2007. London: Play England/National Children's Bureau.

Fonagy, P, Gergely, G and Target, M (2007) 'The Parent–Infant Dyad and the Construction of the Subjective Self', *Journal of Child Psychology and Psychiatry*, 48(3/4): 288–328.

Forbes, E and Dahl, R (2005) 'Neural systems of positive affect: Relevance to understanding child and adolescent depression', *Development and Psychopathology*, 17: 827-850.

Fox, K (2003) 'Childhood obesity and the role of physical activity', *Journal of the Royal Society for the Promotion of Health*, 124(1): 34-39.

Fox, N, Hane, A and Pine, D (2007) 'Plasticity for Affective Neurocircuitry: How the environment affects gene expression', *Current Directions in Psychological Science*, 16(1): 1-5.

France, A and Utting, D (2005) 'The Paradigm of "Risk and Protection-Focused Prevention" and its Impact on Services for Children and Families', *Children and Society*, 19: 77-90.

Franklin, A (2002) *Accidents, Risk and Play in Adventure Playgrounds in Lambeth, Southwark and Lewisham: Findings from research carried out by the National Children's Bureau (NCB) on behalf of Lambeth Lifelong Learning Service*. London: National Children's Bureau.

Frederickson, B (2006) 'Unpacking Positive Emotions: Investigating the seeds of human flourishing', *The Journal of Positive Psychology*, 1 (2): 57-59.

Freeman, N and Brown, B (2004) 'Reconceptualizing Rough and Tumble Play', *Advances in Early Education and Day Care*, 13: 219-234.

Frost, J (2006) 'The Dissolution of Outdoor Play: Cause and consequences', conference paper delivered at The Value of Play: A forum on risk, recreation and children's health. Washington, DC.

Fry, D (2005) 'Rough-and-Tumble Social Play in Humans', in Pellegrini, A and Smith, P (eds) *The Nature of Play. Great Apes and Humans.* London: Guildford Press.

Fuhrer, U (2004) *Cultivating Minds: Identity as meaning-making practice.* London: Taylor and Francis.

Furedi, F (2002) *The Culture of Fear.* London: Cassell.

Furedi, F (2005) 'Cultivating Suspicion', in Waiton, S and Baird, S *Cotton Wool Kids? Making Sense of 'child safety'.* Glasgow: Generation Youth Issues, papers from a one-day conference held on 20 September 2005.

Gabhainn, S and Sixsmith, J (2006) 'Children Photographing Well-being: Facilitating participation in research', *Children and Society*, 20: 249-259.

Gallese, V (2003) 'The Manifold Nature of Interpersonal Relations: The quest for a common mechanism', *Transactions of the Royal Society*, 358: 517-528.

Gallese, V, Keysers, C and Rizzolatti, G (2004) 'A unifying view of the basis of social cognition', *Trends in Cognitive Sciences*, 8(9): 396-403.

Gallese, V and Lakoff, G (2005) 'The Brain's Concepts: The role of the sensory-motor system in conceptual knowledge', *Cognitive Neuropsychology*, 22(3/4): 455-479

Garcia, R and Baltodano, E (2005) 'Healthy Children, Healthy Communities and Legal Services', *Journal of Poverty, Law and Policy*, 39(1-2) 52-64.

Gayler, K and Evans, I (2001) 'Pretend Play and the Development of Emotion Regulation in Preschool Children', *Early Child Development and Care*, 166: 93-108.

Gentile, D, Lynch, P, Linder, J and Walsh, D (2004) 'The Effects of Violent Video Game Habits on Adolescent Hostility, Aggressive Behaviours, and School Performance', *Journal of Adolescence*, 27: 5-22.

Gervais, M and Wilson, D (2005) 'The Evolution and Actions of Laughter and Humour: A synthetic approach', *The Quarterly Review of Biology*, 80(4): 395- 429.

Gibson, J (1986) *The Ecological Approach to Visual Perception.* New Jersey: Laurence Erlbaum.

Giddens, A (2002) *Sociology, 4th edition.* Cambridge: Polity Press.

Giddings, R and Yarwood, R (2005) 'Growing Up, Going Out and Growing Out of the Countryside: Childhood experiences in rural England', *Children's Geographies*, 3(1): 101-114.

Gill, T (2006) *Growing Adventure: Final report to the Forestry Commission.* Cambridge: Forestry Commission England.

Gill, T (2007a) *Can I Play Out…? Lessons from London Play's Home Zones Project.* London: London Play.

Gill, T (2007b) *No Fear: Growing up in a risk-averse society.* London: Calouste-Gulbenkian Foundation.

Gilligan, R (2000) 'Adversity, Resilience and Young People: The protective value of positive school and spare time experiences', *Children and Society*, 14: 37-47.

Ginsberg, K (2007) 'The Importance of Play in Promoting Healthy Child Development and Maintaining Strong Parent Bonds', *American Academy of Pediatrics*, 119(1) 182-191.

Giuliani, MV and Feldman, R (1993). 'Place attachment in a developmental and cultural context', Journal of Environmental Psychology, 13: 267-274, cited in Manzo, L (2003) 'Beyond House and Haven: Toward a revisioning of emotional relationships with places', *Journal of Environmental Psychology*, 22: 47-61

Gmitrova, V and Gmitrov, J (2004) 'The Primacy of Child-Directed Pretend Play on Cognitive Competence in a Mixed-age Environment: Possible interpretations', *Early Child Development and Care*, 174(3): 267–279.

Godfrey, A and Cole-Hamilton, I (2006) *Children's Play Council Play Indicators Project: Consultation report and draft indicators*. London: National Children's Bureau.

Goldson, B (2002) 'New Labour, Social Justice and Children: Political calculation and the deserving-undeserving schism', *British Journal of Social Work*, 32: 683-695.

Goldstein, A and Russ, S (2001) 'Understanding Children's Literature and its Relationship to Fantasy Ability and Coping', *Imagination, Cognition, and Personality*, 20: 105–126.

Goncu, A, Mistry, J and Mosier, C (2000) 'Cultural Variations in the Play of Toddlers', *International Journal of Behavioural Development*, 24(3): 321-329.

Goodwin, M and Armstrong-Esther, D (2004) 'Children, Social Capital and Health: Increasing the well-being of young people in rural Wales', *Children's Geographies*, 2(1): 49-63.

Gordon, G and Esbjorn-Hargens, S (2007) 'Are we having fun yet? An exploration of the transformative power of play', *Journal of Humanistic Psychology*, 47: 198-222.

Gordon, N, Burke, S, Akil, H, Watson, S and Panksepp, J (2003) 'Socially-Induced Brain "Fertilisation": Play promotes brain derived neurotrophic factor transcription in the amygdala and dorsolateral frontal cortex in juvenile rats', *Neuroscience Letters*, 17-20.

Gosso, Y, Morais, M and Otta, E (2007) 'Pretend Play of Brazilian Children: A window into different cultural worlds', *Journal of Cross-Cultural Psychology*, 38(5): 539-558.

Gould, SJ (1996) *Full House: The spread of excellence from Plato to Darwin*. New York: Harmony Books. Cited in Sutton-Smith, B (1997) *The Ambiguity of Play*. Cambridge, MA: Harvard University Press.

Grayling, T, Hallam, K, Graham, D, Anderson, R and Glaister, S (2002) *Streets Ahead: Safe and liveable streets for children*. London: Institute for Public Policy Research.

Gray, J (2004) 'Integration of Emotion and Cognitive Control', *Current Directions in Cognitive Science*, 13(2): 46-48.

Green, H, McGinnity, A, Meltzer, H, Ford, T and Goodman, R (2005) *Mental Health of Children and Young People in Great Britain, 2004. A National Statistics Publication*. Hampshire: PalgraveMacmillan.

Greenberg, N (2004) 'The Beast at Play: The neuroethology of creativity', in Clements, R and Fiorentino, L (eds) *The Child's Right to Play: A Global Approach*. Westport: Praeger.

Gritti, A, Vescovi, A and Galli, R (2002) 'Adult Neural Stem Cells: Plasticity and developmental potential', *Journal of Physiology*, 96(1-2): 81-90.

Grugeon, E (2004) 'Outside the Classroom: Children's talk and play on the playground,' ESRC Research Seminar Series, Children's Literacy and Popular Culture, University of Sheffield, 2002-2004.

Guss, F (2005) 'Reconceptualising Play: Aesthetic self-definitions', *Contemporary Issues in Early Childhood*, 6(3): 233-243.

Hackett, G (2007) 'All Work, No Play at Blair Flagship School' *The Times*, 6 May 2007.

Haglund, M, Nestadt, P, Cooper, N, Southwick, S and Charney, D (2007) 'Psychobiological Mechanisms of Resilience: Relevance to prevention and treatment of stress-related psychopathology', *Development and Psychopathology*, 19: 889-920.

Haiat, H, Bar-mor, G and Shochat, M (2003) 'The World of the Child: A world of play even in the hospital', *International Paediatric Nursing*, 1(3): 209-214.

Hakarrainen, P (1999) 'Play and Motivation', in Engeström, Y, Miettinen R and Punamäki R-L (eds) *Perspectives in Activity Theory*. Cambridge: Cambridge University Press.

Halden, M and Anastasiou M (2007) 'How to Become Invisible While Flying Through the Air', *Play Right*, 2/07: 17-19.

Hallsworth, S and Sutton, A (2004) *Impact Assessment of Changes and Proposed Changes to the Provision of Children's Playscheme Services in Islington. A Research Report for Islington Children's Fund*. London: Centre for Social and Evaluation Research, London Metropolitan University.

Hansard (Westminster Hall) 4 November 2003, column 241 WH.

Hansen, K and Plewis, I (2004) *Children at Risk: How evidence from British Cohort Data can inform the debate on prevention*. Centre for Longitudinal Studies, Bedford Group for Lifecourse and Statistical Studies, Institute of Education, University of London and National Evaluation of the Children's Fund.

Harker, C (2005) 'Playing and Affective Time Spaces', *Children's Geographies*, 3: 47-62, cited in Meire, J (2007) *Qualitative Research on Children's Play: A review of recent literature*. Belgium: Childhood and Society Research Centre.

Harms, K and Dunaevsky, A (2007) 'Dendritic Spine Plasticity: Looking beyond development', *Brain Research*, 1184: 65-71.

Hart, R (1979) *Children's Experience of Place*. New York: Irvington.

Hart, R (2002) 'Containing Children: Some lessons on planning for play from New York City', *Environment and Urbanization*, 14(2): 135-149.

Hartley, D (2006) 'Excellence and Enjoyment: The logic of a "contradiction"', *British Journal of Educational Studies*, 54(1): 3-14.

Haywood, C and Mac an Ghaill, M (2001) 'The Significance of Teaching English Boys: Exploring social change, modern school and the making of masculinities', in Marino, W and Meyen, B (eds) *What About the Boys? Issues of Masculinity in School*. Buckingham: Open University Press, cited in Browne, N (2004) *Gender Equity in the Early Years*. Maidenhead: Open University Press.

Head, T (2001) *Making Sense: Playwork in practice*. London: PLAYLINK.

Head, T and Melville, S (2001) *Wonderful Places to Play*. London: PLAYLINK.

Heft, H (1997) 'The Relevance of Gibson's Ecological Approach to Perception for Environment-Behaviour Studies,' in Moore, G and Marans, R (eds) *Advances in Environment, Behaviour and Design*. New York: Plenum Press.

Hendrick, H (1997) *Children, Childhood and English Society 1880-1990*. Cambridge: Cambridge University Press.

Henricks, TS (2006) *Play Reconsidered: Sociological perspectives on human expression*. Urbana and Chicago: University of Illinois Press.

Hester, R (2004) *Services Provided to Gypsy/Traveller Children: A review of the current literature for the National Evaluation of the Children's Fund*. Birmingham: NECF.

Hill, D (2003) 'The Kids Aren't Alright', *The Guardian*, 11 November 2003.

Hillman, M (2006) 'Children's Rights and Adults' Wrongs', *Children's Geographies* 4(1): 61-67.

Hine, J (2005) 'Early Multiple Intervention: A view from on track', *Children and Society*, 19: 117-130.

HM Treasury and the DfES (2007a) *Aiming High for Children: Supporting families*. London: The Stationery Office.

HM Treasury and the DfES (2007b) *Aiming High for Disabled Children: Better support for families.* London: The Stationery Office.

HM Treasury, Department for Education and Skills, Department for Work and Pensions and the Department of Trade and Industry (2004) *Choice for Parents, the Best Start for Children: A ten year strategy for childcare.* Norwich: HMSO.

Hobcraft, J (2007) *Child Development, the Life Course, and Social Exclusion: Are the frameworks used in the UK relevant for other countries?* Manchester: Chronic Poverty Research Centre.

Hofer, M (2006) 'Psychobiological Roots of Early Attachment', *Current Directions in Psychological Science*, 15(2): 84-88.

Hofferth, S and Sandberg, J (2001) 'Changes in American Children's Use of Time 1981-1997', in Owens, T and Hofferth, S (eds) *Children at the Millenium: Where have we come from, where are we going?* Amsterdam: Elsevier press. Cited in Burdette, H and Whitaker, R (2005) 'Resurrecting Free Play in Young Children: Looking beyond fitness and fatness to attention, affiliation, and affect', *Archives of Pediatric Adolescent Medicine*, 159: 46-50.

Hoggart, S (2005) 'Grimm Reading… but not fairy tales', *The Guardian*. 12 March 2005.

Holland, J, Reynolds, T and Weller, S (2007) 'Transitions, Networks and Communities: The significance of social capital in the lives of children and young people', *Journal of Youth Studies*, 10(1): 97-116.

Holland, P (2003) *We Don't Play with Guns Here: War, weapon and superhero play in the early years.* Maidenhead: Open University Press.

Holloway, K and Suter, B (2003) 'Play Deprivation Without Social Isolation', *Developmental Psychobiology*, 44(1): 58-67.

Holmes, R and Geiger, C (2002) 'The Relationship Between Creativity and Cognitive Abilities in Preschoolers', in Rooparine, J (ed) *Conceptual Social-Cognitive, and Contextual Issues in the Fields of Play. Play and Culture Studies*, 4. Westport: Ablex.

Holmes, R, Pellegrini, A and Schmidt, S (2006) 'The Effects of Different Recess Timing Regimens on Preschoolers' Classroom Attention', *Early Child Development and Care*, 176 (7): 735-743.

Hood, S (2004) *The State of London's Children Report.* London: Greater London Authority.

Hood, S (2007) 'Reporting on Children's Well-being: The State of London's Children Report', *Social Indicators Research*, 80: 249-264.

Hough, M and Roberts, JV (2004) *Youth crime and youth justice: Public opinion in England and Wales.* Bristol: Policy Press.

Howard, J, Bellin, W and Rees, V (2002) *Eliciting Children's Perceptions of Play and Exploiting Playfulness to Maximise Learning in the Early Years Classroom.* Paper presented to BERA Annual Conference, 2002.

Howard, J, Jenvey, V and Hill, C (2006) 'Children's Categorization of Play and Learning Based on Social Context', *Early Child Development and Care*, 176(3-4): 379-393.

Howard, M (2007) 'Children of War: The generation traumatised by violence in Iraq; growing up in a war zone takes its toll as young play games of murder and mayhem', *The Guardian*, 6 February 2007.

Howard-Jones, P, Taylor, J and Sutton, L (2002) 'The Effect of Play on the Creativity of Young Children During Subsequent Activity', *Early Child Development and Care*, 172(4): 323-328.

Hsi, S (2007) 'Conceptualizing Learning from the Everyday Activities of Digital Kids', *International Journal of Science Education*, 29(12): 1509-1529.

248

Hubbs-Tait, L, Nation, J, Krebs, N and Bellinger, D (2006) 'Neurotoxicants, Micronutrients, and Social Environments: Individual and combined effects on children's development', *Psychological Science in the Public Interest*, 6(1): 57-121.

Hughes, B (1996a) *A Playworker's Taxonomy of PlayTypes*. London: PLAYLINK.

Hughes, B (1996b) *Play Environments: A question of quality*. London: PLAYLINK.

Hughes, B (2001) *Evolutionary Playwork and Reflective Analytical Practice*. London: Routledge.

Hughes, B (2002) *A Playworker's Taxonomy of Play Types, 2nd edition*. London: PLAYLINK.

Hughes, B (2003) 'Play Deprivation, Play Bias and Playwork Practice', in Brown, F (ed) *Playwork Theory and Practice*. Buckingham: Open University Press.

Hughes, B (2006) *PlayTypes: Speculations and Possibilities*. London: London Centre for Playwork Education and Training.

Hull City Council (c2005) *Hull Children and Young People's Plan 2006-2008*. Hull: Hull City Council.

Hume, C, Salmon, J and Ball, K (2005) 'Children's Perceptions of Their Home and Neighborhood Environments, and Their Association with Objectively Measured Physical Activity: A qualitative and quantitative study', *Health Education Research*, 2(1): 1-13.

Hunt, C and Kapasi, H (2005) *The Power of Play. Addressing Community Cohesion through Play*. Devon and Cornwall Housing Association.

Hutchby, I (2005) 'Children's Talk and Social Competence', *Children and Society*, 19: 66-73.

Hyder, T (2005) *War, Conflict and Play*. Maidenhead: Open University Press.

Isen, A and Reeve, J (2006) 'The Influence of Positive Affect on Intrinsic and Extrinsic Motivation: Facilitating enjoyment of play, responsible work behaviour and self-control', *Motivation and Emotion*, 29(4): 297-325.

Islington Play Association (2007) *IPA Annual Report 2006*. London: IPA.

Jack, G (2006) 'The Area and Community Components of Children's Well-being', *Children and Society*, 20: 334-347.

James, A (1998) 'Play in Childhood: An anthropological perspective', *Child Psychology and Psychiatry Review*, 3(3): 104-109.

James, A and James, AL (2004) *Constructing Childhood: Theory, policy and social practice*. Basingstoke: Palgrave Macmillan.

James, A, Jenks, C and Prout, A (1998) *Theorising Childhood*. London: Polity.

James, A and Prout, A (eds) (1997) *Constructing and Reconstructing Childhood: Contemporary issues in the sociological study of childhood*. London: Falmer Press.

Jans, M (2004) 'Children as Citizens: Towards a contemporary notion of child participation', *Childhood*, 11(1): 27-44.

Jarrett, O and Duckett-Hedgebeth, M (2003) 'Recess in a Middle School: What do the students do?' in Lytle, D (ed) *Play and Educational Theory and Practice. Play and Culture Studies 5*. Westport: Praeger.

Jarrold, C (2003) 'A Review of Research into Pretend Play in Autism', *Autism*, 7 (4): 379-390.

Jenkins, N (2006) '"You Can't Wrap Them Up in Cotton Wool!" Constructing risk in young people's access to outdoor play', *Health, Risk and Society*, 8(4): 379-393.

John, A and Wheway, R (2004) *Can Play, Will Play: Disabled children and access to outdoor playgrounds*. London: NPFA.

249

Johnson, M (2005) 'Sensitive Periods in Functional Brain Development: Problems and prospects', *Developmental Psychobiology*, 46: 287-292.

Johnston, M (2004) 'Clinical Disorders of Brain Plasticity', *Brain and Development*, 26: 73–80.

Jones D (2004 and forthcoming) *The Singing Playground*. Interactive mixed media painting in Bethnal Green Museum of Childhood.

Jones, O, Williams, M and Fleuriot, C (2003) 'A New Sense of Place?' *Children's Geographies*, 1(2): 165-180.

Jordan, A, Hersey, J, McDivitt, J and Heitzler, C (2006) 'Reducing Children's Television-Viewing Time: A qualitative study of parents and their children', *Pediatrics*, 118(5): 1303-1310.

Jotangia, D, Moody, A, Stamatakis, E and Wardle, H (2005) *Obesity Among Children Under 11*. London: Royal Free and University College Medical School/ National Statistics.

Jutras, S and Lepage, G (2006) 'Parental Perceptions of Contributions of School and Neighbourhood to Children's Psychological Wellness', *Journal of Community Psychology*, 34(3): 305-325.

Kalliala, M (2006) *Play Culture in a Changing World*. Berkshire: Open University Press.

Kapasi, H (2002) *Playing in Parallel: A study of access to play provision by Black and minority children in London*. London: London Play.

Kapasi, H (2006a) *Neighbourhood Play and Community Action*. York: Joseph Rowntree Foundation and National Children's Bureau.

Kapasi, H (2006b) *Equal in Play? A survey of employment of Black and other minority ethnic staff in playwork*. London: London Play.

Kaplan, R and Kaplan, S (2005) 'Preference, Restoration, and Meaningful Action in the Context of Nearby Nature', in Barlett, P (ed) *Urban Place: Reconnecting with the natural world*. Cambridge: MIT Press.

Karsten, L (2003) 'Children's Use of Public Space. The gendered world of the playground', *Childhood*, 10(4): 457-473.

Karsten, L (2005) 'It All Used to be Better? Different generations on continuity and change in urban children's daily use of space', *Children's Geographies*, 3(3): 275-290.

Karsten, L and van Vliet, W (2006a) 'Increasing Children's Freedom of Movement: Introduction', *Children, Youth and Environments*, 1(1): 69-73.

Karsten, L and van Vliet, W (2006b) 'Children in the City: Reclaiming the street', *Children, Youth and Environments*, 16(1): 151-167.

Kearney, M (2007) 'Productive Spaces: Girls' bedrooms as sites of cultural production', *Journal of Children and Media*, 1(2): 126-141.

Kelley, N (2006) 'Children's Involvement in Policy Formation', *Children's Geographies*, 4(1): 37-44.

Kerawalla, L and Crook, C (2002) 'Children's Computer Use at Home and at School: Context and continuity', *British Educational Research Journal*, 28 (6) 751-771.

Keverne, E (2004) 'Understanding Well-being in the Evolutionary Context of Brain Development', *Philosophical Transactions of the Royal Society of London B*, 359: 1349–1358.

Keyes, C (2006) 'Subjective Well-being in Mental Health and Human Development Research Worldwide: An introduction', *Social Indicators Research*, 77:1–10.

Kirby, P and Bryson, S (2002) *Measuring the Magic: Evaluating and researching young people's participation in public decision making*. London: Carnegie Young People Initiative.

Kirby, P, Lanyon, C, Cronin, K and Sinclair, R (2003) *Building a Culture of Participation: Involving children and young people in policy, service planning, delivery and evaluation.* London: DfES.

Korpela, K, Kytta, M and Hartig, T (2002) 'Restorative Experience, Self-Regulation and Children's Special Place Preferences', *Journal of Environmental Psychology*, 22: 387 – 398.

Kreppner, J, O'Connor, T, Dunn, J, Andersen-Wood, L and the English and Romanian Adoptees (ERA) Study Team (1999) 'The Pretend and Social Role Play of Children Exposed to Early Severe Deprivation', *British Journal of Developmental Psychology*, 17: 319–332.

Kuo, F and Sullivan, W (2001) 'Aggression and Violence in the Inner City: Effects of environment via mental fatigue', *Environment and Behaviour* 33(4): 543-571.

Kuo, F and Taylor, A (2004) 'A Potential Natural Treatment for Attention Deficit/Hyperactivity Disorder: Evidence from a national study', *American Journal of Public Health*, 94(9): 1580-1586.

Kuo, F and Taylor, A (2005) 'Kuo and Taylor respond.' *American Journal of Public Health*, 95(3): 372.

Kylin, M (2003) 'Children's Dens', *Children, Youth and Environments* 13(1).

Kytta, M (2004) 'The Extent of Children's Independent Mobility and the Number of Actualized Affordances as Criteria for Child-friendly Environments', *Journal of Environmental Psychology*, 24: 179–198.

Lacey, L (2007a) *Street Play: A literature review.* London: National Children's Bureau.

Lacey, L (2007b) *Playday: Our Streets Too! Street Play Opinion Poll Survey.* London: Play England/ National Children's Bureau.

Lammy, D (2007) *Making Space for Children: The big challenge for our public realm.* London: Compass.

Lareau, A (2000) 'Social Class and the Daily Lives of Children. A study from the United States', *Childhood*, 7(2): 155-171.

Lawrence, P (2005) Gypsy and Traveller Children, *Highlight No 221.* London: National Children's Bureau.

Learning Through Landscapes (2006) 'Playground Design for Better Behaviour', *Groundnotes*, 6(1) Schoolgrounds-UK.

Leckman, J and Mayes, L (2007) 'Nurturing Resilient Children', *Journal of Child Psychology and Psychiatry*, 48(3/4): 221–223.

Leonard, M (2005) 'Children, Childhood and Social Capital: Exploring the links', *Sociology*, 39(4): 606-622.

Lester, S and Maudsley, M (2006) *Play, Naturally.* London: Play England/National Children's Bureau.

Levin, I and Hart, S (2003) 'Risk Preferences in Young Children: Early evidence of individual differences in reaction to potential gains and losses', *Journal of Behavioural Decision Making*, 16: 397-413.

Levin, P (1979) *Making Social Policy: Mechanisms of government and politics and how to investigate them.* Buckingham: Open University Press.

Levinson, M (2005) 'The Role of Play in the Formation and Maintenance of Cultural Identity: Gypsy children in home and school contexts', *Journal of Contemporary Ethnography*, 34(5): 499-532.

Lewis, M (2004) 'Environmental Complexity and Central Nervous System Development and Function', *Mental retardation and Developmental Disabilities Research Review*, 10: 91-95.

251

Lewis, M (2005) 'Self-Organising Individual Differences in Brain Development', *Developmental Review*, 25: 252-277.

Lewis, M and Stieben, J (2004) 'Emotion Regulation in the Brain; Conceptual issues and directions for developmental research', *Child Development*, 75(2): 371-376.

Libby, S, Powell, S, Messer, D and Jordan, R (1998) 'Spontaneous Play in Children with Autism: A reappraisal', *Journal of Autism and Developmental Disorder*, 28 (6): 487-497.

Lindsey, E and Colwell, M (2003) 'Preschoolers' Emotional Competence: Links to pretend and physical play', *Child Study Journal*, 33.

Lindquist, G (2001) 'Elusive Play and its Relations to Power', *Focaal – European Journal of Anthroplogy*, 37: 13-23, cited in Meire, J (2007) *Qualitative Research on Children's Play: A review of recent literature*. Belgium: Childhood and Society Research Centre.

Lindqvist, P and Nordanger, U (2007) 'Better Safe Than Sorry? Risk and educational research', *Educational Studies*, 33(1): 15-27.

Little, H (2006) 'Children's Risk-taking Behaviour: Implications for early-childhood policy and practice', *International Journal of Early Years Education*, 14(2): 141-154.

Little, M Axford, N and Morpeth, L (2004) 'Research Review: Risk and protection in the context of services for children in need', *Child and Family Social Work*, 9: 105-117.

Livingstone, S (2003) 'Children's Use of the Internet: Reflections on the emerging research agenda', *New Media and Society* 5(2): 147-166.

Livingstone, S (2006) 'Drawing Conclusions from New Media Research: reflections and puzzles regarding children's experience of the internet', *The Information Society*, 22: 219–230.

Livingstone, S (2007) 'Do the Media Harm Children? Reflections on new approaches to an old problem', *Journal of Children and Media*, 1(1): 5-14.

Livingstone, S and Bober, M (2003) *UK Children Go Online: Listening to young people's experiences*. London: LSE Research Online. http://eprints.lse.ac.uk/archive/0000388 [Accessed 12/10/07].

Livingstone, S and Bovill, M (eds.) (2001) *Children and Their Changing Media Environment: A European comparative study*. Mahwah, NJ: Laurence Erlbaum.

Lloyd, G, Stead, J and Cohen, C (eds) (2006) *Critical New Perspectives on ADHD*. London: Routledge.

Lofdahl, A (2005) 'Preschool Teachers' Conceptions of Children's "Chaotic Play"', in McMahon, F, Lytle, D and Sutton-Smith, B (eds) *Play: An Interdisciplinary Synthesis*. Maryland: University Press of America.

Lofdahl, A and Hagglund, S (2006) 'Power and Participation: Social representations among children in pre-school', *Social Psychology of Education*, 9: 179–194.

Lohr, V (2007) 'Benefits of Nature: What we are learning about why people respond to nature', *Journal of Physiological Anthropology*, 26(2): 83–85.

Loizou, E (2005) 'Infant Humor: The theory of the absurd and the empowerment theory', *International Journal of Early Years Education*, 13: 43-53.

Lord, P, Wilkin, A, Kinder, K, Murfield, J, Jones, M, Chamberlain, T, Easton, C, Martin, K, Gulliver, C, Paterson, C, Ries, J, Moor, H, Stott, A, Wilkin, C and Stoney, S (2006) *Analysis of Children and Young People's Plans 2006*. Slough: NFER.

Loughry, M, Ager, A, Flouri, E, Khamis, V, Afana, AH and Qouta, S (2006) 'The Impact of Structured Activities among Palestinian Children in a Time of Conflict', *Journal of Child Psychology and Psychiatry* 47(12): 1211-1218.

Louv, R (2005) *Last Child in the Woods: Saving our children from nature-deficit disorder*. Chapel Hill: Algonquin.

Luckett, T, Bundy, A and Roberts, J (2007) 'Do Behavioural Approaches Teach Children with Autism to Play or Are They Pretending?' *Autism*, 11(4): 365-388.

Ludvigsen, A, Creegan, C, and Mills, H (2005) *Let's Play Together: Play and Inclusion. Evaluation of Better Play Round Three*. Ilford: Barnardo's.

Luthar, S and Brown, P (2007) 'Maximizing Resilience Through Diverse Levels of Analysis: Prevailing paradigms, possibilities and priorities for the future', *Development and Psychopathology*, 19: 931-955.

Lynch, K (1980) *The Image of the City*. Cambridge, MA: MIT Press.

Lytle, D (2005) 'Ludic Pathologies and Their Links to Play: Cultural and neurocognitive perspectives', in Lytle, D (ed) *Play and Educational Theory and Practice. Play and Culture Studies 5*. Westport: Praeger.

Maan, N (2005) *Delivery of Better Play Projects to Culturally Diverse Communities (Briefing 3)*. Ilford: Barnardo's.

Mac an Ghaill, M (1999) *Contemporary Racisms and Ethnicities: Social and cultural transformations*. Buckingham: Open University Press.

MacIntyre, I (2007) 'Notes From a Playworker Who Wanted Children to Play his Game', in Russell, W, Handscomb, B and Fitzpatrick, J (eds) *Playwork Voices: In celebration of Bob Hughes and Gordon Sturrock*. London: London Centre for Playwork Education and Training.

Mackett, R and Paskins, J (2004) *Increasing Children's Volume of Physical Activity Through Walk and Play*. Contribution to the Department of Culture, Media and Sport and Department of Health Consultation on Choosing Health, Choosing Activity.

Mackey, T and Ullman, A (2006) *Creative Partnerships: Survey of head teachers*. London: British Market Research Bureau.

Madge, N (2006) *Children These Days*. Bristol: The Policy Press.

Mahoney, P and Hextall I (2000) *Reconstructing Teaching*. London: Falmer Routledge, cited in Browne, N (2004) *Gender Equity in the Early Years*. Maidenhead: Open University Press.

Manwaring, B (2006) *Children's Views 2006: Children and young people's views on play and playworkers*. London: SkillsActive.

Manwaring, B and Taylor, C (2006) *The Benefits of Play and Playwork*. London: SkillsActive and CYWU.

Manzo, L (2003) 'Beyond House and Haven: Toward a revisioning of emotional relationships with places', *Journal of Environmental Psychology*, 22: 47-61.

Marsh, J, Brooks, G, Hughes, J, Ritchie, L, Roberts, S and Wright, K (2005) *Digital beginnings: Young children's use of popular culture, media and new technologies*. Report of the Young Children's Use of Popular Culture, Media and New Technologies Study. Literacy Research Centre University of Sheffield.

Martin, C, Fabes, R, Hanish, L and Hoolenstein, T (2005) 'Social Dynamics in the Preschool', *Developmental Review*, 25: 299-327.

Martin, R (2007) *The Psychology of Humour: An integrative approach*. Burlington, MA: Elsevier Academic Press

253

Masey, H (2004) *Playwork People, Research Report 1*, London: Skillsactive.

Mason, P and Broughton K (2007) 'Gypsy/ Traveller Children and Families: The potential of working with networks', *Social Policy and Society*, 6 (2): 243-253.

Masselos, G (2003) '"When I Play Funny it Makes Me Laugh": Implications for early childhood educators in developing humour through play', in Lytle, D (ed) *Play and Educational Theory and Practice. Play and Culture Studies, 5*. Westport: Praeger.

Masten, A (2001) 'Ordinary Magic: Resilience processes in development', *American Psychologist*, 56(3): 227-238.

Masten, A (2006) 'Developmental Psychopathology: Pathways to the future', *International Journal of Behavioral Development*, 30(1): 47-54.

Masten, A (2007) 'Resilience in Developing Systems: Progress and promise as the fourth wave rises', *Development and Psychopathology*, 19: 921-930.

Masten, A and Obradovic, J (2006) 'Competence and Resilience in Development', *Annals of the New York Academy of Science*, 1094: 13-27.

Mathers, S, Sylva, K and Joshi, H (with others) (2007) *Quality of Childcare Settings in the Millennium Cohort Study*. Nottingham: DfES.

Mathur, R and Berndt, T (2006) 'Relations of Friends' Activities to Friendship Quality', *Journal of Early Adolescence*, 26(3): 365-388.

Matthews, H, Limb, M and Taylor, M (2000b) 'The "Street" as Thirdspace', in Holloway, S and Valentine, G (eds) (2000) *Children's Geographies*. London: Routledge.

Matthews, H and Tucker, F (2006) 'On the Other Side of the Tracks: The psychogeographies and everyday lives of rural teenagers in the UK', in Spencer, C

and Blades, M (2006) *Children and Their Environments*. Cambridge: Cambridge University Press.

Maudsley, M (ed) (2005) *Playing on the Wildside*. Cheltenham: Playwork Partnerships.

Mayall, B (2002) *Towards A Sociology for Childhood: Thinking from children's lives*. Buckingham: Open University Press.

Mayall, B (2003) *Sociologies of Childhood and Educational Thinking: Professorial lecture*. London: Institute of Education

Mayall, B (2005) 'Values and Assumptions Underpinning Policy for Children and Young People in England', *Children's Geographies*, 4(1): 9-17.

Mayall, B and Hood, S (2001) 'Breaking Barriers – Provision and Participation in an Out of School Centre', *Children and Society*, 15: 70-81.

Maybin, J (2003) 'Language, Relationships and Identities', in Kehily, M and Swann, J (eds) *Children's Cultural Worlds*. Chichester: John Wiley and Son.

Mayhew, E, Uprichard, E, Beresford, B, Ridge, T and Bradshaw, J (2004) 'Children and Childhood in the United Kingdom' in An-Magritt Jensen, Asher Ben-Arieh, Cinzia Conti, Dagmar Kutsar, Máire Nic Ghiolla Phádraig and Hanne Warming Nielsen (eds) *Children's Welfare in Ageing Europe, Volume 1*. Trondheim: Norway Centre for Child Research.

McArdle, P (2001) 'Children's Play, Child: Care', *Health and Development*, 27 (6): 509-514.

McEwen, B (2007) 'Physiology and Neurobiology of Stress and Adaptation: Central role of the brain', *Physiological Review*, 87: 873-904.

McGhee, P (1989) 'The Contribution of Humor to Children's Social Development', in McGhee, P (ed) *Humor and Children's*

Development. A guide to practical applications. New York: Haworth Press. Cited in Loizou, E (2005) 'Infant humor: the theory of the absurd and the empowerment theory', *International Journal of Early Years Education*, 13(1): 43–53

McIntyre, S and Casey, T (2007) *People Play Together More* (P.inc) Research Report. Edinburgh: The Yard.

McKendrick, JH, Bradford, MG and Fielder, AV (2000) 'Kid Customer?: Commercialisation of play space and the commodification of childhood', *Childhood*, 7(3): 295-314.

McNeish, D and Gill, T (2006) Editorial: 'UK Policy on Children: Key themes and implications', *Children's Geographies*, 4(1): 1-7.

Meire, J (2007) *Qualitative Research on Children's Play: A review of recent literature.* Belgium: Childhood and Society Research Centre.

Melman, S, Little, S and Akin-Little, K (2007) 'Adolescent Overscheduling: The relationship between levels of participation in scheduled activities and self-reported clinical symptomology', *The High School Journal*, Feb/March 2007: 18-30.

Meltzer, H, Gatward, R, Corbin, T, Goodman, R and Ford, T (2003) *The Mental Health of Young People Looked After by Local Authorities in England.* London: TSO.

Melville, S (2004) *Places for Play.* London: PLAYLINK.

Middleton, E (2006) 'Youth Participation in the UK: Bureaucratic disaster or triumph of child rights?' *Children, Youth and Environments*, 16(2): 180-190.

Millie, A, Jacobson, J, McDonald, E and Hough, M (2005) *Antisocial Behaviour Strategies: Finding a balance.* Bristol: The Policy Press.

Milligan, C and Bingley, A (2004) *Climbing Trees and Building Dens: Mental health and wellbeing in young adults and the long-term effects of childhood play experience.* Lancaster: Lancaster University Institute for Health Research.

Min, B and Lee, J (2006) 'Children's Neighborhood Place as a Psychological and Behavioral Domain', *Journal of Environmental Psychology*, 26: 51–71.

Mindham, C (2005) 'Creativity and the Young Child', *Early Years*, 25 (1): 81-84.

Mitchell, C and Reid-Walsh, J (2002) *Researching Children's Popular Culture.* London: Routledge.

Mohaupt, H, Holgersen, H, Binder, P and Nielsen, G (2006) 'Affect Consciousness or Mentalization? A comparison of two concepts with regard to affect development and affect regulation. *Scandinavian Journal of Psychology*, 47: 237–244.

Mooney, A and Blackburn, T (2003) *Children's Views on Childcare Quality.* Nottingham: DfES.

Moore, M and Russ, S (2006) 'Pretend Play as a Resource for Children: Implications for pediatricians and health professionals.' *Journal of Developmental and Behavioural Pediatrics.* 27(3): 237-248.

Moore, R (1986) *Childhood's Domain.* London: Croom Helm.

Morgan, A and Kennewell, S (2006) 'Initial Teacher Education Students' Views on Play as a Medium for Learning – A divergence of personal philosophy and practice', *Technology, Pedagogy and Education* 15(3): 307–320.

MORI (2004) *Media Image of Young People.* Available online from www.ipsos-mori. com/polls/2004/young-people-now.shtml [accessed 10 March 2008].

Morley-Fletcher, S, Rea, M, Maccari, S and Laviola, G (2003) 'Environmental Enrichment During Adolescence Reverses the Effects of Prenatal Stress on Play Behaviour and HPA in Rats', *European Journal of Neuroscience*, 18: 3367-3374.

Morris, K, Warren, S, Hek, R, Mason, P, and Plumridge, G (2006) *Preventative Services for Black and Minority Ethnic Children: A final report of the National Evaluation of the Children's Fund. Research Report* RR778. London: DfES.

Morrongiello, B and Matheis, S (2004) 'Determinants of Children's Risk-Taking in Different Social-Situational Contexts: The role of cognitions and emotions in predicting children's decisions', *Applied Developmental Psychology*, 25: 303-326.

Morrow, V (2004) 'Children's "Social Capital": Implications for health and well-being.' *Health Education*, 104(4): 211-225.

Morrow, V (2006) 'Understanding Gender Differences in Context: Implications for young children's everyday lives', *Children and Society*, 20(2): 92-104.

Morrow, V and Connolly, P (2006) 'Gender and Ethnicity in children's Everyday Lives', *Children and Society*, 20(2): 87-91.

Moss, P (2003) 'Beyond Caring: The case for reforming the childcare and early years workforce', *Facing the Future Policy Paper 5*, London: Daycare Trust.

Moss, P (2007) 'Meetings Across the Paradigmatic Divide', *Educational Philosophy and Theory*, 39 (3): 229-245.

Moss, P and Petrie, P (2002) *From Children's Services to Children's Spaces: Public policy, children and childhood.* London: RoutledgeFalmer.

Mota, J, Silva, P, Santos, M, Ribeiro, J, Oliviera, J and Duarte, J (2005) 'Physical Activity and School Recess Time: Differences between the sexes and the relationship between children's playground physical activity and habitual physical activity', *Journal of Sports Sciences*, 23(3): 269-275.

Mouritsen, F (1998) *Children's Play-culture and the Concept of Development.* National Advisory Committee on Creative and Cultural Education.

Moyles, J, Adams, S and Musgrove, A (2002) *SPEEL: Study of Pedagogical Effectiveness in Early Learning.* Norwich: HMSO.

Mullineaux, P and DiLalla, L (2006) *'Child Temperament and Mother-Child Interactions in Infant Twins'*, paper presented to the Conference on Human Development, April 2006, Louisville KY.

Murray, R and O'Brien, L (2005) *Such Enthusiasm – a Joy to See: An evaluation of Forest School in England.* Surrey: Forest Research and New Economics Foundation.

Nairn, K, Panelli, R and McCormack, J (2003) 'Destabilizing Dualisms: Young people's experiences of rural and urban environments', *Childhood*, 10(1): 9-42.

Nandy, L (2005) 'The Impact of Government Policy on Asylum-seeking and Refugee Children', *Children and Society*, 19: 410-413.

National Advisory Committee on Creative and Cultural Education (1999) *All Our Futures: Creativity, culture and education*, Report to the Secretary of State for Education and Employment and the Secretary of State for Culture, Media and Sport.

National Association of Early Childhood Specialists in State Departments of Education (2002) *Recess and the Importance of Play: A position statement.* Illinois, USA: NAECSSDE.

National Scientific Council on the Developing Child (2005) *Excessive Stress Disrupts the Architecture of the Developing Brain. Working Paper No 3.* www.developingchild.net/pubs/wp-abstracts/wp3.html [accessed 13 March 2008].

National Institute for Health and Clinical Excellence (2006) *Methylphenidate, Atomoxetine and Dexamfetamine for Attention Deficit Hyperactivity Disorder (ADHD) in Children and Adolescents: Review of Technology Appraisal 13.* London: NICE.

National Union of Teachers (2007) *Time to Play: NUT Play Policy.* National Union of Teachers.

National Union of Teachers (2007b) *Time to Play: Putting play into practice.* National Union of Teachers.

Neighbourhood Renewal Unit (2004) *Street Games: A report into young people's participation in sport.* Wetherby: ODPM.

New Economics Foundation (2000) *Prove It! Measuring the effect of neighbourhood renewal on local people.* London: NEF.

New Economics Foundation (2004) *The Power and Potential of Well-being Indicators: Measuring young people's well-being in Nottingham.* London: NEF.

New Opportunities Fund (NOF) (1999) *Out of School Hours Childcare: Information for applicants.* London: New Opportunities Fund.

Newman, M, Woodcock, A and Dunham, P (2006) 'Playtime in the Borderlands: Children's representations of school, gender and bullying through photographs and interviews', *Children's Geographies*, 4(3): 289-302.

Nilsen, RD and Rogers, B (2005) '"That's not a good idea, mom": Negotiating children's subjectivity while constructing "home" as a research site', *Children's Geographies*, 3(3): 345-362.

NPFA, Children's Play Council and PLAYLINK (2000) *Best Play: What play provision should do for children.* London: NPFA.

Oakley, A (2000) *Experiments in Knowing: Gender and method in the social sciences.* Cambridge: Polity Press.

O'Brien, M, Jones, D and Rustin, M (2000) 'Children's Independent Spatial Mobility in the Public Realm', *Childhood*, 7(3) 257-277.

Odling-Smee, F, Laland, K and Feldman, M (2003) *Niche Construction: The Neglected Process of Evolution.* Princeton: Princeton University Press.

Office of the Deputy Prime Minister (2002a) *Living Places: Cleaner, Safer, Greener.* London: ODPM.

Office of the Deputy Prime Minister (2002b) *Planning Policy Guidance 17: Planning for open space, sport and recreation.* London: ODPM.

Office of the Deputy Prime Minister (2003) *Developing Accessible Play Space: A good practice guide.* London: ODPM.

Office of the Deputy Prime Minister (2005) *Sustainable Communities: People, places and prosperity. A five year plan from the Office of the Deputy Prime Minister.* London: ODPM.

Ofsted (2006) *Extended Services in Schools and Children's Centres.* London: Ofsted.

Oliver, M (1990) *'The Individual and Social Model of Disability'*, paper presented at Joint Workshop of the Living Options Group and the Research Unit of the Royal College of Physicians.

Olshansky, J, Passaro, D, Hershow, R, Layden, J, Carnes, B, Brody, J, Hayflick, L, Butler, R, Allison, B and Ludwig, D (2005) 'A Potential Decline in Life Expectancy in the United States in the 21st Century', *The New England Journal of Medicine*, 352: 1138-1145.

Opie, I and Opie, P (1959) *The Lore and Language of Schoolchildren.* Oxford: Oxford University Press.

Opie, I and Opie, P (1969) *Children's Games in Street and Playground*, Oxford: Oxford University Press.

Opie, I (1993) *The People in the Playground.* Oxford: Oxford University Press.

Orr, D (1994) *Earth in Mind: On Education, Environment and the Human Prospect.* Washington: Island Press.

Oyama, S (2000) *Evolution's Eye: A systems view of the biology-culture divide.* Durham: Duke University Press.

Pace, C (2006) *Extended Schools and the South West: Early research into the development of extended services and playwork in the South West region.* Cheltenham: Playwork Partnerships.

Pahl, K (2006) 'An Inventory of Traces: Children's photographs of their toys in three London homes', *Visual Communication*, 5(1): 95-114.

Pahl, R and Spencer, L (2004) 'Personal Communities: Not simply families of "fate" or "choice"', *Current Sociology*, 52(2): 199–221.

Palagi, E, Coroni, G and Borgognini Tarli, S (2004) 'Immediate and Delayed Benefits of Play Behaviour: New evidence from chimpanzees (Pan troglodytes)', *Ethology*, 110: 949-962.

Palmer, S (2006) *Toxic Childhood: How the modern world is damaging our children and what we can do about it.* London: Orion Books.

Panksepp, J (1997) Interview with Stephen Edelson. Autism Research Institute. Available online at: www.autism.org/interview/panksepp.html [accessed 14 March 2008].

Panksepp, J (1998) 'Attention Deficit Hyperactivity Disorders, Psychostimulants and Intolerance of Childhood Playfulness: A tragedy in the making?' *Current Directions in Psychological Science*, 7(3) 91-98.

Panksepp, J (2001) 'The Long Term Psychobiological Consequences of Infant Emotions: Prescriptions for the twenty-first century', *Infant Mental Health Journal*, 22(1-2): 132-173.

Panksepp, J (2002) 'On the Animalian Values of the Human Spirit: The foundational role of affect in psychotherapy and the evolution of consciousness', *European Journal of Psychotherapy and Health*, 5(3): 225-245.

Panksepp, J (2007) 'Can Play Diminish ADHD and Facilitate the Construction of the Social Brain?' *Journal of the Canadian Academy of Child and Adolescent Psychiatry*, 16(2): 57-66.

Panksepp, J (2007) 'Neuroevolutionary Sources of Laughter and Social Joy: Modeling primal human laughter in laboratory rats', *Behavioural Brain Research* (in press).

Pascoe-Watson, G (2007) 'Britain's Failing its Kids, say UN', *The Sun Online*, 14 February 2007.

Payne, L, Renton, Z and Mcneish, D (2006) *Report for Play England: Review of Children and Young People's Plans.* London: Play England/National Children's Bureau.

Pearce, I (2006) *Equipe: Final external evaluation report.* Cheltenham: Playwork Partnerships.

Pellegrini, AD (2002) 'Perceptions of Playfighting and Real Fighting: Effects of ex and participant status', in Roopnarine, JL (ed) *Conceptual, Social-cognitive and Contextual Issues in the Fields of Play. Play and Culture Studies*, 4. Westport, Connecticut: Ablex Publishing.

Pellegrini, A, Blatchford, P, Kato, K and Baines, E (2004) 'A Short-term Longitudinal Study of Children's Playground Games in Primary School: Implications for adjustment to school and social adjustment in the USA and the UK', *Social Development*, 13(1) 107-123.

Pellegrini, AD and Bohn, C (2005) 'The Role of Recess in Children's Cognitive

Performance and School Adjustment', *Research News and Comment*, AERA, Jan/Feb 2005: 13-19.

Pellegrini, A, Dupuis, D and Smith, P (2007) 'Play in evolution and development', *Developmental Review*, 27: 261-276.

Pellegrini, A and Smith, P (eds) (2005) *The Nature of Play. Great apes and humans.* London: Guildford Press.

Pellis, S and Pellis, V (2007) 'Rough-and-Tumble Play and the Development of the Social Brain', *Current Directions in Psychological Science*, 16(2): 95-98.

Penedo, F and Dahn, J (2005) 'Exercise and Well-being: A review of mental and physical health benefits associated with physical activity', *Current Opinion in Psychiatry*, 18(2): 189-193.

Penn, H (2005) 'Spaces Without Children', in Dudek, M (ed) *Children's Spaces.* London: Architectural Press.

Percy-Smith, B (2002) 'Contested Worlds. Constraints and opportunities in city and suburban environments in an English Midlands city', in Chawla, L (ed) *Growing Up in an Urbanising World.* London: Earthscan.

Petrie, P, Boddy, J, Cameron, C, Heptinstall, E, McQuail, S, Simon, A and Wigfall, V (2005) *Pedagogy – A Holistic, Personal Approach to Work with Children and Young People, Across Services: European models for practice, training, education and qualification.* London: Thomas Coram Research Unit.

Petrie, P, Storey, P and Candappa, M (2002) *Inclusive Play: Supporting provision for disabled children.* London: Institute of Education.

Phillips, J (2006) PPG17: 'A View from a Parkie', *Leisure Manager*, April 2006, 21-22.

Philo, C (2003) 'Memories, Imaginations and Reveries of Childhood', *Children's Geographies*, 1: 7-23.

PlayBoard (2007) *Giving Priority to Play.* Belfast: PlayBoard.

Play England (2006) *The Good Childhood Inquiry: Evidence submitted by Play England.* London: Play England.

Play England (2008) *Local Play Indicators: An Implementation Guide.* London: Play England/National Children's Bureau [forthcoming].

PlayToday (2003) 'Get out and Play for Playday 2003'. *PlayToday* 53: September/October 2003.

PlayToday (2007) 'Play Features in Local Area Agreements', *PlayToday*, 57, April 2007.

PLAYLINK (2002) *Play as Culture: Incorporating play in cultural strategies.* London: PLAYLINK.

PLAYLINK (2007) Comments on Play England's Draft Play Indicators Quality Assessment Tool. [online] London: PLAYLINK. Available from www.playlink.org.uk/articles/?p=19#note1 [accessed 14 March 2008].

Play Principles Scrutiny Group (2005) *Playwork Principles.* Cardiff: Play Wales.

Play Wales (2001) *First Claim: A framework for playwork quality assessment.* Cardiff: Play Wales.

Postman, N (1983) *The Disappearance of Childhood.* London: W.H. Allen.

Poulsen, A and Ziviani, J (2004) 'Health Enhancing Physical Activity: Factors influencing engagement patterns in children', *Australian Occupational Therapy Journal*, 51: 69-79.

Powell, S and Wellard, I (2008) Policies and play: The impact of national policies on children's opportunities for play. London: Play England/National Children's Bureau.

Power, T (2000) *Play and Exploration in Children and Animals.* New Jersey: Erlbaum.

Pramling Samuelsson, I and Johansson, E (2006) 'Play and Learning – Inseparable Dimensions in Preschool Learning', *Early Child Development and Care*, 176(1): 47-65.

Pressman, S and Cohen, S (2005) 'Does positive affect influence health?' *Psychological Bulletin*, 131(6): 925-971.

Preston, G with Robertson, M (2006) *Out of Reach: Benefits for disabled children*. London: Child Poverty Action Group.

Preston, S and de Waal, F (2002) 'Empathy: Its ultimate and proximate bases', *Behavioral and Brain Sciences*, 25: 1–72.

Pretty, J, Peacock, J, Hine, R, Sellens, M, South, N and Griffin, M (2007) 'Green Exercise in the UK Countryside: Effects on health and psychological well-being, and implications for policy and planning', *Journal of Environmental Planning and Management*, 50(2): 211-231.

Prezza, M and Pacilli, G (2007) 'Current Fear of Crime, Sense of Community, and Loneliness in Italian Adolescents: The role of autonomous mobility and play during childhood', *Journal of Community Psychology*, 35(2): 151-170.

Prilleltensky, I (2005) 'Promoting Well-being: Time for a paradigm shift in health and human services', *Scandinavian Journal of Public Health*, 33 (Suppl 66): 53-60.

Primary Review (2007) *Community Soundings: The Primary Review regional witness sessions*. Cambridge: University of Cambridge Faculty of Education.

Prout, A (2002) 'Researching Children as Social Actors: An introduction to the Children 5–16 Programme', *Children and Society*, 16: 67-76.

Prout, A (2005) *The Future of Childhood*. London: RoutledgeFalmer.

Provine, R (2004) 'Laughing, Tickling and the Evolution of Speech and Self', *Current Directions in Psychological Science*, 13(6): 215-218.

Punch, S (2003) 'Childhoods in the Majority World: Miniature adults or tribal children', *Sociology*, 37(2): 277-295.

Putnam, R (1995) 'Bowling Alone: America's declining social capital', *Journal of Democracy*, 6(1): 64-78.

Pyle, R (2002) 'Eden as a Vacant Lot', in Kahn, P and Kellert, S (eds) *Children and Nature*. Cambridge: MIT Press.

Qualifications and Curriculum Authority (2000) *Curriculum Guidance for the Foundation Stage*. London: QCA.

Qualifications and Curriculum Authority (QCA) *National Curriculum in Action. Creativity: Find it, promote it*. Available at: www.ncaction.org.uk/creativity/index.htm [accessed 14 March 2008].

Qualter, P and Munn, P (2005) 'The Friendships and Play Partners of Lonely Children', *Journal of Social and Personal Relationships*, 22(3): 379-397.

Rasmussen, K and Smidt, S (2003) 'The Neighbourhood in the Children', in Christensen, P and O'Brien, M (eds) *Children in the City*. London: RoutledgeFalmer.

Rasmussen, K (2004) 'Places for Children – Children's Places', *Childhood*, 11(2): 155-173.

Ratner, H, Chiodo, L, Covington, C, Sokol, R, Ager, J and Delaney-Black, V (2006) 'Violence Exposure, IQ, Academic Performance, and Children's Perception of Safety: Evidence of protective effects', *Merrill-Palmer Quarterly*, 52(2): 264-287.

Reay, D and Lucey, H (2000) '"I Don't Really Like it Here But I Don't Want to be Anywhere Else": Children and inner city council estates', *Antipode*, 32(4): 410-428.

Reed, T (2005) 'A Qualitative Approach to Boys' Rough and Tumble Play: There is more than what meets the eye,' in McMahon, F, Lytle, D and Sutton-Smith, B (eds) *Play: An interdisciplinary synthesis*. Maryland: University Press of America.

Rees-Jones, D (ed) (2007) *The Play Ranger Guide*. Radstock: Wansdyke Play Association.

Reeves, R (2003) 'The Battle for Childhood', *New Statesman*, 20 October 2003, 18-20.

Reid, V and Belsky, J (2002) 'Neuroscience: Environmental influences on child development', *Current Paediatrics*, 12: 581-585.

Renold, E (2004) '"Other" Boys: Negotiating non-hegemonic masculinities in the primary school', *Gender and Education*, 16(2): 247-266.

Renold, E (2006) 'They Won't Let Us Play … Unless You're Going Out with One of Them: Girls, boys and Butler's "heterosexual matrix" in the primary years', *British Journal of Sociology of Education*, 27(4): 489-509.

Renold, E (2007) 'Primary School "Studs". (De)constructing young boys' heterosexual masculinities', *Men and Masculinities*, 9(3): 275-297.

Ridgers, ND, Stratton, G and Fairclough, SJ (2005a) 'Assessing Physical Activity During Recess Using Accelerometry', *Preventative Medicine*, 41: 102-107.

Ridgers, ND, Stratton, G, Curley, J and White, G (2005b) 'Liverpool Sporting Playgrounds Project', *Education and Health*, 23(4): 50-52.

Ridgers, ND (2007) 'Playtime Research in Liverpool – update', presentation given to Play Research Network meeting, 27 January, London.

Riihela, M (2004) 'Joint Pretend Play Originates in Imitation and Creativity. Three examples of children's own play', seminar paper presented to the Children are Telling Conference, National Research and Development Centre for Welfare and Health (STAKES), Helsinki, Finland, 17 June 2004.

Rissotto, A and Giuliani, V (2006) 'Learning Neighbourhood Environments: The loss of experience in the modern world', in Spencer, C and Blades, M (eds) *Children and Their Environments*. Cambridge: Cambridge University Press.

Rizzolatti, G, Fogassi, L and Gallese, V (2001) 'Neurophysiological Mechanisms Underlying the Understanding and Imitation of Action', *Nature Neuroscience Review*, 2: 661-670.

Roberts, A (1980) *Out to Play: The middle years of childhood*. Aberdeen: Aberdeen University Press. Cited in Factor, J (2004) 'Tree Stumps, Manhole Covers and Rubbish Tins. The invisible play lines of a primary school playground', *Childhood*, 11(2) 142-154.

Roberts, H and Petticrew, M (2006) 'Policy for Children and Young People: What is the evidence and can we trust it?' *Children's Geographies*, 4 (1): 19-36.

Roberts, M (2001) 'Childcare Policy', in Foley, P, Roche, J and Tucker, S (eds) *Children in Society: Contemporary theory, policy and practice*. Basingstoke: Palgrave.

Roberts, N, Beer, J, Werner, K, Scabini, D, Levens, S, Knight, R and Levenson, R (2004) 'The Impact of Orbitofrontal Damage on Emotional Activation to Unanticipated and Anticipated Acoustic Startle Stimuli', *Cognitive, Affective and Behavioural Neuroscience*, 4(3): 307-316.

Robson, C (2002) *Real World Research, 2nd edition*, Oxford: Blackwell Publishing.

Roe, M (2006) '"Making a wish": Children and the local landscape', *Local Environment*, 11(2): 163-181.

Rolfe, H (2006) 'Where Are the Men? Gender segregation in the childcare and early years sector', *National Institute Economic Review*, 195: 103-117.

Rolfe, H, Metcalfe, H, Anderson, T and Meadows, P (2003) *Recruitment and Retention of Childcare, Early Years and Playworkers, Research Report RR409*. Nottingham: DfES.

Rogers, S (2005) *Role Play in Reception Classes: Pupil and teacher perspectives*. Swindon: ESRC.

Rose, S (2005) *The 21st-Century Brain: Explaining, mending and manipulating the mind*. London: Jonathan Cape.

Rosenberg, M (1965) *Society and the Adolescent Self-image*. Princeton, NJ: Princeton University Press.

Ross, N (2004) '"That Tree Used to be Everything to Us": The importance of natural and unkempt environments to children', paper presented to Open Space, People Space Conference.

Rubenstein, D (2002) 'On the Evolution of Juvenile Lifestyles in Mammals', in Pereira, M and Fairbanks, L (eds) *Juvenile Primates: Life History, Development and Behaviour*. Chicago: Chicago University Press. Cited in Prout, A (2005) *The Future of Childhood*. Abingdon: RoutledgeFalmer.

Rubin, K, Burgess, K and Hastings, P (2002) 'Stability and Social Behavioral Consequences of Toddlers' Inhibited Temperament and Parenting Behaviors', *Child Development*, 73: 483-495.

Russ, S (2004) *Play in Child Development and Psychotherapy*. New Jersey: Lawrence Erlbaum Associates.

Russell, W (2005) 'The Unnatural Art of Playwork', in Sturrock, G and Else, P (eds) (2005) *Therapeutic Playwork Reader 2, 2000-2005*. Sheffield: Ludemos Associates.

Russell, W (2006) *Reframing Playwork, Reframing Challenging Behaviour*. Nottingham: Nottingham City Council.

Rutter, M (2006) 'Implications of Resilience Concepts for Scientific Understanding', *Annals of the New York Academy of Science*, 1094: 1-12.

Rye, J (2006) 'Rural Youths' Images of the Rural', *Journal of Rural Studies*, 22: 409-421.

Saakslahti, A, Numminen P, Varstala V, Helenius H, Tammi A, Viikari J and Valimaki I (2004) 'Physical Activity as a Preventive Measure for Coronary Heart Disease Risk Factors in Early Childhood', *Scandinavian Journal of Medicine and Science in Sports*, 14(3): 143-149.

Salovey, P, Rothman, A, Detweiler, J and Steward, W (2000) 'Emotional States and Physical Health', *American Psychologist*, 55: 110-121.

Sandberg, A (2002) 'Children's Concepts of Teachers' Ways of Relating to Play', Australian Journal of Early Childhood, 27(4): 18-23.

Santer, J and Griffiths, C, with Goodall, D (2007) *Free Play in Early Childhood: A literature review*. London: Play England/National Children's Bureau.

Sawyer, R (2003) 'Levels of Analysis in Pretend Play Discourse: Metacommunication in conversational routines', in Lytle, D (ed) *Play and Educational Theory and Practice. Play and Culture Studies*, 5. Westport: Praeger.

Schore, A (2001) 'Minds in the Making: Attachment, the self-organising brain and developmentally orientated psychoanalytic psychotherapy', *British Journal of Psychotherapy*, 17(3): 299-328.

Schott, G and Hodgetts, D (2006) 'Health and Digital Gaming' *Journal of Health Psychology*, 11(2): 309-316.

Scott, E and Panksepp, J (2003) 'Rough-and-Tumble Play in Human Children', *Aggressive Behaviour*, 29: 539-551.

Selden, S (2004) 'Tickle', *Journal of the American Academy of Dermatology*, 50: 93-97.

Sharma, N (2002) *Still Missing Out. Ending Poverty and Social Exclusion: Messages to government from families with disabled children*. Ilford: Barnardo's.

Sharma, N and Dowling, R (2004) *Postcards From Home: The experience of disabled children in the school holidays*. Ilford: Barnardo's.

Shatwell, S (2003) *We're Just Like Other Kids: A report into the needs of homeless children and families in Leeds*. Leeds: Homeless Families Project.

Sheets-Johnstone, M (2003) 'Child's Play: A multi-disciplinary perspective', *Human Studies*, 26(4): 409-430.

Shelter (2006) *Against the Odds: An investigation comparing the lives of children on either side of Britain's housing divide*. London: Shelter.

Sherrat, D (2002) 'Developing Pretend Play in Children with Autism: A case study', *Autism*, 6 (2): 169-179.

Shiota, M, Campos, B, Keltner, D and Hertensetein, M (2004) 'Positive Emotion and the Regulation of Interpersonal Relationships', in Philippot, P and Feldman, R (eds) *The regulation of emotion*. Mahwah, NJ: Lawrence Erlbaum. Cited in Martin, R (2007) *The Psychology of Humour: An integrative approach*. Burlington, MA: Elsevier Academic Press.

Shola Shobowale (2006) 'Reactions from the Sector: A young person's perspective', *PlayToday*, 54, September 2006.

Shonkoff, J and Phillips, D (2000) *From Neurons to Neighbourhoods: The science of early child development*. Washington: National Academy Press.

Shore, R (2003) *Rethinking the Brain: New insights into early development*. New York: Families and Work Institute.

Siegel, D (2001) 'Towards an Interpersonal Neurobiology of the Developing Mind: Attachment relationships, "mindsight" and neural integration', *Infant Mental Health Journal*, 22(1-2): 67-94.

Singer, D, Golinkoff, R and Hirsh-Pasek, K (eds) (2006). *Play=Learning: How play motivates and enhances children's cognitive and social-emotional growth*. New York, NY: Oxford University Press.

Singer, J (2006) 'Epilogue: Learning to play and learning through play', in Singer, D, Golinkoff, R and Hirsh-Pasek, K (eds) *Play=Learning: How play motivates and enhances children's cognitive and social-emotional growth*. New York, NY: Oxford University Press.

Singh, I (2002) 'Biology in Context: Social and cultural perspectives on ADHD', *Children and Society*, 16: 360-367.

Sinha, C (2005) 'Blending Out of the Background: Play, props and staging in the material world', *Journal of Pragmatics*, 37: 1537-155.

Siviy, S (1998) 'Neurobiologiocal Substrates of Play Behaviour', in Bekoff, M and Byers, J (eds) *Animal Play: Evolutionary, Comparative and Ecological Perspectives*. Cambridge: Cambridge University Press.

Siviy, S, Love, N, DeCicco, B, Giordano, S and Seifert, T (2003) 'The Relative Playfulness of Juvenile Lewis and Fischer-344 Rats', *Physiology and Behaviour*, 80: 385-394.

SkillsActive (2002) *Assumptions and Values of Playwork*. London: SkillsActive.

SkillsActive (2005) *Choosing Playwork: Working with children in out of school settings*. London: SkillsActive.

SkillsActive (2006a) Key Facts and Figures. Available online from www.skillsactive. com/playwork [accessed 14 March 2008].

SkillsActive (2006b) *Playwork People 2: Research into the characteristics of the playwork workforce*. London: SkillsActive.

Skivenes, M and Strandbu, A (2006) 'A Child Perspective and Children's Participation', *Children, Youth and Environments*, 16(2): 10-27.

Sleek, S (1998) 'After the Storm, Children Play Out Fears', *APA Monitor*, 29(6).

Smith, A (2002) *The Brain's Behind It*. Stafford: Network Educational Press.

Smith, A (2007) 'Fit for Play?' *Education 3-13*, 35(1): 17-27.

Smith, A (2007) 'Attacks on Teachers Rising, Says Survey', *The Guardian*. 23 February 2007.

Smith, J (2007) '"Ye've got to 'ave balls to play this game sir". Boys, Peers and Fears: The negative influence of school-based "cultural accomplices" in constructing hegemonic masculinities', *Gender and Education*, 19(2) 179-198.

Smith, MK (2005) 'Background to the Green Paper for Youth 2005', *The Encyclopedia of Informal Education*. www.infed.org/youthwork/green_paper_2005_background.htm (accessed June 2008).

Smith, PK (1988) 'Children's Play and its Role in Early Development: A re-evaluation of the "play ethos"', in Pellegrini, AD (ed) *Psychological Bases for Early Education*. Chichester: Wiley.

Smith, PK (2005) 'Social and Pretend Play in Children', in Pellegrini, AD and Smith, PK (eds) *The Nature of Play: Great apes and humans*. London: The Guildford Press.

Smith, PK, Smees, R and Pellegrini, A (2004) 'Play Fighting and Real Fighting: Using video playback methodology with young children,' *Aggressive Behaviour*, 30: 164-173.

Smith, PK, Smees, R, Pellegrini, AD and Menesini, E (2002) 'Comparing Pupil and Teacher Perceptions for Playful Fighting, Serious Fighting and Positive Peer Interaction', in Roopnarine, JL (ed) *Conceptual, Social-cognitive and Contextual Issues in the Fields of Play, Play and Culture Studies*, 4. Westport, Connecticut: Ablex Publishing.

Smith, F and Barker, J (2000) '"Out of School", In School', in Holloway, S, and Valentine, G (2000) *Children's Geographies: Playing, living, learning*. London: Routledge.

Smith, F and Barker, J (2004) 'Inclusive Environments? The expansion of out-of-school child care in the UK', *Children, Youth and Environments*, 14(2) 1-20.

Smith, S and Willans, B (2007) 'There's No Place Like the Play Space: An appreciation of disability and playwork', in Russell, W, Handscomb, B and Fitzpatrick J (eds) *Playwork Voices: In celebration of Bob Hughes and Gordon Sturrock*. London: London Centre for Playwork Education and Training.

Sobel, D (2002) *Children's Special Places*. Detroit: Wayne State University Press.

Sorensen, B, Danielsen, O and Neilsen, J (2007) 'Children's Informal Learning in the Context of Schools of the Knowledge Society', *Education and Information Technologies*, 12(1): 17-27.

Spencer, C and Blades, M (eds) (2006) *Children and Their Environments*. Cambridge: Cambridge University Press.

Spilsbury, J (2005) '"We Don't Really Get to Go Out in the Front Yard" – Children's Home Range and Neighbourhood Violence', *Children's Geographies*, 3(1): 79-99.

Spinka, M, Newberry, R and Bekoff, M (2001) 'Mammalian Play: Training for the unexpected', *The Quarterly Review of Biology*, 76(2): 141-168.

SQW and NOP (2002) *The 2001 Childcare Workforce Surveys*. London: DfES.

Stefanotos GA and Baron IS (2007) 'Attention-Deficit/Hyperactivity Disorder: A neuropsychological perspective towards DSM-V', *Neuropsychology Review*, 17: 5-38.

Strauss, G and Allen, P (2006) 'The Experience of Emotion is Associated With the Automatic Processing of Positive Emotional Words', *Journal of Positive Psychology*, 1(3): 150-159.

Strayhorn, J (2002) 'Self-control: Towards systematic training programmes', *Journal of American Academy of Child and Adolescent Psychiatry*, 41:17-27. Cited in Russ (2004).

Street, C (2001) 'The Value of Children's Play and Play Provision', in Cole-Hamilton, I, Harrop, A and Street, C (2002) *Making the Case for Play: Gathering the evidence*. London: Children's Play Council, New Policy Institute and National Children's Bureau.

Sturrock, G (2003) 'Towards a Psycholudic Definition of Playwork', in Brown F (ed) *Playwork Theory and Practice*. Buckingham: Open University Press.

Sturrock, G and Else, P (1998) *The Playground as Therapeutic Space: Playwork as healing (The Colorado Paper)*. Leigh-on-Sea: Ludemos Press.

Sturrock, G and Else, P (2005) *Therapeutic Playwork Reader 1, 1995-2000*. Sheffield: Ludemos Associates.

Sturrock, G and Else, P (eds) (2005) *Therapeutic Playwork Reader 2, 2000-2005*. Sheffield: Ludemos Associates.

Sturrock, G, Russell, W and Else, P (2004) *Towards Ludogogy Parts I, II and III: The art of being and becoming through play*. Sheffield: Ludemos Associates.

Suadicani, P (2004) 'Physical Activity in Young Children – Does it Matter?' *Scandinavian Journal of Medicine and Science in Sports*, 14: 137.

Suomi, SJ (2006) 'Risk, Resilience, and Gene- Environment Interactions in Rhesus Monkeys', *Annals of the New York Academy of Science*. 1994: 52-62.

Sutton, L, Smith, N, Dearden, C and Middleton, S (2007) *A Child's Eye View of Social Difference*. York: Joseph Rowntree Foundation.

Sutton-Smith, B (1997) *The Ambiguity of Play*, Cambridge, MA: Harvard University Press.

Sutton-Smith, B (1999) 'Evolving a Consilience of Play Definitions: Playfully', *Play and Culture Studies*, 2: 239-256.

Sutton-Smith, B (2001) 'Reframing the Variability of Players and Play', in Reifel, S (ed) *Theory in Context and Out: Play and Culture Studies*, 3. Westport: Ablex Publishing.

Sutton-Smith, B (2002) 'Recapitulation Redressed', in Rooparine, J (ed) *Conceptual Social-Cognitive, and Contextual Issues in the Fields of Play. Play and Culture Studies*, 4. Westport: Ablex.

Sutton-Smith, B (2003) 'Play as a Parody of Emotional Vulnerability', in JL Roopnarine (ed) *Play and Educational Theory and Practice, Play and Culture Studies*, 5. Westport, Connecticut: Praeger.

Sutton-Smith, B (2004) 'Cultivating Courage Through Play', *Voices: The Journal of New York Folklore*, 30, Spring/Summer 2004.

Sutton-Smith, B, Mechling, J, Johnson, T and McMahon, F (eds) (1999) *Children's Folklore*. Logon: Utah State University Press.

Swain, J (2005) 'Sharing the Same World: Boys' relations with girls during their last year of primary school', *Gender and Education*, 17(1): 75-91.

Swain, J, Lorberbaum, J, Kose, S and Strathearn, L (2007) 'Brain Basis of Early

Parent-Infant Interactions: Psychology, physiology, and in vivo functional neuroimaging studies', *Journal of Child Psychology and Psychiatry*, 48(3/4): 262-287.

Sylva, K, Melhuish, E, Sammons, P, Siraj-Blatchford, I and Taggart, B (2004) *The Effective Provision of Pre-School Education Project Final Report*. London: Sure Start and DfES.

Tamminen, B, and Bailey, LF (2001) *Establishing and Operating a Playwork Facility for Children Visiting Prisons*. Leeds: Leeds Metropolitan University.

Tapscott, D (1998) *Growing Up Digital: The rise of the net generation*. New York: McGraw Hill.

Targeton, A (2005) 'Play in Lower Primary Schools in Norway', in McMahon, F, Lytle, D and Sutton-Smith, B (eds) *Play: An Interdisciplinary Synthesis*. Maryland: University Press of America.

Taylor, A, Kuo, F, and Sullivan, W (2001). 'Coping with ADD: The surprising connection to green play settings', *Environment and Behaviour* 33(1): 54-77.

Taylor, D and Balloch, S (eds) (2005) *The Politics of Evaluation: Participation and policy implementation*. Bristol: The Policy Press.

Taylor, T (2006) *Play Between Worlds: Exploring online game culture*. Cambridge: MIT Press.

Thayer, J and Brosschot, J (2005) 'Psychosomatics and Psychopathology: Looking up and down from the brain', *Psychoneuroendocrinolgy*, 30: 1050-1058.

The Children's Society (2006) *Good Childhood: A question for our times?* London: The Children's Society.

The Children's Society (2006) *The Good Childhood: A national inquiry launch report*. London: The Children's Society.

The Children's Society (2007a) *Childhood Friendships at Risk Reveals New Survey*. Press release, 5 June 2007.

The Children's Society (2007b) *Learning and Me: Good Childhood evidence summaries*. London: The Children's Society.

Thomas, G and Hocking, G (2003) Other People's Children: Why their quality of life is our concern. London: Demos.

Thomas, G and Thompson, G (2004) *A Child's Place: Why environment matters to children*. London: Green Alliance/Demos.

Thompson, C, Aspinall, P and Montarzino, A (2008) 'The Childhood Factor. Adult Visits to Green Places and the Significance of Childhood Experience', *Environment and Behaviour*, 40:1: 111-143.

Thompson, E and Varela, F (2001) 'Radical Embodiment: Neural dynamics and consciousness', *Trends in Cognitive Sciences*, 5 (10): 418-425.

Thompson, J and Philo, C (2004) 'Playful Spaces? A social geography of children's play in Livingston, Scotland', *Children's Geographies*, 2(1): 111-130.

Thompson, P, Hall, C and Russell, L (2006) *Promoting Social and Education Inclusion Through the Creative Arts. Final Report: ESRC RES-000-22-0834 (2004-2006)*. Swindon: Economic and Social Research Council.

Thompson, R and Nelson, C (2001) 'Developmental Science and the Media', *American Psychologist*, 56(1): 5-15.

Thomson, S (2005) '"Territorialising" the Primary School Playground: Deconstructing the geography of playtime', *Children's Geographies*, 3(1): 63-78).

Thorne, B (1993) *Gender Play*. Buckingham: Open University Press. Cited in Swain, J (2005) 'Sharing the Same World: Boys' relations with girls during their last year of primary school', *Gender and Education*, 17(1): 75-91.

Thornton, K and Cox, E (2005) 'Play and the Reduction of Challenging Behaviour in Children with ASD and Learning Disabilities', *Good Autism Practice*, 6(2): 75-80.

Tillberg Mattsson, K (2002) 'Children's (In)dependent Mobility and Parents Chauffering in the Town and Countryside', *Tijdschrift voor Economische en Sociale Geograffe*, 93(4): 443-453.

Timimi, S (2006) 'Children's Mental Health: The role of culture, markets and prescribed drugs', *Public Policy Research*, 13(1): 35-42.

Timperio, A, Salmon, J, Telford A and Crawford, D (2005) 'Perceptions of Local Neighborhood Environments and Their Relationship to Childhood Obesity', *International Journal of Obesity*, 29(2): 170-175.

Tomanovic, S (2004) 'Family Habitus as the Cultural Context for Childhood', *Childhood*, 11(3): 339-360.

Tonucci, F (2005) 'Citizen Child: Play as welfare parameter for urban life', *Topoi*, 24: 183-195.

Trageton, A (2005) 'Play in Lower Primary School in Norway', in McMahon, F, Lytle, D and Sutton-Smith, B (eds) *Play: An interdisciplinary synthesis*. Maryland: University Press of America.

Tranter, P and Malone, K (2004) 'Geographies of Environmental Learning: An exploration of the children's use of school grounds', *Children's Geographies*, 2(1): 131-155.

Trevlas, E, Grammatikopoulos, V, Tsigilis, N and Zachopoulou, E (2003) 'Evaluating Playfulness: Construct validity of the children's playfulness scale', *Early Childhood Education Journal*, 31(1): 33-39.

Tugade, M, Frederickson, B and Barrett, L (2004) 'Psychological Resilience and Positive Emotional Granularity: Examining the benefits of positive emotions on coping and health', *Journal of Personality*, 72(6): 1161-1190.

Turnbull, J and Jenvey, B (2004) 'Criteria Used by Adults and Children to Categorize Subtypes of Play', *Early Child Development and Care*, 176(5): 539-551.

Turner, JH and Stets, JE (2005) *The Sociology of Emotions*. Cambridge: Cambridge University Press.

UK Government (2007) The Consolidated 3rd and 4th Periodic Report to the United Nations Committee on the Rights of the Child. London: DCSF.

Unicef (2007) 'Child Poverty in Perspective: An overview of child well-being in rich countries', *Innocenti Report Card 7*. Florence: Unicef Innocenti Research Centre.

Vaillant, G (2003) 'Mental Health', *American Journal of Psychiatry*, 160(8): 1371-1384.

Valentine, G (2000) 'Exploring Children and Young People's Narratives of Identity', *Geoforum*, 31: 257-267.

Valentine, G (2004) *Public Space and the Culture of Childhood*. Aldershot: Ashgate.

Valentine, G and Holloway, S (2002) 'Cyberkids? Exploring children's identities and social networks in on-line and off-line worlds', *Annals of the Association of American Geographers*, 92(2): 302-319.

Valkenburg, P, Schouten, A and Peter, J (2005) 'Adolescents' Identity Experiments on the Internet', *New Media and Society*, 7(3): 383-402.

Van der Hoek, T (2005) 'Through Children's Eyes: An initial study of children's personal experiences and coping strategies growing up poor in an affluent Netherlands', *Innocenti Working Paper No. 2005-05*. Florence, UNICEF Innocenti Research Centre.

Van Praag, H, Shubert, T, Zhao, C, and Gage, F (2005) 'Exercise Enhances Learning and Hippocampal Neurogenesis in Aged Mice', *Journal of Neuroscience*, 25(38): 8680-8685.

Vanderbeck, R and Dunkley, C (2003) 'Young People's Narratives of Rural-Urban Difference', *Children's Geographies*, 1(2): 241-259.

Vanderbeck, R and Dunkley, C (2004) 'Introduction: Geographies of exclusion, inclusion and belonging in young lives', *Children's Geographies*, 2: 177-183.

Veitch, J Bagley, S, Ball, K and Salmon, J (2006) 'Where Do Children Usually Play? A qualitative study of parents' perceptions of influences on children's active free-play', *Health and Place*, 12: 383-393.

Vellacott, J (2007) 'Resilience: A psychoanalytical exploration', *British Journal of Psychotherapy*, 23(2): 163-170.

Viera, M, Garcia, M, Rau, D and Prado, A (2005) 'Effects of Different Opportunities for Social Interaction on the Play Fighting Behaviour in Male and Female Hamsters', *Developmental Psychobiology*, 47(4): 345-353.

Visser, JG and Greenwood, IG (2005) 'The Effect of Playground Games, as Agents for Changing Playground Ethos on Playground Disputes', *Education* 3-13, June 2005.

Wade, H and Badham, B (2001) *Hear by Right: Standards for the active involvement of children and young people*. Leicester and London: National Youth Agency and Local Government Association.

Walker, J (2006) *Play for Health: Delivering and auditing quality in hospital play services*. London: National Association of Hospital Play Staff.

Walsh, G, Sproule, L, McGuiness, C, Trew, K, Rafferty, H and Sheehy, N (2006) 'An Appropriate Curriculum for 4-5-year-old Children in Northern Ireland: Comparing play-based and formal approaches', *Early Years*, 26(2): 210-221.

Warburton, D, Nicol, C and Bredin, S (2006) 'Health Benefits of Physical Activity: The evidence', *Canadian Medical Association Journal*, 174(6): 801-809.

Ward, C (1978) *The Child in the City*. London: Penguin Books.

Ward, C (1988) *The Child in the Country*. London: Bedford Square Press.

Ward, L (2007) 'A World of Wolves, Frogs and Knickers', *The Guardian* Education Weekly, online, 8 May 2007. http://education.guardian.co.uk/schools/story/0,,2074233,00.html [accessed 14 March 2008].

Ward, F, Elliott, C and Day, C (2004) *I Want to Play Too: Developing inclusive play and leisure for disabled children and young people*. Ilford: Barbardo's.

Ward Thompson, C, Travlou, P and Roe, J (2006) *Free Range Teenagers: The role of wild adventure space in young people's lives*. Edinburgh: OPENspace.

Webb, S and Brown, F (2003) 'Playwork in Adversity: Working with abandoned children in Romania', in Brown, F (ed) *Playwork Theory and Practice*. Buckingham: Open University Press.

Weller, S (2007a) '"Sticking with your Mates?" Children's friendship trajectories during the transition from primary to secondary school', *Children and Society*, .21(5): 339-351

Weller, S (2007b) *Children Play Key Role in Forging Close Communities*. Swindon: ESRC.

Wheway, R (2007) 'Couch Prisoners?' *Spaces and Places*, 25, 26-27.

Willcutt, E and Carlson, C (2005) 'The Diagnostic Validity of Attention-Deficit Hyperactive Disorder', *Clinical Neuroscience Research*, 5(5): 219-232.

Williams, S and Williams, L (2005) 'Space Invaders: The negotiation of teenage boundaries through the mobile phone', *The Sociological Review*, 53(2): 314-331.

Williams, Z (2006) *The Commercialisation of Childhood*. London: Compass.

Williamson, D, Dewey, A and Steinberg, H (2001) 'Mood Change Through Physical Exercise in Nine-To Ten-Year-Old Children', *Perceptual and Motor Skills*, 93: 311-316.

Wilson, C and Gray, C (2006) *All Kids Need Play*. Bristol: Bristol Children's Fund and the West of England Centre for Inclusive Living.

Wilson, R (2001) 'A Sense of Place', *EE News*, 18(2): 2-7.

Witte-Townsend, D and Hill, E (2006) 'Lightness of Being in the Primary Classroom: Inviting conversations of depth across educational communities', *Educational Philosophy and Theory*, 38(3): 373-389.

Wohlwend, K (2004) 'Chasing Friendships: Acceptance, rejection and recess play', *Childhood Education*, Winter 2004/2005: 77-82.

Women's Aid Federation of England (2006) *National Standards for Domestic and Sexual Violence*. Bristol: Women's Aid Federation of England.

Wood, P, and Korndorfer, J (2005) *Playing for Real Toolkit. A practical resource for consulting children about outdoor play spaces*. Exeter: Devon Play Association.

Woodhead, M (1997) 'Psychology and the Cultural Construction of Children's Needs', in James, A and Prout, J (eds) *Constructing and Reconstructing Childhood*, 2nd edition. London: RoutledgeFalmer.

Woolley, H (2006) 'Freedom of the City: Contemporary issues and policy influences on children and young people's use of public open space in England', *Children's Geographies*, 4(1): 45–59.

Woolley, H, Armitage, M, Bishop, J, Curtis, M and Ginsborg, J (2006a) *Inclusion of Disabled Children in Primary School Playgrounds*. London: National Children's Bureau and Joseph Rowntree Foundation.

Woolley, H, with Armitage, M, Bishop, J, Curtis, M and Ginsborg, J (2006b) 'Going Outside Together: Good practice with respect to the inclusion of disabled children in primary school playgrounds', *Children's Geographies* 4(3): 303-318.

Worpole, K (2003) *No Particular Place to Go: Children, young people and public space*. Groundwork UK.

Wridt, PJ (2004) 'An Historical Analysis of Young People's Use of Public Space, Parks and Playgrounds in New York City', *Children, Youth and Environments*, 14(1): 86-106.

Wyness, M (2006) *Children and Society: An introduction to the sociology of childhood*. Basingstoke: Palgrave Macmillan.

Youlden, P and Harrison, S (2006) *The Better Play Programme 2000-2005: An evaluation*. London: Children's Play Council and Barnardo's.

Yuill, N, Streith, S, Roake, C, Aspden, R and Todd, B (2007) 'Brief Report: Designing a Playground for Children with Autistic Spectrum Disorders – Effects on Playful Peer Interaction', *Journal of Autism and Developmental Disorders*, 37: 1192-1196.

Yun, A, Bazar, K, Gerber, A, Lee, P and Daniel, S (2005) 'The Dynamic Range of Biological Functions and Variations of Many Environmental Cues May Be Declining in the Modern Age: Implications for diseases and therapeutics', *Medical Hypotheses*, 65: 173-178.

Zeiher, H (2003) 'Shaping Daily Life in Urban Environments', in Christensen, P and O'Brien, M (eds) *Children in the City*. London: RoutledgeFalmer.

Zigler, E, Singer, D, and Bishop-Josef, S (eds) (2004) *Children's Play: The roots of reading*. Washington, DC: Zero to Three Press.

Ziviani, J, Wadley, D, Ward, H, Macdonald, D, Jenkins, D and Rogers, S (2007) 'A Place to Play: Socio-economic and spatial factors in children's physical activity', *Australian Occupational Therapy Journal*, 1-10.

272